WordPerfect 6 for Windows: How Do I . . . ?

Now Available from Prima!

WINDOWS Magazine Presents: Access from the Ground Up
Advanced PageMaker 4.0 for Windows
Adventures in Windows
CompuServe Information Manager for Windows: The Complete Membership Kit & Handbook (with two 3½" disks)
Computers Don't Byte—The Absolute Beginner's Guide to Getting Started with the PC
CorelDRAW! 4 Revealed!
Create Wealth with Quicken
DOS 6.2: Everything You Need to Know
WINDOWS Magazine Presents: Encyclopedia for Windows
Excel 5 for Windows: The Visual Learning Guide
Free Electronic Networks
WINDOWS Magazine Presents: Freelance Graphics for Windows: The Art of Presentation
Improv for Windows Revealed! (with 3½" disk)
Lotus Notes 3 Revealed!
LotusWorks 3: Everything You Need to Know
Making Movies with Your PC
Microsoft Office In Concert, Professional Edition
Microsoft Works for Windows By Example
Novell NetWare Lite: Simplified Network Solutions
1-2-3 for Windows: The Visual Learning Guide
PageMaker 5 for Windows: Everything You Need to Know
PC DOS 6.1: Everything You Need to Know
WINDOWS Magazine Presents: The Power of Windows and DOS Together, 2nd Edition
PowerPoint: The Visual Learning Guide
Quicken 3 for Windows: The Visual Learning Guide
Superbase Revealed!
Windows 3.1: The Visual Learning Guide
Windows for Teens
WinFax PRO: The Visual Learning Guide
Word for Windows 6: The Visual Learning Guide
WordPerfect 6 for DOS: The Visual Learning Guide
WordPerfect 6 for DOS: How Do I…?
WordPerfect 6 for Windows: The Visual Learning Guide

Upcoming Books

CorelDRAW! 5 Revealed!
Cruising CompuServe
Migrating to Windows 4

How to Order:

Individual orders and quantity discounts are available from the publisher, Prima Publishing, P.O. Box 1260BK, Rocklin, CA 95677-1260; phone: (916) 632-4400. On your letterhead include information concerning the intended use of the books and the number of books you wish to purchase. Turn to the back of the book for more information.

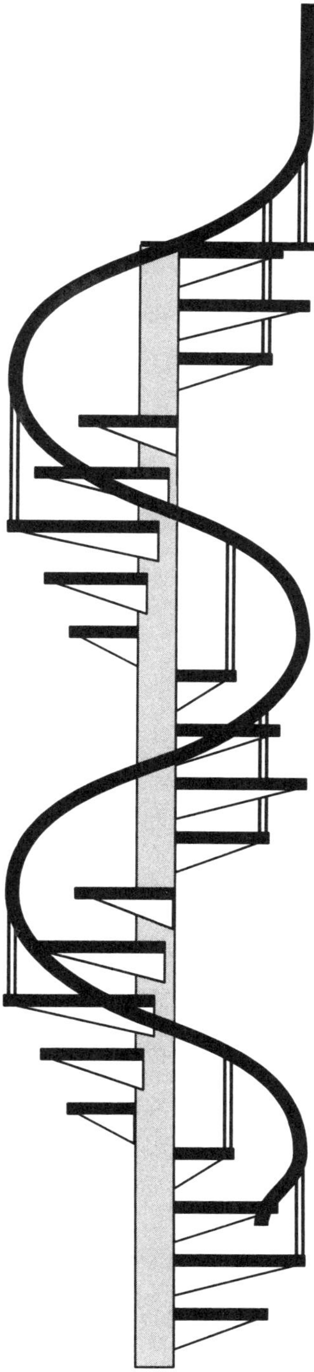

WordPerfect 6 for Windows: How Do I . . . ?

Kristy Clason

Prima Publishing
P.O. Box 1260BK
Rocklin, CA 95677

Prima Computer Books is an imprint of Prima Publishing, Rocklin, California 95677

Executive Editor: Roger Stewart
Managing Editor: Neweleen A. Trebnik
Project Editor: Steven Martin
Cover Production Coordinator: Anne Johnson
Copy Editor: Becky Whitney
Technical Reviewer: Jan Weingarten
Design and Production: Susan Glinert, BookMakers
Cover Design: Page Design, Inc.

ISBN: 1-55958-512-9

Library of Congress Catalog Card Number: 93-087185

Printed in the United States of America

95 96 97 RRD 10 9 8 7 6 5 4 3 2

Contents

Acknowledgments

A very special thanks to the Prima team and all those who worked on this project. To Roger Stewart and Sherri Morningstar for their vision and commitment to this project. To Diane Pasquetti for her timely attention and follow through on all the important details. To Jan Weingarten for her technical insight as well as her much needed work on the screen shots. A very heartfelt thanks to Steven Martin for his professionalism and dedication throughout this project.

As always, the greatest gratitude goes to my family. Their support, patience, and understanding were critical to the success of this book. To Brooke and Tyler for their clever ways to keep me away from the computer (such as paper snowflakes in the disk drive and locating the "master" surge-protector button). To Chris for… everything.

Introduction

How This Book Is Organized

As the title suggests, *WordPerfect 6 for Windows: How Do I...?* is organized around hundreds of questions about WordPerfect—the world's best-selling word processor. The manner in which each question is answered helps you quickly and easily to understand and use the thousands of features and options available in WordPerfect 6 for Windows. Examples of these questions are "How Do I Print a Document?"; "How Do I Create Fancy Text?"; and "How Do I Create a Macro?" Virtually any question that you will have as you work with WordPerfect is answered in *WordPerfect 6 for Windows: How Do I...?*.

Each question is divided into three sections to quickly give you the information you need. The first section, immediately following the "How Do I...?" question, gives a concise description as well as several common applications of the feature. This section is marked with the following icon, so you can quickly find the questions you need answered:

The second section, entitled "Steps," gives detailed, easy-to-follow, step-by-step instructions for accomplishing the task.

The last section, entitled "Tell Me More," gives more detailed information about the feature.

Conventions Used in This Book

The following conventions are used throughout this book to help simplify the step-by-step instructions and examples.

A plus sign joining two keys indicates that the keys should be pressed simultaneously. For example, "press Shift+F1" means you should hold down the Shift key and then press F1.

A comma separating two keys indicates that the first key should be pressed and released and then the second key pressed and released. For example, if you see "Home, ↑" you should press and release the Home key and then press and release the Up Arrow.

An italicized *or* separates mouse and menu functions from their alternative keystrokes. The instructions preceding and following the *or* accomplish the same task. For example, "choose Tools/Speller *or* press Ctrl+F1" indicates that you can choose Tools from the main menu bar and then choose Speller from the Tools pull-down menu or press Ctrl+F1 to achieve the same results.

Menu items appear in the text as they do on-screen. When you need to choose a sequence of menu items, the items are separated with a "➢." For example, to display the Open dialog box, you choose File➢Open. This instructs you first to choose File from the main menu bar, which will display the File pull-down menu, and then to choose Open to display the dialog box.

Within WordPerfect there are several ways to perform the same task. At times you will see the following icons indicating alternatives for the preceding steps:

Notes and Hints appear throughout the book and are designated by the following icons:

Introduction to WordPerfect 6 for Windows

WordPerfect 6 for Windows is being acclaimed as the most advanced word processor ever. WordPerfect lets you work faster, with less effort, and with better results. WordPerfect offers features for users at all levels. If you are new to WordPerfect you will love the Coaches and tutorials that "hold your hand" while you perform various tasks.

If you are a seasoned user of word-processing software you will appreciate the powerful new features WordPerfect offers. The ExpressDocs Templates make it easy to create professional documents without doing all the work yourself. The Button Bar, Power Bar, and QuickMenus give you extra power by providing quick access to those features you use most. And when you need to make sure you have written something just right, you can use the powerful writing tools built into WordPerfect, such as Grammatik and QuickCorrect. WordPerfect has also integrated over 100 of the most common spreadsheet functions right into the Tables feature; and don't forget the amazing power of the drawing tools, including WP Draw, TextArt, and Charts.

If you are a veteran WordPerfect user, you will be thrilled with the hundreds of new and enhanced features. Enhancements have been made to merging, creating envelopes, and labels—just to name a few.

System Requirements

In order to use WordPerfect 6 for Windows you must have Windows 3.1 running in 386 Enhanced Mode and your computer must meet the following requirements:

Minimum Configuration	Recommended/Optimal Configuration
386 PC computer	486 PC computer
11MB free hard disk space for minimum installation	28MB free hard disk space
4–6MB RAM memory	8MB RAM memory
	Mouse

Installing WordPerfect

The first step in using WordPerfect is to correctly install the software on your computer. Installing WordPerfect is easy. In most cases you can simply follow the on-screen prompts that guide you through the installation process. However, if you need a little more information, this section takes you step by step through a standard installation.

To perform a standard installation:

1. Insert the Install 1 disk in the appropriate disk drive.
2. Start Windows and choose File➢Run.
3. Type **a:setup** or **b:setup** and choose OK. The installation program begins and the WordPerfect Setup dialog box displays.

4. Choose Install.
5. Choose Standard.

NOTE

There are several other installation options you can choose from. The Custom option lets you determine what files are installed and the location to which they are installed. The Network option is only applicable if you are installing WordPerfect on the network file server or on a workstation that will be running WordPerfect from the network. The Minimum option is useful if you have very limited disk space, but you will not be able to use all the functionality of the program, such as the Speller, Thesaurus, QuickFinder, and WP Draw. The Update option allows you to update an existing copy of WordPerfect 6 for Windows.

6. After selecting the Standard option, you must select the drive to which you want to install the program. Select the drive and choose OK.

HINT

As the installation begins, informative messages display at the top of you screen. These messages introduce you to various features in WordPerfect and are a great way to begin familiarizing yourself with the program. There is also a dialog box that displays at the bottom of the screen indicating what file is being installed and where the file is being installed. The percentage bars inform you how much of the current disk has been installed and how much of the total program has been installed.

7. Throughout the installation, once a disk has been completely installed, a dialog box is displayed prompting you to insert the next diskette. Insert the appropriate disk and then choose OK. You must choose OK *or* press Enter or the installation program will not continue. You will be prompted to insert both the Installation disks and the Program disks.
8. After the program is installed, you are asked if you want to read the README files. Choose Yes if you want to read these files, choose No if you want to continue with the installation of WordPerfect.

9. A dialog box displays indicating the installation is complete, choose OK. WordPerfect then creates a program group for WPWin 6. Simply click on the WPWin 6 icon to start the program.

The first time you start WordPerfect a QuickStart Coach displays. The QuickStart Coach gives you hints and tips for getting up and running with WordPerfect 6 for Windows. You simply select the item you want to learn more about and choose Continue. If you do not want to use the coach choose Skip this Coach or Quit at any time.

Any time after installing WordPerfect you can use the Setup program (located on the WPWin 6 program group) to install utility disks, additional printers, and fonts. You can also use the Setup program to uninstall WordPerfect from your computer.

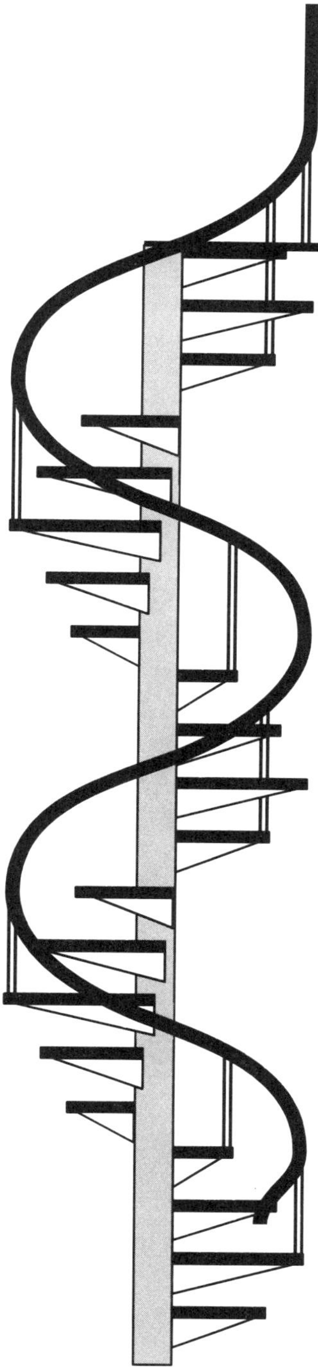

Chapter 1

WordPerfect and Windows: The Basics

This chapter answers questions about the following basic concepts of using WordPerfect with Windows:

- Starting WordPerfect
- Using WordPerfect with Windows
- Using the mouse
- Using the menu bar, Button Bar, and Power Bar
- Moving around in WordPerfect
- Reading the status bar
- Opening a document
- Moving between documents
- Changing the way document windows are displayed
- Changing the size and moving document windows
- Getting help
- Saving a document
- Exiting from WordPerfect

Also in this chapter is a list of some of the most common items you see on-screen along with a definition and an example. If you are new to Windows, these terms help you get quickly up to speed.

HOW DO I... Start WordPerfect?

If you have completed a standard installation of Windows, change to the Windows directory by typing **CD\WINDOWS** and then pressing Enter. To start Windows, type **WIN** and press Enter. You should see a screen similar to the one displayed in Figure 1–1.

During the installation of WordPerfect, the Install program automatically created a WPWin 6.0 program group, similar to the one shown in Figure 1–2. To open the WPWin 6.0 program group, move the mouse pointer to the group icon and double-click on it. You may have to double-click a few times if you are not used to working with your mouse.

HINT

If you are having trouble opening the program group, click and release the mouse button twice as quickly as possible. If you continue to have difficulty double-clicking on items, you may want to slow down the speed of your mouse. See your

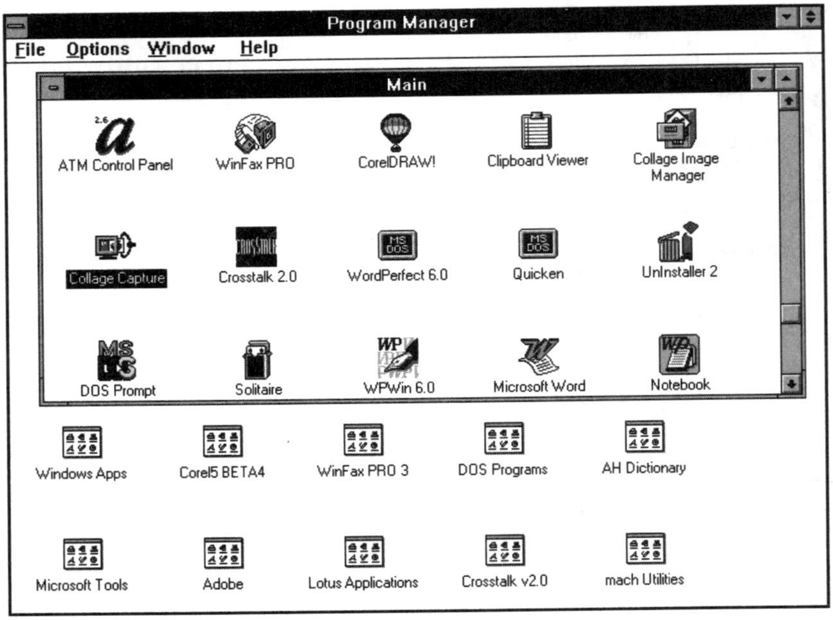

FIGURE 1–1
The Windows Program Manager.

FIGURE 1–2
The WPWin 6.0 program group.

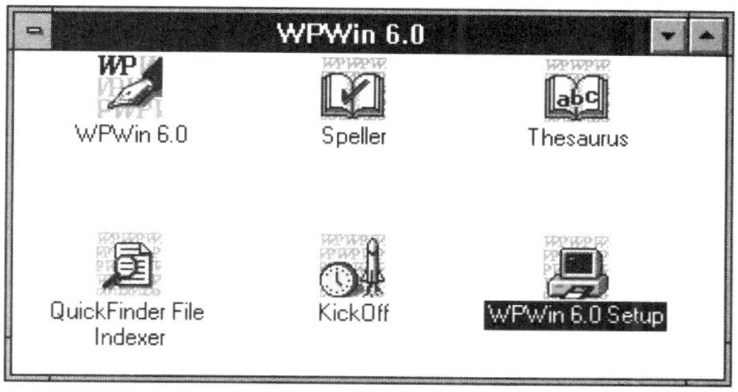

Windows manual for more information. You can also click once on the icon and then press [Enter].

After the WordPerfect program group is open, simply double-click the WPWin 6.0 icon.

After WordPerfect opens, the main screen shown, in Figure 1–3, is displayed. At the top of the window, WordPerfect displays the title bar,

FIGURE 1–3
The main WordPerfect screen.

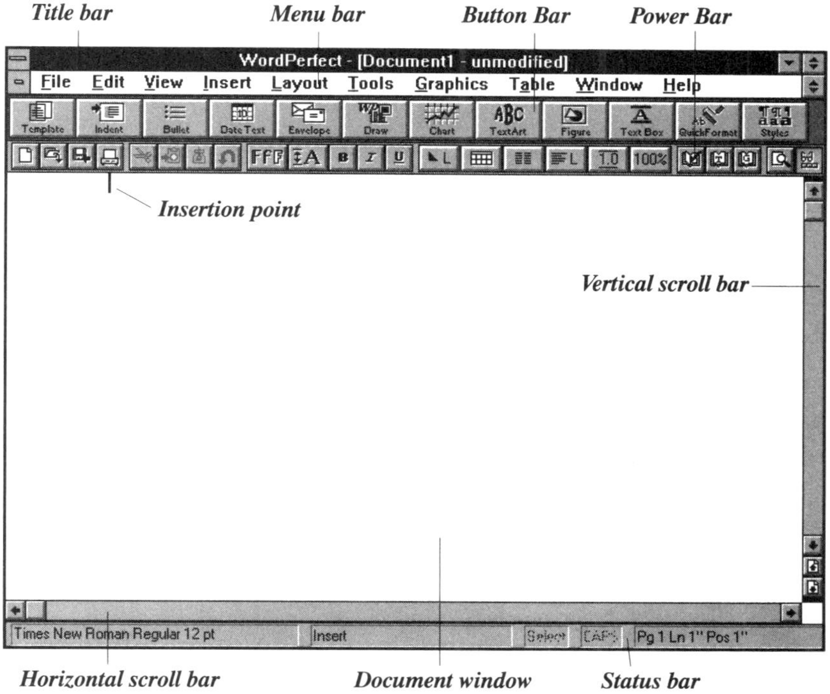

which displays the name of the program. Below the title bar is the menu bar, the WordPerfect Button Bar, and the Power Bar. This part of the screen is sometimes referred to as the *application window.*

Directly below the Power Bar is the document window, in which you can begin typing text or open a document you have already created. The *insertion point,* or cursor (the blinking vertical bar), is displayed in the left corner of the document window. The insertion point lets you know where you are within a document. The document window also has horizontal and vertical scroll bars to aid you in quickly moving through your document.

At the bottom of the document window is the status bar, which displays useful information about your document, such as the font you are using and the current position of the insertion point.

HOW DO I... Use Windows with WordPerfect?

WordPerfect works with Windows to give you the power you need in a word processor. You do not have to know everything about Windows, however, to use WordPerfect for Windows. Many features in Windows are common to all Windows applications, so after you learn some of the Windows basics, you can use that knowledge when you're working with any Windows application.

If you are an experienced Windows user, you probably understand most of the information and terms in this section. If you are a brand-new Windows user, however, this section introduces you to many of the exciting features you have to understand to most effectively use WordPerfect for Windows. Figures 1–4, 1–5, and 1–6 show examples of many of the terms in the following section.

Terms You Need to Know

Button Bar	A series of icons that represent commonly used menu items, features, macros, and other Button Bars. When a Button Bar is displayed, you can simply click the item you want to access rather than remember its location on a menu or the keystrokes to access it. You can move, edit, and create your own Button Bars.
Cancel button	A command button on most dialog boxes that lets you cancel any changes you have made and

FIGURE 1–4
The WordPerfect main screen.

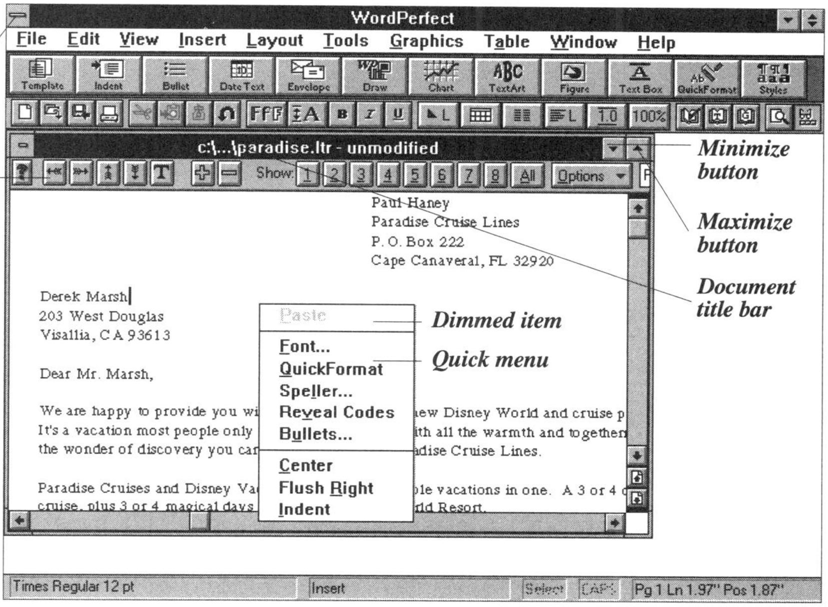

FIGURE 1–5
The WordPerfect main screen with pull-down menu.

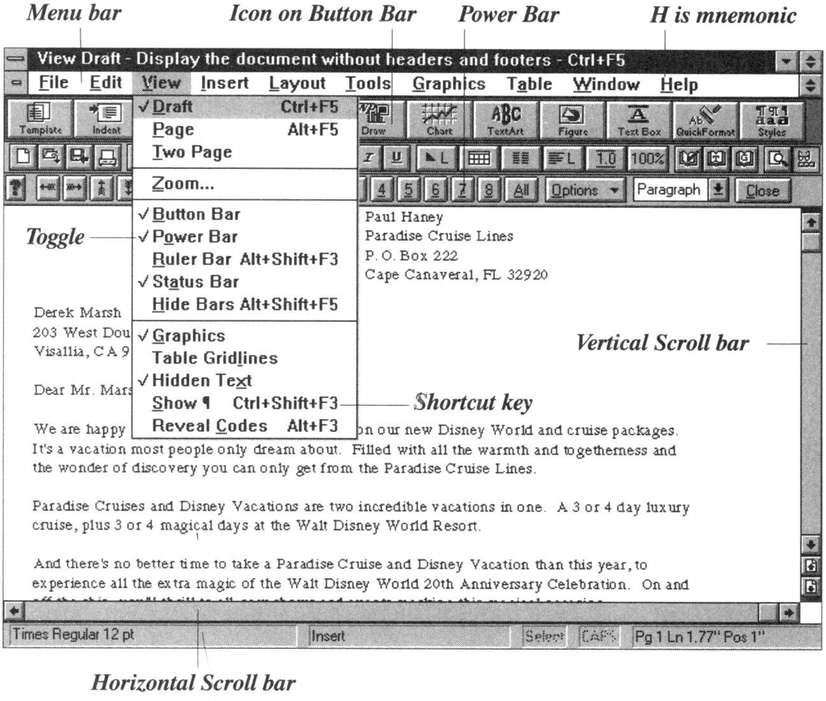

FIGURE 1–6
A typical WordPerfect dialog box.

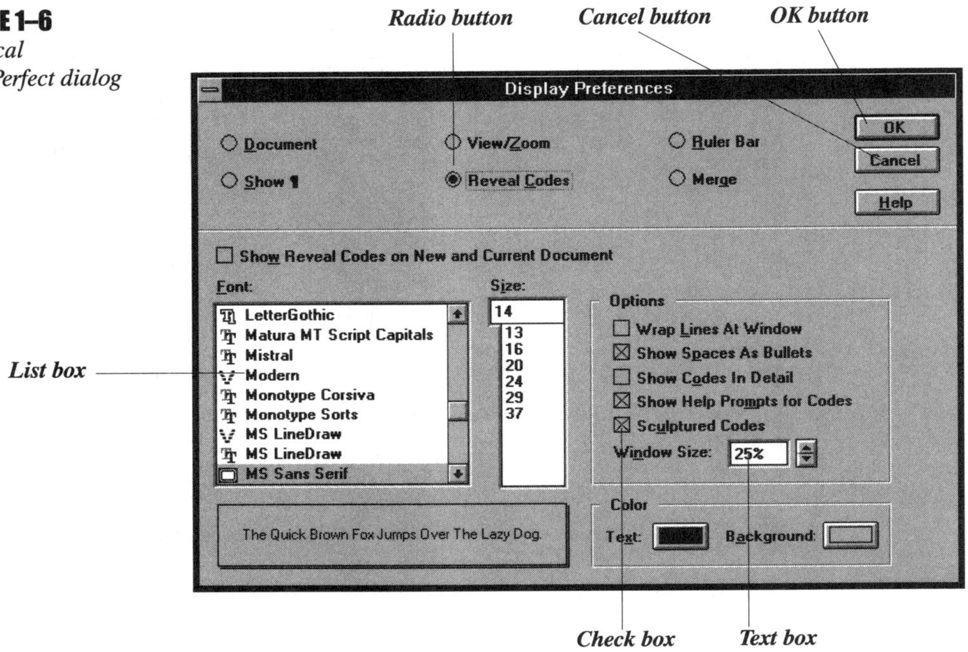

	return to the preceding dialog box or window. You can also press the Esc key to cancel changes and close a dialog box.
Check box	Used to select or deselect an option within a dialog box. When an option is selected, an X is displayed in the corresponding check box.
Click	To press and release the left mouse button. The mouse pointer should be positioned on the option you want to select when you click the mouse.
Close button	A command button on most dialog boxes that lets you close the dialog box.
Control menu	Lets you "control" how a window is displayed. The Control menu is displayed when you click once on the horizontal bar in the upper left corner of a window, called the *Control menu box.* You can move, size, maximize, and minimize windows by using the Control menu. WordPerfect displays a control menu for the application

	that is in the top left corner of the main title bar. In addition, each document window has a Control menu.
Default	The standard settings for options within WordPerfect. For example, the default margins are 1 inch.
Dialog box	Displayed when you're performing certain tasks to enable you to select required options. Can also display messages or warnings about the task you are performing.
Dimmed	An option appears dimmed, or *grayed out,* if it is not available. If you do not have any text selected in your document window, for example, the Copy option on the Edit menu appears dimmed.
Double-click	To press and release the left mouse button twice. If you want to select a word in your document, you can double-click on the word, for example.
Drag	To hold down the mouse button while moving the mouse. You can select a word in your document, for example, and then drag it to a new location.
Drag and drop	To release the mouse button after dragging an item.
Drop-down list box	Displays additional options when you select the down arrow that is displayed to the right of the current option.
Feature Bar	Enables you to quickly access options for a specific feature. The Feature Bar is automatically displayed when you select certain features. When you choose Outline, for example, the Outline Feature Bar is displayed below the Power Bar.
Icon	A graphical picture displayed on-screen. The Button Bar and Power Bar contain icons that represent the various features.
Insertion point	A flashing vertical bar that appears in the document window to let you know your current location. As you type text, your insertion point automatically moves.
List box	Displays a list of selections from which you can select. If there are more choices than can be dis-

	played on-screen, you can click on the list box's scroll bars to see the remaining options.
Maximize button	Enlarges the window to its full or maximum size.
Menu bar	Displays menu options from which you can access various features and commands from within WordPerfect. The menu bar is displayed directly below the title bar.
Minimize button	Reduces or minimizes the window to an icon. To restore a minimized window, you can double-click on the icon.
Mnemonic	The underlined letter in a menu choice. The mnemonic in File, for example, is F. If you are using the keyboard, the mnemonic is the letter you press to access the menu item. If you are accessing the item from the menu bar or dialog box, you have to press the Alt key before the mnemonic.
Mouse pointer	Represents the location of the mouse in the window. The mouse pointer usually is displayed as an I-beam in the document window, depending on the function you are performing; it is usually displayed as an arrow or pointer when you are pointing to an item you can select from a window or dialog box.
OK button	A command button displayed on most dialog boxes. When you click on the OK button, any options you have selected take effect.
Power Bar	A row of icons that represent commonly used menu items and features. When the Power Bar is displayed, you can simply click the item you want to access rather than remember its location on a menu or the keystrokes to access it.
QuickMenu	A QuickMenu displays specific options for a given feature. To display a QuickMenu, click the right mouse button. The QuickMenu that is displayed depends on what your mouse is pointing to when you click the right mouse button.

Radio button	Used to select or deselect an option within a dialog box. When an option is selected, the radio button is filled in. You can select only one option from a group of radio buttons.
Restore button	Restores the window to its previous size. When you first start WordPerfect, the document window displays a Restore button.
Scroll bar	Enables you to move to different locations in a document. There is a horizontal and vertical scroll bar.
Shortcut keys	Keystrokes you can use to access certain commands. Shortcut keys are displayed to the right of an item on a menu. For example, Ctrl+S is the shortcut key for Save.
Template	The formatting codes and setup information used for a document in WordPerfect. Every document you create is based on a template. WordPerfect provides several default templates, such as memos, expense reports, certificates, and fax cover sheets.
Text box	Used to enter information for a specific option inside a dialog box. You enter the information at the insertion point location.
Title bar	Displayed above the menu bar. If you have saved the document in the document window, the name of the file is displayed on the title bar. Help prompts also are displayed in the title bar when you point to items on the Button Bar, Power Bar, or Feature Bar.
Toggle	An option you turn on and off by using the same technique. Bold is an example of a toggle option. Many times, options that are toggles are displayed with a check mark on a menu.

HOW DO I. . . Use the Mouse?

Effective use of your mouse is critical in any Windows application. You can use your mouse to quickly access menus, move around in the document window, and manipulate text. You can choose to use the mouse exclusively while working in WordPerfect or in conjunction with keystrokes. You decide what works best for you.

Steps

When you first start WordPerfect, your mouse should already function properly. WordPerfect uses the settings specified in Windows for your mouse. If your mouse is not working, you have to follow the instructions in your Windows manual for setting up a mouse or changing mouse settings.

Tell Me More

Your mouse pointer is displayed differently depending on where it is positioned on your screen. If you are in the document window, the mouse is displayed as an I-beam, as shown here:

HINT

If you do not want the I-beam displayed on your document window, you can move the mouse pointer off the document window.

In most other locations, the mouse is displayed as a pointer, as shown here:

You may also see the mouse pointer displayed as a hand, indicating that you can "grab" something and move it to a new location, or as an hourglass, indicating that WordPerfect or Windows is processing information.

The mouse pointer does not replace the insertion point; you see both items on your screen at the same time. If you move the mouse pointer to a new location in your document and then click the left mouse button, your insertion point moves to the new location. Moving the mouse pointer in this way makes it easy to move quickly to a line that is displayed on-screen without having to move the insertion point through the text. You can move the mouse pointer only to a section of the document in which text already exists.

The mouse also helps you quickly access items from the menu bar. To use the mouse to select an item from the menu bar, move the mouse pointer anywhere on the menu item (the pointer does not have to point to *the mnemonic,* the underlined letter) and click the left mouse button. To select a radio button or check-box item in a dialog box, simply point to the option you want and click the left mouse button.

HOW DO I... Use the Menu Bar?

The menu bar that appears at the top of your screen lets you easily access all features and menus within WordPerfect. Using the menu bar eliminates the need to memorize keystrokes that correspond to each feature.

Steps

➠To select an item from the menu bar:

1. Move the mouse pointer to the menu item and click the left mouse button.
2. Continue clicking the menu items you want to select.

HINT

To access a specific menu, you can also press Alt+*letter,* where the letter corresponds to the mnemonic on the menu bar.

Tell Me More

Every menu item on the menu bar lists the features that can be accessed from that menu. When you select an item from the menu bar, a *cascading menu* is displayed that lists additional options from which to choose. To help familiarize you with the features associated with each menu, Figure 1–7 shows each of the pull-down menus you can access from the menu bar.

Like all Windows applications, the pull-down menus contain helpful information about the menu items. If the item can be accessed by way of a single keystroke combination (Ctrl+F4, for example), the combination is listed to the right of the item. Many WordPerfect features are available by way of function-key combinations.

Whenever you see three dots (...) listed next to a feature or option, they indicate that a dialog box appears when you choose that feature. A triangle (➤) to the right of an item indicates that a *cascading menu* will

FIGURE 1–7
Pull-down menus.

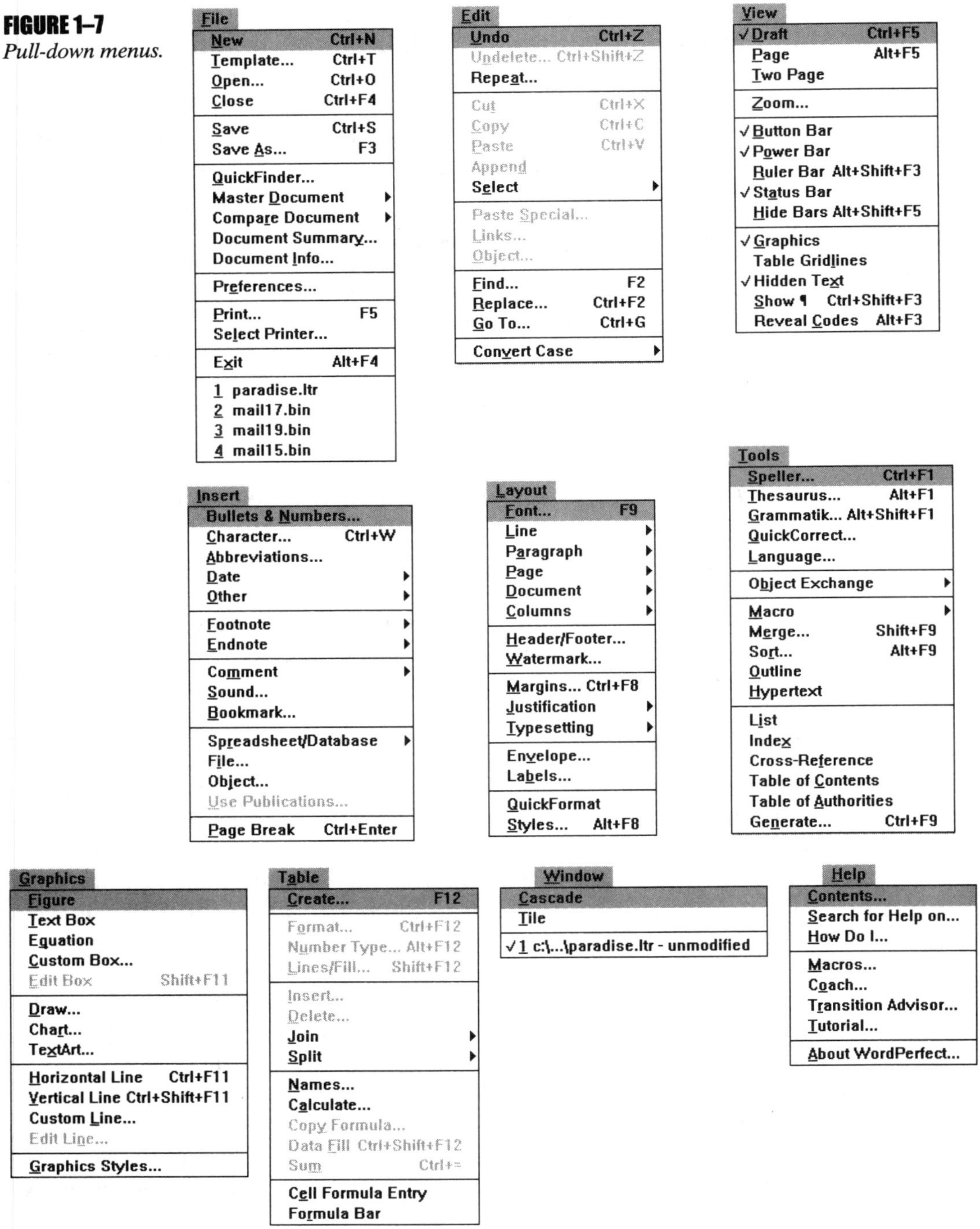

appear. An option that is dimmed is not available in your current mode of operation. If you do not have any text selected, for example, the Cut option is dimmed on the Edit menu. If a check mark appears next to an item, it indicates that the item is turned on or active. If the Button Bar option on the View menu displays a check mark, for example, you know that your Button Bar is displayed. To turn off or deselect an item, you simply click the item.

The default WordPerfect menu bar is displayed every time you start WordPerfect.

HINT

If you do not want to make a selection from a pull-down menu that is displayed, you can click on another selection on the menu bar or you can click anywhere outside the menu to remove the menu.

HOW DO I. . . Use the Button Bar?

The Button Bar is displayed below the menu bar and contains icons that represent commonly used menu items, features, macros, and other Button Bars. When a Button Bar is displayed, you simply click the item you want to access rather than remember its location on a menu or the keystrokes to access it.

Step

➨To access an item on the Button Bar:

1. Move the mouse pointer to the button and click it, as shown here:

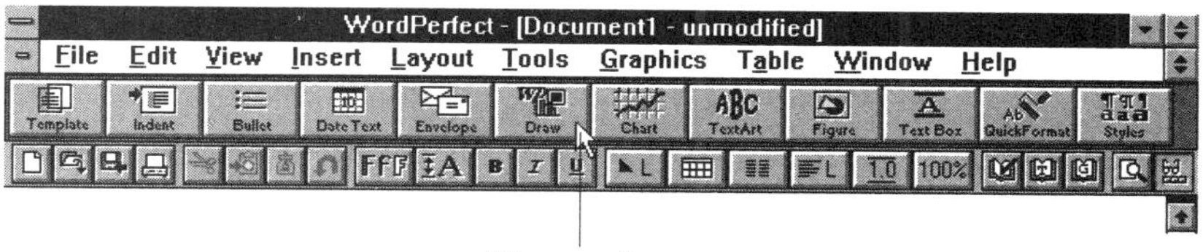

Mouse pointer

Tell Me More

After you click a button, WordPerfect performs the command or displays a dialog box for you to make additional selections for the feature.

The Button Bar is a great way to automate many of the tasks you perform in WordPerfect.

HINT **If you cannot remember the function of a button, you can move the mouse pointer to the button and WordPerfect displays a help message on the title bar at the top of your window.**

HOW DO I... Use the Power Bar?

The Power Bar is displayed below the Button Bar and is similar to the Button Bar. The Power Bar contains icons that represent commonly used features. To access an item on the Power Bar, you can simply click the item you want to access rather than remember its location on a menu or the keystrokes to access it.

Step

➡To access an item on the Power Bar:

1. Move the mouse pointer to the button and click it.

Tell Me More

After you click a Power Bar item, WordPerfect performs the command or displays a list or dialog box for you to make additional selections for the feature. The Power Bar is a great way to automate many of the tasks you perform in WordPerfect. To help familiarize you with the capabilities of the Power Bar, Figure 1–8 describes each button on the Power Bar.

HINT **If you cannot remember the function of a button, you can move the mouse pointer to the button and WordPerfect displays a help message on the title bar at the top of your window.**

For information about customizing the Power Bar, see Chapter 11, "Automating Tasks and Optimizing WordPerfect."

HOW DO I... Move Around the Menus and Dialog Boxes in WordPerfect?

WordPerfect provides several ways to move around in menus and dialog boxes and select options. The lists in this section give you options for

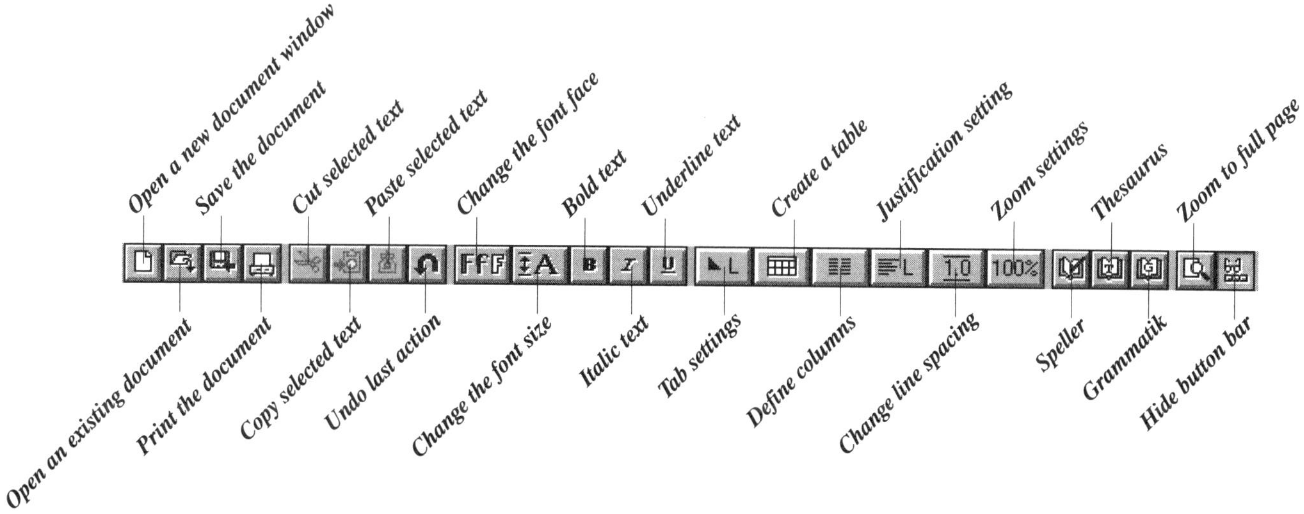

FIGURE 1–8
The Power Bar.

moving around and choosing options from different types of menus and dialog boxes from within WordPerfect.

To select an option from the menu bar, you can:

- Click the option with the mouse.
- Press Alt+*letter,* where the letter corresponds to the mnemonic for the item on the menu bar.

To select a menu item from a pull-down or cascading menu, you can:

- Click the option with the mouse.
- Press the ↑ and ↓ keys to move to the option and then press Enter.
- Press the mnemonic that corresponds to the item you want to select.

To select an option from a dialog box, you can:

- Click the option with the mouse.
- Press Alt+*letter,* where the letter corresponds to the mnemonic for the option.
- Press the Tab key to move through the list of options. If the option allows input, pressing the Tab key moves you directly to the input area. If the option takes you to another dialog box, move to the option by pressing the Tab key or the arrow keys and then pressing Enter.

HINT

A dotted line appears around the option that is active in a dialog box.

To select an option from a list box or drop-down list, you can:

- Click the option with the mouse.
- Press the arrow keys to highlight the option and then press Enter.

To select an option from a pop-up list, you can:

- Hold down the left mouse button, point to the option you want to choose, and then release the mouse button.

To close and exit from a dialog box, you can:

- Choose the OK button to accept the changes you have made and exit from the dialog box.

NOTE **In some instances, you may have to choose OK or Close several times to return to the document window.**

- ➤ Choose the Cancel button *or* press the Esc key to cancel any changes you have made and exit from the dialog box.
- ➤ Double-click the control button in the top left corner of the dialog box to cancel any changes you have made and exit from the dialog box.

Because WordPerfect offers a variety of ways to navigate through its menus and options, you might want to try different methods and see which ways are the easiest and most effective for you.

HOW DO I. . . Read the Status Bar?

The status bar shown in Figure 1–9 is displayed on the bottom line of your screen. It lists useful information about the current document. In the left corner of the status bar, the name and size of the current font are displayed. The middle portion of the status bar displays different types of information, depending on which features you are using. If you are just typing text, you see the word *Insert,* indicating that you are in Insert mode for entering text.

NOTE **If you are in Typeover mode, the word *Typeover* replaces the document name or font name. When you are using Typeover mode, the text you enter overwrites the text on the screen.**

The status bar also displays other useful information, depending on the features you are using. If you are using columns, the current column number is displayed. If you are using tables, the current cell number is displayed.

FIGURE 1–9
The status bar.

The right corner of the status bar displays the page number of the current document and the current position of the insertion point from the top of the page and from the left edge of the page.

HOW DO I. . . Open a Document?

When you open a document, you retrieve a copy of the document into an empty document window. You can also open a new document window so that you can begin creating a new document. If you want to combine two files, you can insert an existing document into the currently displayed document. If you have a document that contains a table, for example, and you want to incorporate that table into a marketing brochure you are creating, you can simply insert the table into your brochure.

Steps

➡To open a new document for which you know the filename:

1. Choose File➢Open *or* press Ctrl+O. The Open File dialog box is displayed, as shown in Figure 1–10.
2. In the Filename text box, enter the name of the document you want to open, (be sure to include the directory in which the

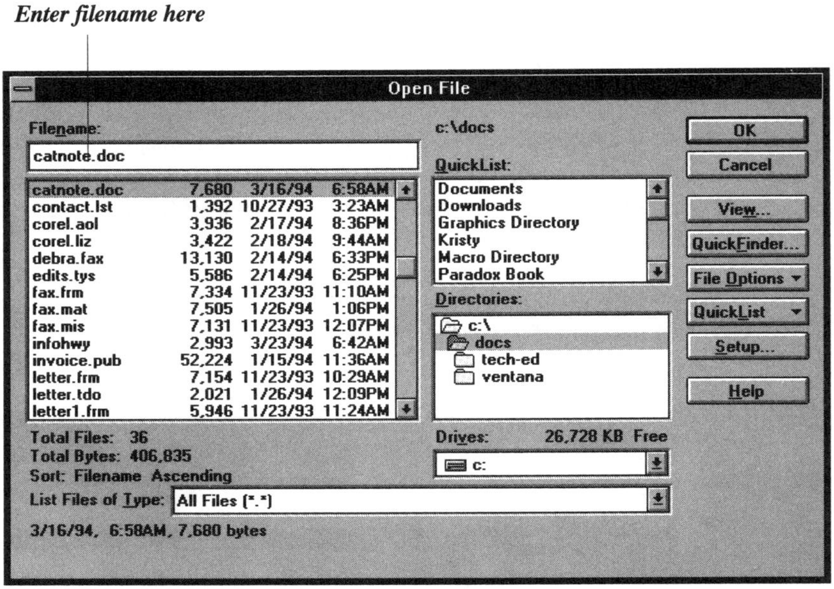

FIGURE 1–10
The Open File dialog box.

file is located) and choose OK. If you already have other documents open, the document is opened in a new document window.

➠**To open a new document for which you do not remember the filename:**

1. Choose File➢Open *or* press Ctrl+O. The Open File dialog box appears.
2. In the Filename text box, type the name of the directory in which the file is located and press Enter. The files listed directly below the Filename text box will now show all the files in that directory.
3. Double-click the filename. The file is now opened in a document window.

➠**To retrieve a document into an existing document:**

1. Position the insertion point where you want the document to be retrieved.
2. Choose Insert➢File to open the Insert File dialog box.
3. In the Filename text box, enter the name of the document you want to retrieve and choose OK.

Tell Me More

When you first start WordPerfect, an empty document window is displayed. WordPerfect allows you to open as many as nine document windows.

WordPerfect makes it quick and easy to open one of the last four documents you have retrieved. You simply choose the File menu, and the names of the last four documents you have opened are displayed at the bottom of the menu, as shown in Figure 1–11. Click on the file and it is opened into a new document window.

When you installed WordPerfect, a default directory for storing documents was created for you. WordPerfect looks for your documents in this directory unless you specify otherwise.

If you do not remember what your default document directory is or if you want to change your default document directory, follow these steps:

1. Choose File➢Preferences and then double-click the File icon.
2. If necessary, select Documents/Backup.

FIGURE 1–11
The File menu lists the last four documents that were opened.

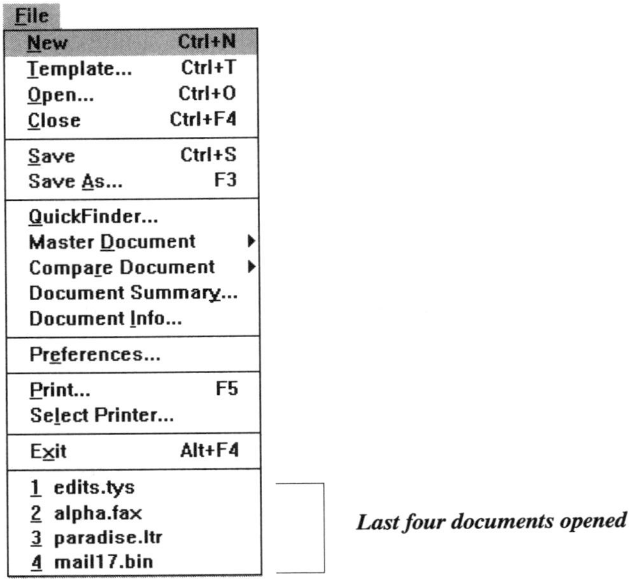

3. In the Default Directory text box, enter the name of the new default directory.
4. Choose OK and Close to return to the document window.

If you want to create a new document and you already have one or more documents open, you can open a new window by choosing File➢New *or* pressing Ctrl+N. This step opens the next available document window so that you can begin creating a new document.

HOW DO I. . . Move Between Document Windows?

WordPerfect allows you to have as many as nine document windows open at a time. Working with multiple document windows gives you great flexibility in using WordPerfect. You can open multiple documents, for example, and cut and copy information between them. If you are working with several documents or just a few documents, you need a quick way to move between them.

Steps

If the window containing your document is displayed on-screen:

1. Click anywhere in the document window you want to switch to.

If the document window is not displayed on-screen, you can display a list of all open document windows and then switch to the window you want:

1. Choose Window from the menu bar. The Window menu is displayed, as shown here:

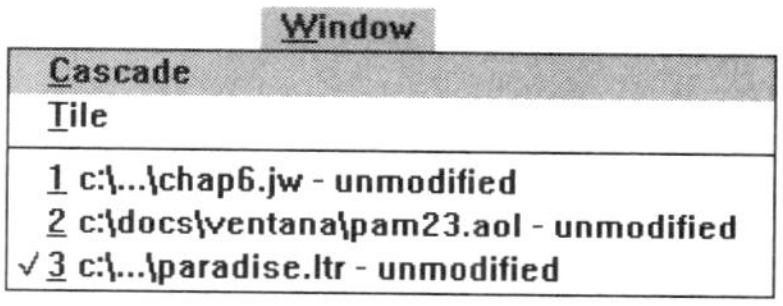

2. Click on the document you want to switch to.

NOTE **If you want to cycle through all your documents, you can press Ctrl + F6.**

Tell Me More

The Window menu displays information about all nine document windows (if they are all opened). The name of the document is displayed next to the document number if the document has been saved. If the document has never been saved, the **Document#** label is displayed. The (unmodified) label indicates that you have not made any changes to the document since the last time it was saved.

If you are going to switch frequently between document windows, you might want to use either the tile or cascade arrangement to display the document windows. When you use either of these arrangements, you can simply click anywhere on the document window to which you want to switch. This capability makes frequent switching between documents quick and easy. For information about using the tile or cascade features, see the following section.

HOW DO I... Change the Way My Document Windows Are Displayed?

Windows and WordPerfect give you great flexibility in arranging the way your document windows are displayed. You can maximize, minimize, tile, and cascade your windows. By default, the document window is *maximized,* which means that it is as large as it can become.

Minimizing a window reduces the window to an icon, as shown in Figure 1–12. Minimizing a window lets you move it out of the way without completely closing the window so that you can quickly open the document when necessary.

You can also change the arrangement of the document windows by using the tile and cascade features. Tiling or cascading windows lets you view multiple documents at the same time. Figure 1–13 shows a tiled window arrangement, and Figure 1–14 shows a cascaded window arrangement.

FIGURE 1–12
A minimized document window.

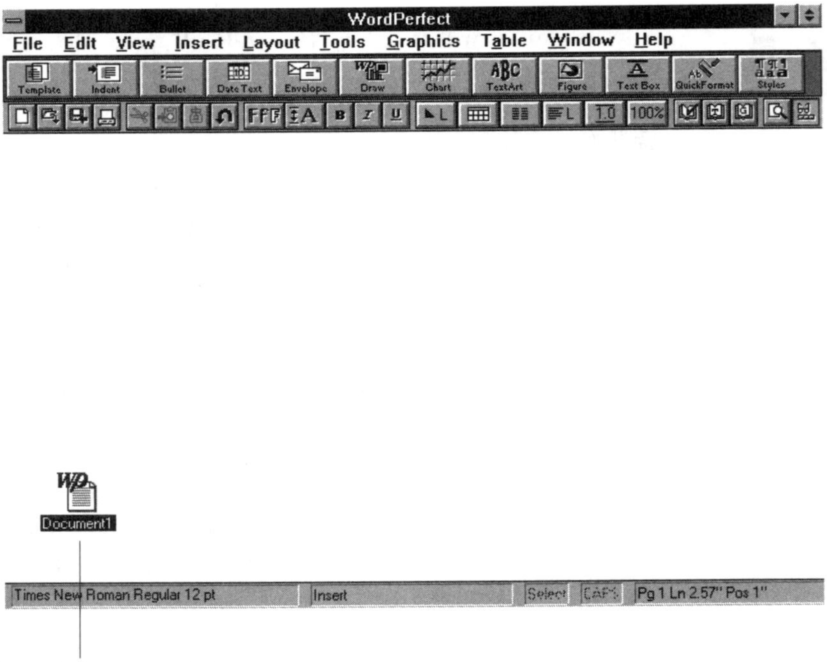

Minimized document window

FIGURE 1–13
A tiled window arrangement.

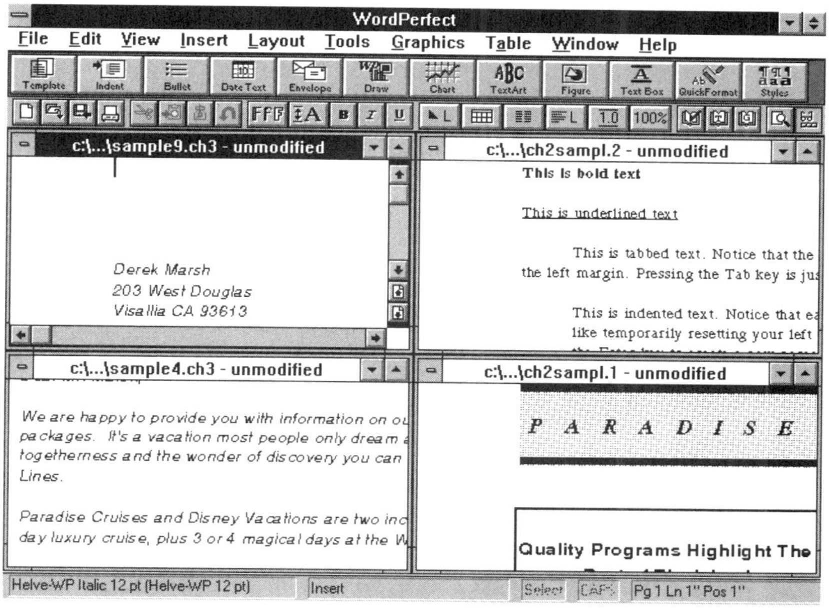

FIGURE 1–14
A cascaded window arrangement.

Document title bar

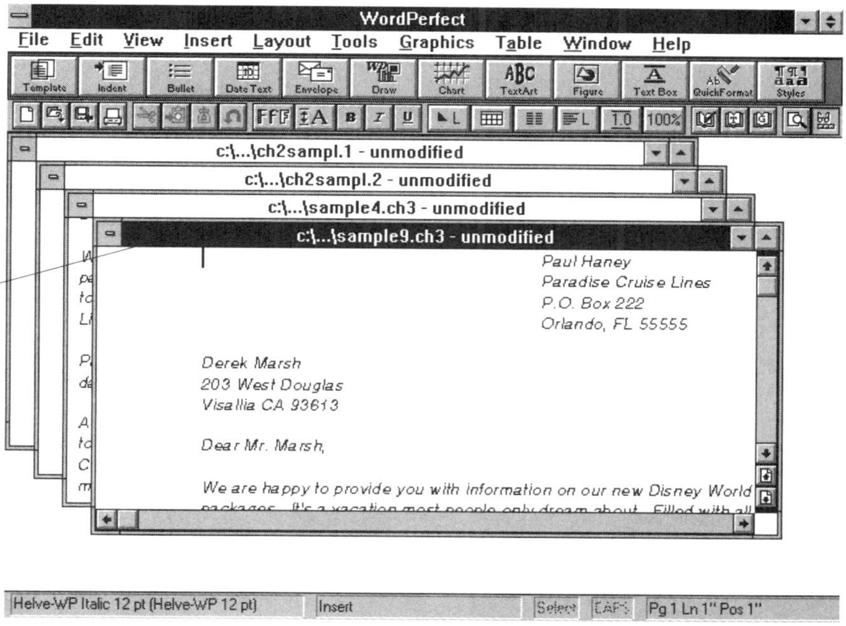

Steps

➡To minimize or maximize a document window:

1. Click the Minimize or Maximize icon shown here:

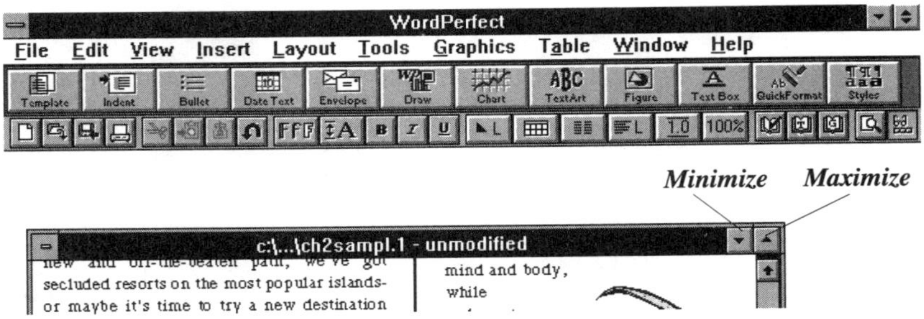

➡To tile or cascade your document windows:

1. Choose Window➢Tile or Window➢Cascade.

Tell Me More

The following sections explain more about the maximizing and minimizing capabilities and tiling and cascading windows.

Maximizing and Minimizing Windows

Maximizing a window lets you take advantage of the entire document window. Whenever you maximize a window, WordPerfect removes the document title bar so that the document window uses the maximum amount of space available on your screen. When you are working on only one or two documents at a time, maximizing the windows is probably the most useful method because you can quickly move between the two documents by using the Ctrl+F6 shortcut key.

Minimizing a window reduces the window to an icon. Below the icon is the name of the file. WordPerfect places the icon in the lower left corner of your window; however, you can drag the icon to any location within the document window.

NOTE **If a document is minimized, WordPerfect still displays it on the Window menu.**

The document title bar displays the name of the document in the top center (refer to Figure 1–14). If the document has not been saved, the title is replaced by the Document number. In the upper right corner of the frame are the Minimize and Maximize buttons. The button in the top left corner of the title bar is the Control menu. Double-clicking on the Control menu lets you quickly close the document window. When you close a window that contains a document to which you have made changes, WordPerfect prompts you to save the document before you close the window. If no text is in the document window, the window automatically closes. If only one document window is open, the text is saved or cleared and the window remains open. If multiple document windows are open, WordPerfect returns to the previous document window.

Tiling and Cascading Windows

Using the tile and cascade arrangements enables you to see parts of all your documents on-screen and switch quickly between the document windows. When your documents are arranged by using the tile or cascade features, you can simply click the mouse pointer somewhere in the window to which you want to switch.

When you are using these arrangements, it is important to know which document window is active. The title bar of the active document window is displayed in color, or shaded if you are using a noncolor monitor.

HOW DO I. . . Change the Size and Move Document Windows?

At times you may want to customize the way document windows are displayed on your screen. You can do this by changing the size and location of the document windows. WordPerfect lets you size and move the document windows just as you do with any other Windows application. You cannot move or size a maximized window; you must minimize it before you can size or move a document window. The easiest way to do this is to tile or cascade your document windows or click the Restore button.

Steps

➨To change the size of a document window:

1. Position the mouse pointer on the outermost line of the horizontal or vertical scroll bar. After the mouse is in the right location, it is displayed as a double arrow, as shown here:

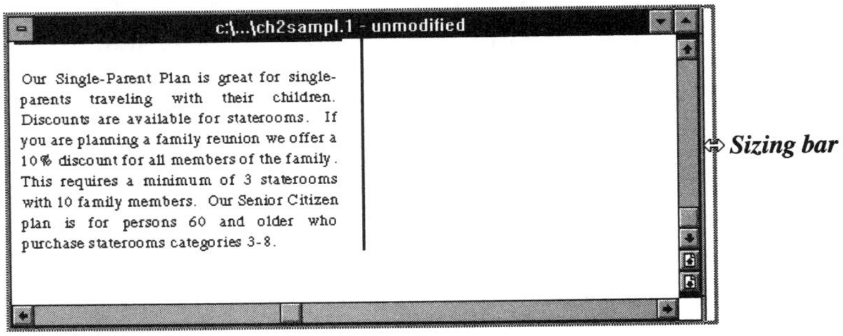

2. While holding down the left mouse button, drag the line until the window becomes the size you want and then release the mouse button.

➡ **To move a document window by using the mouse:**

1. Position the mouse pointer on the title bar of the document window and hold down the left mouse button. A dashed border appears around your screen.
2. While holding down the left mouse button, drag the line until the window is in the location you want and then release the mouse button.

Tell Me More

The ways in which you size and move document windows work independently of each other. At times you may have to size the document first, move it to a new location, and then size it again. You cannot move a full-size document window—it must be sized down first.

HOW DO I. . . Get Help?

WordPerfect has an extensive on-line Help feature to aid you in obtaining useful information while using WordPerfect. The Help feature includes context-sensitive help, a searchable topic list, macro information, HOW DO I. . . topics, coaches, the Transition Advisor, tutorials, and information about your individual WordPerfect setup. In addition,

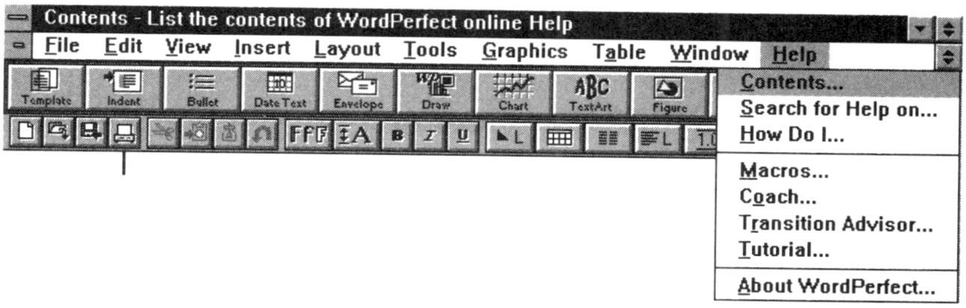

FIGURE 1–15
The main Help menu.

other Help topics include a glossary, menu commands, keystrokes, and new features.

Steps

➡ **To choose an option from the main Help menu, shown in Figure 1–15:**

1. Choose Help from the menu bar.
2. Choose the option you want.
3. Double-click on the Control menu when you're finished.

➡ **To view Help information while using a feature:**

1. Press F1 while the item on a menu is highlighted or while a dialog box is displayed. In addition, many of the dialog boxes contain Help buttons you can choose.
2. Choose the Close button when you're finished.

HINT

You can choose the Print button from any Help screen in WordPerfect to print useful information.

Tell Me More

The Help Contents dialog box, shown in Figure 1–16, displays a variety of useful Help topics from which you can choose. To display this menu, choose Help➢Contents *or* press F1 from the main screen. You can also access this menu from any WordPerfect Help screen by choosing the Contents button.

HINT

When you're using Help, you can choose the Back button to go back to the preceding help screen. You can also choose History to display a list of all the help screens you have viewed in the current Help session.

FIGURE 1–16
The Help Contents dialog box.

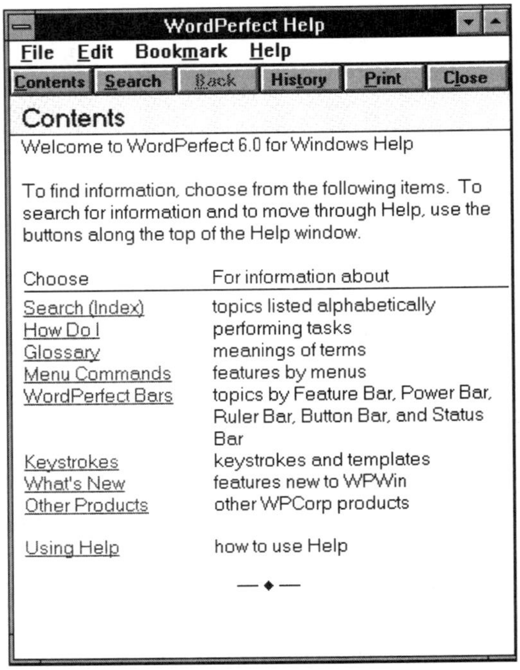

The Search for Help On option is an extensive index that lets you find information about any term, feature, or command in WordPerfect. You simply type the word you want information about, choose Show Topics to display the topics, select the topic you want to view information for, and then choose Go To. The index is useful if you want to find specific information about a certain feature. The information for each topic is the same information you see when you choose Help from a menu or dialog box for that feature.

The HOW DO I. . . help menu lists a few common tasks you can perform in WordPerfect. This information is similar to what you find in the WordPerfect reference manual. The feature name, keystrokes, purpose, Steps , and additional references are listed for the HOW DO I help topics.

The Macros help menu is the only place you can find all the advanced information about WordPerfect macros. The Macros Help information includes these topics:

- Macro command index
- System variable index

- Macro basics
- Programming basics
- DDE basics
- Shipping macros
- Macro conversion (from 5.1 macros)
- Glossary

The Coach feature included with WordPerfect Help guides you through common tasks. To use Coach, choose Coach from the Help menu and then select a task you want to perform. The Coach option shows you how to perform the task and lets you perform it while you are being coached.

The WordPerfect Help tutorials are useful for those who are new to WordPerfect. The tutorials take you through several basic word-processing functions.

Transition Advisor is a great tool for those who have been using other word processors or other versions of WordPerfect. The first thing you do is select your previous word processor and then select a feature. When you select a feature, WordPerfect displays the name of the feature in WordPerfect for Windows 6, lists keystrokes to access the key and the menu on which you can find the feature, and explains the purpose of the feature. You can also have WordPerfect demonstrate the feature by choosing Show Me; better yet, you can have WordPerfect use the feature by choosing Do It. The Transition Advisor is a great way to quickly get up to speed when you transfer from another version of WordPerfect or another word processor.

The About WordPerfect Help dialog box, shown in Figure 1–17, displays useful information about your system. This information can come in handy when you are troubleshooting problems within WordPerfect. If your setup information has changed since the last time you used WordPerfect, for example, you can look at the location of your private BIF setup file that WordPerfect is using and verify that it is correct. You can also see how much memory is available when you are using WordPerfect. Another important item on the WP Info screen is your version number and date. This information is extremely important when you call WordPerfect's Customer-Support department.

FIGURE 1–17
The About WordPerfect Help dialog box.

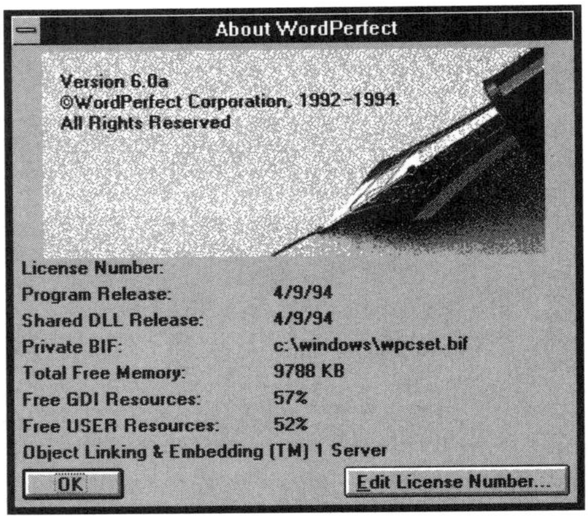

HOW DO I. . . Save a Document?

Saving a document lets you store the document on disk for future use. You can save a document to a directory on your hard disk or to a floppy disk. It is important that you save your documents often to avoid losing any information. WordPerfect provides several options for saving a document. You can save a previously saved document with or without confirmation of replacement. Use the Save feature to save without confirmation; use the Save As feature to save with confirmation and change other options associated with the file. If you use Save As, you can save the file with a different filename or in a different location.

Steps

➠**To save a document and automatically replace the existing document:**

1. Choose File➢Save *or* press Ctrl+S.

➠**To save a document and be prompted for a filename:**

1. Choose File➢Save As *or* press F3. The Save As dialog box is displayed, as shown in Figure 1–18.
2. Enter a new filename in the Filename text box. If a document already exists with the same filename, WordPerfect displays a dialog box asking whether you want to replace the existing document with the document on-screen.

3. If necessary, change any of the other options associated with that file.
4. Choose OK.

Tell Me More

Using the Save feature lets you quickly replace an existing document. If you use the Save feature to save a document that has not been saved, the Save As dialog box appears (refer to Figure 1–18), and you must enter a filename.

In addition to using the Save feature to save your document periodically, you can also use the timed-backup feature to have WordPerfect automatically make a backup copy of your document at specified intervals. By default, WordPerfect automatically backs up your document every ten minutes. The backup feature does not replace your existing file—it simply makes a backup copy of the file.

➠**To change or verify your default backup options:**

1. Choose File➢Preferences.
2. Choose File, and the File Preferences dialog box is displayed.
3. Choose Documents/Backup.
4. Verify or change any of the options shown in Figure 1–19.
5. Choose OK and Close to return to the document window.

FIGURE 1–18
The Save As dialog box.

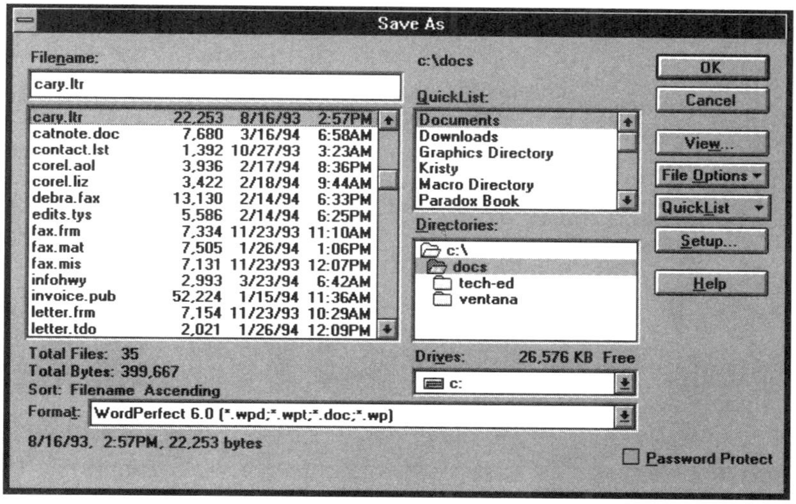

FIGURE 1–19
The File Preferences dialog box.

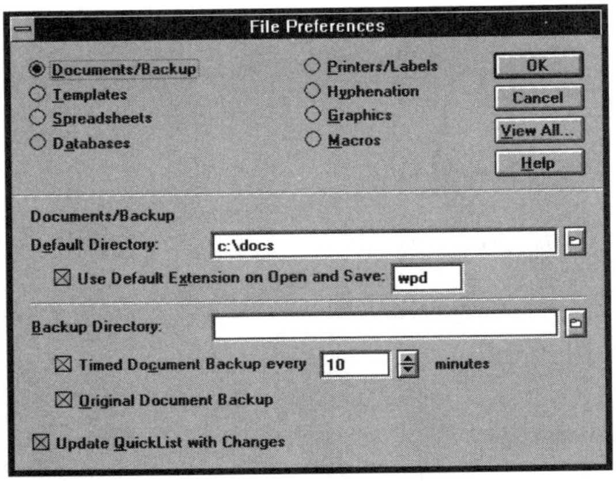

For more information about using the backup feature, see Chapter 2, "Setting Up WordPerfect."

When you are using the Save As feature, you can specify several options when you save a document. You can change the format of a document and assign a password to your document.

By default, WordPerfect saves your document in WordPerfect 6.0 format. If you know that your document will be used with another version of WordPerfect, such as WordPerfect 5.1 or another word processor, you can specify that format from the Save As dialog box.

➨To save a file in a different format:

1. Choose File➢Save As *or* press F3.
2. Click the drop-down list button next to the Format option. A list is displayed that shows all the formats in which a document can be saved.
3. Choose the format you want and choose OK.

From the Save As dialog box, you can also save your documents with a password to add a level of security.

➨To assign a password to your document:

1. Choose File➢Save As *or* press F3.
2. Select Password Protect and choose OK.
3. Enter a password and choose OK, and then reenter the password again when you are prompted to do so.
4. Choose OK to return to the document window.

Every time you retrieve a document with a password, you are prompted for the password. If you do not know the password or do not remember the password, you cannot retrieve the document. You cannot print, copy, move, rename, or look at a file with a password while you are in WordPerfect unless you know the password.

HOW DO I. . . Exit from WordPerfect?

It is important that you properly exit from your documents and from WordPerfect when you finish creating or editing your documents. If you do not exit from WordPerfect properly, you may lose valuable information from your documents. Within WordPerfect, you can close a document or exit from a document.

Closing a document closes the document and the document window. When you use Close, WordPerfect prompts you to save the document only if changes have been made. The Close feature is a quick way to exit from a document and a document window. Exiting from WordPerfect also closes the documents. If no modified documents are open, choosing Exit automatically closes all document windows and exits from WordPerfect without asking for confirmation. If there are modified documents, WordPerfect prompts you to save the documents and then automatically exits from WordPerfect.

Steps

➨To close a document and the current document window:

1. Choose File➢Close *or* double-click the control menu in the upper left corner of a document window (on the same line as the menu bar), as shown here:

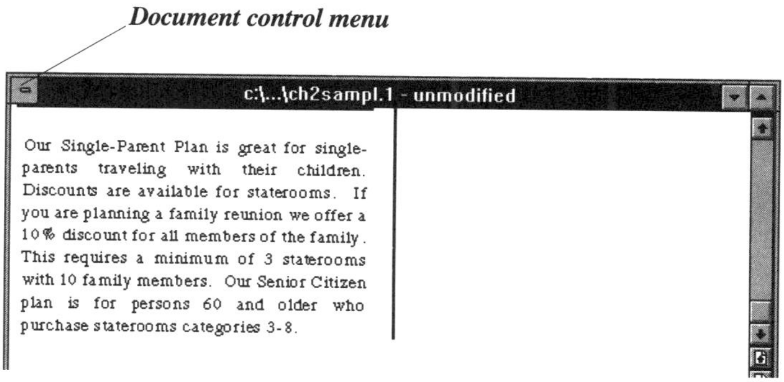

2. If changes have been made to the document or if it is a new document, a prompt is displayed that asks whether you want to save the document. Choose Yes to save the document or No if you do not want to save the document. If you choose Yes, WordPerfect saves the document and closes the document window. If you choose No, WordPerfect does not save the document and closes the document window.

➡To close all document windows and exit from WordPerfect:

1. Choose File➢Exit *or* double-click on the control menu in the upper left corner of the window (on the same line as the title bar), as shown here:

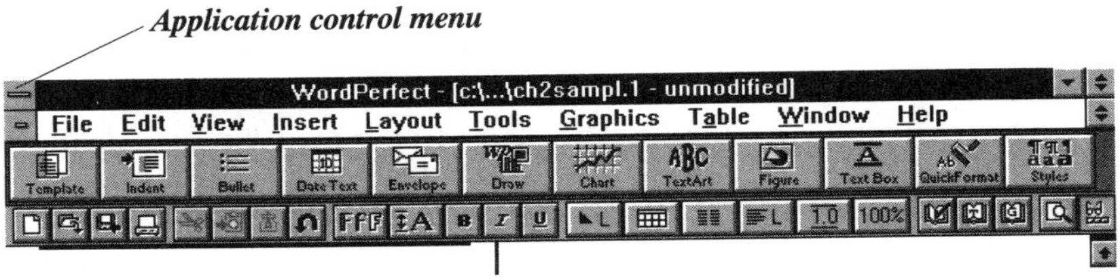

If changes have been made to a document or if it is a new document, a prompt is displayed that asks whether you want to save the document. If you choose Yes, WordPerfect saves the document and then exits from WordPerfect.

Tell Me More

A powerful tool you can use when you exit from WordPerfect is the Save Workspace feature. When you activate Save Workspace, WordPerfect remembers which documents you were working on and displays them the next time you start WordPerfect. This capability is really helpful if you know that you will be working on the same document for an extended period.

➡To activate the Save Workspace feature:

1. Choose File➢Preferences➢Environment.
2. Double-click on the Environment icon.
3. Select the Always, Never, or Prompt on Exit radio button.
4. Choose OK and Close to return to the document window.

The next time you start WordPerfect, the documents you were working on during your last session are opened and your cursor is in the exact location it was when you exited from WordPerfect.

WordPerfect offers many options for saving documents and exiting from document windows. The following table provides a quick overview of all the features associated with saving documents, closing document windows, and exiting from WordPerfect.

FEATURE	KEYSTROKE	DESCRIPTION
Save	Ctrl+S	Saves the document and remains in the current document window; no prompting for document name if it has previously been saved
Save As	F3	Saves the document and remains in the current document window; prompts for the document name and enables you to change Save options
Close	Ctrl+F4 *or* double-click on document Control menu	Closes document window; prompts you to save document if changes have been made
Exit	Alt+F4 *or* double-click on application control menu	Exits from and saves specified documents and exits from WordPerfect

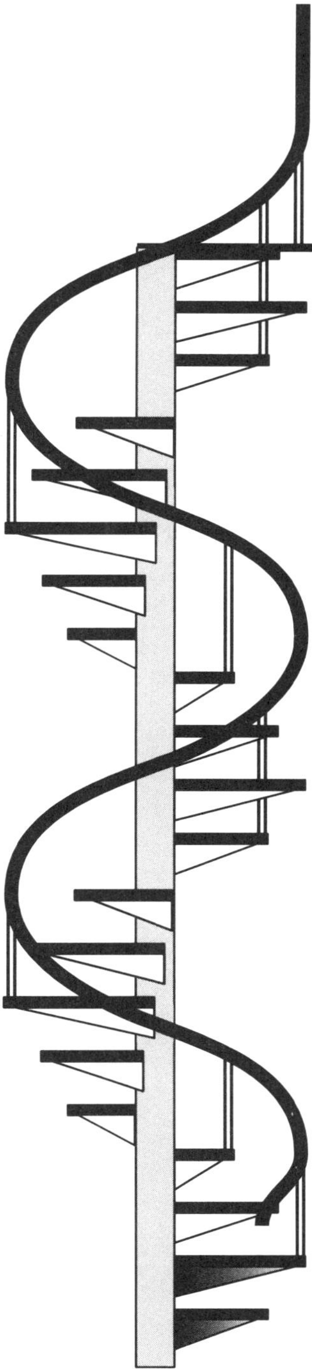

Chapter 2

Setting Up WordPerfect

The questions answered in this chapter help you customize many of the Preferences that make using WordPerfect easier. You learn how to set mouse options and color options from the Windows Control Panel. You also learn how to switch between Draft, Page, and Two Page display modes; also, the advantages of each mode are discussed. This chapter shows you how to customize the display of Button Bars, menu bars, and the Ruler Bar, and how to remove the bars. The chapter also explains how to customize the Backup, Beep, and Units of Measure options, and how to use DOS keystrokes in WordPerfect 6 for Windows. File preferences are discussed so that you know exactly where WordPerfect is looking for and storing your files. Finally, you learn how to display Reveal Codes to help you quickly see formatting codes in your documents.

HOW DO I... Customize Mouse Options?

All the mouse settings in WordPerfect are controlled by Windows. There are several settings you may want to customize if you are having difficulty using your mouse. You can change the double-click interval, which controls the time allowed between clicks in order for a double-click to register. You can change the mouse tracking speed, which controls the speed at which the mouse moves across the screen. You can also switch the functions of the left and right mouse buttons if you are left-handed.

Steps

➡**To change the Windows mouse settings:**

1. From WordPerfect, click on the application Control menu.
2. Choose Switch To and then double-click on Program Manager.
3. Double-click the Main icon and then double-click the Control Panel icon.
4. From the Control Panel, double-click the Mouse icon. A Mouse dialog box is displayed, similar to the one shown in Figure 2–1.
5. Change any settings.

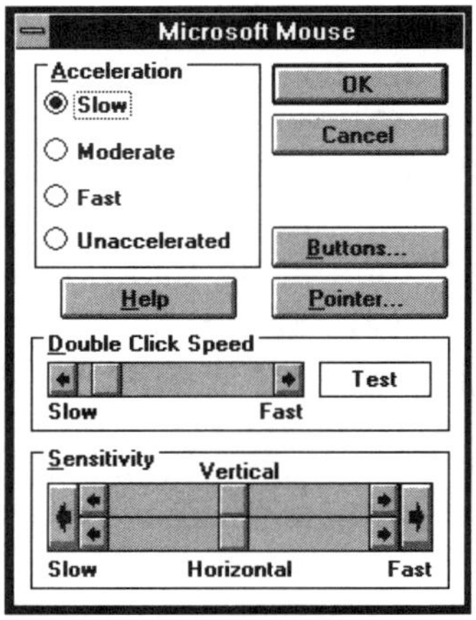

FIGURE 2–1
The Windows Mouse dialog box.

6. Choose OK and then double-click the Control menu buttons until you return to the WordPerfect program group, and then double-click the WPWin 6.0 icon.

Tell Me More

If you are a new mouse user or often have to double-click several times before the action you want occurs, you should try slowing down your double-click speed. After you become more proficient with the mouse, you may want to increase the speed.

If you are a new mouse user and are having trouble controlling the movement of the mouse on-screen, you may want to try slowing down mouse tracking speed or acceleration until you get used to your mouse.

HOW DO I... Change My Screen Colors?

The screen colors displayed in WordPerfect are controlled by Windows. If you want to change the color of any of the screen items, such as the background color of the document window, you must do so through Windows.

Steps

➡To choose a different Windows default color scheme:

1. From WordPerfect, click on the application Control menu.
2. Choose Switch To and then double-click on Program Manager.
3. Double-click the Main icon and then double-click the Control Panel icon.
4. From the Control Panel, double-click the Color icon. The Windows Color dialog box is displayed, as shown in Figure 2–2.
5. Open the drop-down list for Color Schemes by clicking the ↓ next to the Color Scheme and select the color scheme you want. The sample dialog boxes in the middle of the Color dialog box display examples of the color scheme.
6. Choose OK and then double-click the Control menu buttons until you return to the WordPerfect program group, and then double-click the WPWin 6.0 icon.

FIGURE 2–2
The Windows Color dialog box.

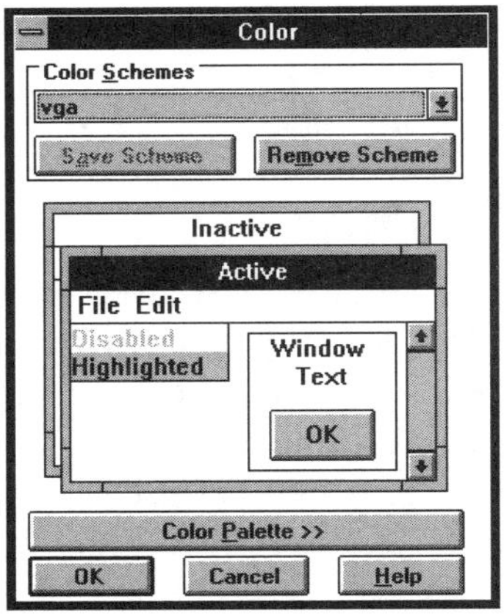

NOTE

Windows also enables you to create your own color scheme. For more information about setting up customized color schemes, see your Windows manual.

Tell Me More

Any text you enter in the document window is displayed according to the Windows system colors. If you are using a color printer, however, and you want the text to be displayed in the color in which it will be printed, you can turn off the Windows system colors.

➠To turn off the Windows system colors:

1. Choose File➢Preferences and then double-click the Display icon.
2. Select Document.
3. Deselect Windows System Colors if an X is in the check box.
4. Choose OK and Close to return to the document window.

The Windows System Colors option affects only text in the document window; it does not affect any other screen elements.

HOW DO I. . . Change the Way Documents Are Displayed in the Document Window?

A WordPerfect document can be created and viewed on-screen in three different display modes: Draft, Page, and Two Page. Draft mode displays your documents very close to the way they appear when they are printed.

You can see fonts and graphics on-screen in Draft mode. Page mode, which is the default mode, is much like Draft mode, but it displays several items that Draft mode does not. In Page mode, you can view headers, footers, page numbers, and footnotes. Using Two Page mode, you can display two pages side-by-side in the document window. To help you see the difference between the display modes, Figure 2–3 shows the same document in Draft mode, Page mode, and Two Page mode.

Steps

➠To view the document window in Draft mode:

1. Choose View➢Draft *or* press Ctrl+F5.

➠To view the document window in Page mode:

1. Choose View➢Page *or* press Alt+F5.

➠To view the document window in Two Page mode:

1. Choose View➢Two Page.

Tell Me More

The first time you start WordPerfect, your document window is displayed in Page mode. You can use another view (Draft or Two Page) as the default view.

➠To change the default view:

1. Choose File➢Preferences and then double-click the Display icon.
2. Select View/Zoom.
3. Select Draft, Page, or Two Page.
4. Choose OK and Close to return to the document window.

HINT **You are not limited to one view for all document windows. You can use Page mode to display document 1, for example, Draft mode to display document 2, and Two Page mode to display document 3.**

It is beneficial to alternate the use of the display modes, depending on what you are trying to accomplish. The following sections explain some of the advantages and disadvantages of using each display mode.

FIGURE 2–3
A document in Draft mode, Page mode, and Two Page mode.

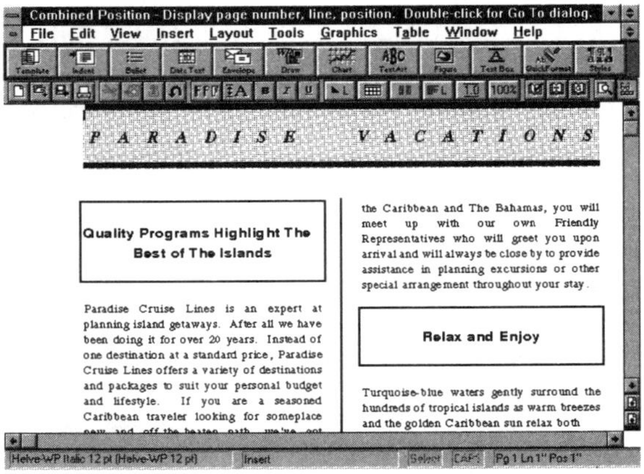

Draft mode

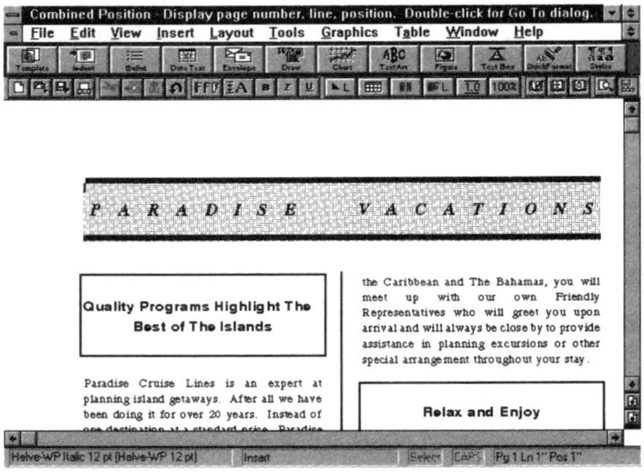

Page mode

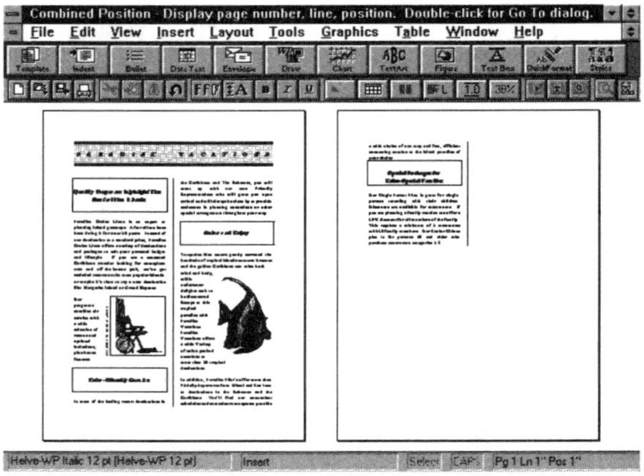

Two Page mode

Using Draft Mode

If your document contains large amounts of text in addition to features that do not display in Draft mode, you may want to enter the text by using Draft mode and then switch to Page mode when you add and edit the other features. In Draft mode, you can see more text at one time in the document window because the margins are not displayed in the window.

Draft mode requires the least amount of memory of the three display modes. If you are trying to use the other display modes and are running into memory errors, you might try using Draft mode. In addition, Draft mode may increase the speed of the program.

Using Page Mode

If you are creating a document, such as a term paper, that includes headers, page numbers, and footnotes, Page mode enables you to see those features in the document window. Page mode lets you see the document almost exactly as it will look when it's printed. Because Page mode represents the entire page, you cannot see as much text in the document window as you can with Draft mode.

Using Two Page Mode

Two Page mode enables you to see two pages of a document side-by-side. All features that are displayed in Page mode also are displayed in Two Page mode. Two Page mode is most useful when you want to see the exact positioning of information on a page and get an idea of how the whole page will look when it's printed.

You can edit your document in Two Page mode; however, the text is so small that it may be difficult to read. If you need to move to another page in your document while in Two Page mode, you can press the PgUp and PgDn keys to move back one page or forward one page. You can also click on the page to which you want to move.

NOTE **You cannot use the Zoom feature, which increases the magnification of the document window, while you're in Two Page mode.**

HOW DO I. . . Select Different Button Bars and Move the Button Bar?

When a Button Bar is displayed, you can quickly click the item you want to access rather than remember where it is on a menu or the keystrokes

FIGURE 2–4
The Button Bar Preferences dialog box.

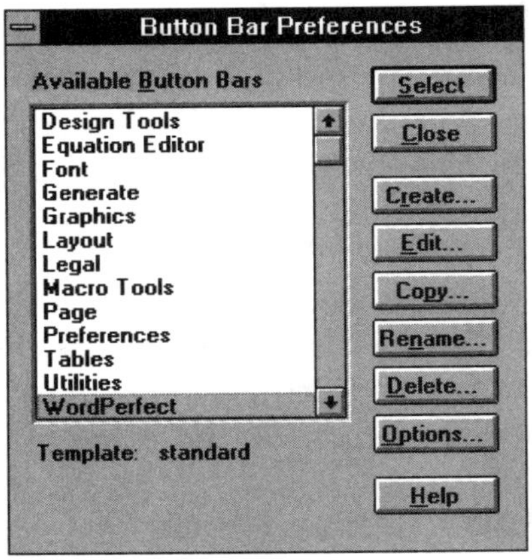

to access it. WordPerfect has several Button Bars you can display; each Button Bar has buttons specific to the accomplishment of certain tasks. In addition to choosing different Button Bars, you can also customize how and where the Button Bar is displayed.

Steps

➡To select a Button Bar other than the default:

1. Click the right mouse button anywhere on the Button Bar and select the Button Bar you want to use *or* choose File➢Preferences and double-click the Button Bar icon. The Button Bar Preferences dialog box is displayed, as shown in Figure 2–4. Highlight the Button Bar you want to use and then choose Select.

HINT

When you're selecting from the Button Bar Preferences dialog box, as you highlight the different Button Bars in the list, the Button Bar on-screen changes to reflect the highlighted Button Bar so that you can easily see which options are available on each Button Bar.

➡To change the position or style of the current Button Bar in your window:

1. Click the right mouse button anywhere on the Button Bar and choose Preferences *or* choose File➢Preferences and double-click the Button Bar icon.

FIGURE 2–5
The Button Bar Options dialog box.

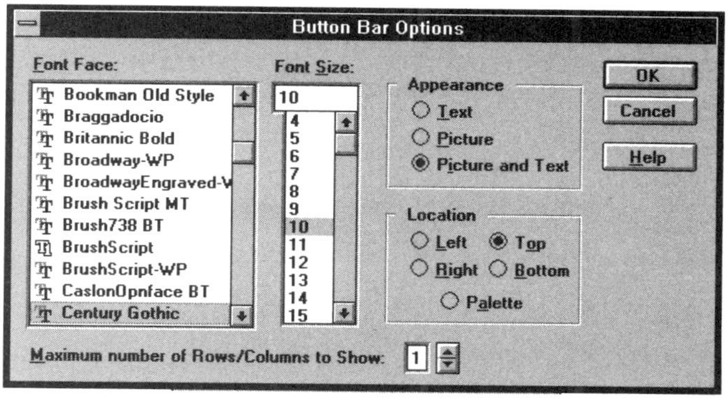

2. Choose Options. The Button Bar Options dialog box is displayed, as shown in Figure 2–5.
3. Select Left, Top, Right, Bottom, or Palette. The Palette option allows you to size and move the Button Bar anywhere in the document window.
4. Select a Font Face if you want to change the style of the text on the Button Bar.
5. Select the Font Size option if you want to change the size of the text on the Button Bar. The smaller the font, the less space the Button Bar takes up in the window.
6. Select Text, Picture, or Picture and Text.
7. Choose OK and Close to return to the document window.

HINT

To move the Button Bar, you can also move the mouse pointer over the edge of the Button Bar until it displays a hand, as shown here:

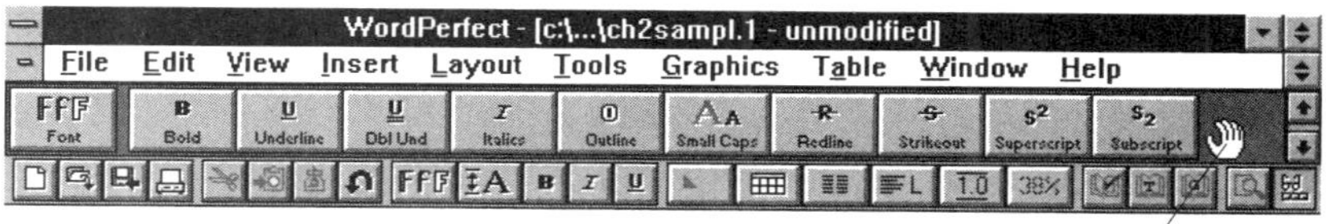

Movement hand

After the hand is displayed, you can hold down the left mouse button and drag the Button Bar to the location you want.

Tell Me More

WordPerfect has 15 predefined Button Bars. Figure 2–6 displays all the Button Bars that are shipped with WordPerfect:

- DESIGN TOOLS
- EQUATION EDITOR
- FONT
- GENERATE
- GRAPHICS
- LAYOUT
- LEGAL
- MACRO TOOLS
- PAGE
- PREFERENCES
- TABLES
- UTILITIES
- WORDPERFECT
- WORDPERFECT 5.2
- WORK GROUP

The FONT Button Bar, for example, displays several font attributes and sizes that are useful when you create flyers or posters. The PREFERENCES Button Bar makes it quick and easy to change any or all of the Preference options available in WordPerfect.

If you use a large font size or a Button Bar that has more buttons than are displayed on one line and you want to display more than one line of the Button Bar, you can increase the maximum number of Rows/Columns to Show option on the Button Bar Options dialog box.

HOW DO I... Customize Menu Bar Options?

When you select a menu bar item, by default WordPerfect displays all available shortcut keys next to the item on the pull-down menu. In addition, when you highlight an item on a pull-down menu, a help prompt describing the item automatically is displayed on the title bar. WordPerfect also displays the names of the last four files you have

FIGURE 2–6
WordPerfect's predefined Button Bars.

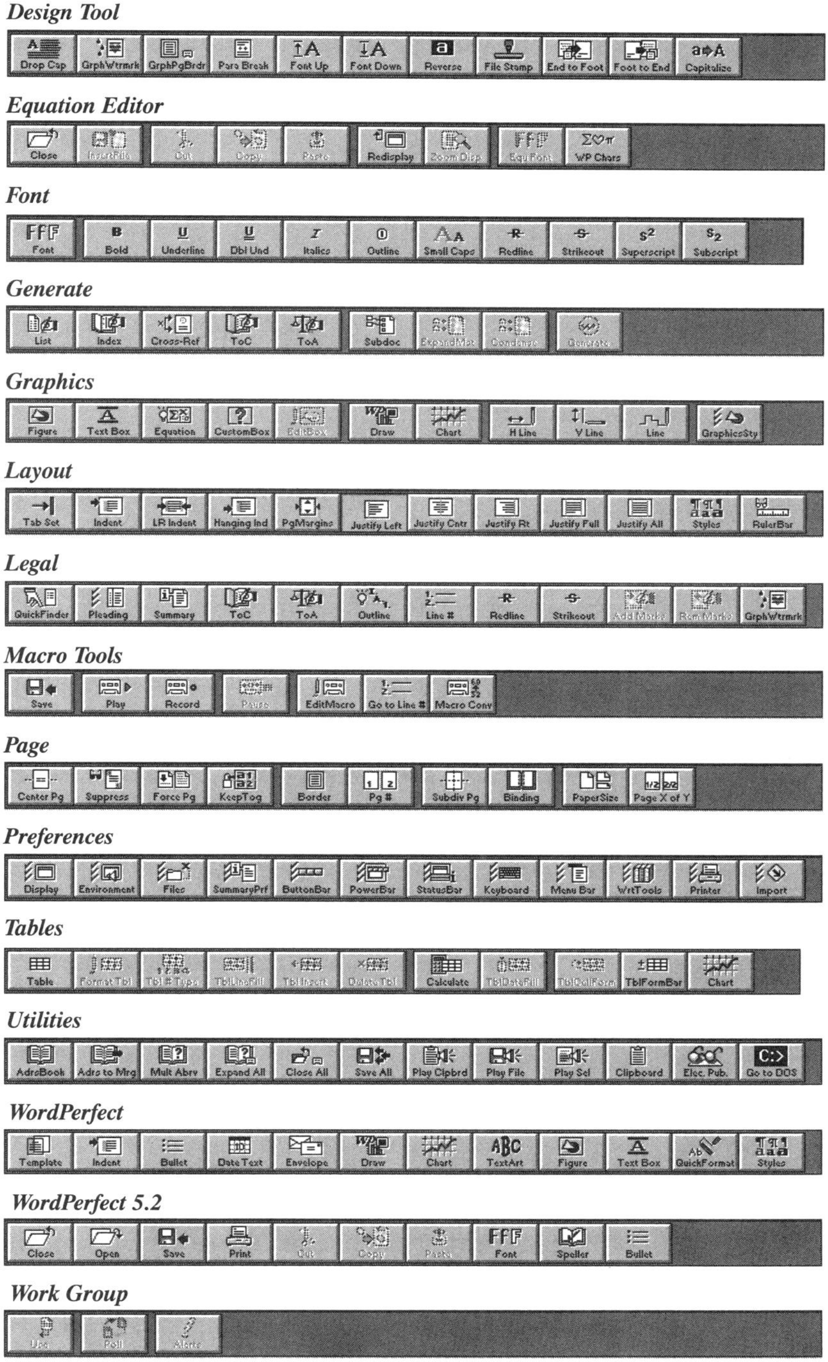

opened on the File menu so that you can quickly open a file you were working with. You can deactivate any of these options by using the Environment Preferences.

Steps

➨To change the menu bar options:

1. Choose File➢Preferences and then double-click the Environment icon.
2. Deselect Display Last Open Filenames, Display Shortcut Keys, or Show Help Prompts. An X in the check box indicates that the item is selected.
3. Choose OK and Close to return to the document window.

Tell Me More

In addition to customizing display options for the menu bar, you can also customize and create your own Shortcut Keys. For information about creating your own menu bars, see Chapter 11, "Automating Tasks and Optimizing WordPerfect."

HOW DO I... Display the Ruler Bar?

The Ruler Bar is a powerful tool that helps you easily view, create, and modify tabs, margins, column settings, and tables. The Ruler Bar is displayed at the top of the document window, as shown in Figure 2–7. With the Ruler Bar displayed, you can simply double-click on the location where you want to set a tab or decrease a column in a table by dragging the column-dividing line and much, much more. Using the Ruler Bar makes performing many task within WordPerfect much simpler.

Step

➨To display or remove the Ruler Bar:

1. Choose View➢Ruler Bar *or* press Alt+Shift+F3. A check mark next to Ruler Bar on the View menu indicates that the option is turned on.

FIGURE 2–7
The Ruler Bar.

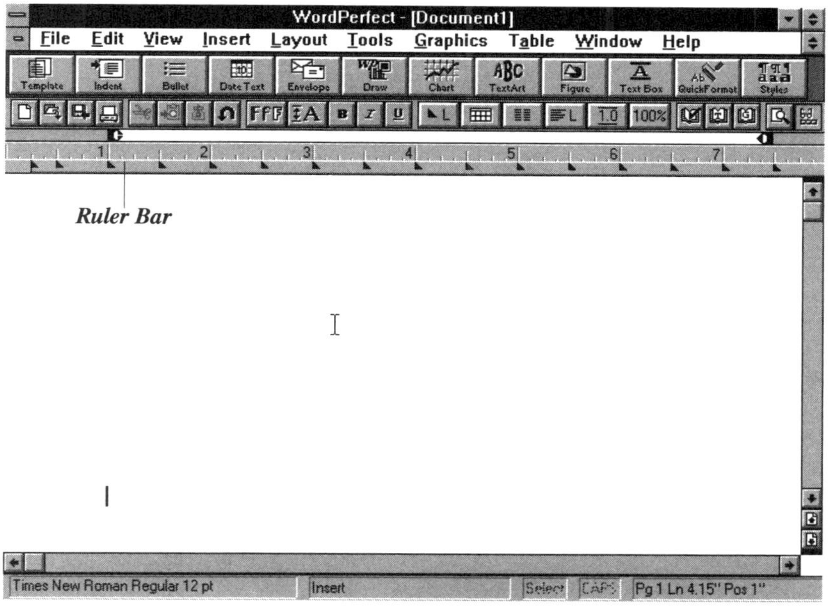

Tell Me More

The Ruler Bar is especially useful when you're creating a document that contains many formatting codes. With the Ruler Bar displayed, you can view and modify many of these individual settings right from the document window.

The Ruler Bar has two QuickMenus that make formatting a document even easier. When you click the right mouse button on a tab setting, you can quickly choose the type of tab settings you want to set. When you click the right mouse button on the Ruler Bar, you can quickly access dialog boxes that let you specify tab settings, paragraph formatting, margins, columns, and tables. In addition, both QuickMenus let you hide the Ruler Bar and access Ruler Bar preferences.

➠To change display preferences for the Ruler Bar:

1. Click the right mouse button on the Ruler Bar and choose Preferences, or choose File➢Preferences, double-click the Display icon, and then select Ruler Bar.

2. Select the options you want; an X in the check box indicates that the option is selected.
3. Choose OK and Close to return to the document window.

The following table describes the Display Preferences for the Ruler Bar and what happens when you select them:

OPTION	DESCRIPTION
Show Ruler Bar on New and Current Document	Displays the Ruler Bar every time you start WordPerfect
Tabs Snap to Ruler Bar Grid	Makes tab settings snap or conform to invisible grid lines that occur every $\frac{1}{16}$ of an inch
Show Ruler Bar Guides	Displays a dashed vertical line in the document window when you move or select a tab to aid in correct placement of the tab; this option is especially useful if you want to set a tab in a location where you have text positioned
Sculptured Ruler Bar	Once selected, the Ruler Bar appears three-dimensional.

For more information about using the Ruler Bar, see Chapter 3, "Entering, Deleting, and Arranging Text."

HOW DO I... Remove Bars from the Screen?

Although the many bars within WordPerfect afford you great power, there may be times when you just want to see your text. The Hide Bars option lets you do just that. When you choose this option, all bars are removed from the screen and you can clearly and easily see your text. The Hide Bars option is a great idea if you want to proofread on-screen.

Steps

➨To hide all bars:

FIGURE 2–8
The Hide Bars Information dialog box.

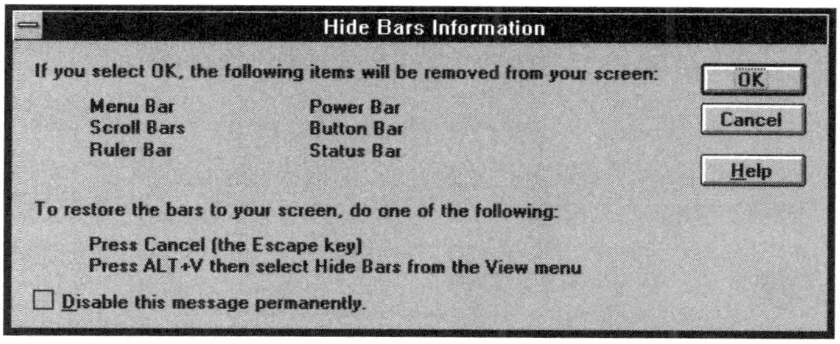

1. Choose View➢Hide Bars *or* press Alt+Shift+F5. The Hide Bars Information dialog box, shown in Figure 2–8, is displayed. If you do not want this dialog box to be displayed every time you choose the Hide Bars option, Select Disable This Message Permanently.
2. Choose OK.

Tell Me More

When you select the Hide Bars option, your screen looks similar to the one shown in Figure 2–9. The active document window occupies the entire screen. This is a great way to unclutter your screen and view your text.

NOTE **When you hide the bars, the menu bar is also removed.**

If you need to restore the bars so that you can access menu items, just press Alt+Shift+F5 or press Alt+V and then choose Hide Bars. Even when the menu bar is not displayed, you can still access all menu bar options, by using the Alt+*mnemonic key* (press Alt+F, for example, to view the File menu).

From the View pull-down menu, you can remove the Button Bar, Power Bar, Ruler Bar, and status bar individually or remove all bars.

➨**To remove the scroll bars used to move through your document:**

1. Choose File➢Preferences and then double-click the Display icon.
2. Select Document.
3. Deselect Vertical or Horizontal; an X in the check box indicates that the option is selected.

FIGURE 2–9
A document window with Hide Bars selected.

Notice no bars

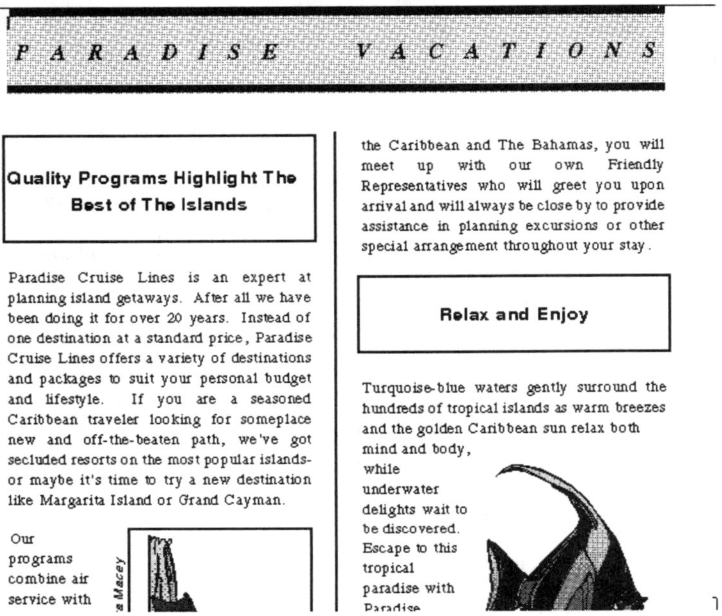

P A R A D I S E   V A C A T I O N S

Quality Programs Highlight The Best of The Islands

Paradise Cruise Lines is an expert at planning island getaways. After all we have been doing it for over 20 years. Instead of one destination at a standard price, Paradise Cruise Lines offers a variety of destinations and packages to suit your personal budget and lifestyle. If you are a seasoned Caribbean traveler looking for someplace new and off-the-beaten path, we've got secluded resorts on the most popular islands- or maybe it's time to try a new destination like Margarita Island or Grand Cayman.

Our programs combine air service with

the Caribbean and The Bahamas, you will meet up with our own Friendly Representatives who will greet you upon arrival and will always be close by to provide assistance in planning excursions or other special arrangement throughout your stay.

Relax and Enjoy

Turquoise-blue waters gently surround the hundreds of tropical islands as warm breezes and the golden Caribbean sun relax both mind and body, while underwater delights wait to be discovered. Escape to this tropical paradise with

4. If you want the horizontal scroll bar to always be displayed, select Show Always; if you want it to be displayed only when necessary to scroll through a document, select When Required.
5. Choose OK and Close to return to the document window.

Any changes you make to the Scroll Bar Display Preferences are stored in the WordPerfect setup file and remain in effect until you change the option again.

HOW DO I... Set Up Backup Options?

WordPerfect provides several options to help you avoid losing data when you work with your documents. One of the first precautions you should take is to save your documents regularly; this step is easy to take with the Save feature (Ctrl+S *or* choosing Save from the Power Bar).

In addition to saving your documents regularly, you should also regularly make backup copies of your files by using a third-party backup

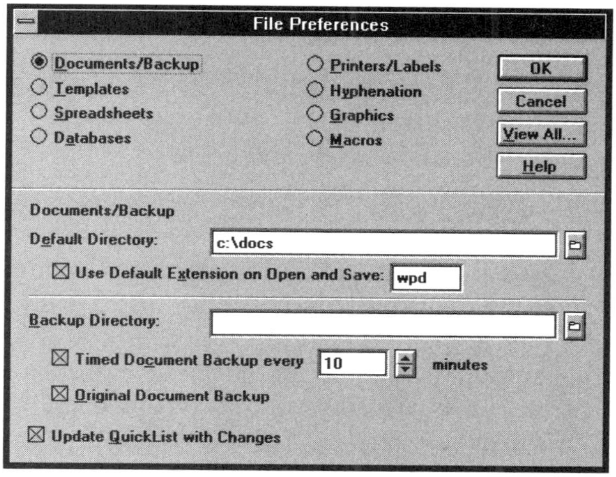

FIGURE 2–10
The File Preferences dialog box displays Document/Backup options.

utility or by simply using the Open File dialog box to copy the files to another disk.

WordPerfect also offers automatic-backup features to protect against the loss of data. Every ten minutes by default, the Timed Document Backup feature automatically makes a backup copy of all your documents currently displayed in a document window to protect you from data loss caused by a power failure or computer failure.

Another backup option is the Original Document Backup feature, which helps you to avoid replacing files with unwanted changes. When you turn on the Original Backup option, WordPerfect saves a copy of the original document after you make changes and replace the original file to protect you from replacing information you may need.

Steps

➠**To turn the Timed Backup or Original Backup features on or off:**

1. Choose File➢Preferences and then double-click the File icon.
2. Select Documents/Backup. The File Preferences dialog box displays the Document/Backup options, as shown in Figure 2–10.
3. Select Timed Document Backup to turn the backup on or off, click the incrementing arrows to change the number of minutes

between backups, or type the number in the Timed Document Backup text box.

4. Select Original Backup Document to turn the option on or off.
5. Choose OK and Close to return to the document window.

Tell Me More

When the Timed Document Backup option is on, WordPerfect briefly displays a dialog box indicating that a backup is being performed. Many times, you may not even notice the dialog box. The timed backup files are automatically saved in the directory in which the WIN.COM file is stored, which is usually your C:\WINDOWS directory unless you specify otherwise.

➡**To specify a different directory for your timed backup files:**

1. Choose File➢Preferences and then double-click the File icon.
2. Select Documents/Backup.
3. Enter the name of the directory in which you want your backup files saved in the Backup Directory text box.
4. Choose OK and Close to return to the document window.

WordPerfect names the Timed Backup files WP{WP}.BK*n* if you are using WordPerfect on your hard drive, or WXXXXX}.BK*n* if you are using WordPerfect on the network, where XXXXX represents your network initials. In both cases, *n* is a number from 1 to 9 that corresponds to the document number. Every time you exit from WordPerfect properly, the backup files are deleted.

If WordPerfect stops its operations and the program has not been exited properly, the next time you start WordPerfect the dialog box displayed in Figure 2–11 informs you that timed backup files exist. From

FIGURE 2–11
The Timed Backup dialog box.

the dialog box, you can rename, delete, or open the backup files. If you rename the files and another copy of the document exists, you can retrieve them later and compare them to the original document to see whether any information is missing.

If you open a backup file, be sure to save it if it contains information that is not in the original document or if it has never been saved. Be sure to save the document with a name other than the WP{WP}.BK*n* temporary name. WordPerfect overwrites the backup files every time it performs a timed backup.

NOTE **WordPerfect backs up files only if you have edited them since retrieving them.**

Original backup files are stored in the same directory as the original file. The files are saved with the same name as the original file and with a .BK! extension.

If you discover that you have replaced a file you need and the Original Document Backup option is on, you can rename an original backup file. See Chapter 10, "Managing Files and Documents," for more information.

NOTE **You must rename the original backup file with an extension other than .BK! to keep it from being replaced if it is retrieved and edited. Also, because WordPerfect uses the .BK! extension for all files, be aware that any files that share the same name are saved to the same original backup file.**

Any changes you make to the Backup Options are stored in the WordPerfect setup file and remain in effect until you change them again.

HOW DO I... Change My Beep Options?

WordPerfect lets you specify whether you want your computer to beep when an error dialog box is displayed, when hyphenation is needed, or when a search fails. By default, WordPerfect beeps only when a word requires hyphenation.

Steps

➡ **To change your beep options:**

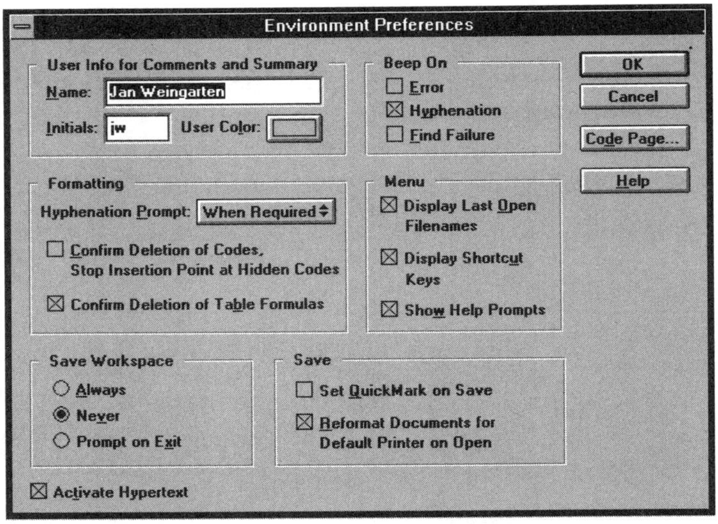

FIGURE 2–12
The Environment Preferences dialog box.

1. Choose File ➢ Preferences and then double-click the Environment icon. The Environment Preferences dialog box is displayed, as shown in Figure 2–12.
2. Select Error, Hyphenation, or Find Failure from the Beep On options.
3. Choose OK and Close to return to the document window.

Tell Me More

Any changes you make to the Beep On options are stored in the WordPerfect setup file and remain in effect until you change them again.

HOW DO I... Change the Units of Measure to Something Other Than Inches?

When you start WordPerfect, the status bar and all measurement-entry fields display the measurements in inches. You can change the way measurements for the status bar are displayed and the format in which you enter numerical data.

Steps

➡ **To change the units of measure:**

1. Choose File ➢ Preferences and then double-click the Display icon.
2. Select Document.
3. Click on the pop-up list for Units of Measure and select the type of measurement you want from the pop-up list shown here:

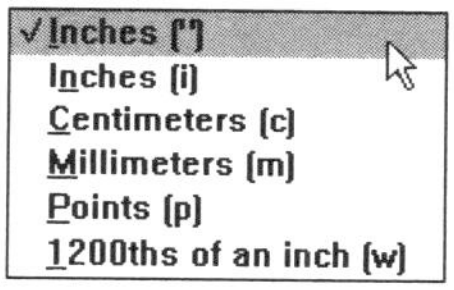

4. Click on the pop-up list for Status/Ruler Bar Display and select the type of measurement you want from the pop-up list.
5. Choose OK and Close to return to the document window.

Tell Me More

WordPerfect has numerous places where you enter measurements: Margin settings, graphics sizes, table measurements, and column widths are just a few of the places that require information entered in measurements. Regardless of the type of measurement you choose for Units of Measure, you can always enter a number in any type of measurement as long as you include the first letter of the measurement. If you select inches for the type of measurement, for example, you can enter 5c (for centimeters) and WordPerfect automatically converts it to 1.97".

Any changes you make to the units of measurement are stored in the WordPerfect setup file and remain in effect until you change them again.

HOW DO I... Use DOS Keystrokes in WordPerfect for Windows?

If you are new to Windows and are accustomed to standard DOS keystrokes or if you are a long-time WordPerfect for DOS user,

WordPerfect for Windows can accommodate you and make the transition to WordPerfect for Windows very smooth. WordPerfect for Windows provides a special keyboard for those who just can't get used to pressing F5 for Print rather than Shift+F7 or who keep displaying Help every time they try to cancel something. Using the WPDOS-compatible keyboard enables you to use all the powerful features in WordPerfect for Windows without the obstacle of learning new keystrokes.

Steps

➠To select the WPDOS-compatible keyboard:

1. Choose File➢Preferences and then double-click the Keyboard icon.
2. Click <WPDOS Compatible> and choose Select.
3. Choose OK and Close to return to the document window.

Tell Me More

Any changes you make to the Keyboard Preferences are stored in the WordPerfect setup file and remain in effect until you change the option again.

After you are more familiar with WordPerfect for Windows, you may want to use the WPWin 6.0 keyboard so that you can begin learning the common Windows keystrokes that are shared among all Windows applications.

HOW DO I... Specify Where I Want WordPerfect to Find and Store My WordPerfect Files?

In addition to the WordPerfect main program files, WordPerfect uses several other files to provide the features that make WordPerfect so powerful. Some of these files are installed during the installation process, such as graphics files and printer files. Other files are created by the user, such as spreadsheets, macros, and documents. WordPerfect gives you great flexibility in deciding where you can store these files, but you must use the Files Preferences dialog box to tell WordPerfect where to find and store specific files.

FIGURE 2–13
The File Preferences dialog box.

File type radio buttons

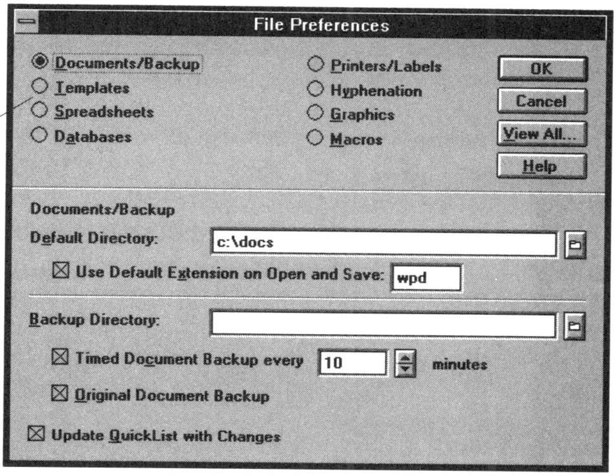

Steps

➡To change or verify the location of files:

1. Choose File➢Preferences and then double-click the File icon. The File Preferences dialog box, shown in Figure 2–13, appears.
2. Select the type of files you want to change by clicking the appropriate radio button. The information in the lower half of the dialog box changes to reflect the type of files you have selected.
3. Enter the appropriate directory in the Directory text box. If you do not remember the name of a directory, you can click the Folder list button to the right of the text box to display the Select Directory dialog box. From the Select Directory dialog box, you can select a directory by clicking the appropriate directory in the Directories list box.
4. If you want to update the QuickList with the changes you have made, select Update QuickList with Changes. For more information about the QuickList, see Chapter 10, "Managing Files and Documents."
5. Select or change any additional options.
6. Choose OK and Close to return to the document window.

NOTE

If you enter a directory that is different from the default location, you must copy the necessary files to the new location. If you do not copy the files, you may see a "File Not Found" error.

Tell Me More

The following table lists the options in the Location of Files dialog box, the default location used by the Install program, and a description of the types of files in the directory.

HINT

If you want to see all your File Preferences at one time, choose View All from the File Preferences dialog box.

File Type	Default Location	Description
Documents	C:\WPWIN60\WPDOCS	WordPerfect documents (*.WPD, by default)
Template	C:\WPWIN60\TEMPLATE	Template files (*.WPT)
Spread-sheets	None	Personal spreadsheet files
Database	None	Personal database files
Printers/ Labels	C:\WPC20	Printer files and label (*.PRS and *.LAB)
Hyphen-ation	C:WPC20	Hyphenation files used to determine word hyphenation
Graphics	C:\WPWIN60\GRAPHICS	WordPerfect graphics files (*.WPG)
Macros	C:\WPWIN60\MACROS	Predefined macros and all macros you create (*.WCM)

When you're changing file preferences for templates, spreadsheets, databases, printers and labels, graphics, and macros, you can enter a Default and Supplemental Directory. If you are running WordPerfect on a network, you may want to enter both locations, the Default on the network and the Supplemental on a personal drive. WordPerfect looks for the file in the Default directory first and then in the Supplemental directory if it does not find the file. If you are not running on a network, you can still use the Supplemental directory if you want to store files in two different locations. You can put business-related graphics in the main graphics directory, for example, and then put "for fun" graphics in a separate directory and specify that directory as the Supplemental directory.

When you're specifying Document/Backup preferences, you can also specify a default extension for documents. WordPerfect uses .WPD as the default extension. Whenever you open and save a document, you can just enter the prefix, such as MEMO, and WordPerfect automatically adds the .WPD. Using this option standardizes filenaming conventions and is helpful if you are going to use DDE and OLE to link WordPerfect documents to other applications.

When you're specifying Templates preferences, you can specify a default template filename and extension. WordPerfect uses templates to store formatting and setup information for documents. The default template is STANDARD.WPT; the default extension is .WPT. For more information about templates, see Chapter 5, "Creating Documents: The Basics."

HOW DO I. . . View Formatting Codes in My Document?

WordPerfect provides a Reveal Codes window that enables you to see the formatting codes in your document. When the Reveal Codes window is displayed, it displays at the bottom of your document window. Reveal Codes displays the formatting codes that are automatically inserted in your document when you choose certain features or menu items or change the format of your document. When Reveal Codes is not displayed, you cannot see these codes. You can display the Reveal Codes window so that you can see and edit specific codes in your document. Displaying Reveal Codes can also help you find and correct formatting errors with greater ease than by just looking through your document.

Steps

➡**To turn the Reveal Codes feature on or off:**

1. Choose View➢Reveal Codes *or* press Alt+F3. A check mark next to Reveal Codes on the View menu indicates that the option is turned on.

Tell Me More

Using Reveal Codes is similar to using the regular document window after you become familiar with it. To help familiarize you with Reveal Codes, Figure 2–14 shows a document window with Reveal Codes displaying some common codes. As you move your insertion point through the document, your insertion point simultaneously moves through Reveal Codes. Your insertion point is always in the same place in both your document and in Reveal Codes. All codes appear as buttons to help you easily identify them.

You can delete codes in your document by using Reveal Codes. To delete the bold code for a line of text, for example, in Reveal Codes move the insertion point to the right of the code and then press Backspace. Not only the first [BOLD] code is deleted, but also the ending [BOLD] code.

FIGURE 2–14
The Reveal Codes window.

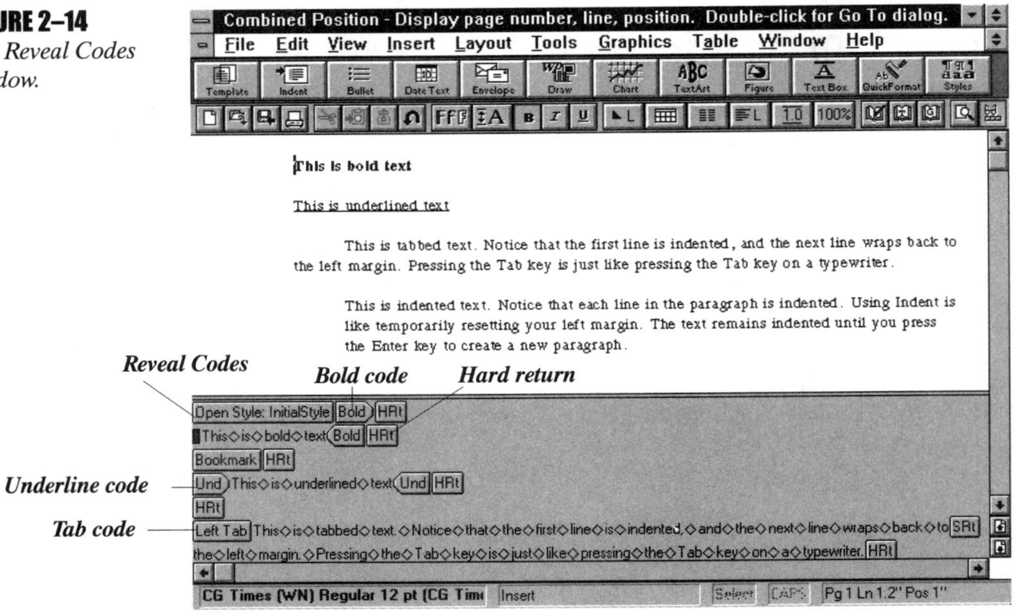

NOTE **When you are deleting paired codes (codes that have an on and off code), you can delete the on or off code.**

To help you recognize and become familiar with codes in Reveal Codes, the following table lists some common codes and the features they represent:

CODE	FEATURE
[HRt]	Hard return
[SRt]	Soft return
[SPg]	Soft page break
[HPg]	Hard page break
[Left Tab]	Left tab
[Left Indent]	Left indent
[Bold]	Bold
[Und]	Underline

There are several Display Preferences you can customize for Reveal Codes.

➡To change these preferences:

1. Choose File➢Preferences and then double-click the Display icon.
2. Select Reveal Codes.
3. Change any of the options you want.
4. Choose OK and Close to return to the document window.

The following table lists the Display Preferences for Reveal Codes and what happens when the option is selected.

Any changes you make to the Reveal Codes Display Preferences are stored in the WordPerfect setup file and remain in effect until you change the option again.

OPTION	DESCRIPTION
Show Reveal Codes on New and Current Document	Displays Reveal Codes every time you start the program or open a new document.
Font	Indicates in which font the text in Reveal Codes is displayed.
Size	Indicates the size of the font in Reveal Codes.
Wrap Lines At Window	Wraps lines with several codes that extend beyond the display to the next line so that you can see all the codes without scrolling.
Show Spaces As Bullets	Displays spaces as bullet characters in the Reveal Codes window; useful for proofreading for spacing errors.
Show Codes In Detail	Displays all the information for the code. Some of the codes displayed in Reveal Codes show only a skeleton of the code. The first header in a document, for example, displays only the code [Header A]. After you click on the code, all the information contained in the header is displayed. Footers, styles, tables, columns, footnotes, endnotes, and tab settings all are examples of codes that appear in skeleton form in Reveal Codes.
Show Help Prompts for Codes	Displays a help prompt explaining what the code is on the title bar whenever you point to a code.
Sculptured Codes	Displays codes as shown in Figure 2–14. If this option is not selected, codes are displayed as one-dimensional.
Window Size	Indicates the percentage of the document window that Reveal Codes will occupy; cannot be greater than 90 percent or smaller than 10 percent.
Color	Indicates the color of text and background in the Reveal Codes window.

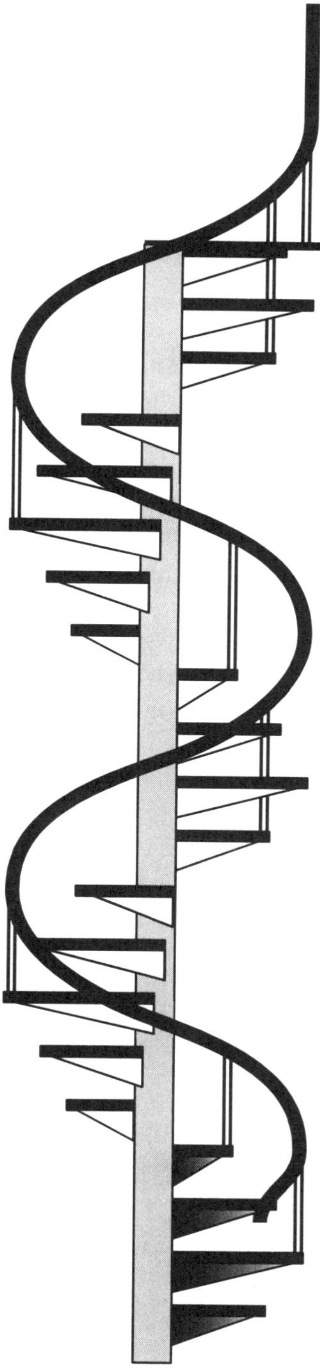

Chapter 3

Entering, Deleting, and Arranging Text

This chapter answers your questions about entering, formatting, and manipulating your text. Questions about the following features are answered:

- Entering text
- Moving around in the document
- Deleting text and codes
- Undeleting and undoing changes
- Selecting text
- Copying text
- Moving text
- Finding text and codes
- Replacing text and codes
- Setting margins
- Changing justification

- Setting tabs
- Aligning text
- Using hyphenation
- Changing line spacing
- Centering a page

HOW DO I... Enter Text?

Entering text in WordPerfect is easy—all you do is type the text. When you type text, the text automatically wraps to the next line when it reaches the end of a line. WordPerfect inserts at the end of the line in Reveal Codes a Soft Return code that looks like this: [SRt]. If you want to end a line of text before it automatically wraps (if you are entering a title, for example), you can press the Enter key on the keyboard. When you press Enter, WordPerfect inserts a Hard Return code that looks like this: [HRt].

When you type text in a document, do not press Enter at the end of each line; if you do, your document does not format properly.

If you want to insert text where text already exists in your document, you simply move the insertion point to the location you want and begin typing. If other text already exists, WordPerfect inserts the text at the location of the insertion point and adjusts the surrounding text. If you want to overwrite existing text, you can press the Insert key to activate Typeover mode. While you are in Typeover mode, the text at the insertion point is deleted and replaced with the new text. When you are in Typeover mode, the word *Typeover* is displayed in the middle of your status bar at the bottom of your screen. To exit from Typeover mode, press the Insert key again. The use of the same key (or menu choice or button) to turn a feature on and off is called a *toggle;* many WordPerfect features use toggles.

HOW DO I... Move Around in My Document?

WordPerfect gives you several methods for moving around in your document: You can use the mouse, cursor keys, Go To command, scroll bars, Find feature, and Bookmarks. Each of these methods is described in this section. Depending on your preferences and needs, you can use one method or a combination of several methods.

Using the Mouse

You can use the mouse to move the insertion point to a position in your document that is displayed on-screen. To move to a specific location, simply move the mouse pointer to the location you want and then click the left mouse button.

If you want to use the mouse to move to a location that is not displayed in the document window, you can use the horizontal and vertical scroll bars, as shown in Figure 3–1.

The scroll arrows enable you to use your mouse to scroll through your document one line at a time or continuously. Clicking once on a scroll arrow moves the text in the document window up or down one line when you are using the vertical scroll bar. Pointing to the scroll arrow and holding down the mouse button continuously moves you through the document until you release the mouse button.

NOTE

Using the scroll bars doesn't move your insertion point—it just changes the view of the document. After you've scrolled to a particular location, you have to click in that portion of the document in order for the insertion point to move.

FIGURE 3–1
Horizontal and vertical scroll bars.

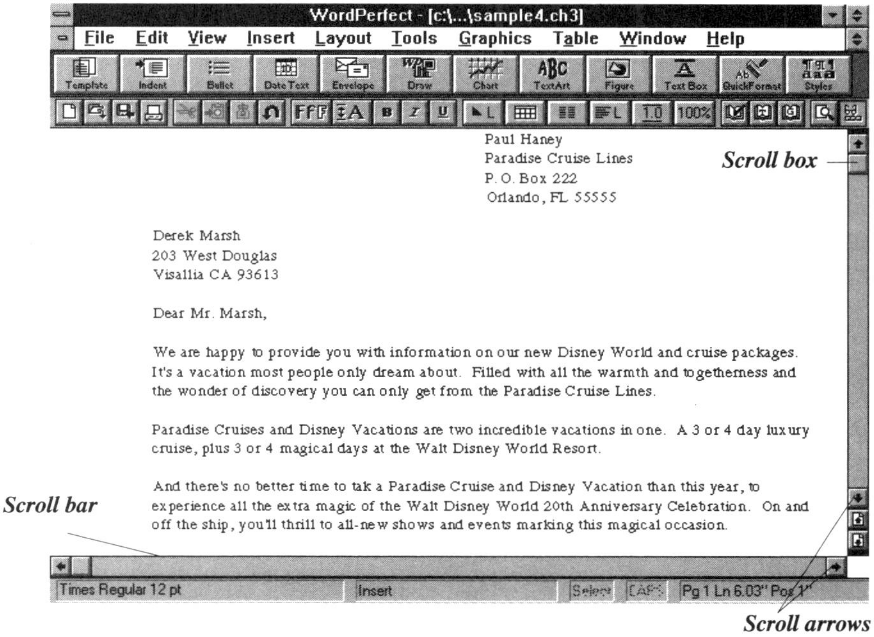

You can move the scroll box by dragging it to any location on the scroll bar. If you move the scroll box to the top of the scroll bar, you see the beginning of the document. If you move the box to the middle of the scroll bar, you see the middle of the document.

HINT

You can also click on either side of the vertical scroll box to move up or down one screen at a time or on the horizontal scroll box to move left or right one screen. You can also click the page buttons to view the preceding or next page.

Using Cursor-Key Movements

Using cursor keys to move around in your document gives you great flexibility. The following table lists some of the keystrokes you can use to move quickly to certain locations in your document and also the action they perform. You may want to experiment with many variations of the keystrokes so that you can see the results for yourself.

KEYSTROKE	MOVES
← or →	Left or right one character
Home	To the beginning of a line
End	To the end of a line
↑ or ↓	Up or down one line
Ctrl + ← or + →	To the preceding or next word
Pg Up or Pg Dn	Up or down one screen
Ctrl + Pg Up or Ctrl + Pg Dn	One screen left or right
Alt + Pg Up or Alt + Pg Dn	To the preceding or next page
Ctrl + Home	To the beginning of the document
Ctrl + Home, Ctrl + Home	To the beginning of the document before any formatting codes
Ctrl + End	To the end of document

FIGURE 3–2
The Go To dialog box.

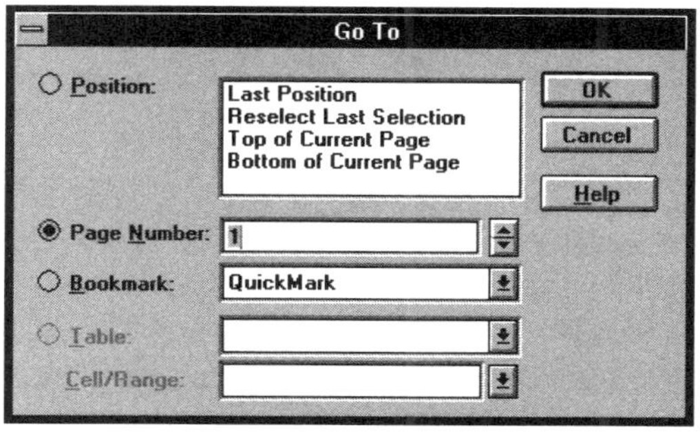

Using Go To

The Go To command enables you to move quickly to a specific location in a document. To use the Go To command, choose Edit➢Go To *or* press Ctrl+G. The Go To dialog box, shown in Figure 3–2, is displayed. You can also access Go To from a QuickMenu by clicking the right mouse button anywhere on a scroll bar and then choosing Go To.

The following table describes the options available on the Go To dialog box and where you move when you choose them:

Option	Moves
Position	To the last position of the insertion point, the top of the current page, or the bottom of the current page. If you have selected text while editing the current document, you can also choose Reselect Last Selection to have WordPerfect select text you had previously selected. If you have selected text, you can also choose to move to the beginning or end of the selected text; for information about selecting text, see the section "HOW DO I. . . Select Text?" later in this chapter.
Page Number	To the top of the specified page.
Bookmark	To the specified Bookmark, which you can choose from the list.
Table	To the specified table. In addition, you can also specify the cell to which you want to move.

FIGURE 3–3
The Find Text dialog box.

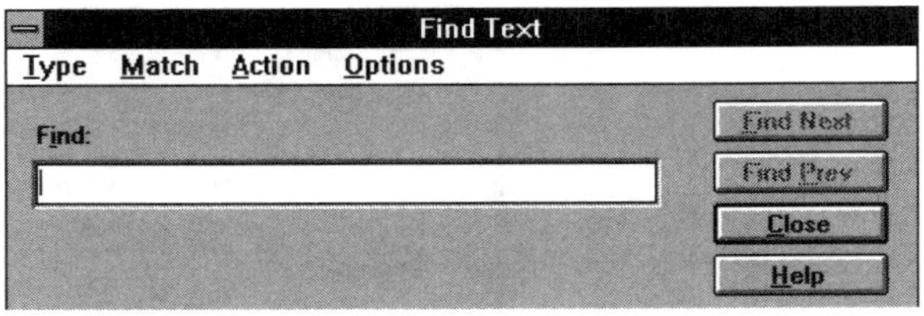

NOTE **You may see additional options for Position, depending on the formatting features used in your document.**

Using Find

The Find feature is useful for moving to a specific location in a document if you don't know the exact page or location within the document but you do know a certain word, phrase, or code in the section.

To use Find to move to a specific location:

1. Position the insertion point at the location where you want to begin searching.
2. Choose Edit➢Find *or* press F2. The Find Text dialog box is displayed, as shown in Figure 3–3.
3. Enter the word or phrase that exists in the location to which you want to move in the Find text field.
4. Choose Find Next to find the next occurrence or Find Prev to find the preceding occurrence.

WordPerfect selects the first occurrence of the word or phrase. If this location is correct, choose Close. If this location is not the right one, choose Find Next or Find Prev and continue the search until the screen displays the location you want. For more information about using the Find feature, see the section "HOW DO I. . . Find Text and Codes in My Document?" later in this chapter.

Using Bookmarks and QuickMarks

The Bookmark feature lets you insert placeholders in your document so that you can return quickly to an exact location. If you are creating a document and you want to go back and edit a certain section, for example, you can place a bookmark where you want to begin editing. When you are ready to edit the section, you can use WordPerfect to find the bookmark rather than scan through the entire document or try to remember the text you want to find.

A QuickMark is the default bookmark for each document. You can insert a QuickMark at any single location in your document.

To insert a QuickMark:

1. Move to the location at which you want to insert the QuickMark, choose Insert➢Bookmark, and then choose Set QuickMark; *or* click the right mouse button anywhere on a scroll bar to display the QuickMenu, choose Bookmark, and then choose Set QuickMark. If you look in Reveal Codes, you see the code [Bookmark].

To find the QuickMark:

1. Choose Insert➢Bookmark and then choose Find QuickMark *or* click the right mouse button anywhere on a scroll bar and choose Bookmark and then Find QuickMark. Your insertion point moves to the location where you inserted the QuickMark.

NOTE

Whenever you insert a QuickMark, WordPerfect deletes the preceding QuickMark.

WordPerfect can automatically insert a QuickMark at the location of your insertion point every time you save a document. To activate this feature:

1. Select File➢Preferences.
2. Double-click the Environment icon.
3. Choose Set QuickMark on Save.
4. Choose OK and then Close to return to the document window.

Setting a QuickMark on Save lets you quickly return to your last position so that you can begin working where you left off.

If you want to insert more than one bookmark, you can create your own bookmarks. They work the same as the QuickMark except that you can set as many as you want. To mark a place in your document where you want to edit information and a place where you want to verify information, for example, you can create an "edit" bookmark and a "verify" bookmark and then insert them in the appropriate locations.

To create and insert a bookmark:

FIGURE 3–4
The Bookmark dialog box.

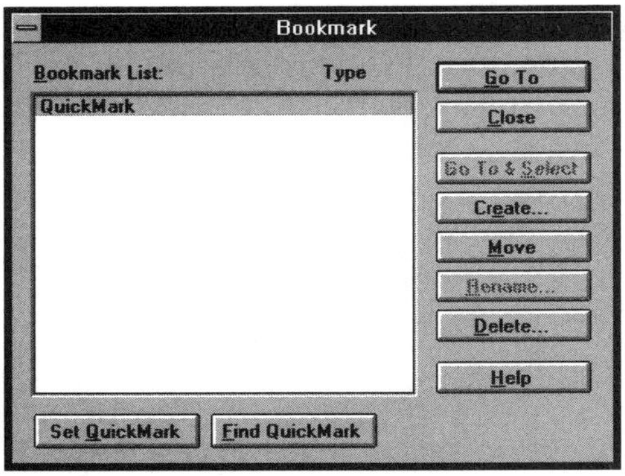

1. Move the insertion point to the location where you want to insert the bookmark.
2. Choose Insert➢Bookmark *or* click the right mouse button anywhere on a scroll bar and choose Bookmark. The Bookmark dialog box is displayed, as shown in Figure 3–4.
3. Choose Create.
4. Enter a name for the bookmark, such as **Edit**. WordPerfect automatically inserts as a default name for the bookmark any text following the insertion point in the Bookmark Name text box. This feature is helpful if you know that you want to move to a certain line in your document.
5. Choose OK.

WordPerfect creates the bookmark and inserts it at the location of the insertion point.

HOW DO I... Delete Text and Codes?

WordPerfect provides a variety of ways for you to delete text and formatting codes. You can delete a single character, a word, an entire line, an entire page, or a selected portion of text.

Steps

The following table lists the keystrokes used for deleting text and codes and describes what those keystrokes do.

KEYSTROKE	DELETES
Delete	Character to the right of the insertion point
Backspace	Character to the left of the insertion point
Ctrl + Backspace	Word at the insertion point
Ctrl + Delete	From the insertion point to the end of the current line
Ctrl + Shift + Delete	From the insertion point to the end of the current page

Tell Me More

You must be careful when you delete text with the keystrokes listed in the preceding table, because WordPerfect does not prompt you for confirmation before deleting the information. If you inadvertently delete text you need in your document, WordPerfect provides a safeguard with the Undelete and Undo features. For information about Undelete and Undo, see the section "HOW DO I. . . Undelete and Undo Changes?" later in this chapter.

In addition to the keystrokes listed in the preceding table, you can select a portion of text and delete it.

➡To select and delete text:

1. Move the insertion point to the beginning of the text you want to delete.
2. Click and hold down the left mouse button as you drag the mouse pointer to the end of the text you want to select. The selected text appears highlighted.
3. Release the mouse button and press Delete or Backspace.

HINT

You can also double-click a word or triple-click a sentence to select them.

If you find that you no longer need an entire file, you can delete it by using the Open File dialog box.

CAUTION

Before you delete a file, be sure that you will never need it again and that it is the correct file, because you cannot undelete a file with WordPerfect. DOS does have an Undelete function that may enable you to salvage a file. For information about undeleting a file, see your DOS manual.

➨To delete an entire file:

1. Choose File➢Open *or* press Ctrl+O.
2. Enter the directory in which the file is located in the Filename text field.
3. Click the file you want to delete.
4. Choose File Options and then choose Delete.
5. At the confirmation dialog box, choose Delete.
6. Choose OK to return to the document window.

For more information about file options, see Chapter 10, "Managing Files and Documents."

If you want to delete codes from your document, you should turn on Reveal Codes first so that you can see exactly what you are deleting. To turn on Reveal Codes, choose View➢Reveal Codes *or* press Alt+F3. After you are in Reveal Codes, move the insertion point to the right of the the code you want to delete, as shown, and then press Backspace:

Insertion Point

Reveal Codes

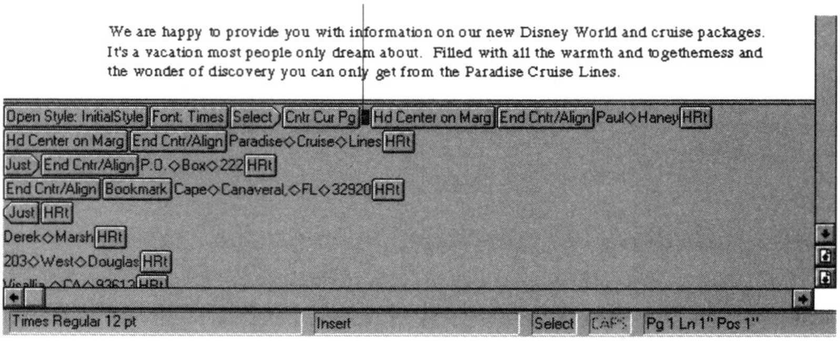

NOTE

When you are deleting text by using any of the keystrokes listed in the preceding table (except for Delete and Backspace), any formatting codes contained in the text also are deleted. If you

press Ctrl+Delete to delete to the end of the line, for example, and that line has a font change, the font change is deleted with the text. If you want to be prompted before the codes are deleted, you can choose File➢Preferences, double-click the Environment icon, and then choose Confirm Deletion of Codes. Choose OK and Close to return to the document window.

HOW DO I... Undelete and Undo Changes?

At times, you may inadvertently delete information or make changes you really didn't want to make. WordPerfect's Undelete feature lets you undelete and restore your last three deletions. The Undo feature lets you "undo" your last editing or formatting change. If you enter a font change, for example, and then decide that you don't like the way the text is formatting, you can use Undo to erase the change without going into Reveal Codes and deleting the font code.

Steps

➨**To undelete text or codes:**

1. Make sure that your insertion point is at the location where you want the text or code restored.
2. Choose Edit➢Undelete *or* press Ctrl+Shift+Z. The Undelete dialog box, shown in Figure 3–5, is displayed with your last deletion highlighted in the document window.
3. Choose Restore if the text you want to undelete appears at your insertion point location. If the correct text is not displayed, choose Previous until the text you want appears and then choose Restore. The Previous option cycles through your last three deletions.

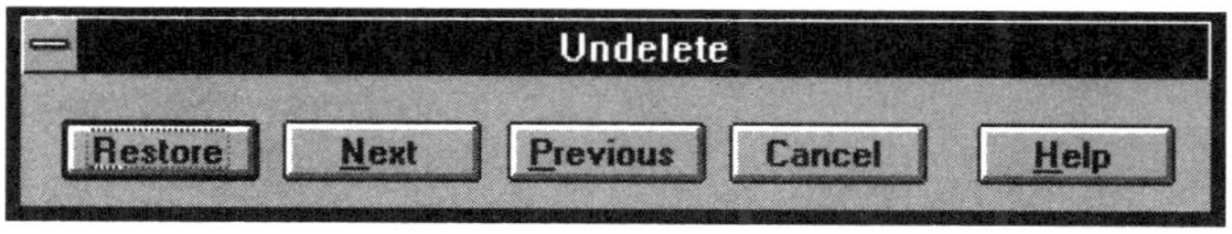

FIGURE 3–5
The Undelete dialog box.

➡**To undo your last change:**

1. Choose Edit➢Undo *or* press Ctrl+Z.

POWER BAR

Choose [Undo button] on the Power Bar.

Tell Me More

Undelete stores your last three deletions in memory. Each deletion consists of an entire deletion action. If you pressed Ctrl+Delete to delete an entire line of text, for example, the entire line is considered one deletion. The last three deletions remain in memory only until you exit from WordPerfect.

You can use Undelete to restore both editing and formatting changes. If you delete a word and then cannot think of a better word to use to replace it, for example, you can undelete the word. Or if you accidentally delete a bold code, you can use Undelete to restore it to the location of the insertion point. If you are restoring a formatting change you have deleted that is not displayed on the text screen, such as a margin change, you may want to turn on Reveal Codes so that you can see the code (or codes) you are restoring.

NOTE

The Undelete buffer contains deleted information from all document windows.

You can use Undelete as a handy shortcut to quickly copy information to multiple locations.

If you are creating a list of requirements for choosing a travel agent, for example, and you want every line to begin with the phrase *A travel agent must,* follow these steps :

1. Type the phrase on the first line.
2. Delete the text.
3. Choose Edit➢Undelete *or* press Ctrl+Shift+Z and choose Restore to restore the first line.
4. Move the insertion point to the next location where you want the phrase to appear.
5. Choose Edit➢Undelete *or* press Ctrl+Shift+Z and choose Restore.
6. Repeat Steps 4 and 5 until you have copied the text to all the desired locations.

Unlike Undelete, Undo restores the information at its original location. Undo works independently on each document window. Undo restores everything since the last time you deleted information, switched document windows, or accessed a menu.

The Undo feature can save you a great deal of time when you are creating and editing documents. If you center text on a line, for example, and then decide that you do not want the text centered, you can simply choose Edit➢Undo *or* press Ctrl+Z, and the center code is automatically deleted. This procedure is much easier than turning on Reveal Codes, finding the code, and then deleting the code.

Another useful application of Undo is with the Replace feature. If you search your document for a word or code and replace it with something else only to find out that you did not want to replace it, you can use Undo to restore the document to its original contents.

Undo can also delete text you insert. Use caution, however, when you are using Undo to delete text, because it deletes all text you have entered since the last time you performed any type of formatting operation or accessed a menu.

CAUTION

Be careful when you use the Undo feature, because the information is not stored in the Undelete buffer (that is, you cannot use Undelete). After you use Undo, the information is deleted permanently unless your next action is Undo.

HOW DO I. . . Select Text?

When you edit documents, you may want to perform a certain function on a portion of text. These functions may include bolding, underlining, sorting, spell-checking, and even printing. By selecting specific text, you have the flexibility to quickly manipulate large amounts of text and to confine certain functionality to small amounts of text. Using the mouse makes selecting text easy. In addition, the Select menu item enables you to quickly select sentences, paragraphs, pages, all text, tabular columns, and rectangles.

Steps

➡**To select text by using the mouse:**

1. Move your mouse pointer to the location where you want to begin selecting text.

2. Hold down the left mouse button and drag the pointer to the end of the portion of text you want to select. The selected text appears highlighted, as shown in Figure 3–6.
3. Release the mouse button and perform the desired function.

➡To select text by using the Select menu item:

1. Choose Edit➢Select.
2. Choose Sentence, Paragraph, Page, All, Tabular Column, or Rectangle.
3. Choose the action you want.

HINT

To quickly select text, double-click to select the current word, triple-click to select the current sentence, or quadruple-click to select the current paragraph. You can also press Shift + click to select all text from the position of the insertion point to the position of the I-beam. If you have trouble selecting the text with the mouse, try clicking faster.

FIGURE 3–6
Selected text.

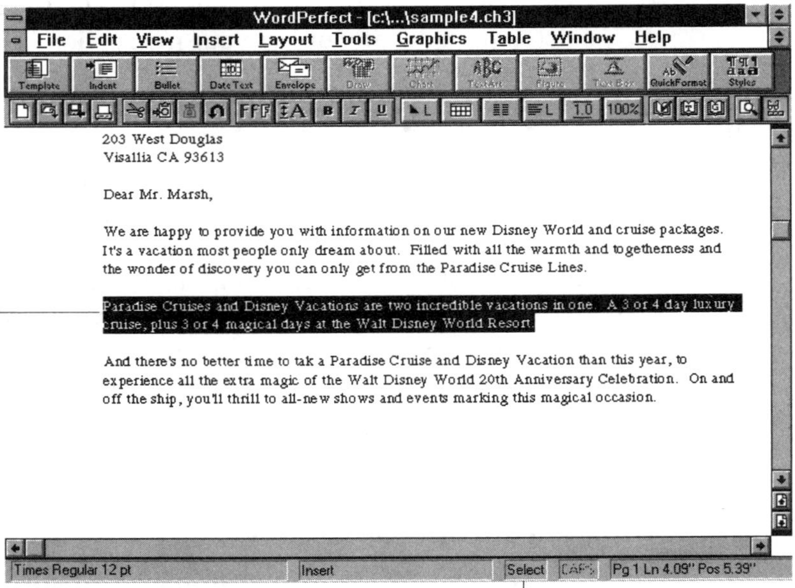

Tell Me More

You can also use several keystroke combinations to quickly select text. The following table lists the selection keystrokes and the text they select.

KEYSTROKE	SELECTED TEXT
Shift + ← or + →	One character to the left or right
Shift + End	To the end of the line
Shift + Home	To the beginning of the line
Shift + Ctrl + ← or →	Preceding or next word
Shift + ↑ or ↓	Up or down one line
Shift + Ctrl + Home	To the beginning of the document
Shift + Ctrl + End	To the end of the document

HINT

You can also double-click Select in the status bar *or* press F8 and then begin selecting text. If you first activate Select, you do not have to press the Shift key with the keystroke combinations in the table.

You can perform many useful tasks when text is selected. Some of the more common tasks are available on the QuickMenu shown here:

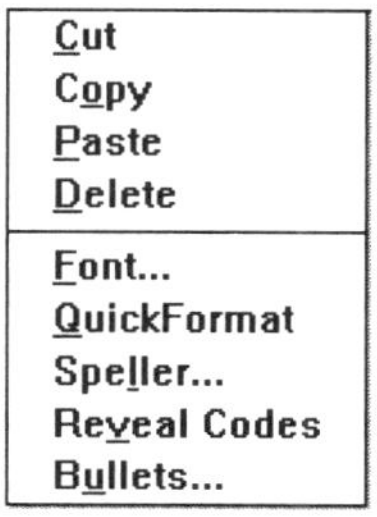

You can access the QuickMenu by clicking the right mouse button anywhere inside the selected text. Many of these features on the QuickMenu are discussed later in this chapter.

You can also save selected text to a new file. You can select parts of your document and save them to a new file. This feature might be useful

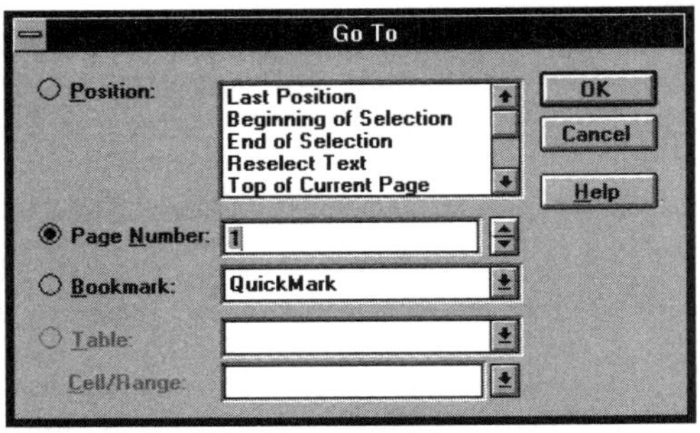

FIGURE 3–7
The Go To dialog box with text selected.

if you have written a letter and you want to use parts of the letter for a letter you want to write later. Simply select the text you want and choose File➢Save As *or* press F3, choose OK, enter the new filename, and then choose OK. The information is saved to the new file for later use.

When you're selecting text, the Go To feature is also helpful. When text is selected and you use Go To, the Position options change (as shown in Figure 3–7), and you can choose to go to the beginning or end of the selected text. You can also quickly reselect text you previously selected by using the Go To feature.

HOW DO I. . . Copy Text to a New Location

The Copy feature helps you quickly copy information to a new location. If you are creating two letters, for example, and the first two paragraphs of each letter are identical, you can copy those paragraphs to the document window containing the second letter. You copy information by selecting the information, copying the information, and then pasting it in the new location.

Steps

➨To copy information to a new location:

1. Select the text you want to copy.
2. Choose Edit➢Copy *or* click the right mouse button and choose Copy *or* press Ctrl+C.
3. Move the insertion point to the new location and choose Edit➢Paste *or* click the right mouse button and choose Paste *or* press Ctrl+V.

You can choose [Copy button] on the Power Bar to copy information and [Paste button] to paste the information.

Tell Me More

When you copy information, you must be sure to paste it in its new location before you copy or move any other information. Only the current information that is being copied or moved is stored. If you copy information and then copy or move more information, the most recent information overwrites the previous information.

If you want to add more information to the information you are copying, you can select the information and then choose Edit➢Append. This step adds the information to what you previously copied.

You can copy information to multiple locations. If you want to insert a heading for several paragraphs, for example, you can copy the heading once and then paste it in multiple locations.

Although you can use the Edit menu to access the Copy feature, it is much faster to use the QuickMenu or the Power Bar for copying and pasting. You can also use the drag-and-drop feature to copy text. You select the text and then click the text and drag it to the new location. Your mouse pointer looks like this:

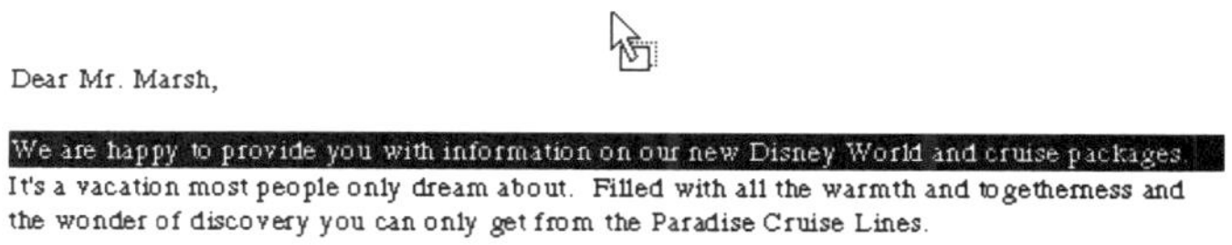

Before releasing the mouse button, hold down the Ctrl key and then release the mouse button. The text remains in the original location, and a copy is inserted at the new location.

Information you copy is stored in the Windows Clipboard. In addition to using this information in WordPerfect, you can also copy this information to any other Windows application.

HOW DO I... Move Text to a New Location?

The Cut feature helps you quickly move information to a new location. Cut is similar to Copy, but when you cut information, it is deleted from its original location. You cut information by selecting and cutting the text and then pasting it in a new location.

Steps

➠To cut information and insert it in a new location:

1. Select the text you want to move.
2. Choose Edit➢Cut *or* click the right mouse button and choose Cut *or* press Ctrl+X.
3. Move the insertion point to the new location and choose Edit➢Paste *or* click the right mouse button and choose Paste *or* press Ctrl+V.

POWER BAR

You can choose  on the Power Bar to cut information and  to paste the information.

Tell Me More

When you are moving information, you can move it to any document window. When you move information, you must be sure to paste it in its new location before you copy or move any other information. Only the current information that is being copied or moved is stored. If you move information and then copy or move more information, the most recent information overwrites the previous information.

Although you can use the Edit menu to access the Move feature, it is much faster to use the QuickMenu or the Power Bar for cutting and pasting. You can also use the drag-and-drop feature to move text. You select the text, click the text and drag it to the new location, and then release the mouse button.

NOTE

Information you move is stored in the Windows Clipboard. In addition to using this information in WordPerfect, you can also move this information to any other Windows application.

HOW DO I. . . Find Text and Codes in My Document?

The Find feature lets you quickly find and move to a specific word, phrase, or code in your document. You can search forward or backward through your documents. You can confine your search to a specific case (uppercase or lowercase) or to a specific whole word. You can also search for codes and for codes with specific values.

Steps

➠To use the Find feature:

1. Choose Edit➢Find *or* press F2. The Find Text dialog box, shown in Figure 3–8, appears.
2. Enter the text for which you want to find or choose Match➢Codes, highlight the code you want to find, and then choose Insert and then Close.
3. Select any additional Find options from the menu bar in the Find Text dialog box.
4. Choose Find Next to search from the insertion point to the end of the document *or* choose Find Prev to search from the insertion point to the beginning of the document.
5. After you have found the text or codes for which you are searching, choose Close.

Tell Me More

You can use the Find feature to help you troubleshoot specific problems. If you print a document, for example, and notice that beginning with the

FIGURE 3–8
The Find Text dialog box.

second page all the text is bolded, you can simply search for a bold code and then delete it.

If WordPerfect finds the information you enter in the Find text field, the text is selected. With the text selected, you can perform any action on the text by using the menu bar or Power Bar, etc. These menu bar and formatting tools are available even when the Find Text dialog box is displayed. If you do not want WordPerfect to select the text, you can choose Action from the Find Text dialog box and choose Position Before or Position After.

NOTE **You can also choose the Extend Selection option if you have selected text before you begin using Find. With this option selected, WordPerfect selects all text from the insertion point up to the information you requested it to find.**

If the information you enter in the Find field does not exist, WordPerfect displays a dialog box letting you know that it cannot find the information.

Specifying Find Conditions

You can specify the exact conditions of what you want to find by using the Match menu. By default, WordPerfect finds all words that contain the characters entered in the Find field. If you enter the word *air,* for example, WordPerfect finds *airplane, airlines,* and *chair.* If you want to find only the entire word and not all forms of the word, choose Match➢Whole Word. Find does not distinguish between upper- and lowercase. Choose Match➢Case if you want to find only the text that matches the case you enter in the Find field. You can also match a specific font by choosing Match➢Font. When you choose this option, you can specify the font face, font style, point size, and any attributes associated with the text for which you are looking.

Using the Options menu, you can change how and which parts of the document WordPerfect searches. When you use Find, WordPerfect searches the entire document, including headers, footers, entry fields, comments, endnotes, footnotes, graphics-box captions, equations, and the Table of Authorities Full Form. If you want to find information only in the document text, choose Options and deselect Include Headers, Footers, etc. in Find.

When you're using Find, the search begins at the insertion point and continues to the end of the document. You can choose Options➢Begin

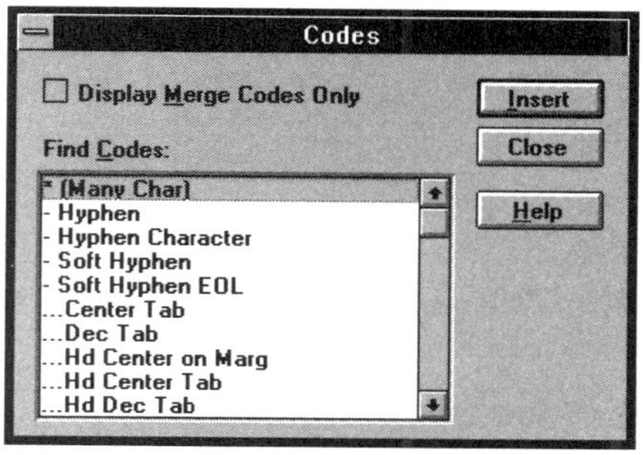

FIGURE 3–9
The Codes dialog box.

Find at Top of Document, Wrap at Beg/End of Document, or Limit Find Within Selection to change where WordPerfect begins and ends its search.

Finding Codes

WordPerfect makes it easy to find codes in your document. With more than 400 formatting codes available, it would be virtually impossible to remember the syntax for specific codes. If you want to search for a code, you just choose Match➢Codes and select it from the Codes dialog box, shown in Figure 3–9. The use of the Find feature to search for codes is much more reliable and much easier than trying to look manually through Reveal Codes.

NOTE **You cannot enter codes directly in the Find field—you must choose the codes from the Codes dialog box.**

You can also search for codes with specific values by choosing Type➢Specific Codes. The Specific Codes dialog box is displayed, as shown in Figure 3–10. After you choose a specific code, you are

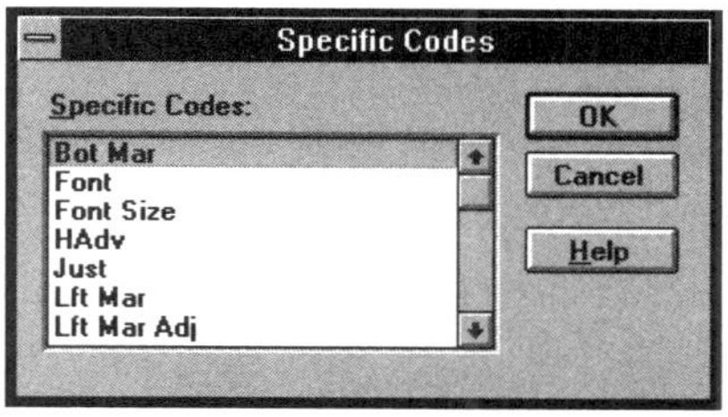

FIGURE 3–10
The Specific Codes dialog box.

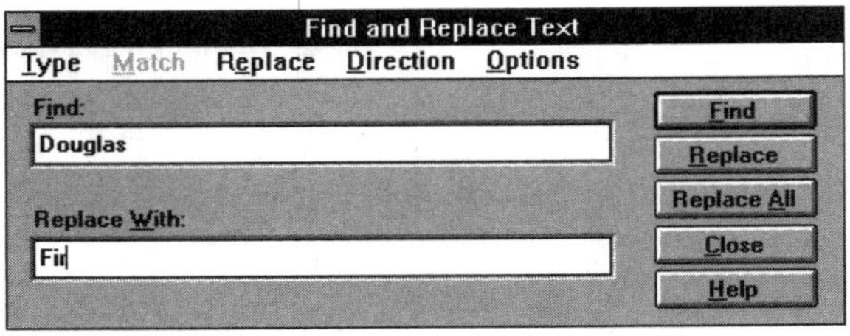

FIGURE 3–11
The Find and Replace Text dialog box.

prompted for the specific value of the code for which you want to search. Using Specific Codes helps customize your search so that you are finding only the exact codes for which you are looking.

HINT

The Find text box always displays the information from your preceding search. This information is useful if you want to repeat a search.

HOW DO I... Replace Text and Codes in My Document?

The Replace feature lets you quickly find a specific word, phrase, or code in your document and replace it with something else. Suppose that you have just created a newsletter and you notice that the font you used for the headings is too small. Rather than manually find each occurrence of the font, delete it, and then insert the new font code, you can use Replace to automatically find the font code and replace it with the new code.

Steps

➡**To find and replace text or codes:**

1. Choose Edit➢Replace *or* press Ctrl+F2. The Find and Replace Text dialog box, shown in Figure 3–11, appears.
2. Enter the text you want to find in the Find field or choose Match➢Codes to choose the codes you want to find.
3. In the Replace With field, enter the text or codes you want to use to replace the original text or codes.

4. Select any of the options you want from the menu bar. For information about each option, see the section "HOW DO I... Find Text and Codes in My Document?" earlier in this chapter.
5. Choose Replace to have WordPerfect stop at each occurrence and select the word. With the word selected, you can choose Replace to replace it with the new information or choose Find to move to the next occurrence. Or choose Replace All to have WordPerfect automatically find and replace each occurrence of the word.

Tell Me More

Find and Replace has numerous uses. Suppose that you write a letter to your travel agent to request information about Alaskan cruises. After writing the letter, you decide that you would rather go on a Caribbean cruise. You simply find the word *Alaskan* and replace it with *Caribbean*.

You not only can find and replace text but also replace specific codes in your document. Finding and replacing codes also increases your efficiency and saves you a great deal of time. You create a newsletter, for example, and bold all the titles, but then you decide that you want the titles in a larger font and bolded. You simply find the [Bold On] codes and replace them with [Font Size:18] and [Bold On].

The menu items available when you use Find and Replace are the same as when you use Find, except for the addition of the Direction menu item. From the Direction menu, you can choose whether you want to search forward or backward through your document.

There is also an additional option on the Options menu. You can choose Options➢Limit Number of Changes and specify how many replacements you want to make when you use the Replace All option.

If you want to search your document and delete all occurrences of a word, phrase, or code, you can leave the Replace With field blank. When you do not enter anything in the Replace With field, it displays <Nothing>, as shown in Figure 3–12.

This global find-and-delete operation is useful. You use an italics font in certain sections of a document, for example. After printing the document, you find that the italics font is too difficult to read, so you want to delete all italics codes. All you have to do is find the [Italc On] codes and replace it with nothing. All occurrences of italics are deleted.

FIGURE 3–12
Finding and Replacing with nothing.

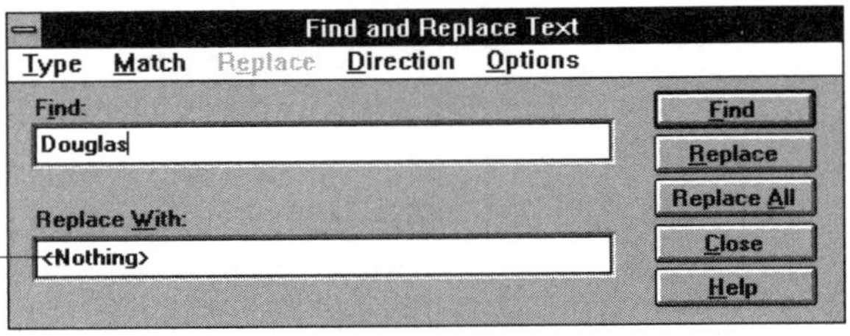

Replace with nothing

NOTE

When you find and replace specific codes, you must do so in pairs. If you want to search for a specific bottom margin code, for example, you must replace it with a new bottom margin code or nothing. You cannot replace it with another code or text.

HOW DO I... Set Margins in My Document?

Margins give you great control over where your text is positioned on the page. Margins enable you to change the distance between the edge of the page and your text. You can use two types of margins in your document: document margins and paragraph adjustments. You can set your left, right, top, and bottom margins for the entire document by using document margins. You can also adjust your margins for paragraphs by using paragraph adjustments. A paragraph adjustment is made to the existing left and right margins.

Steps

➡To set document margins:

1. Place the insertion point where you want to set the new margin.
2. Choose Layout➢Margins *or* press Ctrl+F8. The Margins dialog box is displayed, as shown in Figure 3–13.
3. Choose Left, Right, Top, or Bottom and then type the new margin setting *or* use the incrementing button to select the correct margin.
4. Choose OK to return to the document window. The margin settings remain in effect until you insert new margin settings. When you're setting margins, the sample page or *preview box*

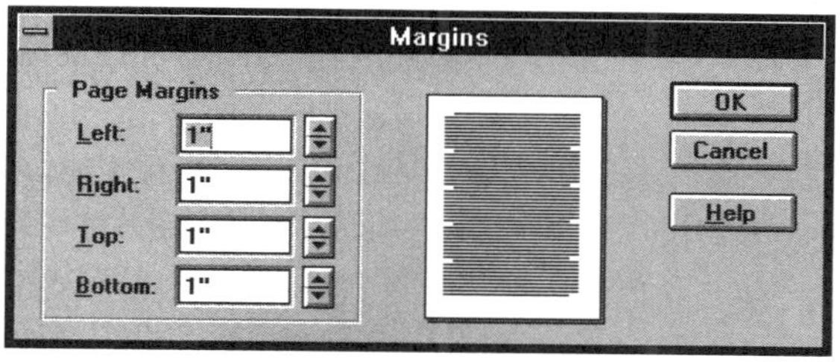

FIGURE 3–13
The Margins dialog box.

on the Margin dialog box shows you how your text will look with the current settings.

You can use the Ruler Bar to quickly change your left and right margins. To display the ruler, choose View➢Ruler Bar *or* press Alt+Shift+F3. The two markers at the top of the ruler indicate the position of the left and right margins:

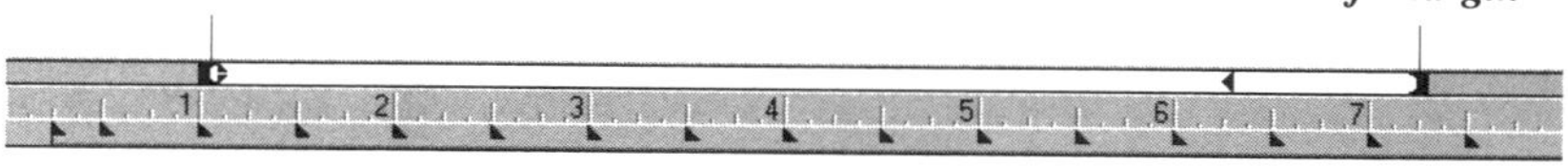

To change the margin settings, drag the markers to the location you want. Be sure to drag the marker that is displayed as a "bracket" shape. The small triangle markers are for changing paragraph settings.

Tell Me More

The default margin setting is 1 inch for top, bottom, left, and right. When you change your margin settings, these changes are reflected on-screen. Changes you make to your document, such as font changes and paper size and type changes, do not affect the margin.

When you insert margin settings, codes are inserted in your document that you can see when you turn on Reveal Codes. Top and bottom margin codes are placed at the top of the current page, and left and right margin codes are placed at the beginning of the current paragraph.

A paragraph adjustment or margin is the space surrounding a paragraph.

➡To adjust the left and right paragraph margins:

1. Select the paragraph you want to change.

2. Choose Layout➢Paragraph➢Format. The Paragraph Format dialog box is displayed, as shown in Figure 3–14.
3. Choose Left Margin Adjustment or Right Margin Adjustment and then type the new margin setting *or* use the incrementing button to select the correct margin.
4. Choose OK to return to the document window.

HINT

When you're setting paragraph adjustments, the sample page or *preview box* on the Paragraph Format dialog box shows you how your text will look with the current settings.

The difference between a left and right document margin and a paragraph adjustment is that the number you enter for the paragraph adjustment is in relation to the current left or right margin. If you enter +1 for the Left Margin Adjustment and your current left margin is set at 1 inch, for example, your new paragraph margin is 2 inches.

In addition to setting a margin adjustment for a specific paragraph, you can also specify how far to indent the first line from the margin adjustment. The First Line Indent is the amount of space between the Left Margin Adjustment and the first character of the first line in the paragraph.

➠To indent the first line of a paragraph:

1. Place the insertion point anywhere in the paragraph you want to change or select the paragraph you want if you want the setting applied to only that paragraph.
2. Choose Layout➢Paragraph➢Format.
3. Choose First Line Indent and then type the new setting *or* use the incrementing button to select the correct setting. This option indents the first line of the paragraph from the margin adjustment when you press [Enter]. If no margin adjustment has been made, the first line is indented from the original document margin.

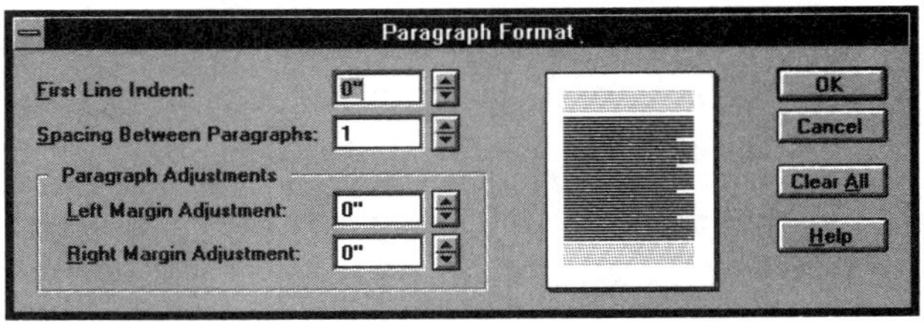

FIGURE 3–14
The Paragraph Format dialog box.

4. Choose OK to return to the document window.

You can also specify the number of lines between the paragraph and other paragraphs.

➨**To specify the paragraph spacing:**

1. Place the insertion point anywhere in the paragraph you want to change or select the paragraph you want if you want the setting applied to only that paragraph.
2. Choose Layout➢Paragraph➢Format.
3. Choose Spacing Between Paragraphs and then type the number of spaces you want between paragraphs *or* use the incrementing button to choose the correct setting.
4. Choose OK to return to the document window.

The use of these margin-formatting features is helpful when you are creating documents. Suppose that you have written a letter to a travel agency requesting information about different Caribbean cruise trip packages. You have included a paragraph in the letter requesting brochures and you want this particular paragraph to stand out. The document margins are set at 1 inch. You can offset the text by moving the paragraph in a half-inch more than the existing left and right margins and also by placing triple spaces both above and below the paragraph, as shown in Figure 3–15.

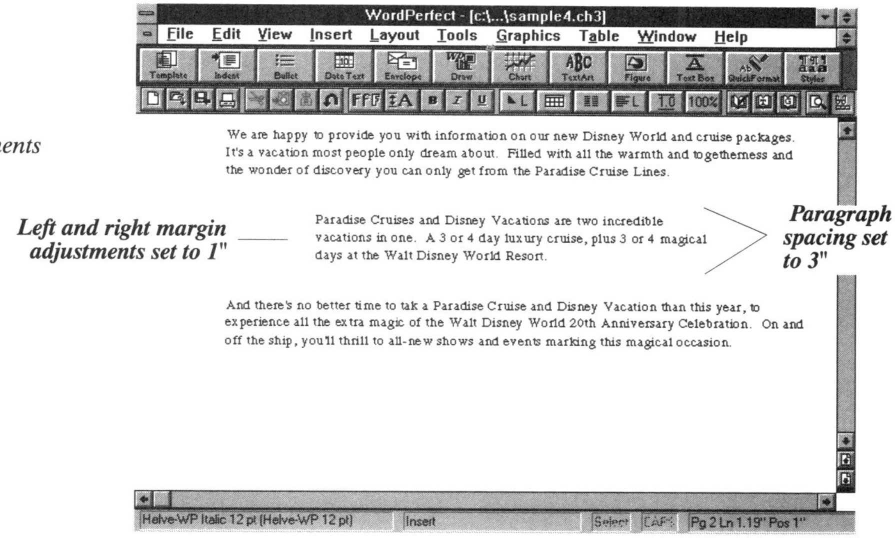

FIGURE 3–15
An example of margin adjustments and paragraph spacing.

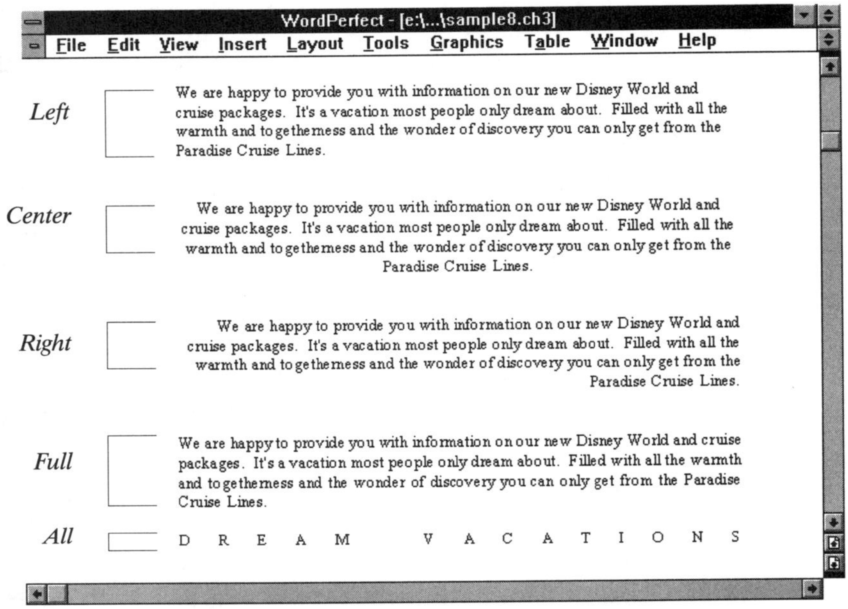

FIGURE 3–16
Examples of justification.

If you do not select text when you're adjusting your paragraph format options, you have to set the paragraph margins back to their original setting when you want the margin to be the same as the document margin.

NOTE

Many printers have an unprintable region. If you specify a margin setting that is less than the minimum margin used to account for the unprintable region for your printer, the minimum margin setting overwrites your setting.

HOW DO I... Change the Justification of Text in My Document?

Justification enables you to specify how you want to align text on a line. You can align text with the left margin, right margin, or both margins, or center text between the right and left margins. You can also set justification to evenly space every letter on the line by using All. Figure 3–16 shows examples of the different ways you justify text.

Steps

➡To set justification:

1. Place the insertion point where you want to set the justification *or* select the text for which you want to change the justification.
2. Choose Layout➢Justification.
3. Choose Left, Center, Right, Full, or All. All text in the current paragraph is justified according to the option you choose and remains in effect until you specify a new justification unless you selected the text, and then only the selected text is affected.

You can also choose  to set justification and then select the setting you want from the pop-up list. The letter on the Justification Power Button indicates your current setting.

Tell Me More

The default justification in WordPerfect is left-justification. When you use this setting, each line in your document has an uneven right edge. You can change the default justification by specifying the justification you want in your Initial Codes setup. For more information about Initial Codes, see Chapter 6, "Advanced Document Creation."

With the All justification setting, WordPerfect evenly spaces each letter on a line between the right and left margins.

➡To make the title on a page evenly spaced across the entire line:

1. Choose Layout➢Justification *or* choose the Justification Power Button.
2. Choose All.
3. Type the text you want to be evenly spaced. Each letter in the title is evenly spaced, as shown here:

C O M E   O N   A   C R U I S E

NOTE Justification does not affect table position in a document. Table position is determined by the options that are set when you format the table.

HOW DO I... Set Tabs?

A tab enables you to move a specified distance when you press the Tab key. You can set the position of tabs, clear tabs, and customize tabs. You can define the way the text aligns on the tab: Left, Right, Center, and Decimal. You can also specify whether the tab is measured from the left margin or from the left edge of the page. Using the Ruler Bar makes modifying tab settings quick and easy.

Steps

➡ **To insert a tab in your document:**

1. Press the Tab key.

RULER BAR

➡ **To specify the tab settings in your document:**

1. Choose View➢Ruler Bar.
2. Place the insertion point in your document where you want the new tab settings to take effect.
3. Click once on the Ruler Bar in the location where you want to set a tab, as shown here:

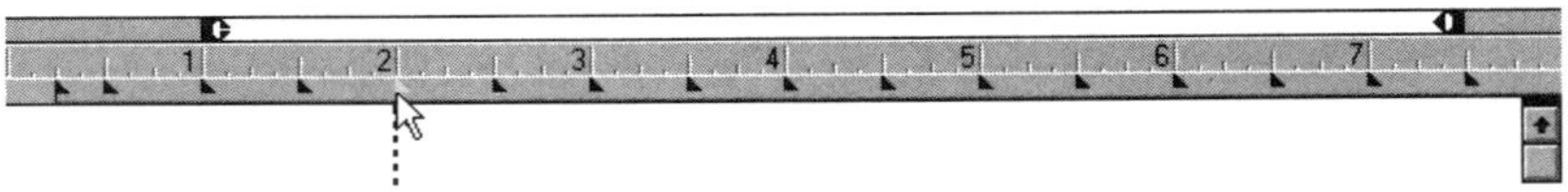

4. To delete a tab, drag it off the ruler.

Tell Me More

Tab settings are displayed on the Ruler Bar. A grid mark helps guide you as you set or move tab settings. If you do not want the grid mark to be displayed, you can click the right mouse button to display the QuickMenu for the Ruler Bar, as shown here:

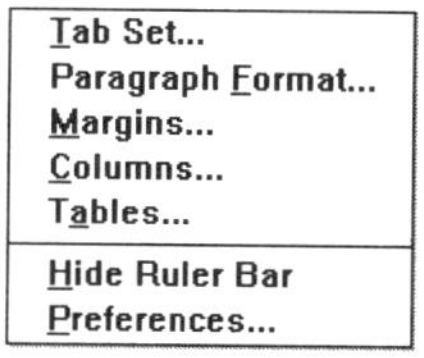

Ruler Bar QuickMenu

With the QuickMenu displayed, you can choose Preferences and then deselect Tabs Snap to Ruler Bar Grid.

By default, tab settings are measured from the left margin, which is called a *relative position* because the tab settings change if the left margin changes. If you want to set absolute tabs, you can click the right mouse button on the Ruler Bar to display the QuickMenu and then select Tab Set and then Left Edge of Paper (Absolute).

If you press Tab while you are in Typeover mode, the insertion point moves through an existing line from one tab setting to another without inserting a new tab.

Specifying Tab Types

Figure 3–17 shows an example of each type of tab setting. The easiest way to specify a tab type is to choose  from the Power Bar and then select the tab type you want from the pop-up list.

HINT

The letter and icon on the Tab Power Button changes to reflect the chosen Tab type. The tab icon on the Ruler Bar also reflects which type of tab is set.

You can also double-click a tab setting on the Ruler Bar to display the Tab Set dialog box and then choose Type and select the tab type you want from the pop-up list.

The following table lists the different tab types and how the text aligns.

TAB TYPE	TEXT ALIGNMENT
Left	Moves the text you type to the right of the tab (default setting)

(continues)

FIGURE 3–17
An example of tab types.

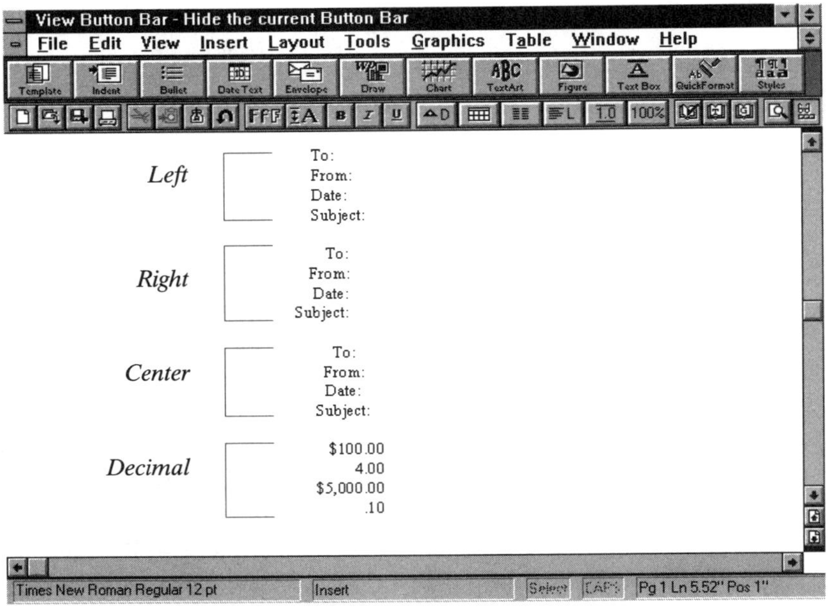

TAB TYPE	TEXT ALIGNMENT
Center	Centers the text around the tab
Right	Moves the text you type backward to the left of the tab
Decimal	Moves the text you type before the align character (such as a decimal point) to the left of the tab; moves the text you type after the align character to the right of the tab
... (Dot Leader)	Inserts a line of dots (periods) for every tab type

Dot leaders are useful if you are creating a document such as a table of contents. When Dot Leader is chosen, every time you press Tab, periods are placed in the document between tab settings, as displayed in this illustration:

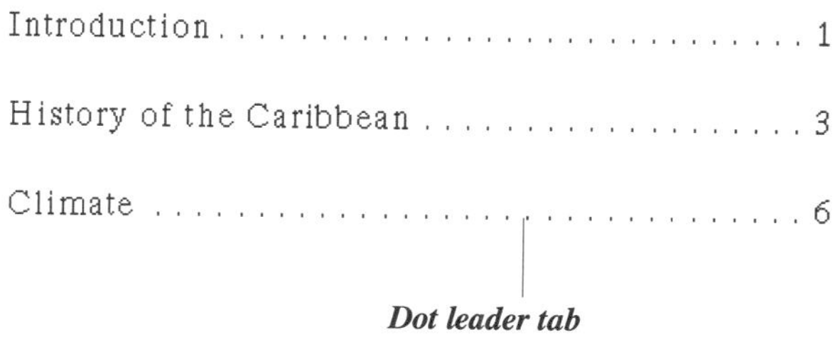

NOTE **From the Tab Set dialog box, you can change the character used for the dot leader and the space between the characters.**

Clearing Tab Settings

Before setting tabs, you may want to clear some or all of the existing tab settings. You can simply drag a tab setting off the Ruler Bar, or if you are displaying the Tab Set dialog box (shown in Figure 3–18), you can specify a position and then choose Clear.

If you want to clear all tab settings, you can right-click a tab setting to display the QuickMenu and then choose Clear All Tabs. From the Tab Set dialog box, you can also choose Clear All.

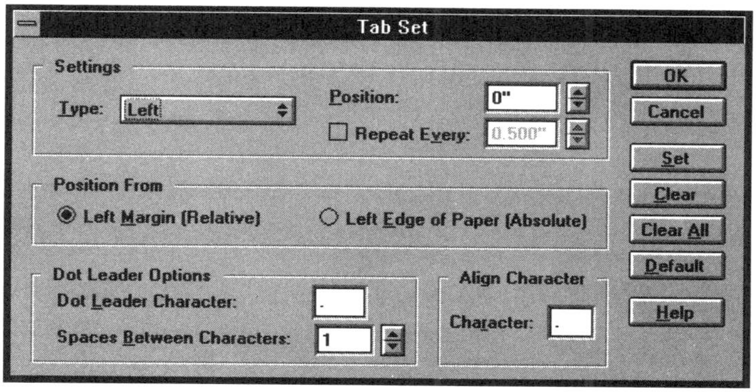

FIGURE 3–18
The Tab Set dialog box.

Setting Evenly Spaced Tabs

You can easily set evenly spaced tabs by using the Repeat Every option on the Tab Set dialog box option. Before setting evenly spaced tabs, be sure to use the Clear All option to remove all previous tab settings.

➠**To set evenly spaced tabs:**

1. Double-click a tab setting on the Ruler Bar *or* choose Layout➢Line➢Tab Set.
2. Choose Position and specify the position where you want the tabs to begin.
3. Select Repeat Every and specify the spacing you want between tabs.
4. Choose OK to return to the document window.

Setting Decimal Tabs

Decimal tabs let you align information based on a character. If you will enter a long column of numbers, for example, you can set tabs so that each number in the column aligns on the decimal point, as shown in Figure 3–19.

FIGURE 3–19
Decimal tabs.

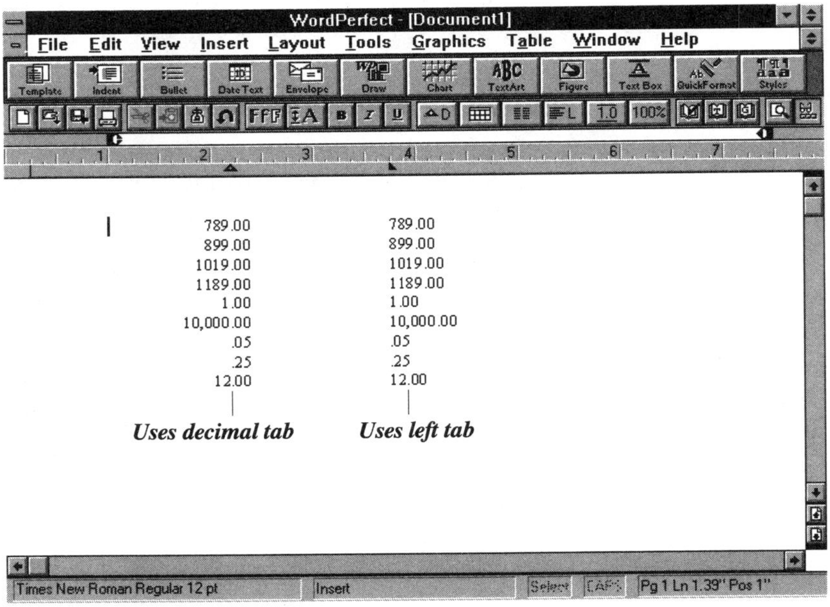

When you set a decimal tab, the text you type before the align character moves to the left of the tab. The text you type after the align character moves to the right of the tab. The alignment characters stay aligned.

The default decimal tab character is a period or decimal point (.). You can use other characters, including those in the WordPerfect character sets.

➡ **To change the decimal tab character:**

1. Place the insertion point where you want to change the decimal tab character.
2. Double-click a tab setting on the Ruler Bar *or* choose Layout➢Line➢Tab Set.
3. Type the character in the Character text box. To enter a character on the keyboard, simply type the character; or to enter a character from a WordPerfect character set special character, press Ctrl+W, specify the character you want, and then choose Insert and Close.
4. Choose OK to return to the document window.

Restoring the Default Tab Settings

If you have made changes to your tab settings and you want to change back to the default tab settings, which are set at every .5":

1. Double-click a tab setting on the Ruler Bar *or* choose Layout➢Line➢Tab Set.
2. Choose Default and then choose OK to return to the document window.

HOW DO I... Align Text in My Document?

WordPerfect gives you great flexibility in aligning text within a document. With a line of text, you can center it or align it with the right margin. With a paragraph, you can indent it or create a hanging indent and a double indent. Figure 3–20 shows examples of different types of text alignment.

Steps

The following table lists the Steps for using different text-alignment options.

Option	Shortcut	Steps	Available Key on QuickMenu
Center	Shift+F7	Layout➢Line➢ Center	Yes
Flush Right	Alt+F7	Layout➢Line➢ Flush Right	Yes
Indent	F7	Layout➢Paragraph➢ Indent	Yes
Hanging Indent	Ctrl+F7	Layout➢Paragraph➢ Hanging Indent	No
Double Indent	Ctrl+Shift+ F7	Layout➢Paragraph➢ Double Indent	No
Back Tab	Shift+Tab	Layout➢Paragraph➢ Back Tab	No

FIGURE 3–20
Examples of line spacing.

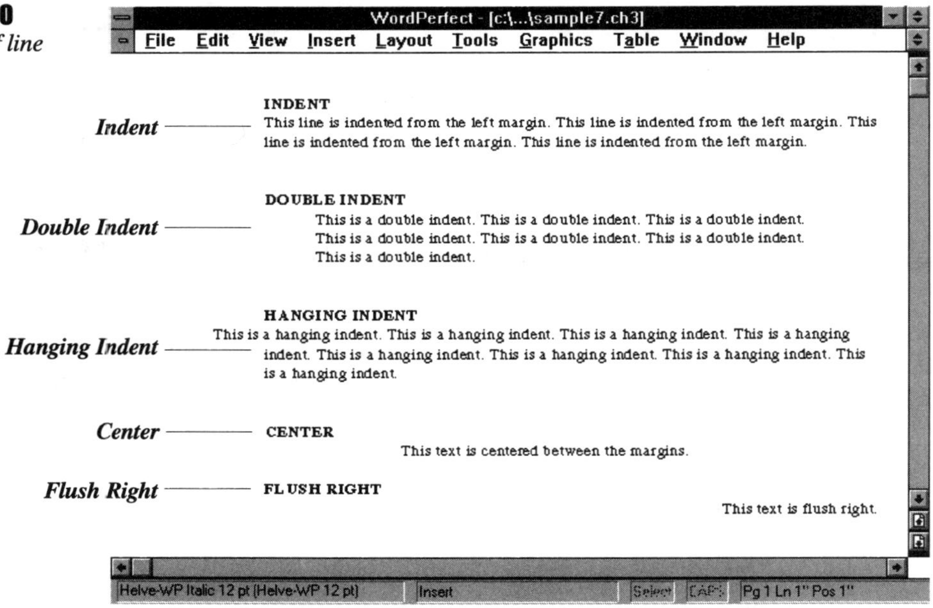

NOTE

To access the QuickMenu, click the right mouse button while pointing to the text in the document window.

Tell Me More

The alignment options in WordPerfect provide quick ways to position text in various locations on the line. You should use the alignment options to position text rather than try to align text by using spaces. When you use spaces to align text, there is no guarantee that the text will align properly when it is printed. The following sections give additional information about each alignment option.

Using Center

The Center option aligns the text between the left and right margins. You can center existing text, position the insertion point in front of the text you want to center, and then choose Center from the QuickMenu *or* press Shift+F7. You can center text on a specific position: To do so, press Tab or move the insertion point to the position, click the right mouse button and choose Center, and then type the text.

Using Flush Right

Flush Right enables you to align text with the right margin. When you use Flush Right to type new text, the text should be one line or shorter. To align existing text by using Flush Right, position the insertion point in front of the text you want to align and then choose Layout➢Align➢Flush Right *or* press Alt+F7. Each selected line aligns at the right margin.

NOTE

You cannot use the QuickMenu to access Flush Right when text is selected.

You can use Flush Right to insert a dot leader. If you are typing a table of contents, for example, pressing Alt+F7 twice fills the entire line with a dot leader, as shown here:

....|

You can then type text.

You can align a partial line of existing text at the right margin by using Flush Right. The line must end with a hard return. Place the insertion point at the beginning of the text you want to move and choose Flush Right from the QuickMenu *or* press Alt+F7.

Using Indent

Although a tab moves just one line of text to the next tab setting, an indent moves all subsequent lines of text in the current paragraph to the next tab setting. The width of each indent is determined by the current tab settings. An indent ends when you press Enter.

The Double Indent feature indents a paragraph one tab stop from the left and right margins (if you are typing a research paper, for example, and you want to use a long quote). Using a double indent sets off the quote and is standard in many research styles.

Hanging indents leave the first line of the paragraph at the margin and then move all subsequent lines one tab stop to the right. If you are creating a bibliography, hanging indents are useful.

You can indent existing text by placing the insertion point in from the first character in the text and then choosing the type of indent you want.

Using Back Tab

Back Tab moves the insertion point and all text on the line to the preceding tab stop. Back Tab also inserts a margin release if the insertion point is already at the left margin.

HOW DO I... Set Up Automatic Hyphenation?

You can choose to have WordPerfect automatically hyphenate words for you. Allowing WordPerfect to automatically hyphenate words gives you the freedom to enter text and not have to worry about long words at the end of lines. By default, WordPerfect wraps words to the next line instead of hyphenating them. You can also specify the parameters of the hyphenation zone. The hyphenation zone determines when words are hyphenated.

Steps

➡ **To turn on automatic hyphenation:**

1. Move the insertion point to the location where you want to turn on hyphenation.

2. Choose Layout➢Line➢Hyphenation. The Line Hyphenation dialog box is displayed, as shown in Figure 3–21.
3. Select Hyphenation On.
4. To change the Hyphenation Zone, choose Percent Left or Percent Right and type new percentages *or* use the incrementing buttons to select a new percent. Increase the percentage to reduce the amount of words hyphenated; decrease the percentage to hyphenate more words.
5. Choose OK to return to the document window.

Tell Me More

When hyphenation is turned on and a word has to be divided, WordPerfect automatically determines where to hyphenate the word. By default, WordPerfect prompts you before hyphenating a word only when it is unable to determine hyphenation.

If you want to be prompted before a word is hyphenated:

1. Choose File➢Preferences.
2. Double-click the Environment icon.
3. Open the pop-up list for Hyphenation Prompt and choose Never, When Required, or Always.
4. Choose OK and Close to return to the document window.

If you choose When Required, WordPerfect hyphenates the word according to the hyphenation dictionary. If the word is not found in the dictionary, you are prompted for the placement of the hyphen. This setting is the default.

If you choose Never, WordPerfect does not prompt you before hyphenating a word. If the word is not found in the dictionary, it is wrapped to the next line.

FIGURE 3–21
The Line Hyphenation dialog box.

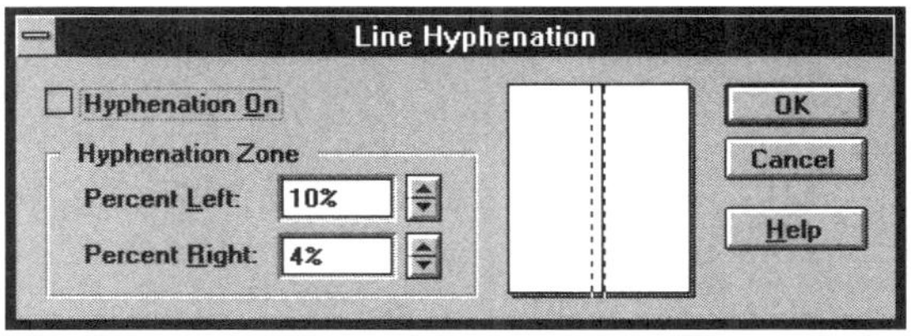

If you choose Always, WordPerfect prompts you regardless of whether the word is found in the dictionary.

HOW DO I... Change the Amount of Space Between Lines of Text?

You can specify how many spaces are inserted between lines of text in your document with the Line Spacing feature. If you want to double-space a report, for example, you can change the Line Spacing to 2.

Steps

➨To change the line spacing:

1. Place the insertion point where you want the new line spacing to begin *or* select the text for which you want to change line spacing.
2. Choose Layout➢Line➢Spacing.
3. Type the amount of space you want between lines *or* click the up and down incrementing buttons. WordPerfect inserts the Line Spacing code at the beginning of the current paragraph.
4. Choose OK to return to the document window.

POWER BAR

You can choose 1.0 from the Power Bar and then select an option from the pop-up list.

Tell Me More

When you start WordPerfect, all text you type is singled-spaced. You are not limited to the use of whole numbers when you use Line Spacing. Figure 3–22 shows examples of different types of line spacing.

Suppose that you have typed a letter and you want to have it proofread before you send it. The letter is singled-spaced, but you want the proofreader to be able to insert comments easily wherever they are necessary. In this instance, it might be beneficial to change the Line Spacing to 1.25 and allow additional space for comments without drastically changing the layout of the letter. After the letter is proofread and you have made any corrections, you can easily change the Line Spacing back to 1.

FIGURE 3–22
Examples of Line Spacing.

Line Spacing set to 1

Line Spacing set to 1.5

Line Spacing set to 2

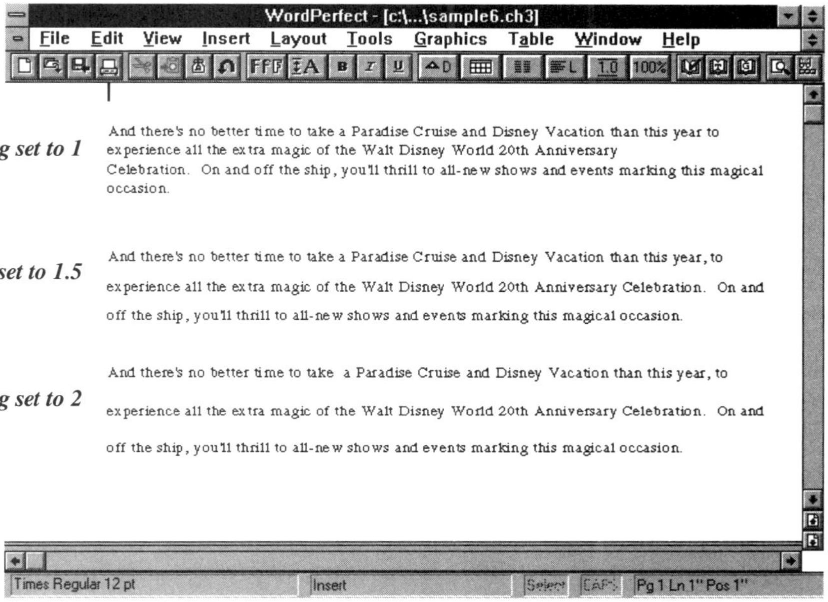

HOW DO I. . . Center a Page?

WordPerfect enables you to not only center text between right and left margins but also center a page between the top and bottom margins. Centering a page is useful if the text does not fill the entire page and you want it centered to approve its appearance, as shown in Figure 3–23.

Steps

➠To center a page or all pages from top to bottom:

1. Place the insertion point on the page you want to center.
2. Choose Layout➢Page➢Center.
3. Select Current Page or Current and Subsequent Pages to center all subsequent pages in the document.
4. Choose OK.

Tell Me More

Center Page enhances the visual appeal of a document. When you use Center Page, WordPerfect automatically calculates where the text

FIGURE 3–23
A centered page.

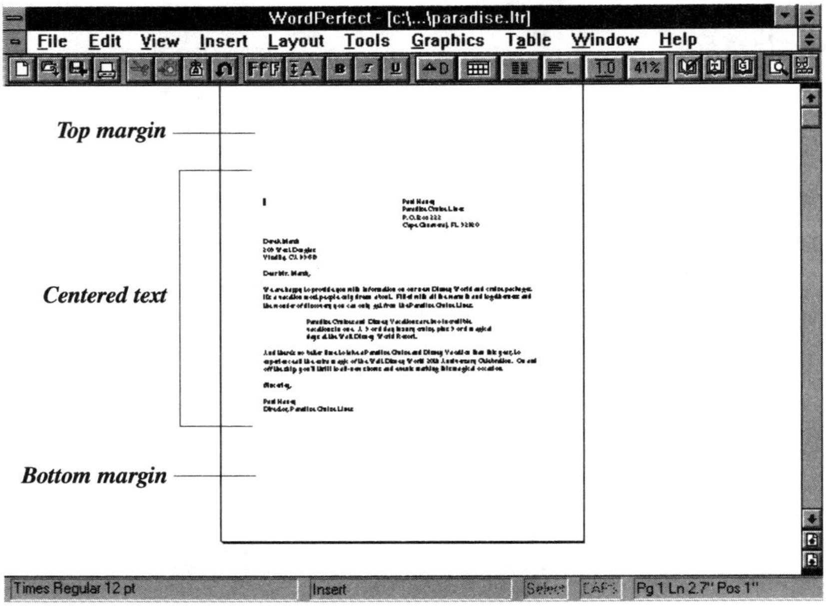

should be placed and readjusts the text if you add or delete text from the page.

When you center a page, the distance between the first line of text and the top margin is the same as the distance between the last line of text and the bottom margin. The location of your insertion point is not important when you center a page as long as the insertion point is on the page you want to center or on the page where you want centering to begin, depending on the option you are using.

You can see the format of the page after centering the page unless you are using Draft mode.

NOTE

The placement of any headers, footers, or footnotes on a page is not affected by Center Page.

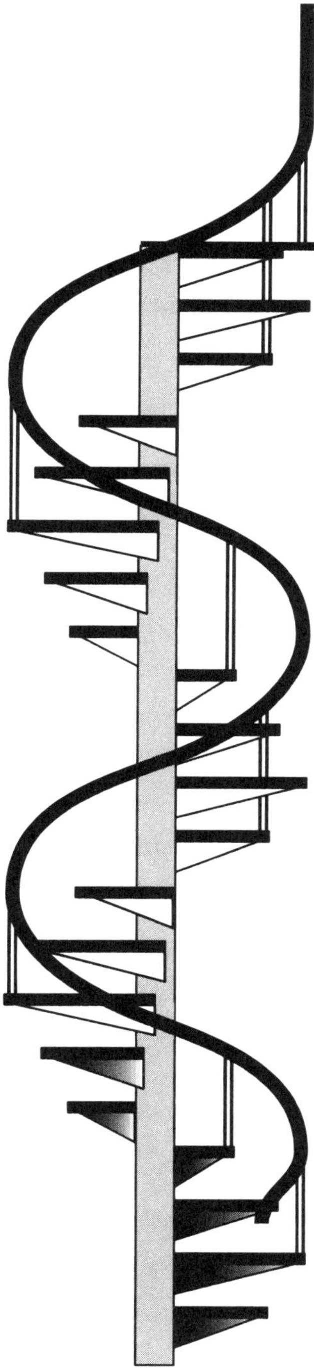

Chapter 4

Advanced Text Management

After you have mastered the basics of formatting text, you are ready for some of the "professional" text-formatting features in WordPerfect. If you do a great deal of layout and typesetting work, the answers to all your questions about text formatting are in this chapter. This chapter answers questions about the following advanced text-formatting features in WordPerfect:

- Advancing text to a specific position
- Numbering lines of text
- Changing characters to upper- or lowercase
- Keeping specific text on the same page
- Changing the space between lines
- Setting the baseline placement
- Adjusting the space between words and letters
- Creating special characters
- Inserting other (special) codes

HOW DO I... Advance Text to a Specific Position?

The Advance feature lets you position text in an exact location on the page. You can advance text to the left or right from the insertion point or from the left edge of the page. You can also advance text up or down from the insertion point or from the top of the page. Advance is useful for filling in preprinted forms and for controlling the exact location of text. If you have entered a heading, for example, and you want to move it down just slightly, you can use the Advance feature to move the heading line down just a few tenths of an inch from the insertion point to improve the appearance of your document.

Steps

➡ **To advance text:**

1. Choose Layout Typesetting.
2. Choose Advance. The Advance dialog box is displayed, as shown in Figure 4–1.
3. Select the option you want and then enter in the appropriate Distance text box the amount of the measurement you want to advance the text.
4. Choose OK to return to the document window.

FIGURE 4–1
The Advance dialog box.

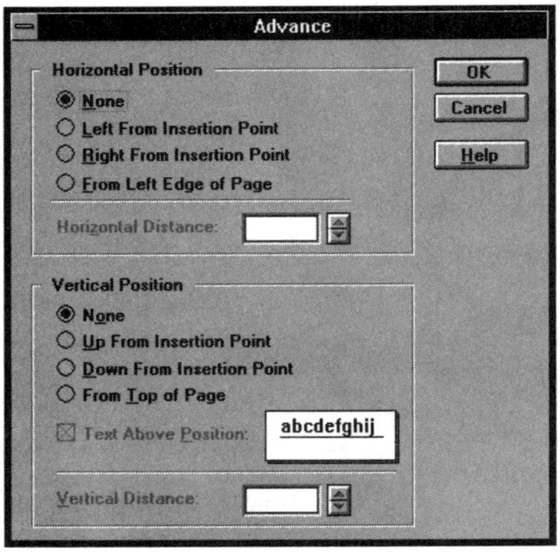

Tell Me More

You can use Advance to have complete control over where text is printed. If you have a preprinted form you want to fill in, for example, you can specify the horizontal and vertical position for each field that has to be filled in. Although this process may be a little time-consuming the first time, you can use the Template feature to create a template document. Then every time you want to fill in the form, you simply open the template you have created and insert the new information. For information about creating templates, see Chapter 11.

Choosing the From Left Edge of Page or From Top of Page option lets you specify an absolute position on the page that is not dependent on the location of the insertion point. When you select From Top Of Page, you can specify whether you want the base of the text above or below the position by selecting or deselecting the Text Above Position check box.

HOW DO I. . . Number Lines of Text?

WordPerfect can automatically number lines in your documents. The line numbers are displayed in the document window and on the printed page. You can customize the position of the numbers, the style of the numbers, and the interval between line numbers, in addition to many other options. Line numbering can be used with legal documents and with any other documents that require numbered lines.

Steps

➠To number lines:

1. Move the insertion point to the line in which you want the line numbering to begin.
2. Choose Layout➢Line.
3. Choose Numbering. The Line Numbering dialog box is displayed, as shown in Figure 4–2.
4. Select Turn Line Numbering On.
5. Make changes to the line-numbering options if you choose.
6. Choose OK to return to the document window.

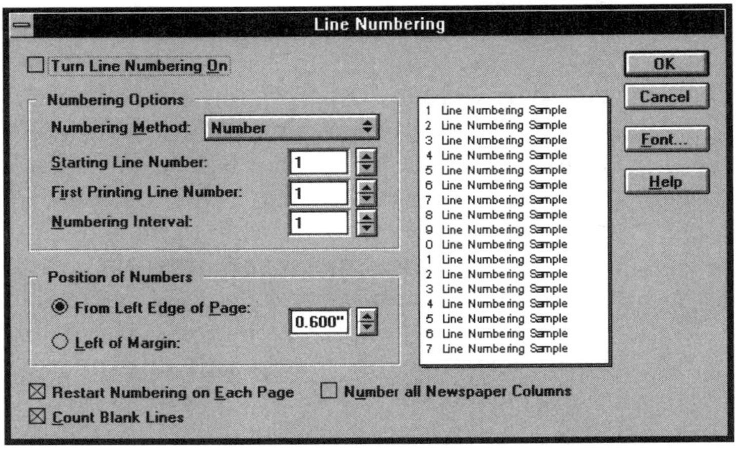

FIGURE 4–2
The Line Numbering dialog box.

Tell Me More

When you use the default line-numbering options, your document looks similar to the one shown in Figure 4–3. The Sample Numbering box on the right side of the Line Number dialog box displays a sample of the line numbering according to the options you have chosen.

WordPerfect provides several options for customizing line numbering to fit the needs of your document. The following table lists the Line Numbering options and describes each one.

OPTION	DESCRIPTION
Numbering Method	Indicates the style of line numbering. You can choose number, upper- or lowercase letters, or upper- or lower-case roman numerals.
Starting Line Number	Indicates the number assigned to the first line on the page.
First Printing Line Number	Indicates the first line number that is printed. If you want to number lines in intervals of 10, for example, and you want line number 10 to be the first line that displays a number, you enter 10 for this option.

Option	Description
Numbering Interval	Indicates the interval for line numbering. Only those numbers at the specified interval are printed on the page. Figure 4–4 shows an example of the Line Numbering Interval set to 5 and the first printed number set to 5.
Position of Numbers	Indicates where the number is printed on the page. You can choose the position from the left edge of the page or from the left margin. Because the numbers by default are printed .6 inches from the edge of the page, which is just inside the left margin, the text placement is not affected by the line numbers.
Restart Numbering on Each Page	Restarts line numbering on each page.
Count Blank Lines	Numbers all lines regardless of whether text is on the line. You must have a Hard Return code on the line in order for the number to print. If you want to print a page that just has line numbers for use with an oral exam or a form that has to be filled out, you turn on line numbering and then just press Enter until the insertion point is at the line number you want.
Number all Newspaper Columns	Numbers lines in each column individually according to the specifications you set.

You can also choose Font to display the Line Numbering Font dialog box, which enables you to select the font face, font size, appearance, and color for line numbering. Line Numbering uses the Document Initial Font unless you change it with this option.

HOW DO I. . . Change Characters to Upper- or Lowercase?

At times, you may want to convert letters quickly to upper- or lowercase. You may type a title in mixed case, for example, and then decide that it would look better if it were in ALL CAPS. With the Convert Case feature, you can quickly convert letters to upper- or lowercase. You can also use Convert Case to convert a line of text to Initial Caps.

FIGURE 4–3
A document window that displays default line-numbering options.

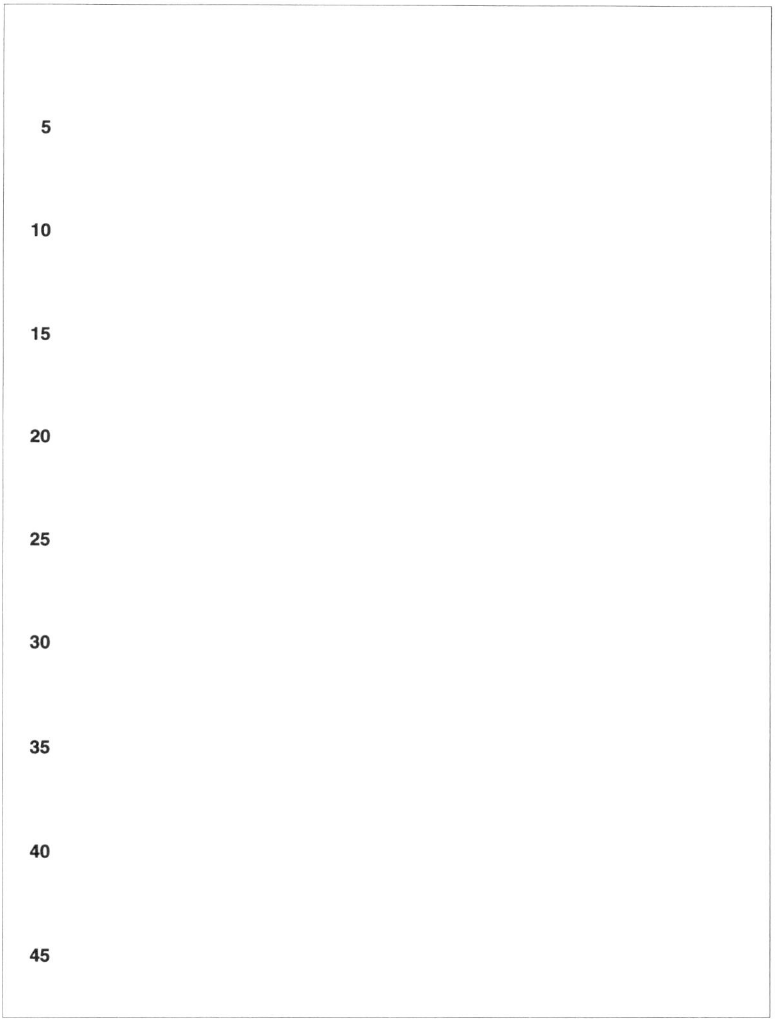

FIGURE 4–4
Line Numbering Interval set to 5 and First Printed Number Set to 5.

Steps

➠To convert case:

1. Select the text you want to convert.
2. Choose Edit➢Convert Case. The Convert Case menu appears.
3. Choose Uppercase, Lowercase, or Initial Capitals.

HINT **You can also press Ctrl+K to convert selected text to ALL CAPS if it is lowercase, or to lowercase if it is in ALL CAPS.**

Tell Me More

When you choose Uppercase or Lowercase, WordPerfect converts all the selected characters to the specified case. When you choose Initial Caps, the first letter of most words is capitalized. Using Initial Caps is helpful for properly capitalizing a title. Words such as *and, the, of,* and *to* are not capitalized unless they occur at the beginning of a sentence.

HOW DO I... Keep Specific Text on the Same Page?

WordPerfect provides several ways to keep text together on the same page and make your documents look more professional. You can keep a block of text and a certain number of lines together on the same page. Keeping specific text together is helpful if you have information that must be viewed together. If you create a list of figures, for example, you can use Block Protect to ensure that the list stays together. You can also prevent single lines of a paragraph, called *widows* and *orphans,* from appearing at the top or bottom of a page.

Steps

➠To keep a block of text together on the same page:

1. Select the text you want to keep together on the same page.
2. Choose Layout/Page/Keep Text Together. The Keep Text Together dialog box is displayed, as shown in Figure 4–5.
3. Select Keep Selected Text Together on Same Page.
4. Choose OK to return to the document window.

➠To keep a certain number of lines together on the same page:

FIGURE 4–5
The Keep Text Together dialog box.

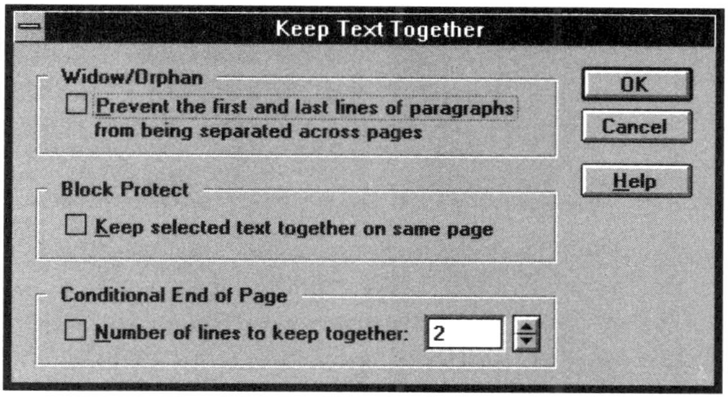

1. Move the insertion point to the first line you want to keep together with other text.
2. Choose Layout/Page/Keep Text Together.
3. Select Number of Lines to Keep Together and then enter the number of lines you want to keep together. Be sure to include blank lines when you are determining the number of lines to keep together.
4. Choose OK and to return to the document window.

➠**To avoid widows and orphans:**

1. Move the insertion point to the page on which you want to activate Widow/Orphan Protect.
2. Choose Layout/Page/Keep Text Together.
3. Select the option Prevent the First and Last Lines of Paragraphs from Being Separated Across Pages.
4. Choose OK to return to the document window.

Tell Me More

Using Block Protect, Conditional End of Page, and Widow/Orphan eliminates the need to continually check your documents for stranded lines and split text. The following sections explain more about each feature.

Using Block Protect

Although you can see where a page will end when you are creating a document, Block Protect guarantees that the selected text always stays together on a page regardless of any editing changes you may make to the document.

Suppose that you have a long quotation you want to keep on the same page in a document. When you first create the document, the quotation is all on one page, but later you add some information in the section before the quotation. If you do not use Block Protect, the quotation will end up on two pages and then you have to move your text around manually. Block Protect is also useful when you are creating long tables you want to keep on the same page.

When you use Block Protect, WordPerfect moves the entire block to the next page if it does not fit on the current page. If you have a large section of text that is block-protected, you may end up with very little text on the preceding page. If you Block Protect more text than will fit on one page, WordPerfect puts as much of the text as possible on a page. When you block-protect a section of text, any text you insert later in that section is also block- protected.

Using Conditional End of Page

Conditional End of Page helps you to avoid leaving headings at the end of a page with no text underneath them. If you are creating a document with headings or section titles, you have to insert a Conditional End Of Page code at the beginning of each heading.

Using Widow/Orphan Protect

With Widow/Orphan Protect turned on, single lines of a paragraph are not left at the top or bottom of the page. When you turn on Widow/Orphan Protect, it is in effect from the current page until you turn it off.

You can also select a section of text in which you want to prevent widows and orphans.

HOW DO I... Change the Space Between Lines?

In addition to Line Spacing, WordPerfect has two other methods for changing the spacing between lines: Line Height and Line Height (Leading) Adjustment. Line Height and Line Height (Leading)

Adjustment are most often used with professionally typeset documents. These features give you complete control over the placement of a line of text. *Line height* is the distance between the top of one line of text to the top of the next line of text. By default, line height is automatically set for you according to the size of the font. By using the Line Height feature, you can increase or decrease the line height.

Line height (leading) adjustment is the amount of space between lines. By default, the Line Height (Leading) Adjustment is automatically set for you according to the size of the font. You can increase or decrease the leading.

Steps

➨To change the line height:

1. Move the insertion point to the line in which you want the line height to change.
2. Choose Layout➢Line➢Height.
3. Select Fixed and enter the new line height.
4. Choose OK to return to the document window.

➨To change the Line Height (Leading) Adjustment:

1. Move the insertion point to the line in which you want the leading adjustment to change.
2. Choose Layout➢Typesetting➢Word-Letterspacing.
   The Word Spacing and Letterspacing dialog box is displayed, as shown in Figure 4–6.
3. Select Adjust Leading and enter the amount of space you want to add or subtract between the bottom of each line of text and the top of the next line of text.
4. Choose OK to return to the document window.

Tell Me More

The Line Height and Line Height (Leading) Adjustment features are most often used when you are creating documents that must meet certain typesetting specifications. You can experiment with these features by re-creating a professionally typeset document and using Line Height and Line Height (Leading) Adjustment to control the space between lines.

Figure 4–7 shows an example of a title in a newsletter with and without Line Height (Leading) Adjustment. You can see that when you

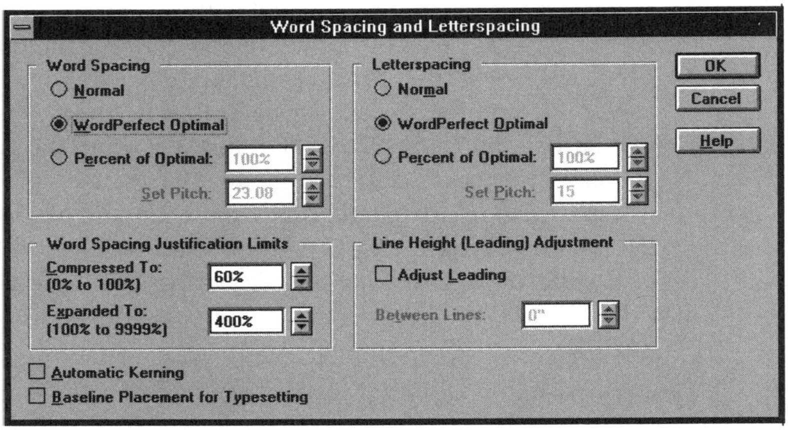

FIGURE 4–6
The Word Spacing and Letterspacing dialog box.

use Line Height (Leading) Adjustment the white space is reduced and the title looks more appealing.

HOW DO I... Set the Baseline Placement?

The *baseline* is the bottom of a line of text. By default, WordPerfect places the top of the first line of text even with the top margin of the document and then places the baseline at the bottom of the first line of text. If you are creating a document that must meet typesetting specifications for the baseline placement, you can use the Baseline Placement for Typesetting option. When this option is chosen, the baseline of the first line of text is at the top margin, so the text is *above* the top margin.

Steps

➡To change the baseline placement:

1. Choose Layout ➢ Typesetting ➢ Word-Letterspacing.
   The Word Spacing and Letterspacing dialog box is displayed.

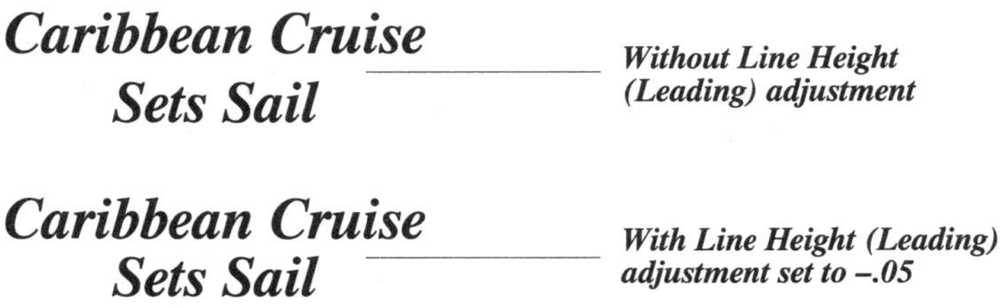

FIGURE 4–7
A title with and without Line Height (Leading) Adjustment.

2. Select Baseline Placement for Typesetting.
3. Choose OK to return to the document window.

Tell Me More

By default, the placement of the first baseline on a page varies depending on the font and font size you are using. Choosing Baseline Placement for Typesetting enables the first baseline to remain constant (the top margin and the first baseline are the same).

HOW DO I. . . Adjust the Spacing Between Words and Letters?

WordPerfect provides several ways to adjust the spacing between words and letters. The Automatic Kerning feature automatically adjusts certain letter pairs so that they have a more appealing amount of space between them. When the letters *W* and *a* are used together, for example, they have a great deal of white space between them. Kerning reduces this white space. You can also manually kern letter pairs to reduce white space.

The Word/Letterspacing feature lets you manipulate the space between letters or words. Word Spacing Justification Limits lets you change the space between words in justified text.

Steps

➡To turn on automatic kerning:

1. Move the insertion point to the location in your document where you want to turn on kerning.
2. Choose Layout➢Typesetting➢Word/Letterspacing.
   The Word Spacing and Letterspacing dialog box is displayed.
3. Select Automatic Kerning.
4. Choose OK to return to the document window.

➡To change the word- and letterspacing:

1. Move the insertion point to the location in your document where you want to change the word and letter spacing.
2. Choose Layout➢Typesetting➢Word/Letterspacing.

3. Select the appropriate Word Spacing or Letterspacing options. Normal uses the settings recommended by the font manufacturer; WordPerfect Optimal uses the settings recommended by WordPerfect; and Percent of Optimal lets you enter a number greater than 100% to increase the spacing, or a number less than 100% to decrease the spacing; or choose Set Pitch and enter the pitch (characters per inch) you want the spacing to use.
4. Choose OK to return to the document window.

➡ **To change the word-spacing justification limits:**

1. Move the insertion point to the location in your document where you want to change the word-spacing justification limits.
2. Choose Layout➢Typesetting➢Word/Letterspacing.
3. Enter the percentages to which justified text can be compressed and expanded for the Compressed To and Expanded To options.

Tell Me More

The following sections give applications and uses for kerning, word spacing and letterspacing, and word-spacing justification limits.

Using Kerning

Kerning takes effect from the insertion-point location or for selected text. WordPerfect automatically adjusts specific letter pairs so that the space between them is more visually appealing. Figure 4–8 shows an example of kerned and unkerned text. Notice the difference between the spacing of the letters *W* and *a*.

If automatic kerning does not take care of specific spacing problems, you can manually kern letter pairs.

➡ **To manually kern a pair of letters:**

Water Sports Included *Unkerned text*

Water Sports Included *Kerned text*

FIGURE 4–8 *Kerned and unkerned text.*

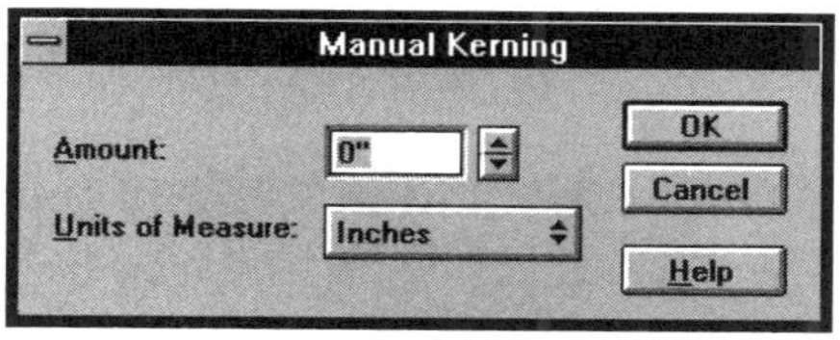

FIGURE 4–9
The Manual Kerning dialog box.

1. Move the insertion point between the two characters you want to kern.
2. Choose Layout➢Typesetting➢Manual Kerning. The Manual Kerning dialog box is displayed, as shown in Figure 4–9.
3. If necessary, select from the pop-up list the Units of Measure you want to use for the Amount.
4. Enter the amount you want to move the letters. A negative amount moves them closer together, and a positive amount moves them farther apart.

HINT

As you enter the amount, you can see the letters moving in the document window.

5. Choose OK to return to the document window.

Using Word- and Letterspacing

You can adjust word spacing or letterspacing or both. You can use this feature to alter the *pitch,* which is the number of characters per inch (of a certain font) on the page. If you have a built-in 14-pitch font in your printer but you want to use a 16-pitch font and don't have one, for example, you can use the Set Pitch option for Word/Letterspacing to make the font appear to be 16 pitch.

Manually adjusting the pitch does not always result in perfect-looking text because letters can become scrunched together. You can also use the Word Spacing feature to evenly space letters to make an attractive title, as shown in Figure 4–10. The second line of the figure shows Word Spacing set to 185 percent of Optimal with a 48-point font size.

FIGURE 4–10
A title using Word Spacing to evenly space letters.

CARIBBEAN

C A R I B B E A N

Word Spacing set to 185% of Optimal with a 48-point font.

Using Word Spacing Justification Limits

The Word Spacing Justification Limits feature determines how your justified text looks when it is printed. You specify how much WordPerfect can compress and expand word spacing to justify the line.

HINT

If you do not like having a lot of additional white space between words, you may want to decrease the percentage specified in the Expanded To option.

HOW DO I... Create Special Characters?

In addition to the standard letters, numbers, and other symbols on your keyboard, WordPerfect gives you the ability to insert many other characters in your document. WordPerfect provides 15 sets of different characters (one of which you can define yourself) you can insert in your document. The character sets include typographic symbols, math and scientific symbols, digraphs and diacritics, Greek and Hebrew characters, and many more.

You can also create your own characters by using Overstrike. Overstrike combines two characters to create a new character, such as the cent symbol (¢), which combines the *c* and the slash mark (/). By using the Overstrike feature, you can change the appearance of the characters.

Steps

➡ **To insert a character from a WordPerfect character set:**

1. Place the insertion point in your document where you want to insert the character.
2. Choose Insert➢Character *or* press Ctrl+W. The WordPerfect Characters dialog box is displayed, as shown in Figure 4–11.
3. Choose a Character Set from the pop-up list. The Characters box displays the characters in the selected character set.

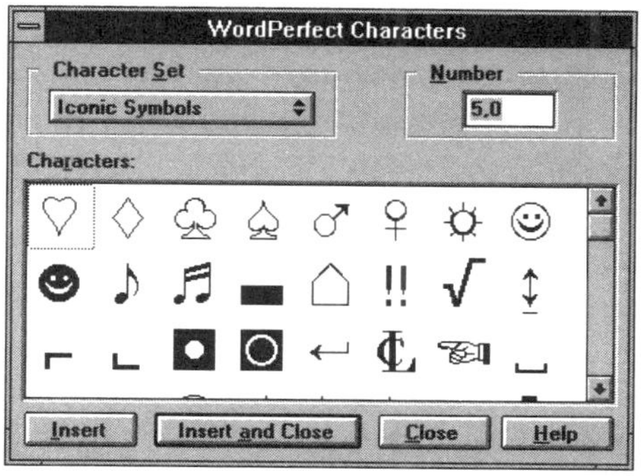

FIGURE 4–11
The WordPerfect Characters dialog box.

4. Double-click the character to insert it in your document and keep the dialog box open *or* click once on the character and then choose Insert and Close. *Note:* You can also choose Insert if you want to leave the dialog box open to add more characters.

➠**To create a character by using Overstrike:**

1. Place the insertion point in your document where you want to insert the overstrike character.
2. Choose Layout➢Typesetting➢Overstrike. The Overstrike dialog box is displayed, as shown in Figure 4–12.
3. Type the characters, without spaces or commas, that you want printed as an overstrike. The order in which you type the characters is not important.
4. To add an attribute to the character, select the pop-up box next to the Characters text box and select the attribute you want for the character.
5. Choose OK to insert the overstrike character and return to the document window.

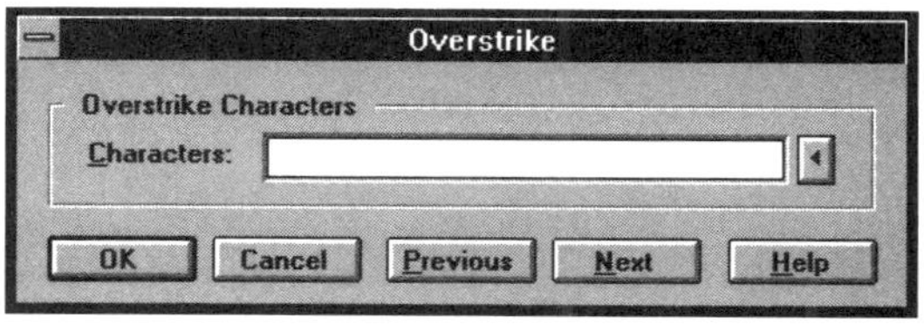

FIGURE 4–12
The Overstrike dialog box.

Tell Me More

If WordPerfect cannot print the character by using your current font, it tries to find another font that contains the character. This is the reason your special characters may appear in a different font from the rest of your text. If your printer does not have any fonts that support the character, WordPerfect prints the character graphically. The print quality for characters also depends on the Print Quality settings you select in the Print dialog box.

Inserting Characters from the WordPerfect Character Sets

The 15 character sets include more than 1,400 characters and symbols. Each character set and character in a set is numbered. This number appears in the upper right corner of the dialog box. The number corresponds to the character around which a dotted box is flashing. The combination of the set number and the character number creates a specific character.

The following table lists the 14 different character sets that are available when you are using WordPerfect characters and shows examples of the characters in each set.

CHARACTER SET	EXAMPLES
ASCII	1 2 3 ! ?
Multinational	ī ź Ö Ö ā
Multinational 2	̦ ̓ ̒ ˚ ̕ ̨ ̧ ˙ ˳ ˆ ˘ ‾ ̉
Box Drawing	╤ ╥ ╤ ╥ ╢ ╫ ╢
Typographic Symbols	⅓ ⌐R ⁿL ⁎ £ ¿ “
Iconic Symbols	⌐ ⌙ ◘ ◙ ← ☞ ☜ ✓
Math/Scientific	≮ ⌣ ⊄ ⊛ ∋
Math/Scientific Extended	⎞ ⎫ ⎠ , ⌊ ⌊ ‖
Greek	Σ ρ Σ Υ Χ

(continues)

CHARACTER SET	EXAMPLES
Hebrew	צץפףעסנ
Cyrillic	ЧЪСчшЫ
Japanese	ざじ ずぜぞた
User-defined	You must define these
Arabic	ت ـجـ ج ـلأ لأ ع خ
Arabic script	ٽ ٿ ٺ ڹ ڵ ڒ ڃ
Phonetic	ɣʄ ɟɞɸɚ

HINT **You can quickly insert a character for which you know the number by pressing Ctrl+W and then enter the numbers. If you often insert bullets in your document, for example, you know that a bullet character is 4,0 in the WordPerfect character sets. You can simply press Ctrl+W and enter *4,0* to insert the bullet and then choose OK. You can also include this information in a macro. For information about creating macros, see Chapter 11.**

Using Overstrike

You can use Overstrike to create digraphs, symbols, and diacritics. A *digraph* is a combination of two letters that represent a single sound, such as the schwa A (æ). An example of a *symbol* is the paragraph symbol (¶). A *diacritic* is an accent mark used with a character to change the way the character is pronounced. An example of a diacritic is in the word résumé.

When you use Overstrike, WordPerfect uses the current font to print the character. If your printer fonts do not have the characters that are necessary, you should use the WordPerfect character sets to insert the special character.

NOTE **If the combination of characters does not form a digraph, diacritic, or symbol, nothing is displayed on-screen.**

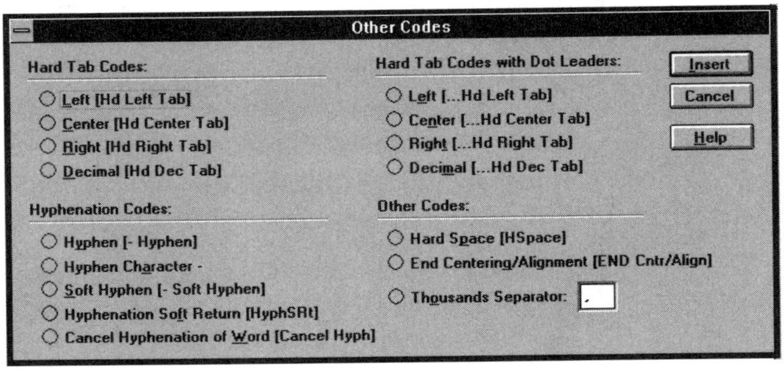

FIGURE 4–13
The Other Codes dialog box.

After creating an overstrike character, you can edit it. To edit an overstrike character:

1. With the Overstrike dialog box displayed, choose Previous to display the first overstrike character to the left of the insertion point or choose Next to display the first overstrike character to the right of the insertion point.
2. Add or delete any characters or text-appearance attributes in the text box.
3. Choose OK to insert the new character in the document window.

HOW DO I. . . Insert Other Codes?

WordPerfect has several special codes that enable you to control tab codes, hyphenation codes, and spacing. If you want to make sure that your company name always stays on the same line, for example, you can use a hard space. A *hard space* forces the two words on each side of the hard space to stay together. You can insert some of these codes by using a keystroke combination (such as Ctrl+Spacebar for a hard space) or from the Other Codes dialog box.

Steps

➡To insert other codes:

1. Choose Layout➢Line➢Other Codes. The Other Codes dialog box is displayed, as shown in Figure 4–13.
2. Select the option you want and choose Insert.

Tell Me More

Hard tab codes let you change the type of tab one time without changing the tab settings. If your tabs are set up as left tabs and you want a center tab at the next tab stop, for example, you can use the Other Codes feature to insert the hard center tab. You can also change the tab type with dot leader tabs.

Hyphenation codes are also included in the Other Codes dialog box. You can insert a hyphen code or a hyphen character. The hyphen code is just the dash key on the keyboard. Although the hyphen code and the hyphen character appear the same on-screen, the difference between them is that words joined by a hyphen character remain on the same line. If you want to keep names or phone numbers from being separated on two lines, use the hyphen character.

HINT **To insert a hyphen character from the keyboard, press** Ctrl+-.

You can also insert soft hyphens from the Other Codes dialog box. A soft hyphen lets you specify the position where you want WordPerfect to hyphenate the word if hyphenation is necessary. You see a soft hyphen on-screen only if hyphenation is necessary. You can also specify Hyphenation Soft Return, which divides a word without using a hyphen when hyphenation is necessary. The Cancel Hyphenation of Word option moves the entire word, if necessary, to the next line instead of hyphenating the word.

You can also insert a Hard Space code from the Other Codes dialog box. Insert a hard space wherever you want to keep two words together. Hard spaces are particularly useful between names, titles, and dates. If you want the date August 9, 1995, to remain on the same line, for example, you can insert a hard space after the word *August* and after the comma (,) to ensure that the date stays together.

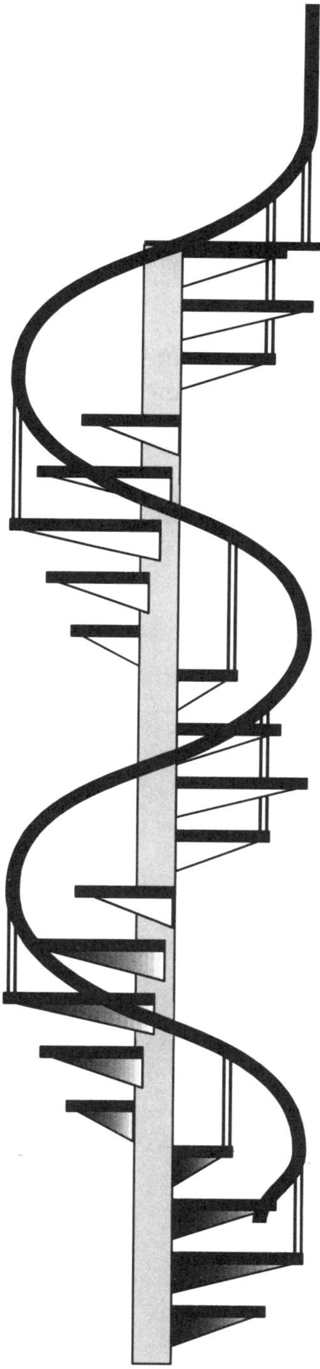

Chapter 5

Creating Documents: The Basics

This chapter answers questions about the following document-formatting features:

- Document templates
- Inserting new pages
- Changing paper sizes
- Creating new paper sizes
- Creating an envelope
- Numbering pages
- Changing print styles
- Changing the Printer and Document Initial Font
- Inserting the date in a document
- Creating headers and footers
- Spell-checking a document
- Using supplementary dictionaries

- ➤ Using the Thesaurus
- ➤ Using Grammatik
- ➤ Using QuickCorrect
- ➤ Displaying statistical document information

HOW DO I... Use Document Templates?

All documents in WordPerfect use a template as the pattern for a document. Specific macros, Button Bars, menus, keyboards, and styles can be associated with a template. WordPerfect has provided more than 75 templates from which to choose. Memos, title pages, calendars, newsletters, and résumés are a few examples of the predefined templates. These templates help you format and arrange the information in your document. The default template is called Standard and does not have any specific items associated with it.

Steps

➠To select a template to use for your document:

1. Choose File➢Template *or* press Ctrl+T. The Templates dialog box is displayed, as shown in Figure 5–1.
2. Select the template you want to use and choose OK. The Description at the bottom of the dialog box displays information about the template.

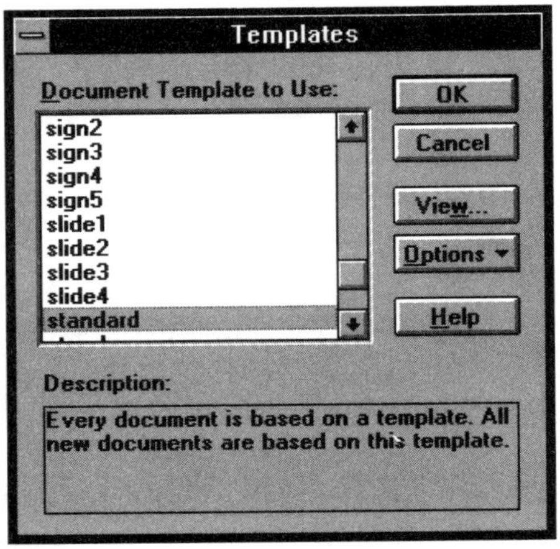

FIGURE 5–1
The Templates dialog box.

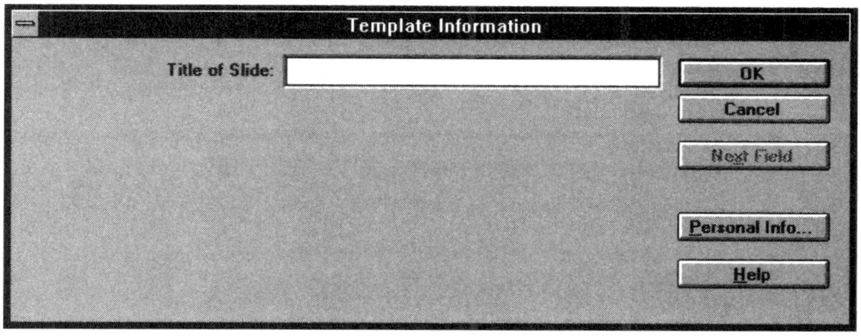

FIGURE 5–2
The Template Information dialog box.

HINT

You can choose View to see what the template looks like.

3. If this is the first time you have used the template feature, you are prompted to personalize your templates. Choose OK at the prompt, enter the necessary information, and choose OK.
4. A Template Information dialog box is displayed, similar to the one shown in Figure 5–2. It requests specific information for the template you chose. Enter the necessary information and choose OK.
5. The template is displayed on the screen with the information you entered. You can continue to enter information just as you would with any other document.

BUTTON BAR

Choose the Template icon from the Button Bar to open the Templates dialog box.

Tell Me More

The predefined templates can save you a great deal of time because the formatting is already done for you. All you have to do is enter the necessary information. Figures 5–3, 5–4, and 5–5 show examples of a few of the predefined templates.

In addition to document templates, there are also several "transition" templates. These transition templates help you convert from other word processors, such as Microsoft Word 2.0 or WordPerfect 5.1 for DOS, by using keystrokes and menu items with which you are already familiar. Each pull-down menu has the item WPWin 6.0 Additions to help you quickly locate new features. These transition templates can greatly

FIGURE 5–3
The Certificate template (CERT2).

reduce your learning curve and get you up and running with WordPerfect 6 for Windows.

For information about creating and editing templates, see Chapter 11, "Automating Tasks and Optimizing WordPerfect."

HOW DO I... Insert a New Page in a Document?

WordPerfect automatically inserts page breaks, called *soft page breaks,* in your document when you reach the end of a page. There are times when you want to begin a new page before WordPerfect inserts a page break for you, such as when you want to create a title page or insert a table or chart on its own page. To do this, you must insert a *hard page break,* which creates a new page for you.

Steps

➨**To insert a new page:**

1. Move the insertion point where you want to insert a hard page break.
2. Choose Insert➢Page Break *or* press Ctrl+Enter.

FIGURE 5–4
The Memo template (MEMO).

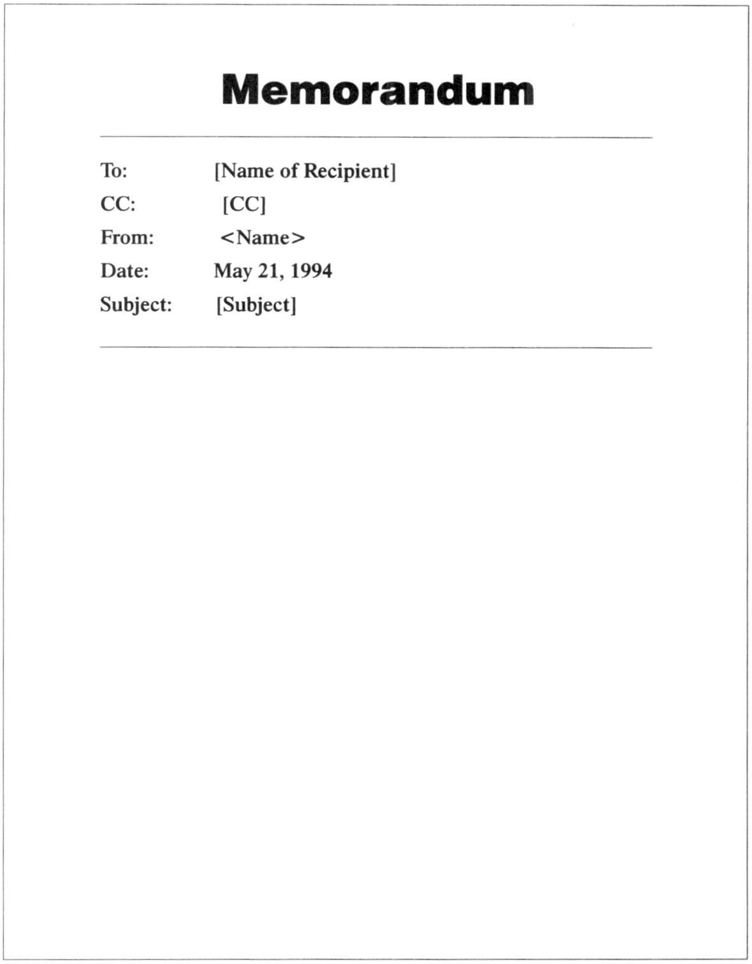

Memorandum

To: [Name of Recipient]
CC: [CC]
From: <Name>
Date: May 21, 1994
Subject: [Subject]

Tell Me More

A hard page break and soft page break both look like this in the document window:

If you switch to Draft mode (View➢Draft), however, a hard page break is displayed as a double line, and a soft page break is displayed as a single line.

FIGURE 5–5 *The Calendar template (CAL_SIDE).*

SUNDAY	MONDAY	TUESDAY	WEDNESDAY	THURSDAY	FRIDAY	SATURDAY

HOW DO I... Change the Paper Size for a Document?

Within WordPerfect, you can create documents for all sizes of paper. You can create standard letter-size documents, legal-size documents, or any other size of document you want, as long as your printer supports the size of paper.

You can also change the orientation of the page. *Orientation* refers to the direction the text prints on a page. Figure 5–6 shows a document in portrait orientation and a document in landscape orientation. By default, WordPerfect formats your documents for an 8½-×-11-inch portrait page. If you want to create a document with a different paper size, you must select a new Paper Definition. Being able to choose different paper definitions provides endless possibilities for creating documents.

Steps

➡ **To select a new paper definition:**

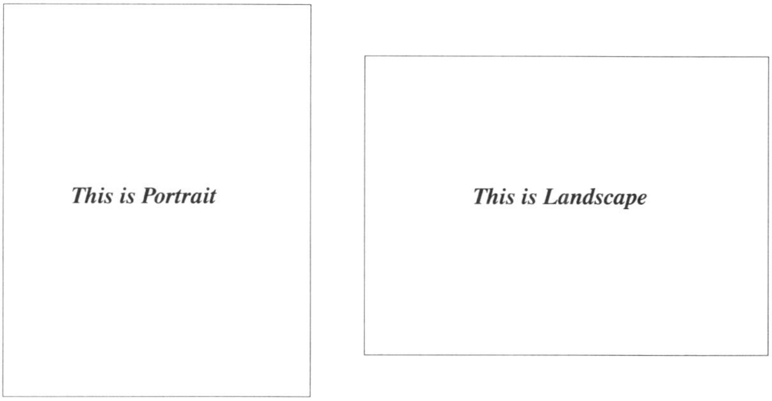

FIGURE 5–6
Portrait and landscape documents.

1. Choose Layout ➢ Page ➢ Paper Size. The Paper Size dialog box is displayed, as shown in Figure 5–7. The Paper Definitions that are displayed depend on the printer you are using.
2. Highlight the Paper Definition you want to use and choose Select. Information about the selected paper size is displayed in the Information box at the bottom of the screen.

HINT

The Orientation box displays a sample of what the printed page will look like.

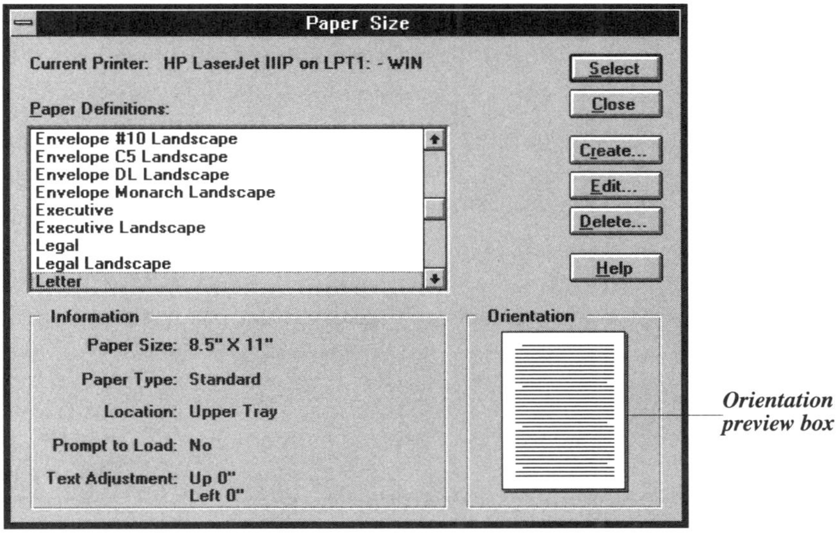

FIGURE 5–7
The Paper Size dialog box.

Tell Me More

When you select a new Paper Definition, it affects the document from the current page forward. WordPerfect automatically moves the code for the Paper Definition to the top of the current page.

You can create a single document that contains multiple paper definitions. If you are creating a marketing brochure, for example, you may want to have the text on an 8½-×-11-inch portrait page but use 8 ½-×-14-inch landscape pages for charts and tables. To do this, you simply follow the preceding steps whenever you want to change the Paper Definition.

Several additional items of information are displayed in the Paper Size dialog box (refer to Figure 5–7). WordPerfect lists the name of the selected printer at the top of the dialog box. The name of the paper definition is listed in the Paper Definition list box. Information about the highlighted definition is displayed in the Information box. The following table describes each item in the Information box.

INFORMATION ITEM	DESCRIPTION
Paper Size	Displays the size of the paper.
Paper Type	Displays the type of paper, such as Standard, Letterhead, or Envelope.
Location	Displays the location from which the paper prints. Depending on your printer, these options include Continuous, Manual Feed, or a specific Sheet Feeder option, such as a bin number.
Prompt to Load	Specifies whether WordPerfect displays a prompt before printing. This option is useful if you want to insert special paper, such as an envelope or letterhead, before printing the job. This option is available only for WordPerfect print drivers.
Text Adjustments	Offsets text for printers that do not print at the correct top or left margin. Some dot-matrix printers automatically scroll the paper before printing, which causes your margins to be incorrect. This option lets you enter the amount of adjustment needed for your printer so that WordPerfect can compensate for it.

HINT If you do not use some of the Paper Definitions listed in the Paper Size dialog box, you can highlight the definition and choose Delete.

HOW DO I. . . Create a New Paper Size?

In addition to choosing predefined paper definitions, you can create your own definitions. This feature is useful when you want to use a size or type of paper that is not included in the list of predefined definitions. If you are creating an invitation on a special size of paper, for example, you have to create a new Paper Definition before creating the document. Your printer must support the paper size you create.

Steps

➨**To create a new paper definition:**

1. Choose Layout ➢ Page ➢ Paper Size.
2. Choose Create. The Create Paper Size dialog box is displayed, as shown in Figure 5–8.
3. Enter a name for the new definition in the Paper Name text box. The name you enter is the name that is displayed as a choice in the Paper Size dialog box. Use a descriptive name so that you know when to use the definition.

FIGURE 5–8
The Create Paper Size dialog box.

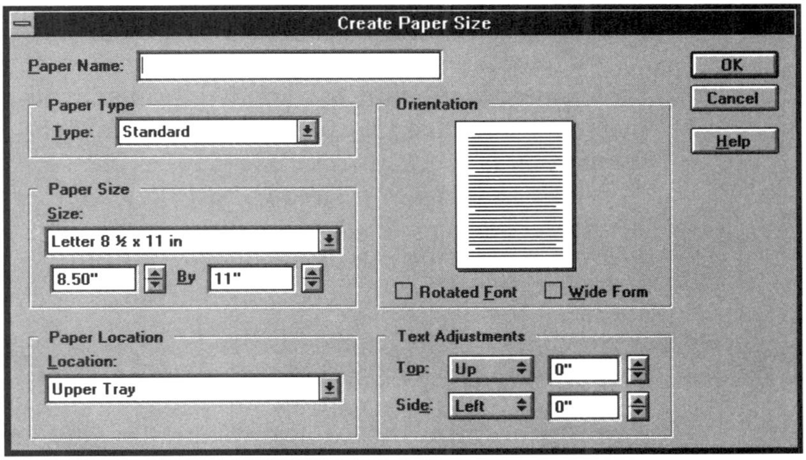

4. Choose Type and select from the drop-down list the type of paper you are using.
5. Choose Size and select the size of paper from the drop-down list. If the correct size is not listed, you can enter it in the measurement text boxes.
6. Choose Location and enter the location of the paper. For tractor-fed dot-matrix and daisywheel printers and most single-bin laser printers, the location is the default or manual feed. If you are using a WordPerfect printer driver and want WordPerfect to prompt you before it prints the document, select Prompt to Load Paper. This option is useful if you want to insert a different type of paper in the printer.
7. Choose Orientation and choose the orientation in which you want the text printed.
8. If necessary, choose Text Adjustments and enter the measurement WordPerfect needs in order to adjust the text to have a correct top and left margin.
9. Choose OK to return to the Paper Size dialog box, choose Select to return to the document window, and select the newly created paper size.

For more information about Paper Size options, see the section "HOW DO I... Change the Paper Size for a Document?" earlier in this chapter.

Tell Me More

Paper definitions are specific for each printer. When you add or delete a paper definition, it is for the selected printer. If you want to add the same paper definition for another printer, you must first select the printer and then add the paper definition. You can create as many paper definitions as you want.

If a paper definition already exists but some of the information just needs to be changed, you can edit the definition. From the Paper Size dialog box, highlight the Paper definition, choose Edit, and then make any necessary changes, as described in the preceding steps.

HOW DO I... Create an Envelope?

WordPerfect makes creating envelopes fast and simple. All you have to do is choose the Envelope option and insert your information. You do not have to remember paper sizes and dimensions, margin codes, or advance codes. If you open the Envelope dialog box from a document window that contains a letter with a mailing address, WordPerfect attempts to automatically insert the mailing address for you. WordPerfect can even keep a list of all your return and mailing addresses. In addition, you can have WordPerfect automatically insert a POSTNET bar code on the envelope. Creating envelopes is *easy!*

Steps

➡To create an envelope:

1. Choose Layout➢Envelope. The Envelope dialog box is displayed, as shown in Figure 5–9.

NOTE

If your printer does not support envelope printing or you do not have an envelope paper definition defined, WordPerfect displays a message indicating that no envelopes are defined for the current printer. You can then define an envelope paper definition.

2. If necessary, enter a return address.
3. If necessary, enter the mailing address. If you opened the Envelope dialog box from a letter containing a mailing

FIGURE 5–9
The Envelope dialog box.

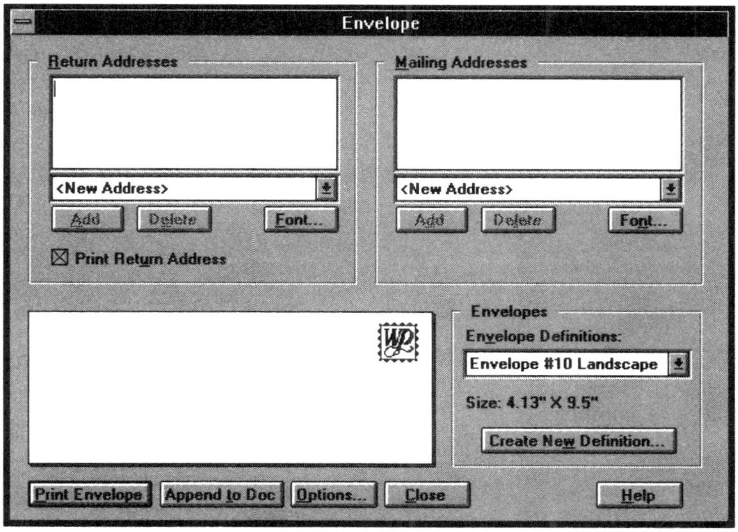

address, the address is automatically inserted in the Mailing Addresses text box.

4. Make sure that the selected envelope definition is correct. If it's not correct, select the correct definition from the Envelope Definitions drop-down list.
5. Choose Append to Doc to place the information for the envelope at the end of the displayed document or choose Print Envelope to print the envelope immediately.

BUTTON BAR

You can also choose the Envelope icon on the Button Bar to access the Envelope dialog box.

Tell Me More

If you always send letters with the same return address, you can choose Add after entering the information for the return address. When you choose Add, WordPerfect adds the address to the drop-down list. If you use several return addresses, you can add each one and then select the correct one from the drop-down list. WordPerfect uses the last address you add as the default.

You can deselect Print Return Address if you do not want the return address to be printed. This option is useful for envelopes that have a preprinted return address.

Just as you can have a list of return addresses, you can also have a list of mailing addresses. If you frequently mail to a certain address, simply choose Add, and the address is added to the drop-down list. This process helps automate the process of creating envelopes.

You can select a font for both the return address and the mailing address. Choose Font for the appropriate address, make the selections you want from the Font dialog box, and choose OK.

Inserting USPS Bar Codes

USPS (United States Postal Service) or POSTNET bar codes help the postal service sort and deliver mail more efficiently. The bar codes are generated from the ZIP code of the mailing address.

To include a POSTNET bar code on an envelope:

1. Choose Options from the Envelope dialog box. The Envelope Options dialog box is displayed, as shown in Figure 5–10.
2. Select Include and Position Above Address or Include and Position Below Address.

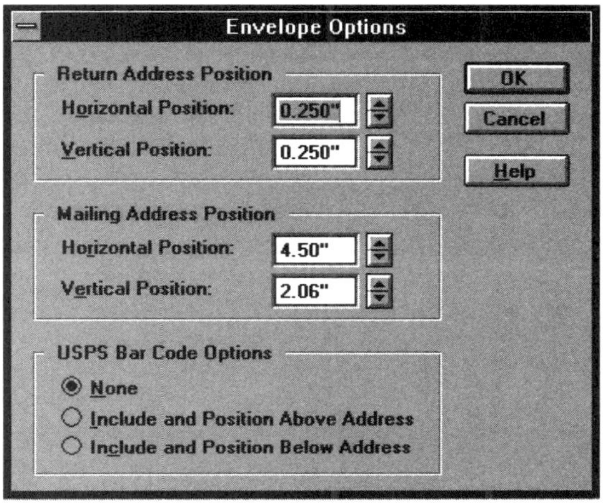

FIGURE 5–10
The Envelope Options dialog box.

3. Choose OK. This change remains in effect until you change it again. After you choose to include the USPS bar code, an additional text box is displayed below the Mailing Addresses for you to enter the POSTNET bar code.

When you include a POSTNET bar code, WordPerfect automatically converts the numbers to a bar code and prints it on the envelope. Figure 5–11 shows an envelope with a 5-digit ZIP code and the bar code printed above the address.

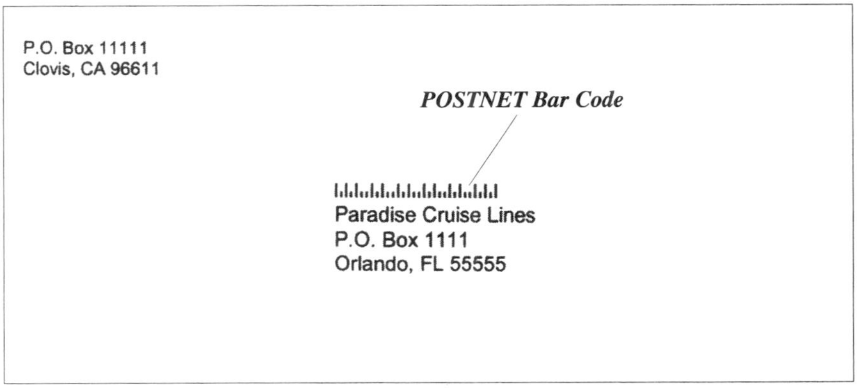

FIGURE 5–11
An envelope with a 5-digit ZIP code and bar code.

Changing the Position of Text and the Size of an Envelope

If you want to change where the text on the envelope is positioned, you can use the Envelope Options dialog box to make the necessary adjustments.

To change the position of text:

1. Choose Options from the Envelope dialog box.
2. Enter the correct measurements for the Return Address Position or the Mailing Address Position.
3. Choose OK. The sample envelope at the bottom of the dialog box reflects any changes you have made so that you can quickly see whether the text is in the proper location. Any changes remain in effect until you change them again.

WordPerfect sets the default envelope size to 4.13 × 9.5 inches. You can select any other Envelope Definition that is defined for the selected printer.

If the size you want is not listed, you must create a new paper definition. When you create the new definition, you must choose Envelope for the Paper Type option. For information about creating paper definitions, see the section "HOW DO I... Create a New Paper Definition?" earlier in this chapter.

HOW DO I... Automatically Number the Pages in a Document?

Numbering pages in WordPerfect is easy and versatile. To have your pages automatically numbered for you, you simply choose the location for the page number, and WordPerfect does the rest. WordPerfect also lets you number chapters and volumes. You can select the format for your page numbering and even add text to the page numbering.

Steps

➡To insert page numbering:

1. Choose Layout➢Page➢Numbering. The Page Numbering dialog box is displayed, as shown in Figure 5–12.
2. Select the position of the page number you want from the Position pop-up list.

FIGURE 5–12
The Page Numbering dialog box.

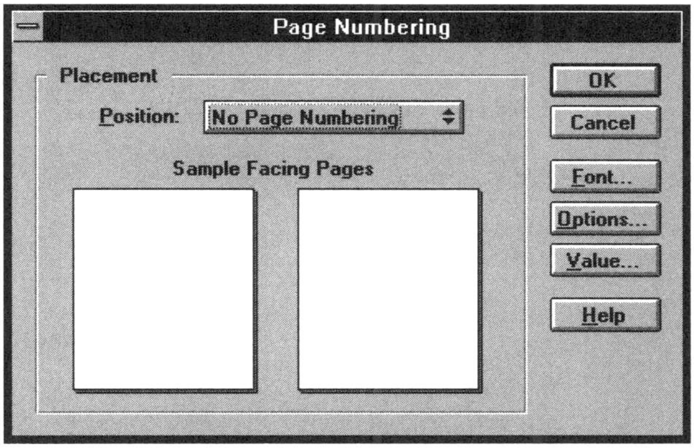

3. Choose Close to return to the document window and view the page numbers.

Tell Me More

It is easy to insert basic page numbering in a document. In addition to basic page numbering, WordPerfect offers several advanced page-numbering features to help you accomplish more sophisticated page numbering. The following sections explain some of the more advanced page-numbering techniques and other functionality associated with page numbering.

Changing the Page Number Format

When you're using page numbering, you can add text and change the appearance of your page numbering. If you want your page numbering to be displayed with the word *Page* in front of the number, for example, you can add text to the page-numbering format.

To add text to your page-numbering format:

1. Choose Options from the Page Numbering dialog box.
2. In the Format and Accompanying Text text box, enter the text you want to add. Text entered before the [Pg#] indicator appears before the page number in your document, and text entered after it appears after the page number. Figure 5–13 displays the page number with the word *Page* inserted before the page number.

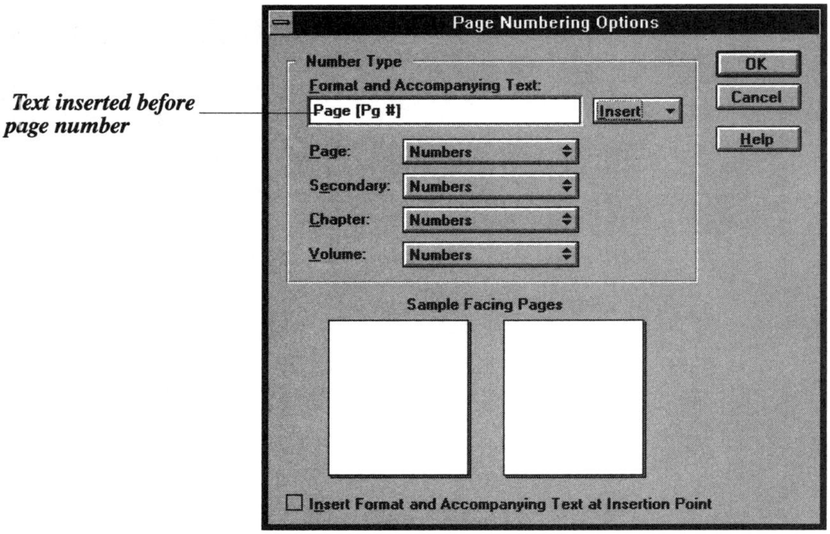

FIGURE 5–13
A Page Number Format example.

3. Choose OK and Close until you return to the document window.

You can also change the appearance of the page numbers in your document. By default, page numbers are always printed in the initial document font no matter how many font changes you have made within the document.

To change the appearance of page numbers:

1. Choose Font from the Page Numbering dialog box.
2. Choose the options you want.
3. Choose OK until you return to the document window.

By default, WordPerfect uses Arabic numbers (1, 10, 55, for example) for all page numbering. You can change the numbering method for page numbers.

To change the numbering method:

1. Choose Options from the Page Numbering dialog box.
2. From the appropriate pop-up list (Page, Secondary, Chapter, or Volume) choose Number, Lowercase Letter, Uppercase Letter, Lowercase Roman, or Uppercase Roman. The Sample Facing Pages reflect any changes you make.
3. Choose OK until you return to the document window.

Changing Page Numbers

You can change the number of a page in a document. If you are creating a term paper, for example, and in the middle of the paper you want to insert some sketches, you can change the pages following the sketches to reflect the added pages.

To insert a new value for a page number:

1. Move the insertion point to the page where you want to change the page number.
2. Choose Layout➢Page➢Numbering.
3. Choose Value from the Page Numbering dialog box. The Numbering Value dialog box is displayed, as shown in Figure 5–14.
4. Specify the New Page Number (or New Secondary Number, Chapter Number, or Volume Number).
5. Choose OK and Close until you return to the document window.

The current page number is changed, and all subsequent page numbers also reflect this change.

NOTE

You can also change page numbers by increasing or decreasing the value of the current number. Follow the preceding steps and, rather than insert a New Page Number, insert the value by which you want to Increase/Decrease the Existing Page Number.

FIGURE 5–14
The Numbering Value dialog box.

Enter new page number here

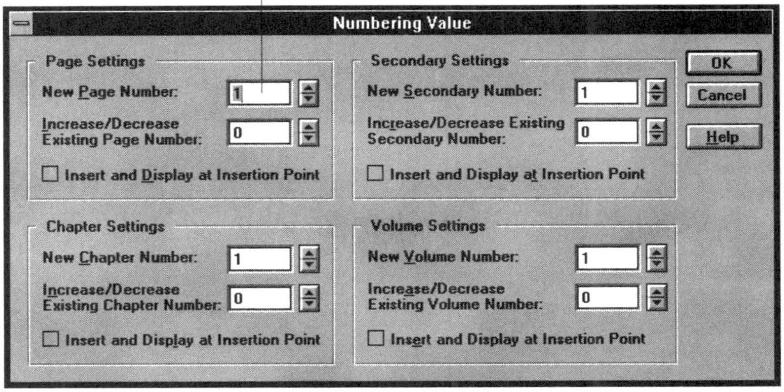

Forcing Page Numbers

You can force a page in a document to have an odd, even, or new page. If you are writing a book, for example, and you want all new chapters to begin on an odd page, the Force Page option enables you to do so.

NOTE **If necessary, WordPerfect inserts a hard page break to ensure that the page number is correct.**

To use the Force Page feature:

1. Move the insertion point to the page you want to force.
2. Choose Layout➢Page➢Force Page.
3. Select Current Page Odd, Current Page Even, or New Page.
4. Choose OK to return to the document window.

Inserting Page Numbers into Document Text

WordPerfect can automatically insert the current page number in the text of your document. If you want the page number to appear somewhere other than at the predefined positions or in addition to the predefined positions, you use this option. The page number is updated automatically if the text moves to another page.

To insert a page number in the text:

1. Move the insertion point to the location where you want to insert the page number.
2. Choose Layout➢Page➢Numbering.
3. Choose Options and then select Insert Format and Accompanying Text at Insertion Point.
4. Choose OK until you return to the document window.

HINT **You can also move your insertion point to the location in your document where you want to insert the number and press** Ctrl+Shift+P.

When you insert a page number in your text, WordPerfect includes all the information you have inserted in the Format and Accompanying Text box.

If you want to insert only the page number:

1. Move the insertion point to the location where you want to insert the page number.
2. Choose Layout➢Page➢Numbering.
3. Choose Value and select Insert and Display at Insertion Point from the appropriate group box.
4. Choose OK until you return to the document window.

Using Chapter, Volume, and Secondary Page Numbers

In addition to numbering pages, you can number chapters, volumes, and secondary pages. If you are writing a book, for example, you can use a chapter number and a page number, such as 1–5, to number your pages.

Volume numbers are often used in newsletters or publications. Using Page Numbering to insert volume numbers eliminates the need to reenter the volume number every time it appears.

Secondary pages let you have two sets of page numbers in a document. If you are creating a document with several sections, for example, and you want to number all the pages in the document and also independently number the pages in each section, you can insert secondary page numbers within the individual sections. To insert chapters, volumes, and secondary pages, you must change the Page Numbering Options.

To insert chapter, volume, or secondary page numbers:

1. Choose Options from the Page Numbering dialog box.
2. Position the insertion point in the Format and Accompanying Text box and choose Insert. Then select the option you want from the drop-down list shown here:

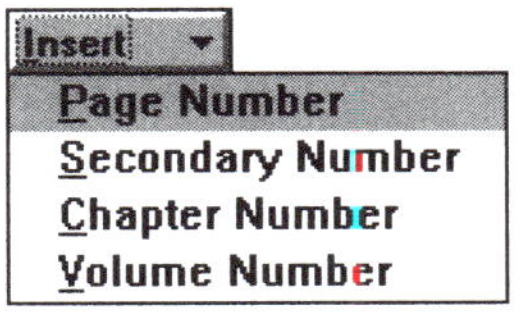

3. Choose OK and Close to return to the document window.

Unlike with page numbers, you must manually set and increment chapter and volume numbers. WordPerfect sets the chapter and volume numbers to 1. The secondary page number is set to the current page number and is incremented automatically.

For information about changing chapter, volume, and secondary page numbers, see the section "Changing Page Numbers" earlier in this section.

Removing Page Numbers

If you do not want a page number to print on a specific page, you can use the Suppress option. This option is useful if you have a title page, for example, and you do not want it to be numbered. Although the page number is not printed, it is still assigned a page number. If you suppress the title page and it is page 1, for example, the next page is printed as page 2.

To suppress a page number:

1. Move anywhere on the page where you do not want the page number to be displayed.
2. Choose Layout➢Page➢Suppress. The Suppress dialog box is displayed, as shown in Figure 5–15.
3. Select Page Numbering *or* select All to turn off all headers, footers, watermarks, and page numbering.
4. Choose OK to return to the document window.

HOW DO I... Change the Style of Print?

WordPerfect provides many different methods for changing the style of your print. You can use different fonts to change the typeface of the

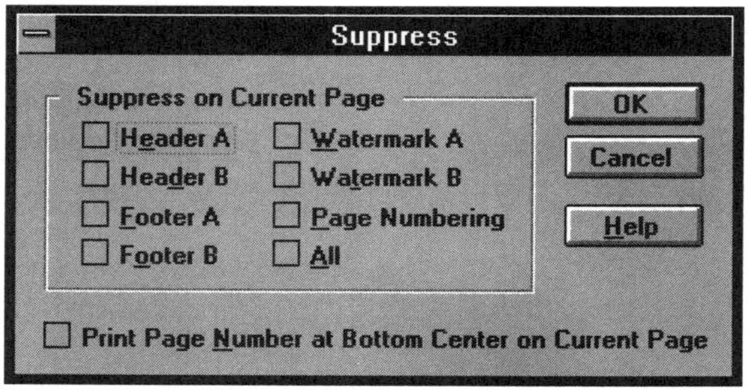

FIGURE 5–15
The Suppress dialog box.

print in your document. A *font* is a set of characters with similar features, such as slant and weight. With some fonts, you can change the size of the font to allow more or less information to fit on a page or to emphasize certain text, such as titles. You can also change the appearance of the font with such attributes as bold, italics, and small caps, and you can change the location of the font by using subscript or superscript.

Changing and varying the typeface, size, appearance, and position of the fonts in your documents greatly enhances the appearance and appeal of your documents. The fonts that are available to you depend on your printer and whether you have purchased additional fonts, such as cartridges or soft fonts. For more information about cartridges and soft fonts, see Chapter 7. WordPerfect also ships TrueType fonts, which you may have installed. These graphical fonts print on any printer that prints graphics.

Steps

➨To change the font:

1. Move the insertion point where you want to change the font.
2. Choose Layout➢Font *or* press F9. You can also choose Font from the document QuickMenu. The Font dialog box is displayed, as shown in Figure 5–16.
3. Select a Font Face.

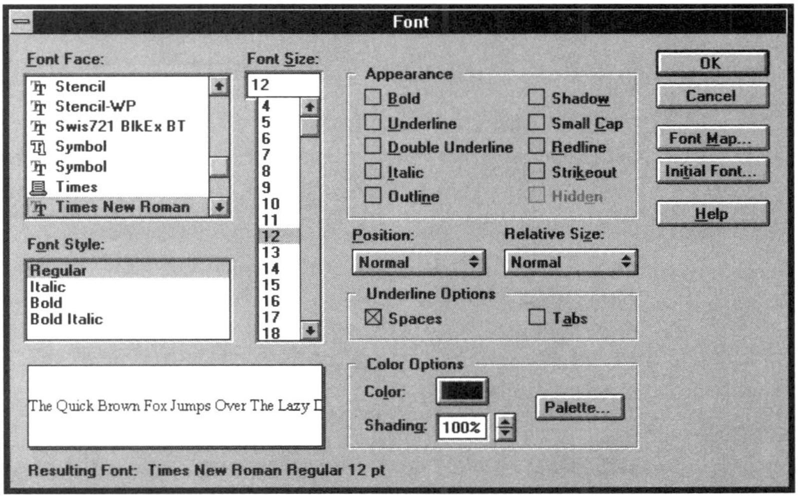

FIGURE 5–16
The Font dialog box.

HINT

When you highlight a font, the preview box in the lower left corner of the Font dialog box shows you what the font looks like.

4. If necessary, select a Font Size. If you are using a printer font that is not *scalable* (it cannot be sized), you cannot change the size of the font.
5. Select any additional options, such as Appearance, Position, Relative Size, Underline Options, and Color Options.
6. Choose OK to return to the document window.

POWER BAR

To change the font face, choose [FFF] from the Power Bar. To change the font size, choose [A] from the Power Bar. The font face and font size buttons on the Power Bar do not list all available options. You can double-click either icon, however, to display the Font dialog box. To insert bold, choose [B]; to insert italics, choose [I]; or to insert underline, choose [U].

HINT

You can also select text and then change the font by using the Font dialog box or the Power Bar.

Tell Me More

When you are using fonts, it is helpful to understand some of the concepts behind fonts. Your printer has certain built-in fonts. The type of printer you have determines the number and style of built-in fonts. In addition to the built-in fonts, WordPerfect provides TrueType graphical fonts to enhance the appearance of your document. To use the graphics fonts, your printer must have the capability to print graphics. Graphics fonts usually print slower than do built-in fonts, but they also enable you to print in any size.

When you display the Font dialog box (refer to Figure 5–16), the icon next to the font face indicates which type of font it is, such as printer, TrueType, or vector. Some printers can also use cartridges and soft fonts to access more fonts. For more information about cartridges and soft fonts, see Chapter 7.

HOW DO I... Change the Default Initial Font?

The *printer initial font* is the default font used when you create documents. This font is specific to the selected printer. The printer initial font is used as the current document font as well as the font for headers, footers, page numbers, text within graphics boxes, and many other elements. You can change the printer initial font at any time for each printer.

The *document initial font* lets you override the printer initial font for one document. If your printer initial font is Times Roman, for example, but you want to print a document in Helvetica, you can do so by changing the document initial font.

Steps

➠**To change the printer initial font:**

1. Choose File➢Select Printer and highlight the printer for which you want to change the font.
2. Choose Initial Font.
3. Select the Font Face, Font Style, and Font Size you want.
4. Choose OK and Close to return to the document window.

➠**To change the document initial font:**

1. Choose Layout➢Font➢Initial Font. The Document Initial Font dialog box is displayed, as shown in Figure 5–17.
2. Select the Font Face, Font Style, and Font Size you want.
3. Choose OK until you return to the document window.

Tell Me More

When you change the document initial font, WordPerfect uses this font for all text in headers, footers, graphics boxes, and so on. Unlike choosing a font from the Font dialog box, choosing a Document Initial Font eliminates the need to reselect the font every time you want to enter text in a location other than the document window.

HOW DO I... Insert the Date in My Document?

WordPerfect makes it quick and easy to insert the current date in your document. You can insert the date in text format so that it remains

FIGURE 5–17
The Document Initial Font dialog box.

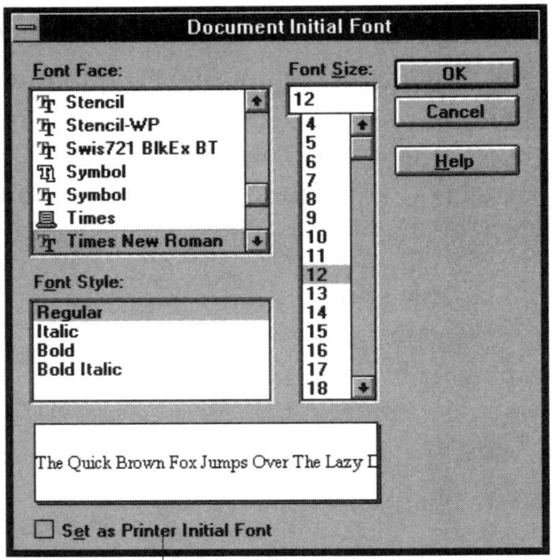

Select this option if you want this font to be the Printer Initial Font

unchanged every time you retrieve or print the document. Or you can insert the date in a code format that is updated automatically every time you retrieve or print a document.

Steps

➠To insert the date:

1. Choose Insert➢Date.
2. Choose Date Text to insert the date in text format or Date Code to insert the date in a code that is updated automatically every time you retrieve a document.

BUTTON BAR

To insert the Date Text, choose the Date icon from the Button Bar.

HINT

You can also press Ctrl+D to insert Date Text or Ctrl+Shift+D to insert the Date Code.

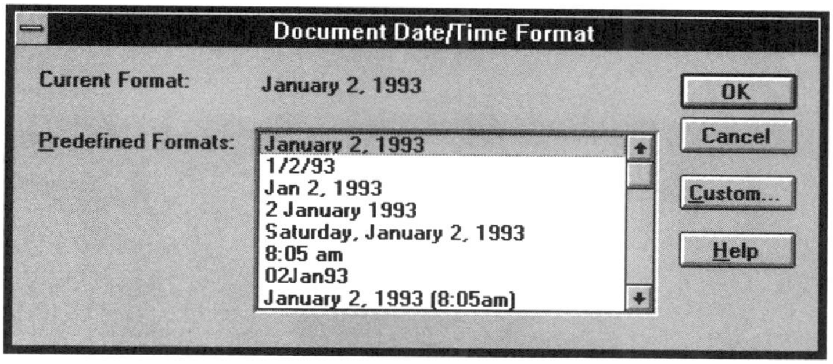

FIGURE 5–18 *The Document Date/Time Format dialog box.*

Tell Me More

The default date format WordPerfect uses is a month-date-year format. Your date is displayed like this: **July 12, 1995**. You can change the date format to meet your specific needs.

To select a new date format:

1. Choose Insert➢Date➢Date Format.
2. Choose an option from the Document Date/Time Format dialog box (see Figure 5–18) and press OK or choose Custom and create your own date format from the date-and-time codes that are displayed.
3. Choose OK to return to the document window.

HOW DO I. . . Create a Header or Footer?

When you want to add the same information to each page or alternating pages in your document, you can use headers and footers. You can create a header or footer, for example, to insert the document name, date, and page number automatically on every page of your document. You can include text and formatting codes in headers and footers.

Steps

➨To create a header or footer:

1. Choose Layout➢Header/Footer. The Headers/Footers dialog box is displayed, as shown in Figure 5–19.
2. Select Header A , Header B, Footer A, or Footer B.

FIGURE 5–19
The Headers/ Footers dialog box.

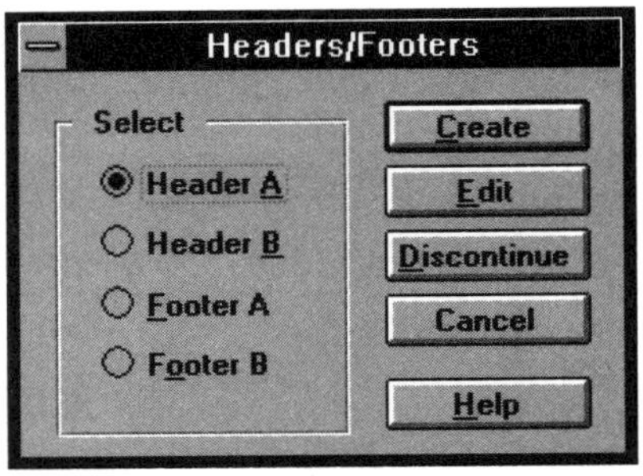

3. Choose Create. The Header/Footer Feature Bar is displayed in the document window, as shown in Figure 5–20.
4. Choose Placement from the Feature Bar and select Odd Pages, Even Pages, or All Pages and choose OK.
5. Enter the text and formatting information you want included in the header or footer. You can use the Feature Bar to insert Page Numbering and Graphics Lines.
6. Choose Close from the Feature Bar to return to the document window.

Tell Me More

The uses for headers and footers are endless. Headers and footers are ideal for term papers, proposals, and legal documents. Figure 5–21 shows an example of a footer in a document.

When you are creating or editing a header or footer, the title bar displays the name of the header or footer you are creating or editing, such as Header A, as shown in Figure 5–20. You can insert text and choose

FIGURE 5–20
The Header/Footer Feature Bar.

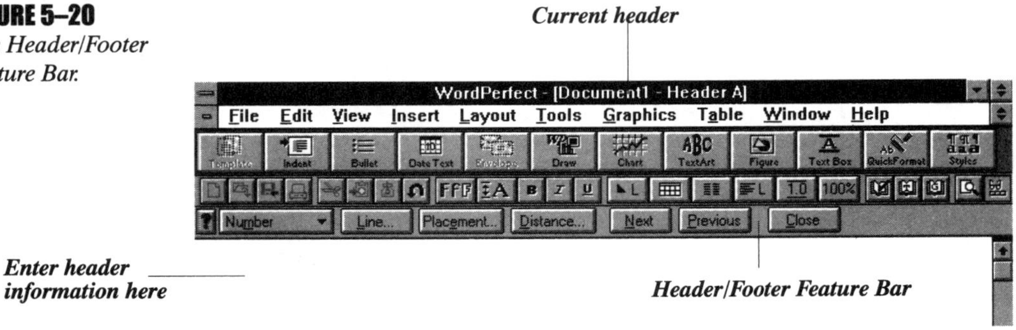

FIGURE 5–21
An example of a footer.

ALL INCLUSIVE VACATION HOTEL FEATURES

Jamaica Grande— A Residence Resort	Windsurfing Sailing Snorkeling Glass bottom boat trip Daily Activities	$958-1024
Enchanted Garden	Spa and Steam Bath Complimentary facial, manicure and massage	$1000-1500
Ciboney Resort	Dunn's River Falls tour Snorkeling Waterskiing Scuba diving Windsurfing Sailing Health Club Paddle Boats Canoes Massages	$1085-1650
Couples	Tennis/Squash Golf Horseback riding Scuba diving	$1200-1300
Boscobel Beach Resort	Snorkeling Windsurfing Scuba Diving Sailing Waterskiing Health Club	$1019-1739

Graphics line to divide footer from document footer

Footer — **May 21, 1995** **1** **A:\FIGURE.4**

formatting codes just as you do when you are creating a document. Features not available are dimmed on the menus.

Headers and footers are printed at the top and bottom margins, respectively. If you want headers and footers to be printed at a different location, you must adjust your top and bottom margins. WordPerfect inserts a space that measures 0.167 inch below a header and above a footer. You can change the amount of space by choosing Distance from the Feature Bar and specifying a new distance.

Editing headers and footers is simple. First make sure that you are viewing your document in Page or Two Page mode. Then simply click on the header or footer area and begin editing. If you want to display the Feature Bar while editing the header or footer, click the right mouse button to display the QuickMenu, and choose Feature Bar.

If you do not want a header or footer to be printed on a specific page, you can use the Suppress feature. This feature is useful if you have a figure, table, or chart in your document that does not need the information contained in the header or footer or if the information clutters the page.

➡To suppress a header or footer:

1. Move to the page where you do not want the header or footer to be displayed.
2. Choose Layout➢Page➢Suppress.
3. Select the items you want to suppress or select All to turn off all headers, footers, watermarks, and page numbering.
4. Choose OK to return to the document window.

In addition to suppressing headers and footers for specific pages, you can turn off a header or footer from the current page forward.

➡To turn off a header or footer:

1. Move to the page where you want to turn off the header or footer.
2. Choose Layout➢Header/Footer.
3. Select the headers and footers you want to turn off.
4. Choose Discontinue.

HOW DO I... Spell-Check a Document?

WordPerfect includes a powerful writing tool to spell-check your documents. With WordPerfect Speller, you can spell-check a word, sentence, paragraph, page, an entire document, selected text, or from the insertion point position forward. You can also look up a specific word. In addition to checking spelling, the Speller checks for duplicate words and irregular capitalization.

Steps

➡To use the Speller:

1. Choose Tools➢Speller *or* press Ctrl+F1 *or* choose Speller from the QuickMenu. The Speller dialog box is displayed, as shown in Figure 5–22.
2. Choose Check and select an option from the pull-down menu shown here:

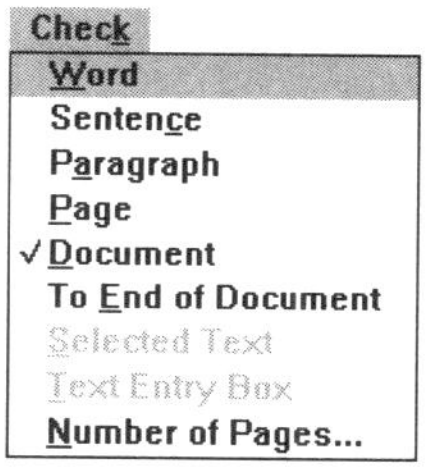

3. Choose Start. If an unrecognized word is found, it is selected in the document window and is also displayed in the Speller dialog box, next to Not Found.
4. Choose Skip Once to skip this occurrence of the word or choose Replace to replace the word with the word in the

FIGURE 5–22
The Speller dialog box.

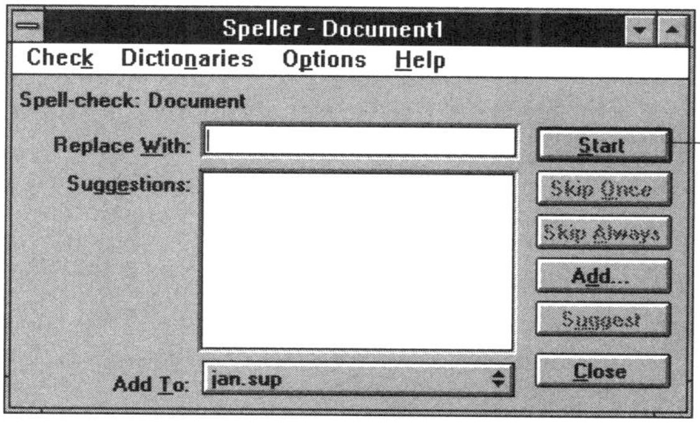

Replace With text box. If the correct word is not displayed in the Replace With text box, click the word in the Suggestions list and then choose Replace. Several other options are available in the Word Not Found dialog box; see the following "Tell Me More" section for information about these additional options.

5. When the spell-check is complete, choose Yes to close the Speller.

POWER BAR

Choose from the Power Bar to open the Speller dialog box.

Tell Me More

The Speller includes two dictionary types: main and Supplementary. The English version of the main dictionary spell-checks a document by comparing words to the word list contained in the dictionary. A *Supplementary* dictionary is a dictionary you create or purchase that lists common words or phrases not found in the main dictionary, such as names, proper nouns, and industry-specific terms. For more information about Supplementary dictionaries, see the section "HOW DO I... Use Supplementary Dictionaries?" later in this chapter.

When you spell-check a document and choose to skip a word in the entire document, you notice that you no longer are prompted to change that word; these words are inserted in the default Supplementary dictionary, the document-specific Supplementary dictionary, or another Supplementary dictionary you have specified.

WordPerfect automatically attaches a document-specific Supplementary dictionary to every document you create and save. After checking the document-specific Supplementary dictionary, WordPerfect checks the default Supplementary dictionary for a word. If a word is not found in the Supplementary dictionary, it looks to the main dictionary. You can change the order in which the supplemental dictionaries are searched by choosing Dictionaries➢Supplementary and changing the order in the list.

The following sections explain more about the powerful capabilities of the Speller.

Options Available During Spell-Checking

When you spell-check a document, you can choose from many different options. The following table briefly describes all the options available on the Speller dialog box during a spell-check.

Option	Description
Start	Begins the spell-check
Replace	Replaces the word found by the Speller with the word in the Replace With text box
Skip Once	Skips one occurrence of a word
Skip Always	Skips all occurrences of a word in the entire document
Add	Adds the word to the specified Supplementary dictionary
Suggest	Enables you to look up words that sound the same or match a specific pattern
Close	Ends the spell-check and closes the dialog box
Add To	Specifies the Supplementary dictionary to which words are added when you choose Add; if you have created a Supplementary dictionary that contains scientific terms, for example, and you are spell-checking a document that contains scientific terms, you select the scientific Supplementary dictionary

HINT

When you're spell-checking a document, you can click in the document window at any time to edit text. After editing the text, choose Resume to restart the spell-check.

Specifying Spell-Check Options

WordPerfect provides several options to help customize a spell-check. You select these options from the Options pull-down menu in the Speller dialog box. The following table briefly describes all the options available on the Options pull-down menu and what happens when you select them.

OPTION	**DESCRIPTION**
Words with Numbers	Checks words even if they include numbers; when this option is deselected, it ignores words that contain numbers, such as *4pm* and *PS/2*
Duplicate Words	Displays duplicate words found together and prompts you to replace them with a single occurrence of the word
Irregular Capitalization	Displays irregular capitalization in your document; if you type the word *cUstomer* and then spell-check the document, the Speller highlights the word and displays suggestions for proper capitalization, as shown in Figure 5–23
Auto Replace	Automatically replaces words found in the selected Supplementary dictionaries; also automatically replaces all occurrences of the replaced word throughout the document
Auto Start	Automatically begins spell-checking when you open the Speller dialog box; eliminates the need to choose Start after the dialog box is opened
Document Dictionary	Uses the document dictionary that is specific to the current document; using a document dictionary can increase the speed of the Speller
Beep On Misspelled	Makes WordPerfect beep every time it finds an error

Any changes you make to the Speller options remain in effect until you change them again.

HOW DO I... Use Supplementary Dictionaries?

WordPerfect's main dictionary contains thousands of words, but you can also add words to a Supplementary dictionary to increase the effectiveness of the Speller. After you start WordPerfect, a default Supplementary dictionary is automatically created for you, but it does not contain any words. Every time you spell-check a document and choose the Add option, by

FIGURE 5–23
Speller suggestions for irregular capitalization errors.

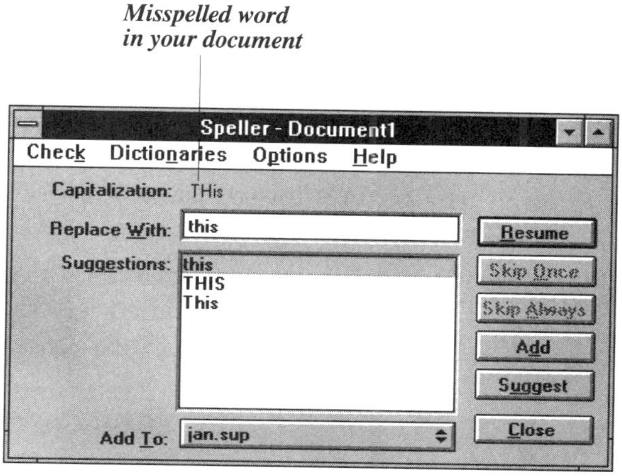

default the word is inserted in this default Supplementary dictionary. You can edit the default Supplementary dictionary, which enables you to add several words at a time, create new Supplementary dictionaries, and even chain together Supplementary dictionaries so that you can use more than one when you spell-check a document.

Steps

➠**To add words to your default Supplementary dictionary:**

1. Choose Tools➢Speller *or* press Ctrl+F1 *or* choose Speller from the QuickMenu.
2. Choose Dictionaries➢Supplementary.
3. Highlight **wpspelus.sup**, which is the filename of the default Supplementary dictionary, and choose Edit. The following dialog box is displayed:

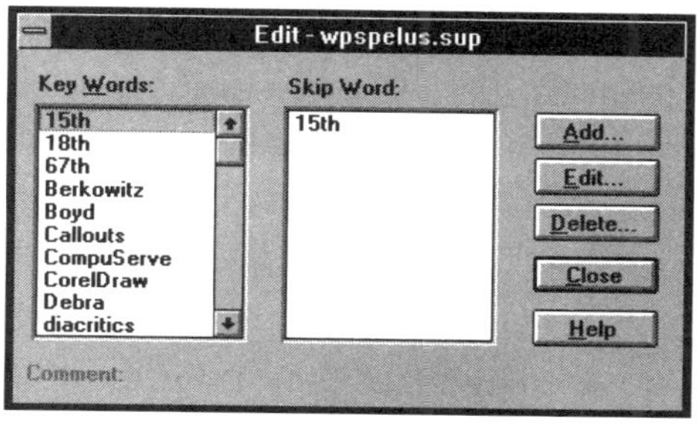

4. Choose Add.
5. Select Skip to add a word or phrase you want to always skip during a spell-check, select Replacement to add a word or phrase you always want to have replaced with another word or phrase, or select Alternatives to add a word or phrase for which you want to display a list of alternatives during a spell-check.
6. Enter the necessary information in the text boxes and then choose OK. For a detailed description of these options, see the following "Tell Me More" section.
7. Choose OK and Close to return to the document window.

Tell Me More

When you are adding words to a Supplementary dictionary, WordPerfect enables you to choose the way the Speller recognizes those words when it spell-checks a document. The following table describes these options:

OPTION	DESCRIPTION
Skip	Ignores the word or phrase
Replacement	Automatically replaces the word or phrase with another word or phrase
Alternatives	In the Suggestions list, lists the alternative words you enter here when Speller finds the word or phrase; you can also enter a comment

Editing Supplementary Dictionaries

You can also edit Supplementary dictionaries. If you inadvertently choose Add during a spell-check, for example, and add to a Supplementary dictionary a word you do not want to include, you can delete it.

To edit a Supplementary dictionary:

1. Choose Tools➢Speller *or* press Ctrl+F1 *or* choose Speller from the QuickMenu.
2. Choose Dictionaries➢Supplementary.
3. Highlight the Supplementary dictionary you want to edit and choose Edit.

4. Highlight the word and choose Delete to delete an entry in the dictionary or choose Edit to edit an entry in the dictionary.
5. Choose Close until you return to the document window.

Creating Supplementary Dictionaries

You can create multiple Supplementary dictionaries. If you create documents that contain medical terms, for example, you can create a specific Supplementary dictionary that contains these terms and use it when you spell-check documents that contain medical terms.

The advantage of creating several specific Supplementary dictionaries is that WordPerfect does not have to check as many words as it spell-checks the document and therefore increases the speed of spell-checking.

To create a new Supplementary dictionary:

1. Choose Tools➢Speller *or* press Ctrl+F1 *or* choose Speller from the QuickMenu.
2. Choose Dictionaries➢Supplementary.
3. Choose Create and type the name of the new Supplementary dictionary in the Filename text box.
4. Choose Yes when you are prompted to create the file.
5. Choose Edit.
6. Choose Add.
7. Select Skip to add a word or phrase you want to always skip during a spell-check, select Replacement to add a word or phrase you always want to have replaced with another word or phrase, or select Alternatives to add a word or phrase for which you want to display a list of alternatives during a spell-check.
8. Enter the necessary information in the text boxes and then choose OK.
9. Choose OK and Close to return to the document window.

Connecting Multiple Supplementary Dictionaries

WordPerfect gives you the ability to chain or connect multiple Supplementary dictionaries so that you can increase the effectiveness of the Speller. If you purchase a supplemental dictionary for medical terms, for example, you can add it to the list of Supplementary dictionaries that are searched.

To add Supplementary dictionaries:

1. Choose Tools➢Speller *or* press Ctrl+F1 *or* choose Speller from the QuickMenu.
2. Choose Dictionaries➢Supplementary.
3. Click the location in the Dictionaries in Search Order list box where you want to insert the Supplementary dictionary. The listed order is the order in which the dictionaries are searched.
4. Choose Add and type the filename for the dictionary you want to add, and then choose OK.
5. Choose Close to return to the document window.

HOW DO I... Use the Thesaurus?

The Thesaurus is included with WordPerfect to enhance your ability to communicate effectively by displaying words that can be used as alternatives to the words you are using. You can easily look up synonyms and antonyms and replace a word in your document with another word.

Steps

➡To replace a word by using the Thesaurus:

1. Position the insertion point on the word you want to look up *or* select the word.
2. Choose Tools➢Thesaurus *or* press Alt+F1. The Thesaurus dialog box is displayed, as shown in Figure 5–24.
3. Click on the word you want to use in your document and then choose Replace. The word in your document is replaced and the Thesaurus is closed.

POWER BAR

Choose the Thesaurus button from the Power Bar to open the Thesaurus dialog box.

Tell Me More

The Thesaurus is a powerful tool when it comes to looking good on paper. Suppose that you are writing a letter and you notice that you continually use the word *optimize.* You can use the Thesaurus to replace the

FIGURE 5–24
The Thesaurus dialog box.

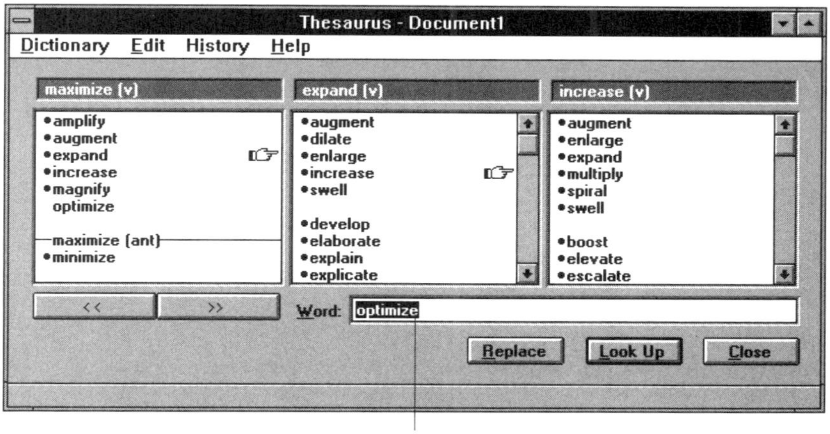

Word from document

word with variations of the word you may not have thought of on your own.

You can also use the Thesaurus to elevate your language in documents. You can type a basic word that has the meaning you want to convey and then use the Thesaurus on that word to display additional words that mean the same thing.

The Thesaurus dialog box is broken up into columns. The first column displays the word the insertion point is on in your document and then lists a group of related words and antonyms underneath it. A word preceded by a bullet indicates that the word is a *headword* and contains a subgroup of additional words. You can display the additional words by double-clicking the headword.

You can display as many headwords as you want. As you open additional headwords, the columns scroll to the right. You can move back and forth between columns by clicking in a column, clicking the right and left arrows, or pressing the → or ← keys on your keyboard.

HINT

You can clear all the columns except for the one you want to view by selecting the word you want to view and choosing Look Up.

The Thesaurus provides a quick and easy way to trace the path of words you have selected. Suppose that you have opened a large amount of subgroups and you know that somewhere along the way you have seen

FIGURE 5–25
The Thesaurus History pull-down menu.

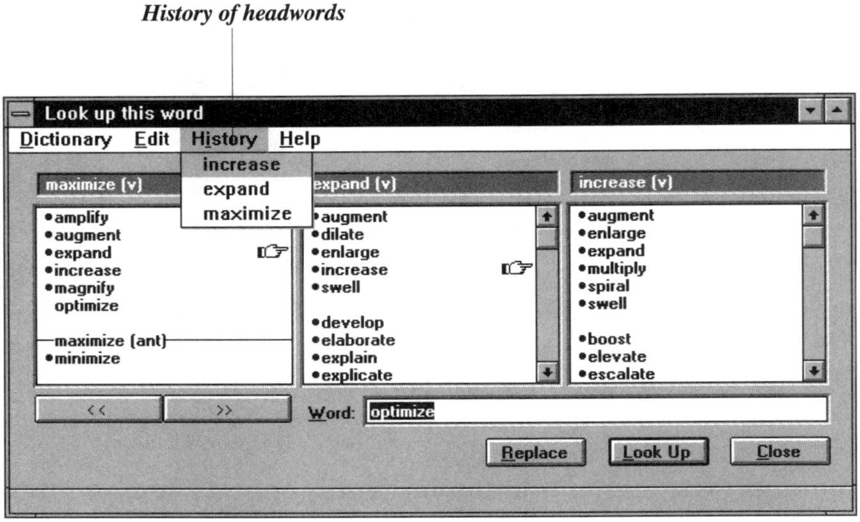

the word you want to use. Rather than scroll back through the columns of subgroups, you can choose History. The Thesaurus History pull-down menu is displayed, as shown in Figure 5–25. You can quickly scroll through the list and click on the word you want to view. The subgroup for the word you selected is displayed.

HOW DO I... Use Grammatik?

In addition to checking your spelling and word usage, you can check your document for grammar, punctuation errors, paragraph problems, passive voice, jargon, style, and much more with Grammatik. You can select the style and rules you want to use to check your document, and then WordPerfect displays errors and suggests way to correct them.

Steps

➡To proofread your document:

1. Choose Tools➢Grammatik *or* press Alt+Shift+F1. The Grammatik dialog box is displayed, as shown in Figure 5–26.
2. Choose Check and select which part of the document you want to check.

FIGURE 5–26
The Grammatik dialog box.

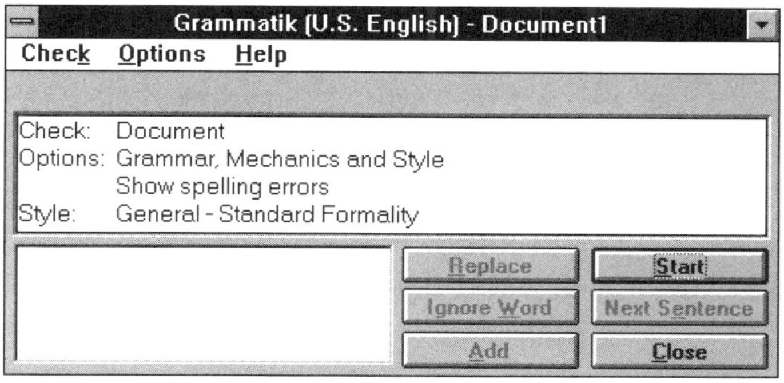

3. Choose Start. Grammatik pauses at each error and allows you to decide what you want to do, as shown in Figure 5–27. The following "Tell Me More" section briefly describes each of the options.
4. When you are finished proofreading, choose Close.

Choose from the Power Bar to open the Grammatik dialog box.

Tell Me More

The following sections explain how to correct errors Grammatik finds and how to customize Grammatik options.

FIGURE 5–27
Grammatik displays an error.

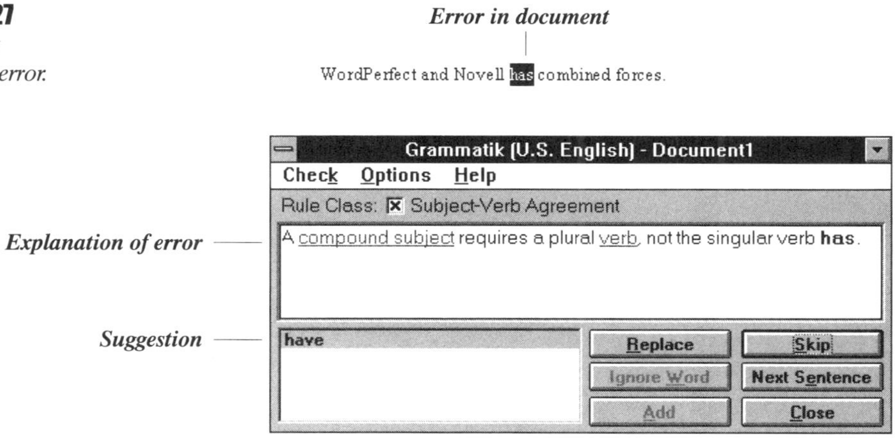

Correcting Errors

When you're proofreading your document, you can choose from several actions when an error is found. The dialog box that was shown in Figure 5–27 shows the information Grammatik displays when it encounters an error. The following table explains the different actions you can perform.

OPTION	DESCRIPTION
Replace	Replaces the error with the highlighted suggestion; most useful for spelling- and number-style errors
Skip	Skips the error and continues to the next error; you can use this option when you do not agree that a problem exists
Resume	Begins checking the document after editing information in the document window
Ignore Word or Phrase	Ignores the highlighted word or phrase throughout the document
Next Sentence	Ignores any errors in the current sentence and moves on to the next sentence
Add	Adds the highlighted word to Grammatik's speller file
Close	Closes the Grammatik dialog box and ends grammar-checking

In addition to the options available on the dialog box, you can also click in the document window and make the corrections you want when an error is encountered. After making the necessary changes, choose Resume.

HINT

If you do not understand the explanation of an error, you can choose Help➢Rule Class to display in-depth information about the error. The Help information, taken from notable grammar reference manuals, is an excellent resource.

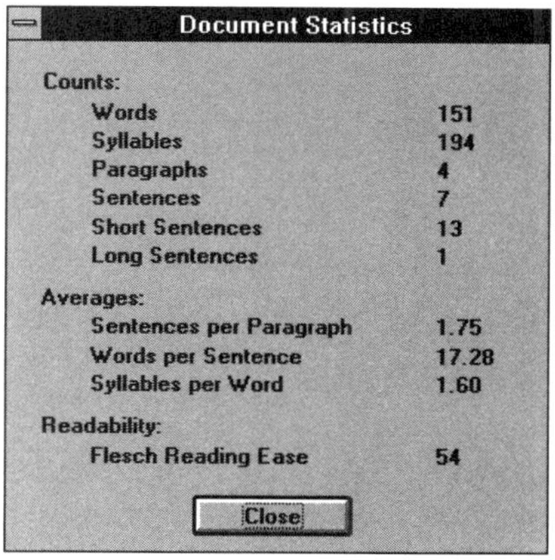

FIGURE 5–28
Document statistics from Grammatik.

Choosing Grammatik Options

Grammatik has several options you can choose to customize the type of checking performed on a document. The following table lists the options available from the Options pull-down menu.

OPTION	DESCRIPTION
Writing Style	Specifies the writing style used to check the document. Grammatik has several different writing styles it can use to edit your documents. The writing style determines the rules Grammatik uses to check a document. The available writing styles are General, Advertising, Business Letter, Documentation, Fiction, Journalism, Memo, Proposal, Report, and Technical. You can also change the Formality Level of the style. If the styles do not meet your needs, you can edit a style and specify the settings you want to use or create your own custom style.
Checking Options	Specifies whether paragraph errors are checked, whether words with periods are ignored, whether suggestions appear for misspelled words, and whether you want the checking to begin as soon as the dialog box opens without choosing Start.

(continues)

OPTION	DESCRIPTION
Show Spelling Errors	Displays spelling errors along with grammatical errors. If you are using the Speller, you may want to deselect this option to speed up Grammatik and avoid repetition.
Grammar, Mechanics, and Style	Checks for errors by using only grammatical, mechanical, and style *rule classes* (groups of standard errors and styles).
Grammar and Mechanics	Checks for errors by using only grammatical and mechanical rule classes.
Statistics	Displays statistical information for a document. Figure 5–28 shows the Document Statistics dialog box, which displays the number of words, paragraphs, sentences, and so on. It also shows statistics about several averages in the document, such as the average number of words per sentence. Finally, it displays a readability statistic.

HOW DO I... Have WordPerfect Automatically Correct Errors?

The QuickCorrect feature automatically corrects errors as soon as you type them. If you type "aparent" and QuickCorrect is active, for example, as soon as you press Spacebar, WordPerfect corrects the mistake and changes the word to "apparent." There are several predefined QuickCorrect errors and replacements. In addition, you can define your own errors and replacements.

Steps

QuickCorrect is activated when you start WordPerfect.

➨**To deactivate QuickCorrect:**

1. Choose Tools➢QuickCorrect.
2. Deselect Replace Errors as You Type.
3. Choose Close to return to the document window.

➡**To add a word to the QuickCorrect list:**

1. Choose Tools➢QuickCorrect.
2. Type in the Replace text field the incorrect word you want to have corrected.
3. In the With Text field, type the word you want to have replace it.
4. Choose Add Entry.
5. Choose Close to return to the document window.

Tell Me More

QuickCorrect is a great tool because, after it is activated, it automatically corrects errors as you type. In addition to correcting commonly misspelled words, QuickCorrect also corrects words that have two uppercase letters at the beginning of the word. For example, "CHoose" automatically becomes "Choose."

HOW DO I. . . Display Statistical Document Information?

WordPerfect lets you quickly and easily access specific information about your document. The Document Information feature displays the number of characters, words, lines, sentences, paragraphs, and pages in your document. It also displays information about word length and words per sentence.

Steps

➡**To display document information:**

1. Choose File➢Document Info. The Document Information dialog box is displayed, as shown in Figure 5–29.
2. Choose OK to return to the document window.

Tell Me More

You can view information that is specific to certain text by selecting the text and then following the preceding steps. The majority of the information displayed is specific to the selected text.

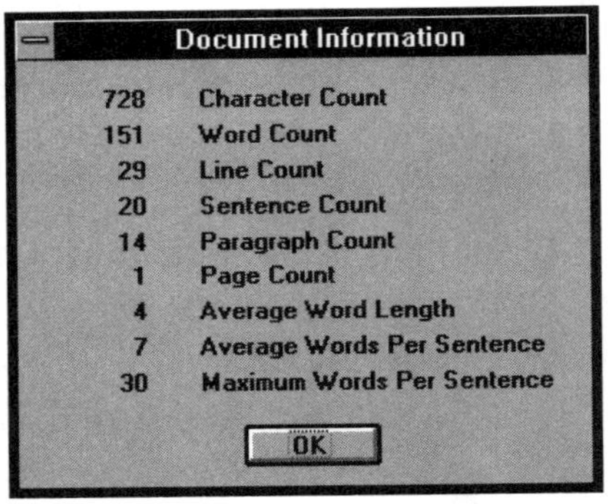

FIGURE 5–29
The Document Information dialog box.

An example of the usefulness of this information is when you are writing a document that has to contain a specific number of words. Rather than print the document and count the words manually, you can simply choose this option to view the number.

Document Information can also help you evaluate your writing. If you have a tendency to write sentences that are very long, for example, you can check the number for Average Words per Sentence to see whether the current document needs some work.

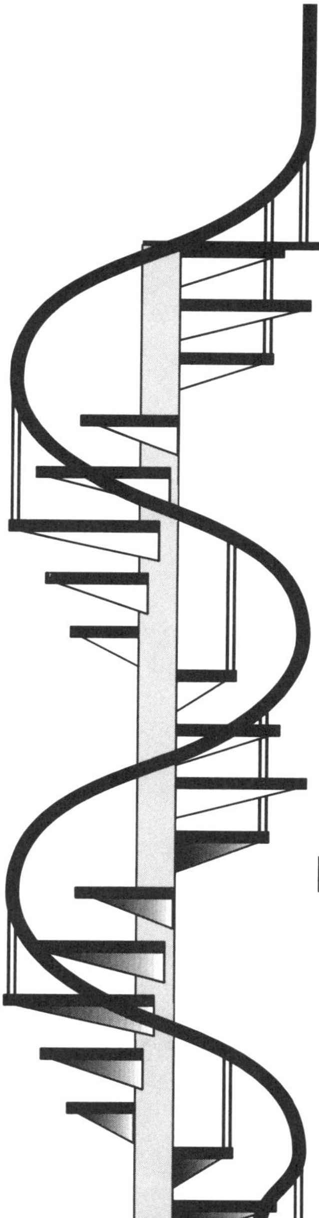

Chapter 6

Advanced Document Creation

This chapter answers questions about the following advanced document-formatting features in WordPerfect:

NOTE **Because of the number of questions answered and features covered, this chapter is organized alphabetically by feature name.**

- Inserting a bar code
- Inserting bullets and numbers
- Creating columns
- Creating comments
- Cross-referencing items
- Using counters
- Delaying codes
- Creating footnotes and endnotes
- Hiding text

- ➤ Creating hypertext links
- ➤ Creating an index
- ➤ Specifying global formatting codes
- ➤ Inserting the filename in a document
- ➤ Creating labels
- ➤ Creating lists
- ➤ Creating outlines
- ➤ Including sound
- ➤ Dividing pages into sections
- ➤ Creating a table of authorities
- ➤ Creating a table of contents

HOW DO I. . . Insert a Bar Code?

You can create POSTNET bar codes in a line of text within a document. This capability is useful if you are creating mailing labels and you want to insert a POSTNET bar code or you are using windowed envelopes and want to insert a POSTNET bar code on the document. POSTNET bar codes are based on ZIP codes that help the postal service sort and deliver mail more efficiently.

Steps

➡**To insert a bar code:**

1. Move your insertion point to the location in the document where you want the bar code inserted.
2. Choose Insert➢Other➢Bar Code. The POSTNET Bar Code dialog box is displayed, as shown here:

3. Enter a 5-, 9-, or 11-digit ZIP code in the Bar Code Digits text field.
4. Choose OK. WordPerfect automatically converts the ZIP code to a bar code and inserts it in your document.

Tell Me More

For information about inserting POSTNET bar codes on an envelope, see the section "HOW DO I... Create an Envelope?" in Chapter 5.

HOW DO I... Insert Bullets and Numbers?

The Bullets and Numbers feature is a great way to number text sequentially as well as mark text with bullets. Figure 6–1 shows a slide created with the Bullets and Number feature. After you select the bullet or number you are going to use, you can choose to have WordPerfect automatically insert it every time you press Enter. When you're using Numbers, the numbers automatically increment for you.

Steps

➡ **To insert a bullet or number:**

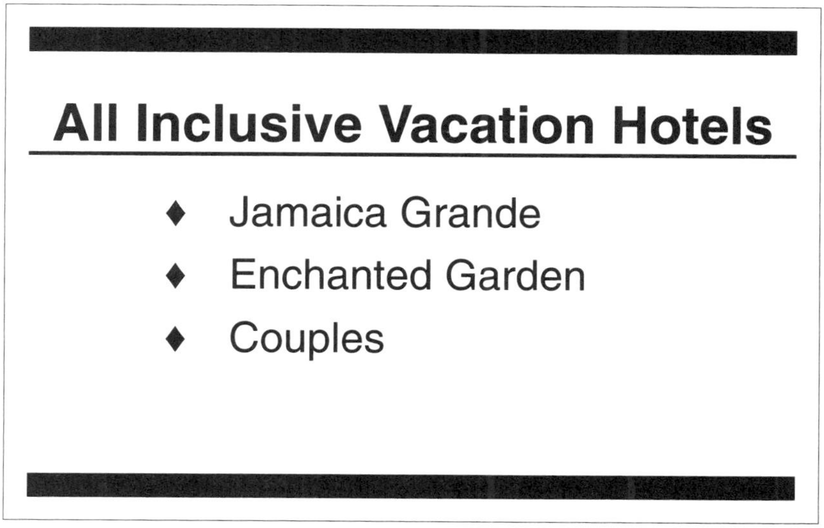

FIGURE 6–1
A slide created with the Bullets and Number feature.

1. Move your insertion point to where you want to begin inserting bullets or numbers.
2. Click the right mouse button and choose Bullets from the QuickMenu *or* choose Insert➢Bullets & Numbers.
3. Highlight the style of bullets or numbers you want to use.
4. If you are using numbers or letters, you can select Starting Value and specify the initial value you want to use. If you are using Numbers and want to start with 5, for example, you can do so with this option.
5. Select New Bullet or Number on ENTER if you want a bullet or number inserted every time you press [Enter].
6. Choose OK.

NOTE

You can also select text and then follow steps 2 through 5

BUTTON BAR

You can choose the 

icon from the Button Bar to access the Bullets & Numbers dialog box.

Tell Me More

Bullets and numbers are helpful for creating bulleted lists and single-level numbering. Unlike the Outline feature, bullets and numbers do not number multiple levels deep (I, A, 1, a, for example). If you use the Uppercase Roman style, for example, you number items as I, II, III, and so on.

If you did not select the option to have a bullet or number inserted when you press [Enter], you can press [Ctrl]+[Shift]+[B] to quickly insert the next number or bullet at the insertion point.

NOTE

You can also insert numbers in text and have them automatically increment by using the Counters feature (see the section "HOW DO I... Use Counters," later in this chapter).

HOW DO I... Create Columns?

Columns let you easily align text in rows in your documents. Columns are useful when you are creating newsletters, lists, definitions, scripts, or other documents in which you want to align text side by side. Word-

Perfect has two types of columns: newspaper and parallel. With newspaper columns, the text automatically moves to the next column as soon as the current column is full. With parallel columns, you choose the column in which the text is placed. When you create a column, you position the insertion point where you want the column to begin and define the Column options. To end columns, you simply turn Columns Off. You can insert text, tables, and graphics boxes in columns.

Steps

➠**To create columns:**

1. Choose Layout➢Columns➢Define. The Columns dialog box is displayed, as shown in Figure 6–2.
2. Specify the Number of Columns.
3. Select the Column Type: Newspaper, Balanced Newspaper, Parallel, or Parallel w/Block Protect.
4. Specify the Spacing Between Columns. If you selected Parallel or Parallel w/Block Protect, specify the Line Spacing Between Rows In Parallel Columns to change the line spacing of the text within columns. If you want all text in the columns to have a line spacing of 1.5, for example, you can specify that setting.

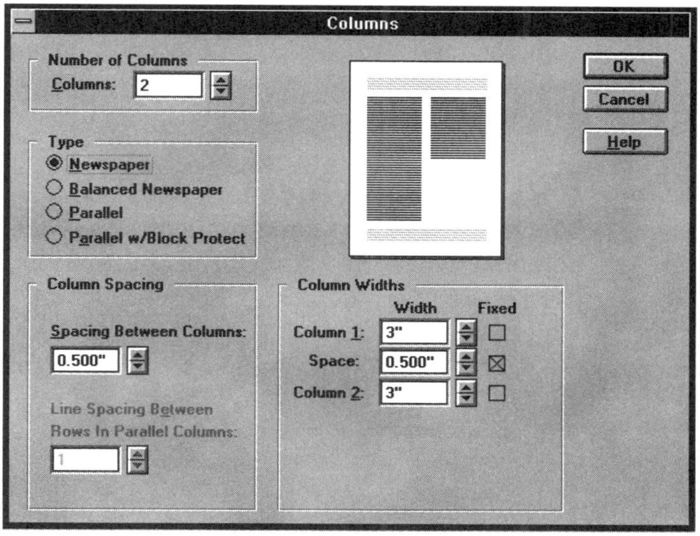

FIGURE 6–2
The Columns dialog box.

5. Make any necessary adjustments to the Column Widths settings.
6. Choose OK.

NOTE

You can insert text first and then turn on Columns. Your text is then reformatted in column format. You have to be aware of your insertion point position if you turn columns on after you've entered text. The column definition code is inserted at the beginning of the current paragraph. You can also select text and then turn on Columns. Selected text or existing text is inserted in the first column. To move the text to the next column, position the insertion point at the beginning of the text you want to move and press Ctrl + Enter.

➡**To turn off Columns:**

1. Choose Layout➢Columns➢Off.

POWER BAR

Choose the icon from the Power Bar and then select the number of columns you want to create. You can also double-click the icon to open the Columns dialog box and make changes to the column settings.

Tell Me More

Figure 6–3 shows an example of newspaper columns, and Figure 6–4 shows an example of parallel columns. There are two types of newspaper columns and two types of parallel columns. Balanced newspaper columns ensure that each column is of equal length. Parallel columns with Block Protect ensure that column rows are kept on the same page.

Moving Around in Columns

To enter text in a column, simply type the text. If you are using parallel columns and you want to insert text in the next column, press Ctrl + Enter *or* click the Column icon on the Power Bar and select Column Break.

After a new column is created, you can move to a column by simply clicking in the column. You can also use the keystrokes shown on page 181 to move to a specific column.

FIGURE 6–3
An example of newspaper columns.

Bay Area Living

One of the pleasures of living in the Bay Area is the wide range of recreational and cultural activities one can enjoy year-round. The following are some suggestions from area residents and Relocation Consultants.

PARKS: For outdoor lovers, your entire five years could be spent just exploring the parks within the Bay Area. There are over 100 parks on over 200,000 acres surrounding the metropolitan area, with thousands of walking, hiking, riding, and bike trails; lakes for boating, fishing and swimming; as well as camping and nature programs.

OPERA: The San Francisco Opera performs in their own Opera House, the Marin Opera at the Civic Center, and the West Bay Opera in Palo Alto.

OCEAN: Sand beaches nestled between towering cliffs follow the coastline from Marin through Carmel. Almost all is public land and one can go beachcombing or sunbathe year-round. Because they are so extensive, you can generally find a quiet spot.

SAN FRANCISCO BAY: Almost the entire Bay is ringed by public land with marinas, fishing piers, and nature study areas, as well as bike and jogging trails.

LAKES and RESERVOIRS: Close to 100 lakes and reservoirs, open to the public, are within a 100-mile radius of the Bay Area. They support such activities as fishing, boating, swimming, waterskiing, picnicking, and camping.

NARROW GAUGE RAILROAD: One of the last surviving steam logging railroads is found in the Santa Cruz Mountains at Felton. Ride the train through Redwood forests, over wood trestles and yawning canyons.

PLANETARIUMS: Featuring Laserium and other astronomic shows and exhibits. Morrison Planetarium, Minolta Planetarium, and Chabot Observatory.

MARINE RESERVE: At low tide, walk out onto the wide limestone shelf and view sea anemones, sea urchins, crabs, and other creatures at Moss Beach.

WILDLIFE SANCTUARY: Herons and egrets are just a few of the over 100 species of birds living at the Audobon Canyon Ranch in Bolinas. You can also watch big birds at the Lake Merritt sanctuary in Oakland.

Text automatically flows to next column

FIGURE 6–4
An example of parallel columns.

ALL INCLUSIVE VACATION HOTEL FEATURES

Jamaica Grande— A Residence Resort	Windsurfing Sailing Snorkeling Glass bottom boat trip Daily Activities	$958-1024
Enchanted Garden	Spa and Steam Bath Complimentary facial, manicure and massage	$1000-1500
Ciboney Resort	Dunn's River Falls tour Snorkeling Waterskiing Scuba diving Windsurfing Sailing Health Club Paddle Boats Canoes Massages	$1085-1650
Couples	Tennis/Squash Golf Horseback riding Scuba diving	$1200-1300
Boscobel Beach Resort	Snorkeling Windsurfing Scuba Diving Sailing Waterskiing Health Club	$1019-1739

KEYSTROKE	DESCRIPTION
Ctrl + Enter	Creates next column and moves to it
Alt + →	Moves one column to the right
Alt + ←	Moves one column to the left
Alt + Home	Moves to the top of the current column
Alt + End	Moves to the bottom of the current column

Using the Ruler with Columns

You can quickly and easily size columns by using the ruler.

To display the ruler, choose View➢Ruler *or* press Alt + Shift + F3. The Ruler Bar displays the column markers, as shown in Figure 6–5. To change the size of a column, simply drag the marker to the new location. If you have selected Fixed for the Column Width settings (which is the default), the other columns remain in their original position.

FIGURE 6–5
The Ruler Bar displays column markers.

Column markers

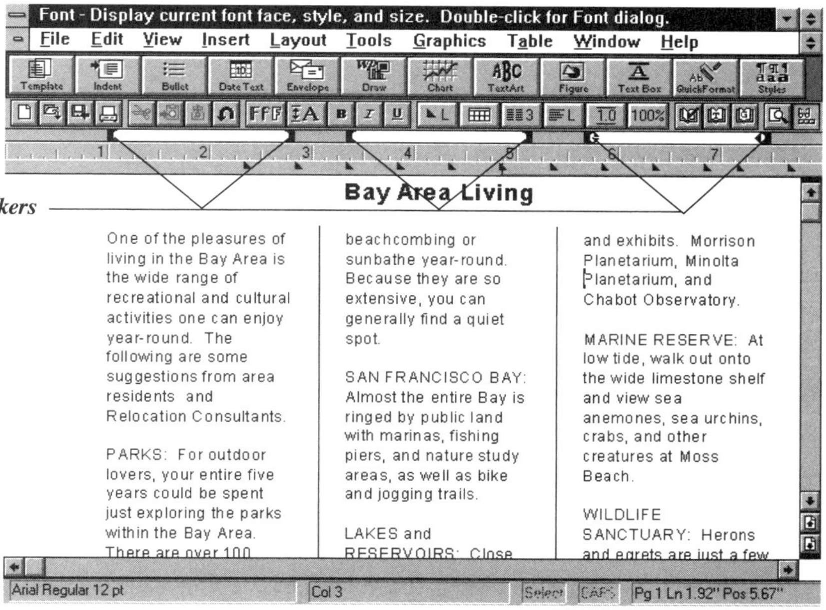

Inserting Column Borders

You can insert borders between columns to offset each column. Figure 6–6 shows an example of column borders.

To insert column borders:

1. Choose Layout➢Columns➢Border-Fill.
2. Select Column Between or Column All from the Border Style drop-down list.
3. Choose OK to return to the document window.

When you select Column Between, a vertical line is placed between your columns. If you select Column All, a border is placed around the outside and inside of columns.

HOW DO I. . . Create a Comment in a Document?

WordPerfect enables you to insert comments in your documents that are not part of the text. Comments are useful for inserting on-line editing comments, instructions for filling in on-line forms created with WordPerfect, and notes to yourself.

Suppose that you are creating a travel brochure about the Bahamas and you want to include the average temperature in the Climate section. Because you are not certain what the temperature is, you insert a comment to remind yourself to add the information later. You can edit comments and convert them to text. Comments are not printed with the document.

Steps

➡**To create a comment:**

1. Move the insertion point to the location where you want to insert the comment.
2. Choose Insert➢Comment➢Create. The Comment Feature Bar is displayed at the top of the document window.
3. Enter the information you want in the comment. You can include formatting features, such as bold, center, and underline.
4. Choose Close to close the Comment Feature Bar and return to the document window.

FIGURE 6–6
Column borders.

Bay Area Living

One of the pleasures of living in the Bay Area is the wide range of recreational and cultural activities one can enjoy year-round. The following are some suggestions from area residents and Relocation Consultants.

PARKS: For outdoor lovers, your entire five years could be spent just exploring the parks within the Bay Area. There are over 100 parks on over 200,000 acres surrounding the metropolitan area, with thousands of walking, hiking, riding, and bike trails; lakes for boating, fishing and swimming; as well as camping and nature programs.

OPERA: The San Francisco Opera performs in their own Opera House, the Marin Opera at the Civic Center, and the West Bay Opera in Palo Alto.

OCEAN: Sand beaches nestled between towering cliffs follow the coastline from Marin through Carmel. Almost all is public land and one can go beachcombing or sunbathe year-round. Because they are so extensive, you can generally find a quiet spot.

SAN FRANCISCO BAY: Almost the entire Bay is ringed by public land with marinas, fishing piers, and nature study areas, as well as bike and jogging trails.

LAKES and RESERVOIRS: Close to 100 lakes and reservoirs, open to the public, are within a 100-mile radius of the Bay Area. They support such activities as fishing, boating, swimming, waterskiing, picnicking, and camping.

NARROW GAUGE RAILROAD: One of the last surviving steam logging railroads is found in the Santa Cruz Mountains at Felton. Ride the train through Redwood forests, over wood trestles and yawning canyons.

PLANETARIUMS: Featuring Laserium and other astronomic shows and exhibits. Morrison Planetarium, Minolta Planetarium, and Chabot Observatory.

MARINE RESERVE: At low tide, walk out onto the wide limestone shelf and view sea anemones, sea urchins, crabs, and other creatures at Moss Beach.

WILDLIFE SANCTUARY: Herons and egrets are just a few of the over 100 species of birds living at the Audobon Canyon Ranch in Bolinas. You can also watch big birds at the Lake Merritt sanctuary in Oakland.

Column borders set to Column Between

HINT

You can convert existing text to a comment by selecting the text and following step 2.

➡**To read a comment in a document:**

1. Click the comment icon shown here to display the text of the comment:

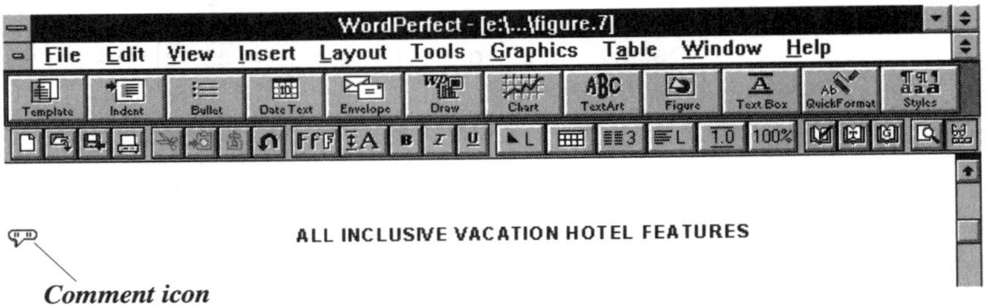

Comment icon

2. Click anywhere in the document window to close the comment.

NOTE

If you are in Draft display mode, the text of the comment is visible in the document window.

Tell Me More

Figure 6–7 shows an opened comment in the document window. The pointer points to the location where the insertion point was when the comment was created. This pointer gives you a reference for the comment.

Using the Comment Feature Bar

When you're creating a comment, the Comment Feature Bar, displayed here, has several buttons that automatically insert information in a comment for you:

To use the Initials and Name options, you must insert this information in the Environment Preferences dialog box.

To insert your name and initials:

FIGURE 6–7
An opened comment.

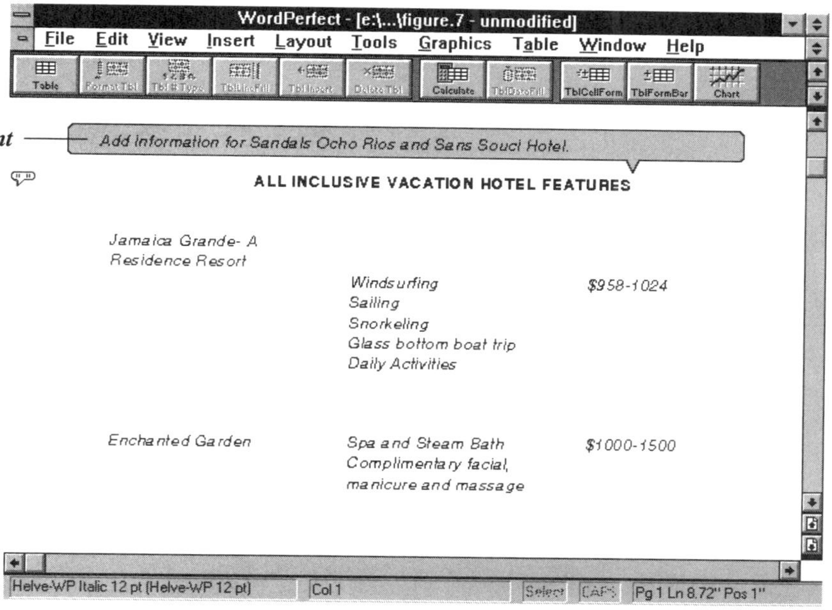

1. Choose File➢Preferences.
2. Double-click the Environment icon.
3. Insert your name and initials in the appropriate text boxes. If you want to change the color in which your comment is displayed, select a new color from the User Color palette.

After you insert this information, you can quickly insert your name or initials in a comment. This feature is most useful when multiple people will insert comments in a document. The Date and Time buttons insert the current date and time as they are set on your computer.

When you enter your initials, all comments you insert in a document display your initials, as shown here:

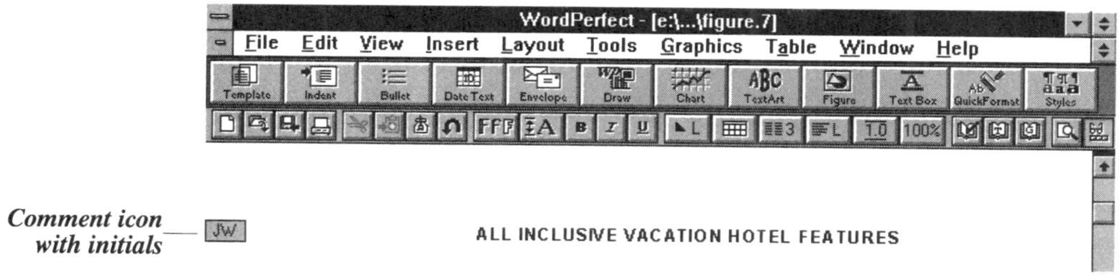

Editing, Deleting, and Converting Comments

If you need to make changes to a comment, you can edit it.

To edit a comment:

1. Position the insertion point on the comment you want to edit.
2. Click the right mouse button to display the QuickMenu and then choose Edit.
3. Edit the information.
4. Choose Close from the Feature Bar to return to the document window.

To remove a comment, you can delete it entirely or convert it to text.

To delete a comment:

1. Position the mouse on the comment and click the right mouse button to display the QuickMenu.
2. Choose Delete.

To convert a comment to text:

1. Position the insertion point just below the comment you want to convert. You must convert each comment individually.
2. Choose Insert➢Comment➢Convert to Text.

HINT **The only way to print a comment is to convert it to text.**

If you don't want to delete your comments but you don't want them to be displayed, you can do so with the following steps:

1. Choose File➢Preferences.
2. Double-click the Display icon and select the Document radio button.
3. Deselect Comments from the Show group box.
4. Choose OK to return to the document window.

The comments are no longer displayed in the document window, but they are not deleted from the document. If you want to view your comments later, follow the preceding steps.

HOW DO I... Use Counters?

The Counters feature lets you insert counters *or numbers* in your document. With Counters, you can control where the number is displayed and when it increments and decrements.

Counters are especially useful in documents in which you have an ongoing numbering sequence that spans throughout the document. If you are numbering illustrations in the text of your document, for example, you can use counters to insert and automatically increment the number every time you want to reference a new illustration in the document.

If you delete or add an illustration, the Counters feature automatically adjusts all the other illustration numbers. Using counters prevents you from having to manually renumber each occurrence of an illustration number when you make changes to a document. When you use the Counters feature, you must first create the counter, display it in your document, and then increment and display it every time you want to insert a number in the document.

Steps

➨**To create and insert the first counter:**

1. Choose Insert➢Other➢Counter. The Counters dialog box is displayed, as shown in Figure 6–8.
2. Choose Create. The Create Counter Definition dialog box is displayed.
3. Specify a name for the counter, such as **illustrations** (the name is not seen in the document text).
4. If you will have only one level of counting, select Numbers, Lowercase Letters, Uppercase Letters, Lowercase Roman, or Uppercase Roman from the Single Level Method pop-up list.
5. If you want more than one level of counting, specify the number for Levels and specify a Numbering Method for each level.
6. Choose OK.
7. Choose Display in Document. WordPerfect inserts the number in your document at the location of the insertion point.

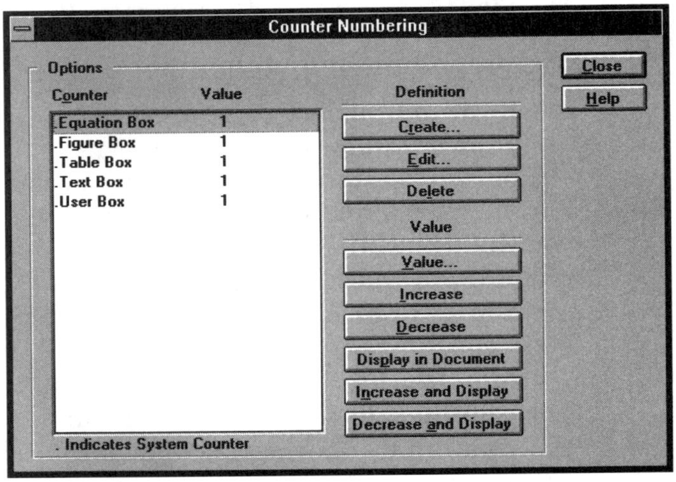

FIGURE 6–8
The Counter Numbering dialog box.

➡**To increment the counter in your document:**

1. Place the insertion point where you want to display the next counter number.
2. Choose Insert➢Other➢Counter.
3. Choose Increment and Display. WordPerfect automatically increments the number and inserts it in your document at the location of the insertion point.

Tell Me More

When you create a counter, it is saved with the document. When you insert a counter in your document, WordPerfect inserts a code that displays the counter number at the location of the insertion point. You want to be careful and not delete the code. The Counter code allows WordPerfect to automatically recount when you insert or delete another counter.

You can set a specific value for the counter. If you are numbering illustrations in a document. for example, and you want the first illustration to be number 5 rather than 1, you can set the value for the counter. From the Counter dialog box, choose Value, specify the number and choose OK, and then choose Display in Document. You can change the value for the Counter at any time.

HINT You can use numbers to specify a value regardless of the numbering method. If your Numbering Method is set to Upper Roman and you type 1, for example, an I is displayed instead.

NOTE In addition to creating your own counters, you can use one of WordPerfect's many system counters. These counters are used in numbering different types of graphics boxes.

HOW DO I. . . Cross-Reference Items in a Document?

A *cross-reference* tells readers where to find additional information. A typical cross-reference in a document might read "See page 14 for more information." When you create a cross-reference, you refer the reader to another location. The location where you refer the reader to another location is the *reference.*

A *target* is the location where you want to refer the reader; pages, footnotes, or caption numbers are examples of targets. In the preceding example, page 14 is the target. If the target changes pages or locations, WordPerfect automatically updates your reference when you generate the document. When WordPerfect generates a document, it reads or makes passes through the document to verify and update specific information, such as the location of cross-references.

Steps

➡To create a cross-reference:

1. Move to the location where you want to create the reference and enter the text you want to precede the reference, such as **see page**.
2. Choose Tools➢Cross-Reference. The Cross-Reference Feature Bar is displayed, as shown here:

3. Choose Reference and select an option from the drop-down list. The Reference specifies what you want to reference, such as a page number, footnote, or chapter.

4. In the Target text box, enter the name of the target. The Target Name, which is only informational, creates a link between the reference and the target.
5. Move the insertion point to the location of the target, such as a specific page or footnote, and choose Mark Target.

NOTE

If your reference is anything other than a page, footnote, or endnote, move the insertion to the right of the code in Reveal Codes before marking the target.

6. Move the insertion point to the location where you want to insert the reference and choose Mark Reference. WordPerfect automatically inserts a question mark (?) at the reference point.
7. Choose Generate to have WordPerfect insert the correct reference.

NOTE

After making any editing changes, be sure to regenerate the document. When you generate a document, all features included in the document are generated (lists, indexes, cross-references, table of contents, and table of authorities). To regenerate, choose Tools➢Generate *or* press Ctrl+F9 and choose OK.

Tell Me More

At times, you may have multiple references to the same target. If you are creating a travel brochure that contains information about the Bahamas and Bermuda, for example, you can create a reference in both sections to a page that contains information about water sports.

To create a cross-reference to the same target:

1. Move to the location where you want to create the second reference and enter the text you want to use to precede the reference, such as **see page**.
2. Choose Tools➢Cross-Reference.
3. Verify that the name in the Target text box is correct. If it is not correct, select the correct name from the drop-down list.
4. Move the insertion point to the location where you want to insert the reference and choose Mark Reference. WordPer-

fect automatically inserts a question mark (?) at the reference point.

5. Choose Generate to have WordPerfect update the reference.

You can also create multiple targets for a reference. You may have several pages, for example, that contain information about a topic to which you want to refer the reader.

To create multiple targets for the same reference:

1. Create the Target by entering the name.
2. Select a Reference Type.
3. Move the insertion point to the location of the target, such as a specific page or footnote, and choose Mark Target.
4. Repeat step 3 for each location to which you want to refer.
5. Move the insertion point to the location where you want to insert the references and choose Mark Reference.

NOTE **Only one question mark appears, but after you generate the document, all references are inserted.**

6. Choose Generate to have WordPerfect update the reference.

HOW DO I... Delay Codes to a Specified Page?

Sometimes you may want to do all your formatting for a document before you create it. Using Delay Codes enables you to insert formatting codes in your document and have them take effect on a certain page. You might create a term paper, for example, in which you want the title page to use a Times Roman 18-point font and, beginning on page 2, you want to use a Times Roman 12-point font. Using Delay Codes, you can insert both font changes at the beginning of the document and have them take effect on the appropriate pages.

Steps

➡ **To delay codes:**

1. Choose Layout ➢ Page ➢ Delay Codes.
2. Specify the Number of Pages to Delay. If the insertion point is on page 1 and you enter 2, for example, the codes take effect on page 3.

3. Insert the codes you want to delay.
4. Choose Close from the Feature Bar to return to the document window.

Tell Me More

You can delay only open codes. *Open codes* take effect until the same code with different settings is inserted in the document; they do not require specific ending codes. Open codes include font changes, margin settings, and paper size and type definitions. Examples of codes you cannot use with Delay Codes are bold, underline, outline, tab, and center.

HINT

When you use Delay Codes, you see a [Delay] code at the top of the page on which you inserted the delayed codes. The code you delayed appears on the page it takes effect as [Delay Codes].

HOW DO I... Create a Footnote or Endnote?

Footnotes and Endnotes are useful when you want to create at the bottom of a page or at the end of a document a note that provides more information about specific items in your text. If you are creating a travel brochure, for example, and you want to enter information about restrictions for a travel package, you can insert that information in a footnote or endnote.

When you create a footnote or endnote, WordPerfect inserts a number by a word in the document. With a footnote, the same number is inserted along with additional information at the bottom of the page, as displayed in Figure 6–9. With an endnote, the number and additional information are placed at the end of the document, as shown in Figure 6–10.

Steps

➡ **To create a footnote:**

1. Place the insertion point directly after the word you want to reference to a footnote.
2. Choose Insert➢Footnote➢Create. The Footnote editing window is displayed.

FIGURE 6–9
A document containing footnotes.

If I were asked which is the area of greatest misunderstanding and confusion in the field of nutrition, I would immediately be forced to reply that it is the failure to understand and interpret properly the symptoms and changes which follow the beginning of a better nutritional program.

What is meant by a better nutritional program? It is the introduction of foods of higher quality in place of lower-quality ones. For example, if a person replaces a protein-rich food such as pork with beef, the beef may be considered the superior of the two due to its easier digestibility, lower and less-saturated fat content, etc. Chicken is superior to beef, and fish is superior to chicken because of its more rapid digestibility and lower saturated fat content. Lima beans, lentils, and chick peas, which are eaten at the same meal with vegetables, are superior in all the nutrients needed to rebuild health. To summarize: the closer the food comes to the natural state in which it occurs, or the closer we come to its raw, unfired form, the higher its quality. In this condition, all enzymes are found intact. The amino acids are in their finest form. The minerals, vitamins, trace elements, carbohydrates, and "life force" are present. This life force in turn is capable of reproducing healthy tissue[1].

This same classification of quality which we analyzed in relation to protein-rich foods applies to carbohydrates (the starches and sugar-rich foods), the fats and the mineral-rich foods[2].

Footnote references

---

1. Brotherson, Jennifer, *What Symptoms to Expect When You Improve Your Diet,* (Lehi: PG Publishing, 1991).
2. Brotherson, Scott, *Don't Fight the Healing Process,* (Lehi: PG Publishing, 1991).

FIGURE 6–10
A document containing endnotes.

Endnotes

1. Brotherson, Jennifer, *What Symptoms to Expect When You Improve Your Diet,* (Lehi: PG Publishing, 1991).

2. Brotherson, Scott, *Don't Fight the Healing Process,* (Lehi: PG Publishing, 1991).

3. Type the text you want in the footnote and then choose Close from the Footnote Feature Bar. The footnote number is displayed in a superscript font directly after the word your insertion point was on. The footnote text is placed at the bottom of the page.

➠**To create an endnote:**

1. Place the insertion point directly after the word you want to reference to an endnote.

2. Choose Insert➢Endnote➢Create. The Endnote editing window is displayed.
3. Type the text you want in the endnote and then choose Close from the Endnote Feature Bar. The endnote number is displayed in a superscript font directly after the word your insertion point was on. The endnote text is placed at the end of the document.

Tell Me More

The following sections explain how to edit footnotes and endnotes, assign numbers to footnotes and endnotes, and change footnote and endnote options.

Editing Footnotes and Endnotes

The editing window for footnotes and endnotes is much like the main document window. You can format your notes by using many of the features available in WordPerfect. If an option is unavailable when you are creating a footnote or endnote, it appears dimmed on the pull-down menu or in the dialog box.

HINT **You can paste information you have cut or copied into the footnote or endnote editing window.**

To edit an existing footnote or endnote:

1. Click anywhere on the text of the footnote or endnote *or* choose Insert➢Footnote or Endnote➢Edit and enter the number of the note and choose OK.
2. Make the necessary changes in the editing window and choose Close from the Feature Bar.

HINT **When you are editing a footnote or endnote, you can quickly move to the next or preceding note by choosing Next or Previous from the Feature Bar.**

Assigning New Numbers to Footnotes and Endnotes

WordPerfect gives you the flexibility to assign new numbers to footnotes and endnotes. You may want to renumber footnotes or endnotes if you want to restart numbering on each page or for each section in a document.

To assign a new number to the next created footnote or endnote:

1. Choose Insert➢Footnote or Endnote➢New Number. The appropriate Number dialog box is displayed, as shown here:

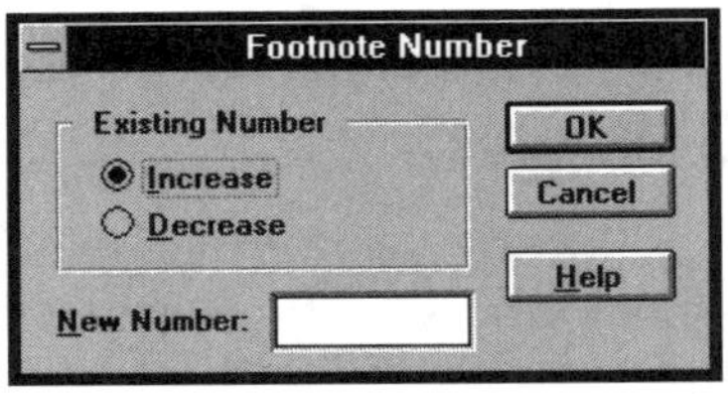

2. Select Increase or Decrease to increment the last number by one or specify a New Number.
3. Choose OK. The next note you create reflects the changes you made.

Changing Footnote Options

You can customize the way your footnotes are displayed in your document by choosing Insert➢Footnote➢Options. The following table describes the options available on the Footnote Options dialog box, displayed in Figure 6–11.

OPTION	DESCRIPTION
Method	Specifies the numbering method: Numbers, Lowercase Letters, Uppercase Letters, Lowercase Roman, Uppercase Roman, or Characters. If you specify Characters, press Ctrl+W while in the Characters text box and insert the character you want. Restart Numbering on Each Page Automatically restarts the footnote numbering at 1 for each page
Edit Numbering Style	Specifies the style of the note number in the text and in the actual note. By default, the notes are superscripted; you can change the font face or attributes with this option. If you want the note numbers to be bold, for example, you can edit the numbering style.

(continues)

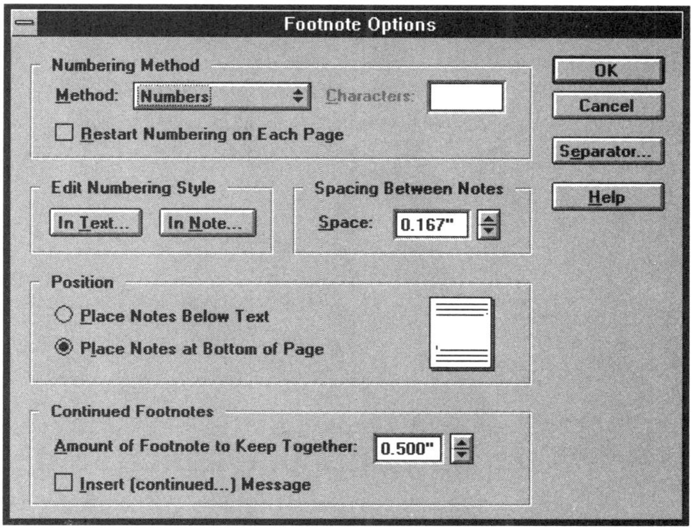

FIGURE 6–11
The Footnote Options dialog box.

Option	Description
Spacing Between Footnotes	Specifies the amount of space between footnotes
Position	Specifies whether the footnote is placed below the last line of text on the page or at the bottom of the page
Amount of Footnote to Keep Together	Specifies how much space the footnote occupies at the bottom of the page; if the amount specified is not available, it forces the footnote to the next page
Insert (continued...) Message	Prints the word **continued** on the last line of footnotes on each page and the first line of footnotes on each subsequent page when a footnote spans to the next page

You can also specify several settings for the line that separates the document text from the footnote by choosing Separator from the Footnote Options dialog box. The Line Separator dialog box is displayed, as shown here, and lists the settings you can change:

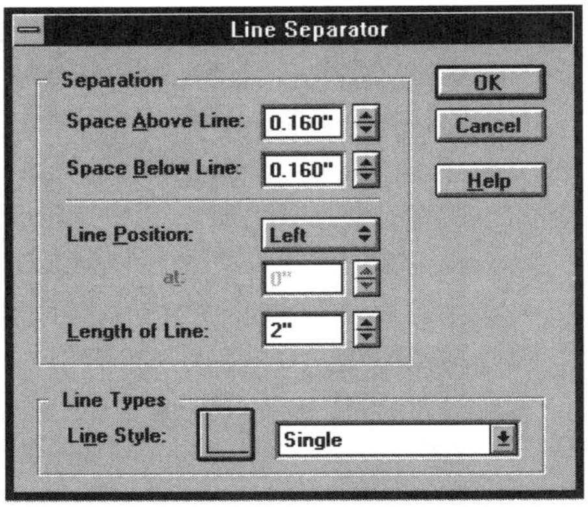

Changing Endnote Options

You can also customize the way your endnotes are displayed in your document by choosing Insert➢Endnote➢Options. The Endnote Options dialog box is displayed, as shown in Figure 6–12.

The following table describes the Endnote options:

OPTION	DESCRIPTION
Method	Specifies the numbering method: Numbers, Lowercase Letters, Uppercase Letters, Lowercase Roman, Uppercase Roman, or Characters. If you specify Characters, press Ctrl+W while in the Characters text box and insert the character you want.

(continues)

FIGURE 6–12
The Endnote Options dialog box.

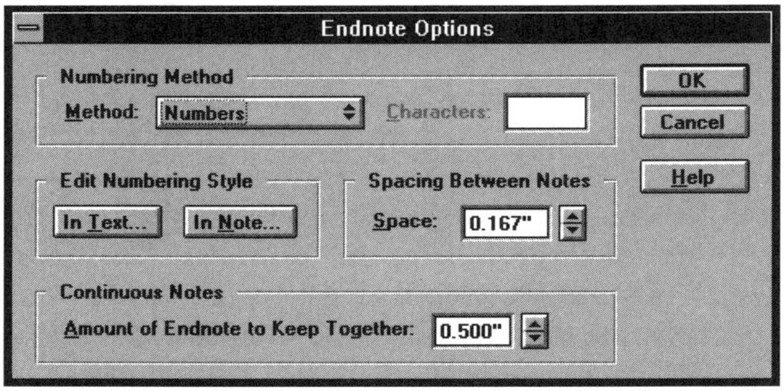

OPTION	DESCRIPTION
Edit Numbering Style	Specifies the style of the note number in the text and in the actual note. By default, the notes are superscripted; you can change the font face or attributes with this option. If you want the note numbers to be bolded, for example, you can edit the numbering style.
Spacing Between Endnotes	Specifies the amount of space between endnotes.
Amount of Endnote to Keep Together	Specifies the minimum amount of space an endnote can occupy; if the amount specified is not available, it forces the endnote to the next page.

HINT

Endnotes are usually printed at the bottom of a document. You can choose where you want to place endnotes, however, by placing the insertion point where you want the endnotes in your document and choosing Insert➢Endnote➢Placement. Select Insert Endnotes at Insertion Point or select Insert Endnotes at Insertion Point and Restart Numbering.

HOW DO I... Insert Hidden Text in a Document?

The Hidden Text feature lets you enter text and choose when you want to hide it and when you want to display it. Hidden text is useful when you do not want certain parts of a document to be displayed. When a document contains information you want all your employees to read, for example, but you want to keep a few sections of the document confidential, you can use the Hidden Text feature to hide the confidential sections and then print the document.

When hidden text is displayed, it looks just like regular document text. Hidden Text is similar to Comments. For information about Comments, see the section "HOW DO I... Create a Comment in a Document?," earlier in this chapter.

Steps

➡**To insert hidden text:**

1. In the document window, type the text you want hidden and then select it.
2. Choose Layout➤Font *or* press Ctrl+F9.
3. From the Appearance group box, select Hidden and choose OK.

➡**To display hidden text:**

1. Choose View➤Hidden Text.

Tell Me More

Hidden text can be used with on-line documents and printed documents. You must be careful when you use it with on-line documents because other users can simply choose View➤Hidden Text and WordPerfect then displays all hidden text. Hidden text prints only when it is displayed.

To convert hidden text to regular document text, select the text and then deselect Hidden in the Font dialog box.

HOW DO I... Create Hypertext Links in My Document?

WordPerfect gives you the ability to create hypertext links in your document. A *hypertext link* is a connection between two locations; it lets you move quickly to a different location when you are viewing a document on-line. If you are creating a document with many technical terms, for example, you can create hypertext links that link the term to a definition on another page or even in another document. With hypertext, you can create links that jump to a specific section (bookmark) of the current document, jump to another document, or play a macro. A *hypertext jump* is the action that occurs when you choose a hypertext link.

NOTE **Bookmarks and macros must exist before you can create hypertext links to them.**

Steps

➡**To create and activate a hypertext link:**

1. Select the text you want to become the hypertext link.
2. Choose Tools➤Hypertext.

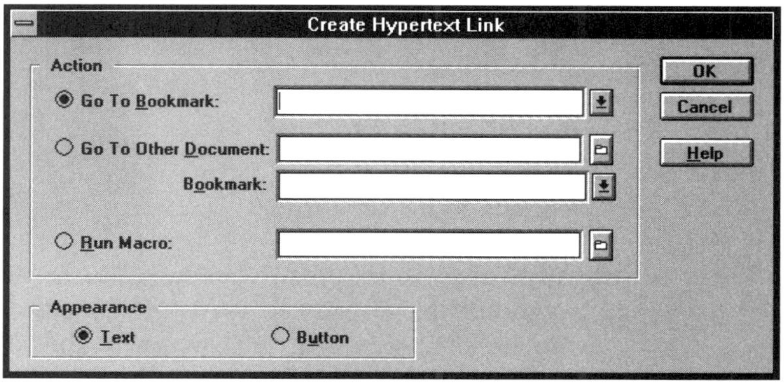

FIGURE 6–13 *The Create Hypertext Link dialog box.*

3. From the Hypertext Feature Bar, choose Create. The Create Hypertext Link dialog box is displayed, as shown in Figure 6–13.
4. Select Go to Bookmark and select the name of the bookmark from the drop-down list; or select Go to Other Document, type the path and filename of the document, and then select the bookmark from the drop-down list; or select Run Macro and then type the path and filename of the macro.
5. Select Text or Button from the Appearance group box.
6. Choose OK.
7. Choose Close from the Hypertext Feature Bar.

Tell Me More

The following sections provide additional information about selecting a hypertext link type, displaying hypertext in documents, moving through hypertext jumps, and deleting hypertext jumps.

Selecting a Hypertext Link Type

When you are creating a hypertext link, you can choose between three link types. The first type is Go to Bookmark. When you select Go to Bookmark and type the bookmark name, WordPerfect inserts a hypertext link that jumps to a bookmark in the current document. Suppose that you are creating a lengthy scientific document that is meant to be read on-line. Some of the terms may be unfamiliar to your readers, so you create a glossary of terms at the end of the document. By creating links throughout the document to bookmarks in the glossary, those who read the document can quickly jump to the information that clarifies the terms.

HINT

You can place hypertext links to jump back to bookmarks where the reader jumped from originally. You can create as many links as you need.

If you choose Go to Other Document, WordPerfect inserts a link that opens another document and goes to a specific bookmark. When the other document is opened, the document that contains the hypertext link is closed. To expand on the preceding example, if a document already exists that contains the additional information, you can create a link to that document. Readers can jump to the other document and obtain the additional information.

If you choose Run Macro, WordPerfect inserts a link that runs the macro you specify. If you want feedback from people who read a document, for example, you can create a link to a macro that prompts your readers for their name and title and any comments. The macro then can save the information in a separate file for you to read at your convenience without adding text to the original document.

Displaying and Deactivating Hypertext in Documents

By default, hypertext is displayed as green and underlined. You can change the hypertext to any font style and appearance you want. The changes you make to the hypertext style affect all hypertext links in the document.

To change the Hypertext style:

1. Choose Style from the Hypertext Feature Bar. The Styles Editor dialog box for the Hypertext style is displayed.
2. Insert or delete in the Contents box the codes you want.
3. Choose OK.

You can also have the hypertext display inside a button, as shown in Figure 6–14. To display the hypertext in a button, simply choose Button for the Appearance when you're creating the link.

While you are creating a document that includes hypertext links, you may want to deactivate hypertext. Deactivating hypertext enables you to edit links without performing the action assigned to the link. You can

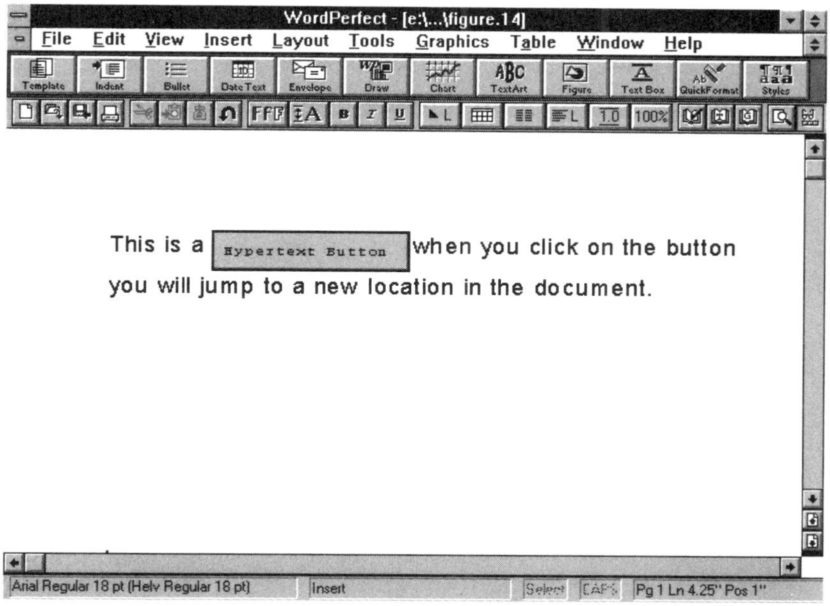

FIGURE 6–14
Hypertext button.

deactivate hypertext by choosing Deactivate from the Hypertext Feature Bar.

Moving Through Hypertext Links

When Hypertext is active, you can use different methods to move through the hypertext links. To move to the jump or run the macro associated with a hypertext jump, click once on the hypertext *or* choose Perform from the Hypertext Feature Bar. After jumping to the new location, choose Back from the Feature Bar to move back to the hypertext. You can also choose Next or Previous to move to the next or previous link in your document.

Deleting Hypertext Links

If you no longer need the hypertext link in a document, you can delete it with the following steps:

1. Place the insertion point on the hypertext link.
2. Choose Delete from the Feature Bar. WordPerfect deletes the link, but the text remains.

HOW DO I... Create an Index?

Indexes are useful when you are creating books, documentation, or any document that needs an alphabetical guide with page numbers for locating information. The Index feature significantly automates the task of creating an index. When you create an index, you mark the entries you want included in it, define the index, and then generate it.

Steps

➡To mark the entries:

1. Choose Tools➢Index. The Index Feature Bar is displayed, as shown here:

2. Select the word or phrase you want to include in the index and then click in the Heading text box. If you want to include a subheading in the index, first create the heading and then select the text for the Subheading and click in the Subheading text box.
3. Choose Mark.
4. Repeat steps 1 through 3 until you have marked all words and phrases you want to include in the index.

➡To define the index:

1. Move your insertion point to the location where you want the index. If you want the index on a new page, press Ctrl+Enter and insert any text you want to precede the index.
2. Choose Define from the Feature Bar.
3. Make any necessary changes to the settings and choose OK.

➡To generate the index:

1. Choose Generate from the Feature Bar.
2. Choose OK. WordPerfect creates or updates the index.

NOTE

You have to generate your index every time you make any editing changes. Regenerating guarantees that the page numbers are correct. When you generate a document, all features included in the document are generated (lists, indexes, cross-

references, table of contents, and table of authorities). You can also generate a document by choosing **Tools➢Generate** *or* pressing Ctrl + F9.

Tell Me More

If you want to include a title, such as "Index," on the top of your index, make sure that you insert the title before the index-definition code. Any text following the definition is deleted every time you generate the document.

When you define an index, you can customize several options to meet your specific needs. The following sections explain additional index options as well as how to create subheadings in an index. Figure 6–15

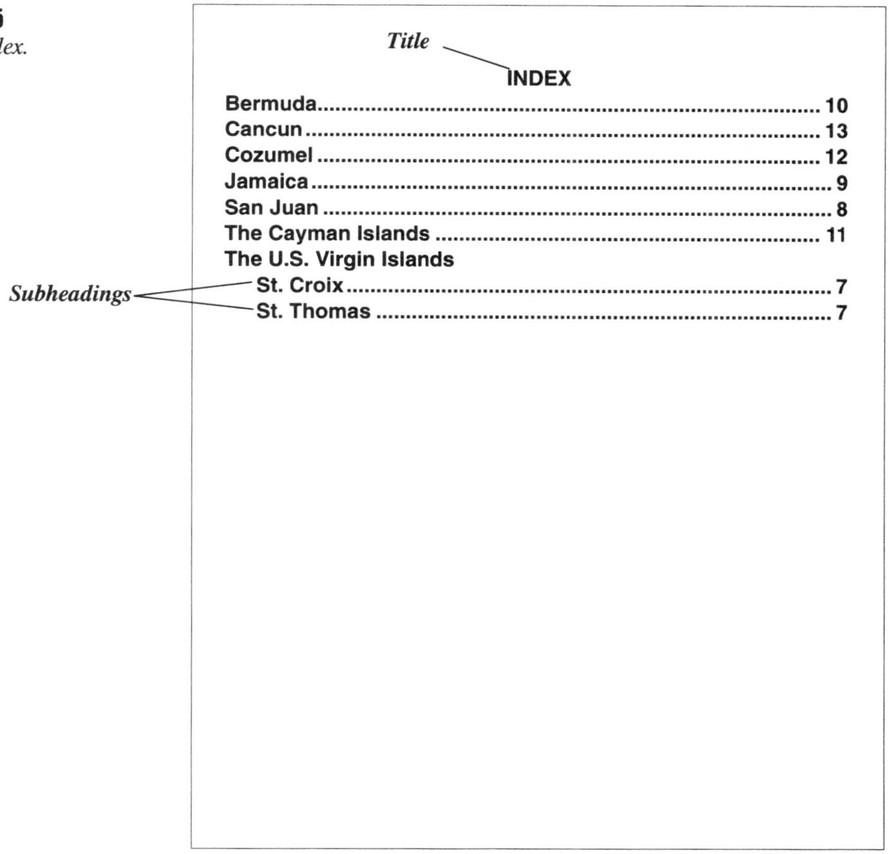

FIGURE 6–15
A sample index.

shows an index created with several of the options discussed in the following sections.

Defining Index Options

The following table describes the options available when you're defining an index.

OPTION	DESCRIPTION
Position	Specifies where the page number is displayed in relation to the text in the index. The Preview box in the middle of the dialog box shows an example of the selected option.
Page Numbering	Specifies whether the page-numbering format in the index uses the document format or a user-defined format.
Use Dash to Show Consecutive Pages	By default, if an index entry is found on multiple pages, WordPerfect lists the page numbers as a span, such as 4–8. If you want each page number listed individually, deselect this option.
Current Style	Enables you to select another style or edit the style used for the headings and subheadings in an index. If you want all headings to be bolded, for example, you can edit the Heading: Index1 style.
Concordance File	You can further automate the task of defining an index by using a *concordance file,* which is a list of all the words or phrases you want to include in the index. When you define a concordance file, WordPerfect automatically finds the occurrences of these words within your document. When you create a concordance file, each word or phrase must be on its own line and should not contain any spacing codes; the words or phrases must also appear exactly as they appear in the document. If you list *cruise,* WordPerfect finds only that form of the word (it does not find *cruises* or *cruise ship,* for example). If you include in your concordance file a word that is not in your document, WordPerfect does not list the word in the index. You can also mark words and phrases manually when you are using a concordance file.

Using Subheadings

Along with the index headings, you can also include subheadings. In Figure 6–15, *St. Croix* and *St. Thomas* are subheadings of *The U.S. Virgin Islands.*

To create a subheading:

1. Select the heading you want to use with the subheading in the heading text box. In the preceding example, it is *The U.S. Virgin Islands.*
2. Specify the subheading in the Subheading text box and choose Mark.

HOW DO I... Specify Formatting Codes for All Documents?

To help you organize and more effectively create documents, you can insert formatting codes in the Initial Codes Style. The Initial Codes Style is useful for inserting codes you always want in all documents. If you always create documents with half-inch top and bottom margins, for example, you can insert this code in the Initial Codes Style one time and then not have to insert it in each document individually. Any formatting features that always deviate from the WordPerfect default should be inserted in the Initial Codes Style.

Steps

➠To insert codes in the Initial Codes Style:

1. Choose Layout➢Document➢Initial Codes Style. The Styles Editor dialog box is displayed for the Initial Style, as shown in Figure 6–16.
2. Insert at the top of the dialog box the codes you want to include in all new documents from the menu bar. The Contents box uses a Reveal Codes-style window to display information.
3. Select Use as Default if you want to copy the Document Initial Style to the default template.

HINT

If you do not select this option, the codes affect only the current document.

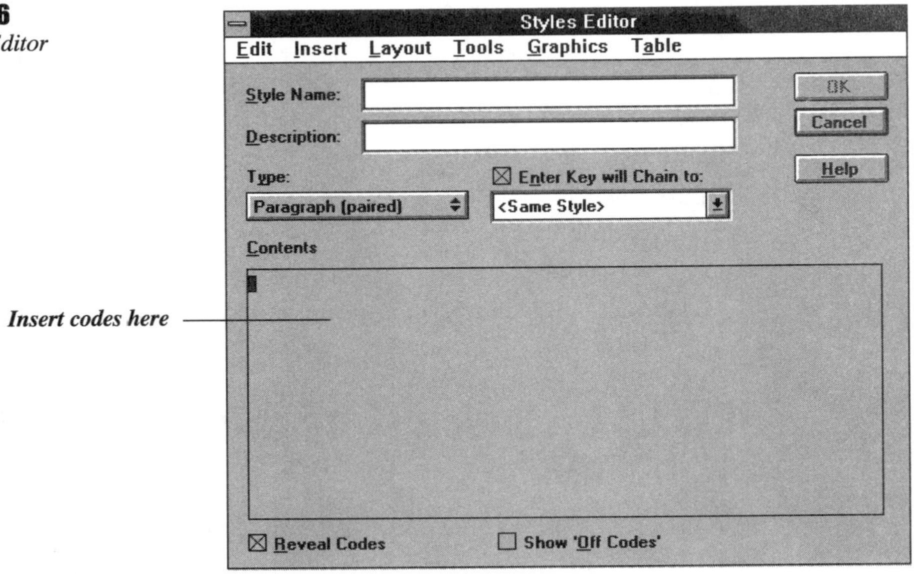

FIGURE 6–16
The Styles Editor dialog box.

4. Choose OK when you have entered all the codes.

Tell Me More

You can insert all types of formatting codes in the Initial Codes Style. For example, you can insert Paper Size ➢ Type definitions, margins, page numbering, and justification settings. Although you can insert codes directly in your current document, placing the codes in the Initial Codes Style inserts them all in one place for ease of editing and organization.

When you insert codes in Initial Codes Style, they are enclosed in the [Open Style:Initial Style] code at the top of the document. Having the codes enclosed in this way prevents them from being deleted accidentally. When you highlight the code, you can see all the codes, as shown here:

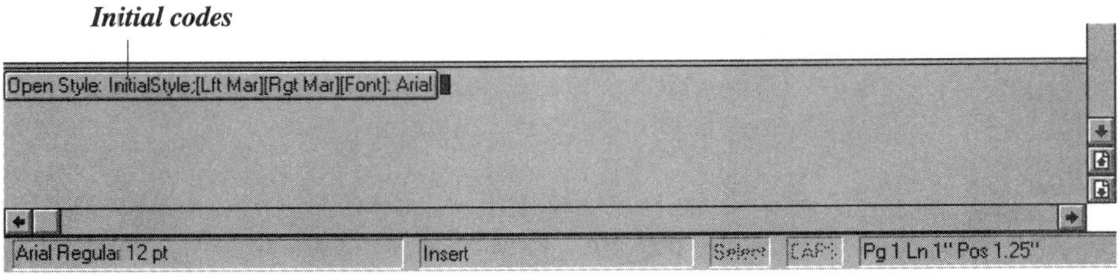

NOTE

When you insert codes in the Initial Codes Style and then insert conflicting codes in the document, the codes in the document take precedence.

You can also enter text in the Initial Codes Style. If you are required to have the author and the creation date listed at the top of all your documents, for example, you can insert that information in the Initial Codes Style. If you enter text in the Initial Codes Style, however, the only way to delete it from a document is to delete it from the Styles Editor dialog box; you cannot edit it from the document window.

HOW DO I... Automatically Insert the Filename in a Document?

WordPerfect lets you automatically insert the filename or the path and the filename in a document. Whenever you change the name of the file, WordPerfect automatically updates it in your document. Inserting the filename in your document helps you easily identify which file you are reading when you print documents.

Steps

➡ **To insert a filename or path and filename:**

1. Move your insertion point to the location where you want to insert the filename of the current document.
2. Choose Insert ➢ Other ➢ Filename or Path and Filename.
3. Choose OK and Close to return to the document window.

HINT

WordPerfect has a predefined macro called FILESTMP.WCM that automatically inserts the filename of a document into a header or footer. For information on this and other predefined macros, see Chapter 11, "Automating Tasks and Optimizing WordPerfect."

Tell Me More

You can insert a filename in a header or footer so that when the document prints, the filename is automatically included on every page with the header. Figure 6–17 displays a document containing the path and filename.

FIGURE 6–17
The Filename option used in a document.

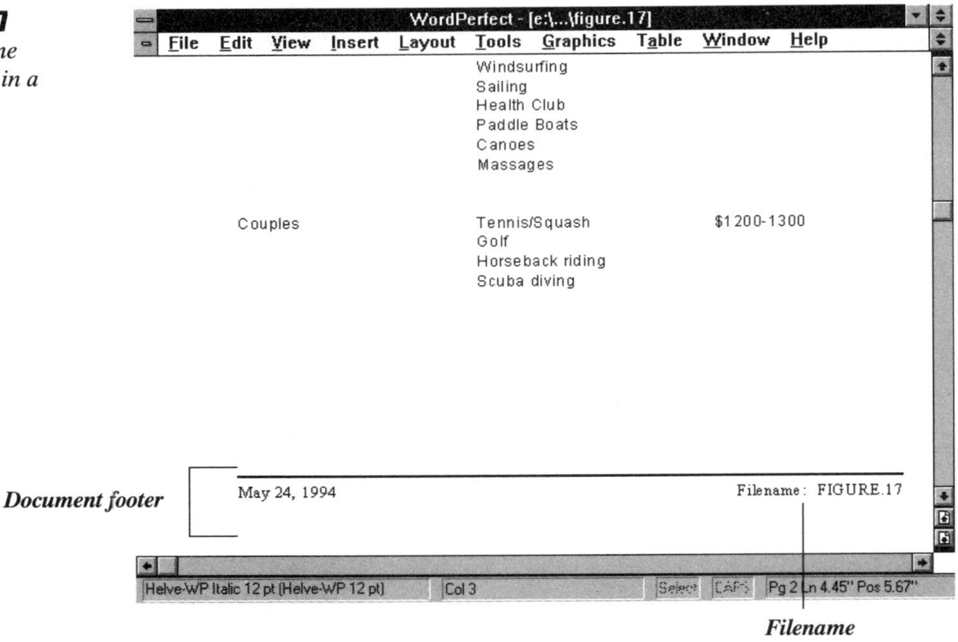

HOW DO I... Create Labels?

WordPerfect makes creating labels simple and fast. You select the type of label you are using, enter the information you want on the label, and then print the labels. WordPerfect provides more than 100 predefined label formats from which to choose, such as Avery 4022 address labels. You can also create your own label definitions.

Steps

➡To create labels:

1. Choose Layout➢Labels. The Labels dialog box is displayed, as shown in Figure 6–18.
2. Select the type of label definitions you want to display: Laser, Tractor-Fed, or Both.
3. Highlight the type of label you are using and choose Select.

HINT

The Preview box in the lower left corner of the dialog box displays a sample of the labels, and the Labels Details box displays information about the label.

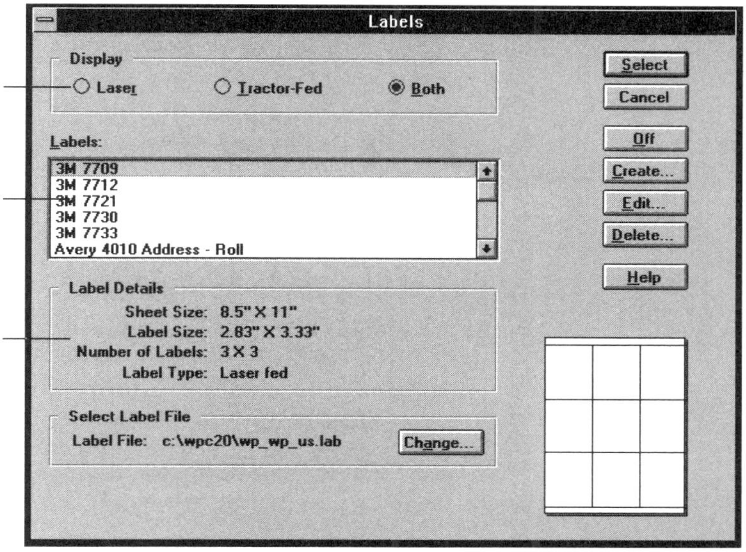

FIGURE 6–18
The Labels dialog box.

4. Type the information you want printed on the label and press Ctrl + Enter to move to the next label.
5. Repeat step 4 until you have entered all the information for all the labels.
6. Print or save the file.

NOTE **If you want to turn off the labels feature in a document, choose Layout ➢ Labels and then choose Off.**

Tell Me More

When you create labels, each label is considered a separate page on the document window and is displayed, as shown in Figure 6–19. To move through your labels, press Alt + Pg Dn to move to the next label or Alt + Pg Up to move to the previous label *or* just click in the label you want.

HINT **If you want to view the labels as normal pages in a document (one page preceding another page), you can choose View ➢ Draft.**

FIGURE 6–19
Labels in a document window.

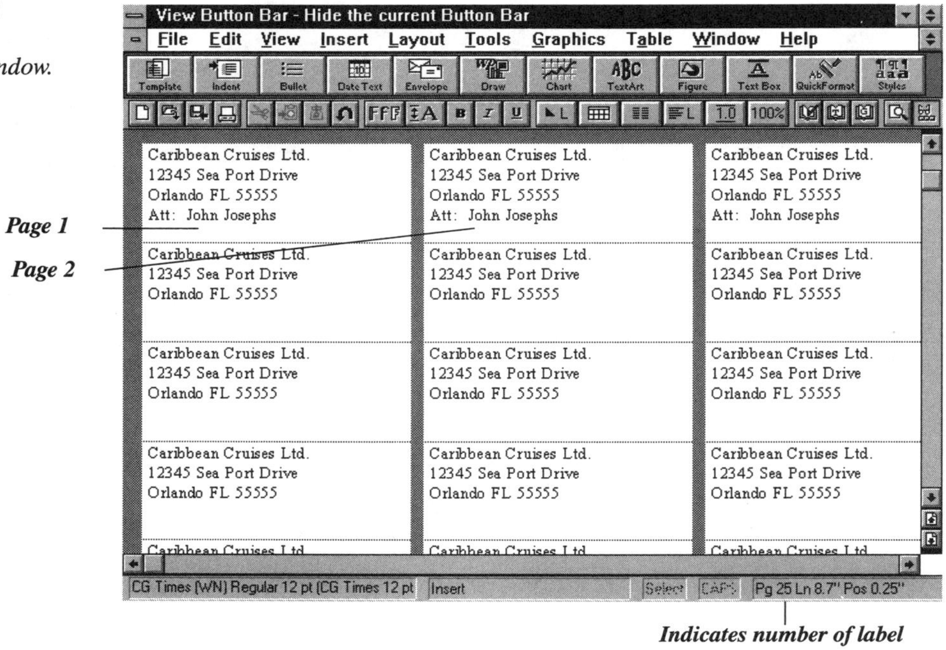

Using Label Files

All the WordPerfect predefined label definitions are contained in the file WP_WP_US.LAB. By default, this label file is displayed in the Labels dialog box. If you intend to create several of your own label definitions, you may want to create your own label file so that you can easily locate your custom definitions. If you put them in their own file, you can easily copy label files from other WordPerfect users.

HINT

It is a good idea to name the file with a .LAB extension so that you can easily identify the file.

Creating and Editing Label Definitions

If WordPerfect does not have a definition for the type of label you are using or if you need to edit one of the definitions, you can do so with the following steps:

HINT

Before creating a label definition from scratch, select a definition similar to the one you are using. You can use the similar definition as a pattern and make modifications. Also, in many cases, you can use one of the existing definitions even if you have a different brand of labels.

1. Choose Layout ➢ Labels.
2. Choose Create or Edit.
3. Enter or edit the descriptions for the label definition.
4. Specify the Label Size by entering the width and height of the individual labels.
5. Specify the Top Edge measurement. This measurement is the amount of space (if any) between the top edge of the page and the top of the first left label. Also specify the Left Edge measurement, which is the amount of space (if any) between the left edge of the paper and the left side of the first label.
6. Specify the number of Labels Per Page by entering the number of columns and rows of labels.
7. Specify the Distance Between Labels by entering the amount of space (if any) between the columns and rows of labels.
8. Specify the Label Margins by entering the margins you want for each individual label.
9. Specify the Label Type: Laser, Tractor-Fed, or Both.
10. Choose OK and Select to select the new definition and return to the document window.

Although this may seem like a great deal of information to enter, most of it should be readily available on your label packaging.

Printing Individual Labels

Because each label is considered a separate page, you can print individual labels.

To print a single label:

1. Create the label and fill in the necessary information as outlined in the preceding steps.
2. Choose File ➢ Print.
3. Select Multiple Pages and then choose Print.

4. From the Multiple Pages dialog box, enter the page number of the label you want to print. If there are several labels, insert a comma after each page number (2,6, for example).
5. Choose Print.

HOW DO I... Create a List?

The List feature in WordPerfect lets you mark items in your document that you want to include in a separate list. You can create a separate list, for example, for figures, charts, tables, and illustrations in a document. When you create a list, you must define the list, mark the entries you want included in the list, and then generate the list. You can also use the List feature to have WordPerfect automatically generate a list of captions from a specified graphics type.

Steps

➠To define a list:

1. Choose Tools➢List. The List Feature Bar is displayed at the top of the document window.
2. Choose Define and then choose Create. The Create List dialog box is displayed, as shown in Figure 6–20.
3. Enter the name of the list, such as **Figures**.

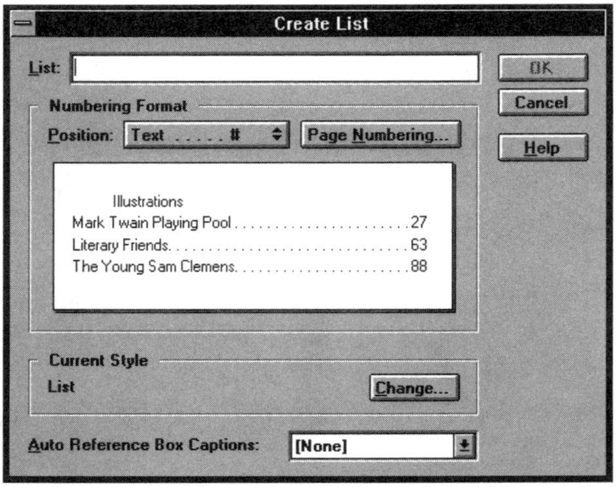

FIGURE 6–20
The Create List dialog box.

4. Choose a Numbering Format by selecting a Position and specifying the Page Numbering Format. The Preview box in the middle of the dialog box displays a sample of the List.
5. Choose OK and Close to return to the document window.

➡ **To mark the entries:**

1. Verify that the correct list name is displayed in the List text box.
2. Select the word or phrase you want to include in the list.
3. Choose Mark from the List Feature Bar.
4. Repeat steps 2 and 3 until you have marked all words and phrases you want to include in the list.

➡ **To insert and generate the list:**

1. Move your insertion point to the location where you want the list. If you want the list on a new page, press Ctrl+Enter and insert any text you want to precede the index, such as **Figure List**.
2. Choose Define from the Feature Bar.
3. Select the list you want to use and choose Insert from the Define List dialog box.
4. Choose Generate from the Feature Bar.
5. Choose OK. WordPerfect creates or updates the list.

NOTE

You have to generate your list every time you make any editing changes. Regenerating guarantees that all the entries are included in the list. When you generate a document, all features included in the document are generated (lists, indexes, cross-references, table of contents, and table of authorities). To regenerate, choose Tools➢Generate *or* press Ctrl+F9 and choose OK.

Tell Me More

If you want to include a title, such as Figure List, on the top of your list, make sure that you insert the title before you define the list in the document. Any text following the definition is deleted every time you generate the document.

In addition to selecting a numbering mode when you define a list, you can also change the page-number format and automatically create a list of graphics captions. WordPerfect uses the page-number format from the current document for the list. If you want to change the format to add text to the numbering or add a chapter or volume, for example, you can do so with the Page Numbering option. Choose Page Numbering from the Create or Edit List dialog box and specify whether the page-numbering format in the index uses the document format or a user-defined format.

Retrieving List Definitions

List Definitions apply to only the current document. You can retrieve a list from another document, however, for use with the current document. From the Define List dialog box, follow these steps:

1. Choose Retrieve and enter the filename of the document that contains the lists.
2. Choose OK and Close to return to the document window and begin marking the entries.

Creating a List for Graphics Captions

If you want a list that contains all the captions for your graphics boxes in a document, the List feature can automatically generate it for you. Move to the page where you want the list to appear and follow these steps:

1. Choose Tools➢List.
2. Choose Define from the Feature Bar.
3. Choose Create from the Define List dialog box.
4. Enter the name of the list, such as **Figures**.
5. Choose a Numbering Format by selecting a Position and specifying the Page Numbering Format.
6. Select the type of graphics box caption you want to list from the Auto Reference Box Captions drop-down list.
7. Choose OK and then choose Insert.
8. Choose Generate from the Feature Bar and then choose OK. WordPerfect creates or updates the list.

HOW DO I... Create an Outline?

The Outline feature is a powerful organizational tool to automate the process of grouping text together. With the Outline feature, you can

FIGURE 6–21
The Outline Feature Bar and the first level of outline.

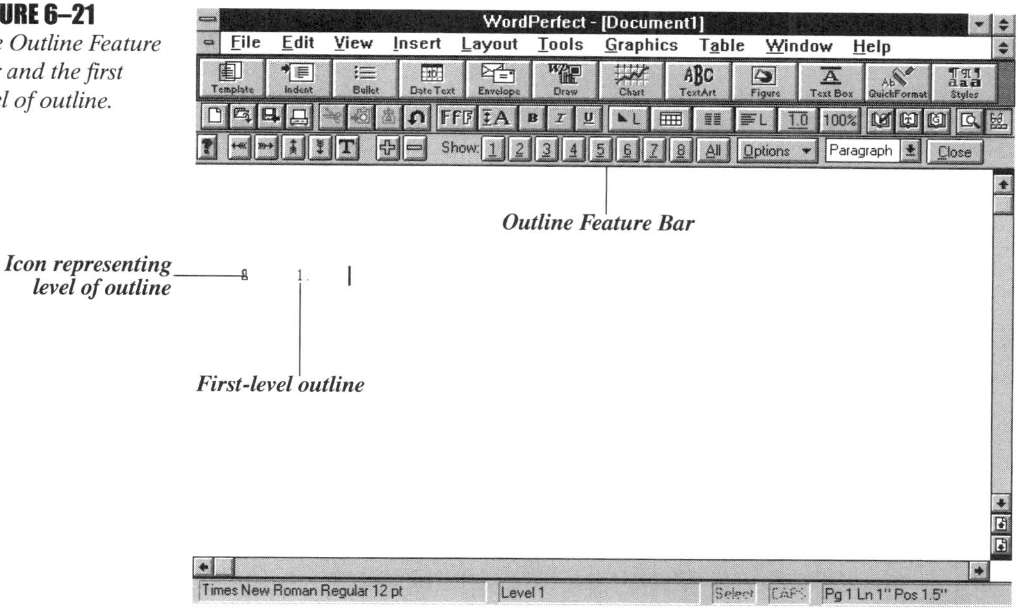

organize your text by choosing from several predefined outline styles or creating different outline styles. When you use Outline, WordPerfect automatically numbers items for you. Outline also automatically adjusts the numbers if you add or delete items from the outline.

Steps

➡**To organize text in an outline format:**

1. Place the insertion point where you want the outline to begin.
2. Choose Tools➢Outline. The Outline Feature Bar is displayed at the top of the document window, as shown in Figure 6–21, and the first level of the outline is inserted.
3. From the drop-down list box that displays "Paragraph," select the style of the outline you want to use.
4. Type the text you want in the first level and press Enter. The Outline levels and text are shown here:

5. Continue inserting the text in the outline. Press Tab to move to the next outline level or press Shift+Tab to move to the preceding outline level.
6. To turn off Outline, choose Options from the Outline Feature Bar and then select End Outline.
7. Choose Close to close the Feature Bar.

Tell Me More

WordPerfect inserts icons in the document window that represent the level of the outline. A number represents the level in the outline. If you insert text that is not part of an outline level, a **T** is displayed to indicate that the line is text and not an outline level. These icons are displayed only in the document window—they do not print. If you do not want the icons to be displayed, choose Options and deselect Show Level Icons from the Outline Feature Bar.

HINT

Clicking on an outline level icon selects all the text in the level. This capability is helpful if you want to cut, copy, or paste information within an outline.

Inserting Text in an Outline

When the Outline feature is turned on, you can easily toggle between outline mode and normal text-entry mode by choosing the icon on the Feature Bar. This option takes you out of Outline mode and enables you to type normal text. You can return to Outline mode by choosing the icon again.

NOTE

If you want to turn off the outline completely, choose Options➢End Outline.

Using Outline Families and the Outline Feature Bar

Outlines are grouped together in *outline families.* Each family consists of the main (parent) level and its accompanying text and various sublevels (children and grandchildren) and their accompanying text. If you create an outline by using the Outline definition I. A. 1. a. (1) (a)…, for example, the *I* is considered the parent, *A* the child, *1* the grandchild, and so on. The second family includes *II* as the parent, *A* as the child, and so on. Each level is considered a family.

The Outline Feature Bar, shown here, provides several options for manipulating the text in the outline:

The following table describes each option:

OPTION	DESCRIPTION
←, →	Change text to next or previous outline level; you can also press Tab or Shift+Tab
↑, ↓	Move selected items or families up or down one level
T	Toggles selected text between body text and outline levels
+	Shows all levels of current outline family
–	Conceals sublevels of a family for greater ease in editing a large outline
1–8	Shows all levels through the level you select here
All	Shows all text in outline (this is default selection)

Renumbering Outlines

You can renumber your outline at any level by setting a number in the outline. Suppose that you create a document which is split into specific sections and that it includes an outline in each section. You want the outlines to be numbered consecutively throughout the document even though you are turning the Outline feature on and off. To renumber the second outline, place the insertion point where you want to begin renumbering and follow these steps:

1. Choose Options from the Outline Feature Bar.
2. Choose Set Number and enter the number you want to begin the outline with (in the preceding example, you enter 2).

The current outline number is replaced with the new number, and the outline is renumbered from that point forward.

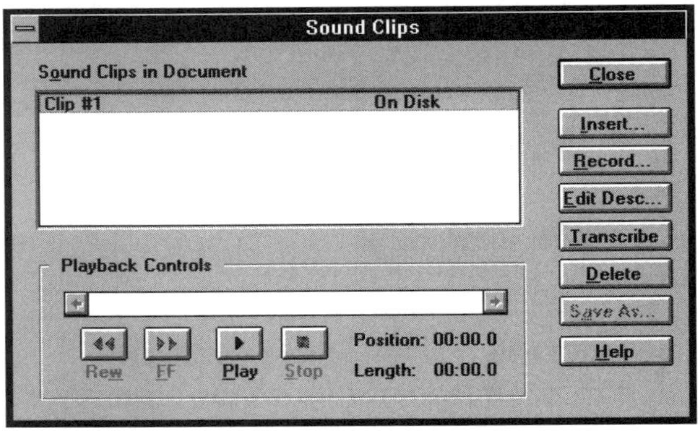

FIGURE 6–22
The Sound Clips dialog box.

HOW DO I... Include Sound in My Document?

WordPerfect lets you include sound in your documents, by using the Sound Clip feature. If you have a sound card in your computer and a sound driver loaded on your hard disk, you can attach voice recordings, music, and sound effects to your document.

Steps

➨To add a sound clip to a document:

1. Choose Insert➢Sound. The Sound Clips dialog box is displayed, as shown in Figure 6–22.
2. Choose Insert and specify the filename of the sound clip.
3. If you want, specify a new Name for the sound clip.
4. Select Link to File on Disk to create a link to the sound file or select Store in Document to save the sound file with the document.
5. Choose OK. A sound icon is inserted in your document, as shown here:

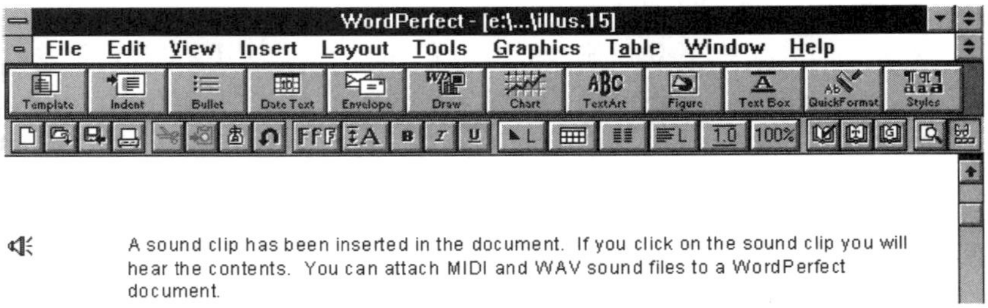

➡**To play an attached sound clip:**

1. Double-click the sound icon *or* choose Insert➢Sound, select the sound clip you want to listen to, and choose Play.

NOTE

The Playback Controls enable you to rewind, fast forward, and stop the sound clip. Your position in the sound clip (how much you have played) in addition to the total length of the clip are displayed in the Playback Controls.

Tell Me More

Before you can use sound in a document, you must first purchase and install a sound card. In addition, you may have to define the sound driver by using the Windows Control Panel. WordPerfect uses the Sound setup information specified in Windows. For specific information about defining a sound driver in Windows, see your Windows manual.

The following sections explain how to record sound clips and transcribe using sound clips.

Recording a Sound Clip

➡**To record a sound clip and attach it to your document:**

1. Choose Insert➢Sound.
2. Choose Record. WordPerfect uses the Windows Sound Recorder.
3. Record the sound. If you need information about recording sound, see your Windows manual.
4. Choose Close. You can then include the recording in your document by choosing Insert from the Sound Clips dialog box.

Transcribing with Sound Clips

Not only is sound beneficial for attaching musical files and sound clips, but also you can attach voice recordings to use as dictation. If someone has sent you a memo, for example, asking you to type a letter from the recording attached to the memo, you can do so by placing your insertion point just before the attached recording and choose the command Insert➢Sound➢Transcribe.

You can toggle between Play and Stop by choosing the appropriate icons. You can repeat the section of a recording you have listened to by choosing Replay. You can also rewind and fast forward the recording. The most beneficial feature of this dialog box is that you can type while the recording is being played.

HOW DO I. . . Divide a Page into Smaller Sections?

The Subdivide Page feature lets you divide your page into smaller sections to create programs, booklets, tickets, and so on. Subdivide Page lets you divide one page into several smaller sections by specifying how many rows and columns you want on the page. Each section of the page is called a *logical page.* Figure 6–23 shows the inside of a program created with the Subdivide feature.

Steps

➠To subdivide a page:

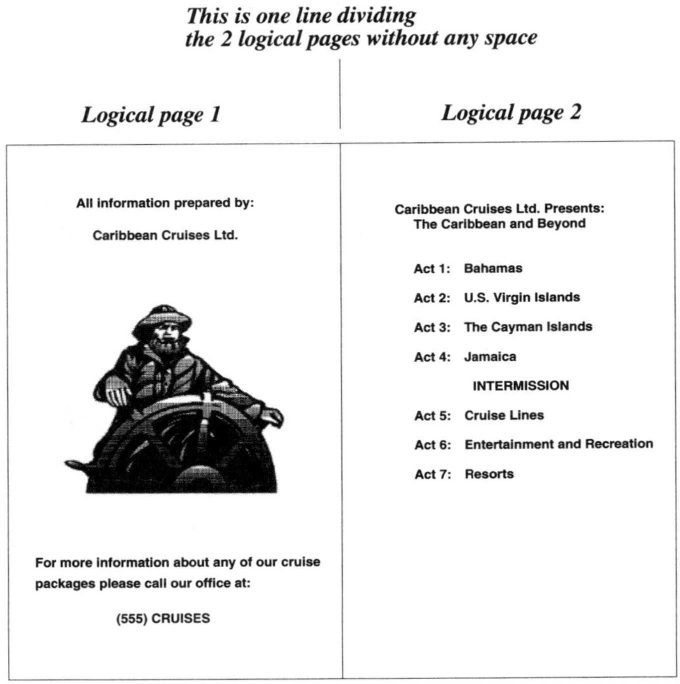

FIGURE 6–23
The inside of a program created with the Subdivide feature.

1. Choose Layout ➢ Page ➢ Subdivide Page. The Subdivide Page dialog box is displayed, as shown here:

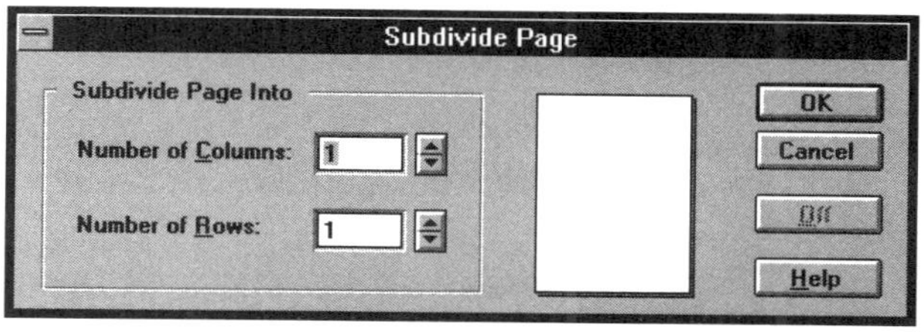

2. Enter the number of rows and columns you want to use to divide your page. The Preview box displays a sample of the page.
3. Choose OK to return to the document window.

Tell Me More

When you're using Subdivide Page, the sections of the page are displayed as they are when they are printed. WordPerfect views each logical page as a physical page for such features as page numbering, margins, and headers and footers. If you include headers, footers, or page numbers in a document with subdivided pages, they are printed on each logical page.

To move to a logical page, you can click the mouse anywhere on the page to which you want to move. You can also use the same keystrokes as you would use to move to a new physical page:

KEYSTROKE	ACTION
Alt + Pg Up	Moves to preceding page
Alt + Pg Dn	Moves to next page
Ctrl + Enter	Begins a new page
Ctrl + G	Moves to a specified page

You can also use the Print as Booklet feature with Subdivide Page if you want to print a booklet. After specifying a 1×2 or 2×1 subdivided page, specifying duplex printing if your printer supports it

(Layout➢Page➢Binding-Duplex), and entering the appropriate text, follow these steps:

1. Choose File➢Print *or* press F5.
2. Choose Options.
3. Choose Booklet Printing
4. Choose OK and then choose Print.

NOTE

If you do not have a printer that supports duplex printing or you have not selected duplex printing, you have to manually reinsert the appropriate physical page in the printer so that it can print on the other side of the page.

HOW DO I... Create a Table of Authorities?

A *table of authorities* is a section of a legal document used to cite references. To create a table of authorities in WordPerfect, you have to decide how you want to categorize the authorities into sections and how many sections you want to have. Examples of different sections include Cases, Constitutional Provisions, Statutory Provisions, Regulatory Provisions, and Miscellaneous. After you have designed the table of authority, you have to mark the first occurrence of the authority and then all subsequent references in the document. You must do this for each authority. You then have to define the table. Finally, you must generate the table.

Steps

➡To mark the authorities or citations for the first time:

1. Choose Tools➢Table of Authorities. The Table of Authorities Feature Bar is displayed, as shown here:

2. Select the text of the authority within the document.
3. Choose Create Full Form from the Feature Bar.
4. Specify a Section Name and enter the name of the section in which you want to insert the citations, such as **Cases**.
5. Specify the Short Form and enter the Short Form name. The selected text appears in the Short Form entry box. The Short

Form name is used when you mark several occurrences of the same citation. See the following set of steps for information about using the Short Form.

6. Choose OK.
7. The short form appears in the editing window. Using the Short Form text as a guide, create the Full Form. Edit the text so that it's exactly how you want it to appear in the table, including any formatting changes (such as bold).
8. Choose Close from the Feature Bar.

➡To mark subsequent occurrences of the same authority:

1. Position the insertion point at the next location of the authority.
2. If necessary, select the correct Short Form from the Short From drop-down list.
3. Choose Mark from the Feature Bar.
4. Repeat steps 1 through 3 for each authority.

NOTE

You can quickly move to the next occurrence of an authority by using the Find feature (Edit➢Find *or* F2).

➡To define the table of authorities:

1. Move your insertion point to the location where you want the table of authorities. If you want the table of authorities on a new page, press Ctrl+Enter and insert any text for the first heading, such as **Cases**, and then press Enter to add some space.
2. Choose Tools➢Table of Authorities to display the Table of Authorities Feature Bar.
3. Choose Define. The Define Table of Authorities dialog box is displayed, as shown in Figure 6–24.
4. Highlight the name of the section and choose Insert.
5. Repeat steps 3 and 4 for each section.
6. Choose Generate from the Feature Bar. WordPerfect creates or updates the table of authorities.

NOTE

You have to generate your Table of Authorities every time you make any editing changes. Regenerating guarantees that the

FIGURE 6–24
The Define Table of Authorities dialog box.

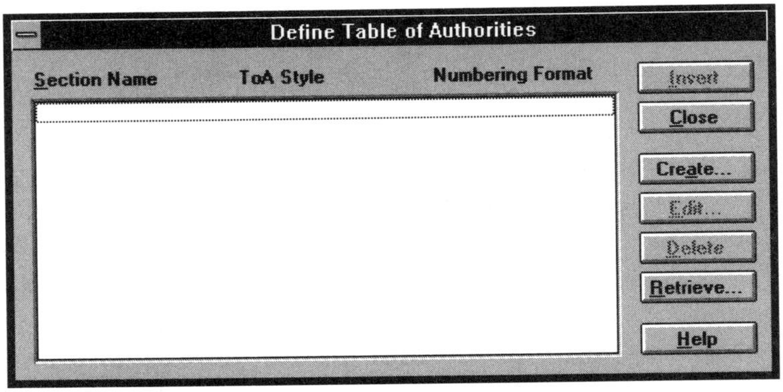

page numbers are correct. When you generate a document, all features included in the document are generated (lists, indexes, cross-references, table of contents, and table of authorities). To regenerate, choose Tools➢Generate *or* press Ctrl+F9 and choose OK.

Tell Me More

When you define a table of authorities section, you can customize several options for the sections within the table. You can specify the Numbering Format, specify whether you want to combine sequential page numbers, allow underlining, and edit the Table of Authority Style.

➨To customize Table of Authority options:

1. Choose Define from the Feature Bar. The Define Table of Authorities dialog box is displayed.
2. Highlight the section you want to modify and choose Edit.

NOTE

You can also create sections for the table from the Define Table of Authorities dialog box.

3. From the Position pop-up list, select the position of the page number.
4. Choose Page Numbering to modify the format of the page number. WordPerfect uses the page-number format from the current document for the table of authorities. If you want to change the format to add text to the numbering or add a

chapter or volume, you can use the Page Numbering option. For specific information about changing the Page Numbering option, see the section "HOW DO I... Automatically Number the Pages in a Document?" in Chapter 5.

5. Select Underlining Allowed if you want to maintain the underlining in the authority. By default, if the authority has any underlining, WordPerfect removes it when it creates the table.
6. Deselect Use Dash to Show Consecutive Pages if you want each occurrence of an authority to have its own page number. By default, if an authority appears on multiple pages, the page numbering is combined, such as 5 through 7.

HINT **If you want to save your selections for steps 5 and 6 and use them every time you create a Table of Authorities, choose Use as Default.**

7. Choose Change if you want to change the way the text is formatted for the table of authorities. You may want to edit or create your own styles for a table of authorities.
8. Choose OK to return to the document window.

HOW DO I. . . Create a Table of Contents?

A table of contents helps readers easily locate information in a document so that they do not have to read an entire document to find specific information. A table of contents can be used with books, documentation, brochures, or any type of document that contains several sections of information. The Table of Contents feature greatly automates the task of creating a table of contents.

Three basic steps are involved in creating a Table of Contents: Define the table of contents, mark the entries you want included in it, and then generate it.

Steps

➡ To define a table of contents:

1. Move your insertion point to the location where you want the table of contents. If you want the table of contents on a new

page, press Ctrl+Enter and insert any text you want to precede the table of contents, such as the title **Table of Contents**.

2. Choose Tools➢Table of Contents. The Table of Contents Feature Bar is displayed, as shown here:

3. Specify the Number of Levels you will have in your table of contents. You can have as many as five levels.
4. Select from the pop-up list the Numbering Format you want for each level.
5. Select Display Last Level in Wrapped Format if you do not want to indent the last level in the table of contents.
6. Choose OK.

➡To mark entries you want to include in the table of contents:

1. Select the word or phrase you want to include in the table of contents.
2. Click the appropriate Mark button on the Feature Bar. To Mark the first level in a table of contents, for example, click on Mark 1.
3. Repeat steps 1 and 2 until you have marked all words and phrases you want to include in the table of contents.

➡To generate the table of contents:

1. Choose Generate from the Feature Bar.
2. Choose OK. WordPerfect creates or updates the table of contents.
3. Choose Close to close the Feature Bar.

NOTE

You have to generate your table of contents every time you make any editing changes. Regenerating guarantees that the page numbers are correct. When you generate a document, all features included in the document are generated (lists, indexes, cross-references, table of contents, and table of authorities). To regenerate, choose Tools➢Generate *or* press Ctrl+F9 and choose OK.

FIGURE 6–25
A sample table of contents.

Bolded Level 1

Level 2

Table of Contents

The Bahamas	**2**
Nassau	2
Exclusive Salt Cay	2
The Private Abacos Out Island	2
The U.S. Virgin Islands	**3**
St. Thomas	3
St. Croix	3
San Juan	**4**
Jamaica	**5**
Bermuda	**6**
The Cayman Islands	**7**
Cozumel	**8**
Cancun	**9**

Tell Me More

If you want to include a title, such as "Table of Contents," on the top of your table of contents, make sure that you insert the title before the codes for the table of contents. Any text following the definition is deleted every time you generate the document.

When you define a table of contents, you can customize several options to meet your specific needs. Figure 6–25 displays a table of contents with several of the options explained in this section.

In addition to selecting the number of levels and the page-number position within a table of contents, you can also edit the table of contents style and define a page-number format.

The Table of Contents styles define the way the text in each level appears. You may want to edit or create your own styles for a table of contents. If you want all first-level headings in the table of contents bolded, for example, you can add a bold code to that style rather than manually bold the entries after the table of contents is generated.

➠To change the style of a Table of Contents level:

1. Choose Define from the Table of Contents Feature Bar.
2. Choose Styles.
3. Highlight the level of the style you want to edit and choose Edit.
4. Make the necessary changes in the Contents box.
5. Choose OK until you return to the document window.

NOTE

You can also change which style is connected to which Table of Contents level. This way, you can define and name your own styles and then attach them to the appropriate Table of Contents levels.

WordPerfect uses the page-number format from the current document for the table of contents. If you want to change the format to add text to the numbering or add a chapter or volume, you can use the Page Numbering option. Choose Page Numbering from the Define Table of Contents dialog box. Select User-Defined Page Number Format and make the changes you want. For specific information about changing the page-number format, see the section "HOW DO I... Automatically Number the Pages in a Document?" in Chapter 5, "Creating Documents: The Basics."

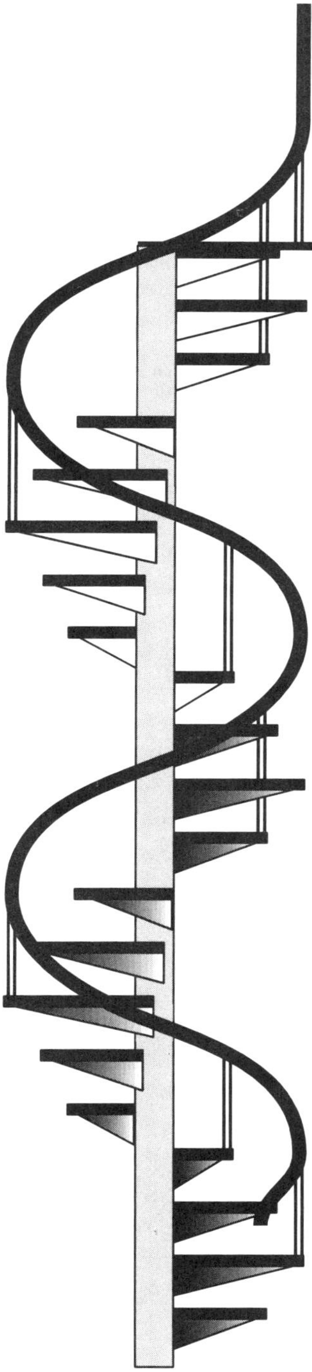

Chapter 7

Printing the Document

One of the most important features to understand in WordPerfect is its capability to print your documents. This chapter answers questions about the following printing features:

- Choosing between Windows and WordPerfect print drivers
- Selecting and adding a printer
- Printing a document
- Previewing a document before printing it
- Changing the print quality
- Viewing the status of print jobs
- Canceling a print job
- Printing multiple copies

- Editing printer setup information
- Printing in color
- Printing on both sides of a page
- Selecting a font cartridge
- Installing additional fonts
- Troubleshooting printer problems

HOW DO I... Choose Between Windows and WordPerfect Print Drivers?

Special software files called *printer drivers* enable WordPerfect to communicate with your printer. Because each printer is different, WordPerfect for Windows includes printer drivers for more than 900 printer models. These drivers include ones for standard laser printers, PostScript printers, dot-matrix and daisywheel printers, and some plotter output devices. Complete font support is included to make the best use of your printer's capabilities. Color printing is also supported for printers with color capabilities.

Most software programs that run under Microsoft Windows use the printer drivers supplied with the Windows program. WordPerfect, however, lets you use the Windows printer drivers or its own WordPerfect printer drivers. If you prefer to work with the Microsoft Windows printer drivers, you can easily change and edit the printer driver from within the WordPerfect program.

If you will share your documents with users who are using a different platform of WordPerfect, such as WordPerfect 6 for DOS, you will want to use the WordPerfect print drivers so that the documents retain their formatting codes when they're retrieved on the other platform.

Because of the advantages of both types of printer drivers, WordPerfect lets you select either driver type at any time while you are working with the program. WordPerfect automatically displays both Windows drivers and WordPerfect drivers. An icon is displayed to the left of each printer name in the Select Printer dialog box, to designate whether the driver is WordPerfect or Windows (see Figure 7–1). This chapter deals mainly with the capabilities of the WordPerfect print drivers.

HOW DO I. . . Select or Add a Printer?

When you install WordPerfect, you are automatically prompted to select one or more printers. If you purchase a new printer or will use a different printer, you can add a printer at any time by using the WPWin Setup program. You can define as many printer definitions as you need.

Steps

➠**To verify or select a new printer:**

1. Choose File ➢ Print *or* press F5. The Print dialog box is displayed, as shown in Figure 7–2.
2. Verify that the correct printer is displayed under Current Printer at the top of the screen. If the correct printer is not displayed, continue with step 3.
3. Choose Select. The Select Printer dialog box is displayed (refer to Figure 7–1).
4. Highlight the printer you want to use and choose Select. If the printer is not displayed on the list, continue with step 5.
5. Choose Add Printer and then select WordPerfect or Windows, depending on which printer drivers you want to use. If

FIGURE 7–1
The Select Printer dialog box.

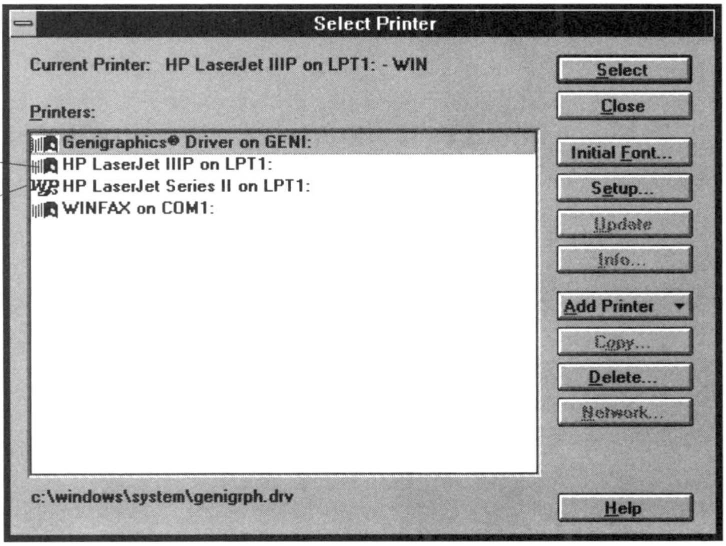

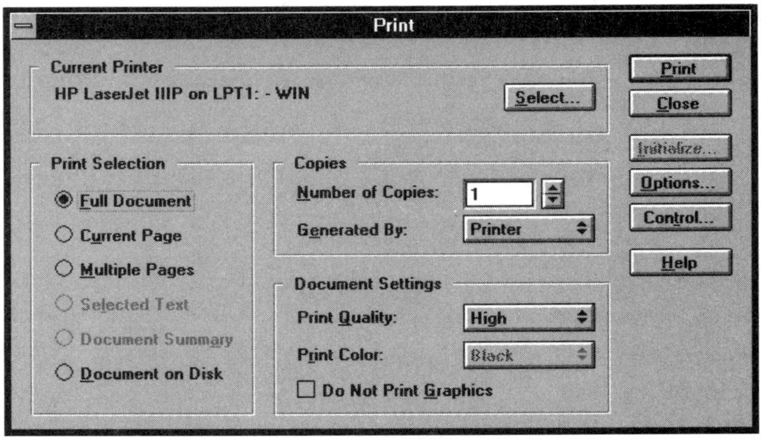

FIGURE 7–2
The Print dialog box.

you select Windows, follow the instructions in your Windows manual for selecting printers. If you choose WordPerfect, the Add Printer dialog box is displayed.

6. Select Additional Printers (*.all) if you want to see all available printer definitions you have installed. Or select Printer Files (*.prs) to see only the printer drivers you have installed.
7. Click on the printer (or printers) you want to add. If you want to view information about a printer, such as dip switch settings, known problems, and color printing options, choose Info.

NOTE

If your printer does not appear on the Printers list, verify that the directory listed for Printer File Directory is correct. If the directory is correct, you use the WPWin Setup program to add the printer.

8. Choose OK.
9. Choose Select to select the new definition as the current printer and return to the Print dialog box.

➡To add a new printer by using the WPWin Setup program:

1. Exit from WordPerfect.
2. From the WPWin 6.0 program group, double-click the WPWin 6.0 Setup icon.
3. Choose Options.

4. Choose Printers. The Select Printer Directory dialog box is displayed.
5. Specify the drive from which you are installing the printer files and where you want to install the printer files and choose OK. By default, printer files are installed in the C:\WPC20 directory. Insert the appropriate disk when you are prompted.
6. Double-click the printer (or printers) you want to install and choose OK. You can install as many printers as you want. You may be prompted to insert a new disk that contains the correct printer information.
7. Choose OK to return to the WordPerfect program group and then start WordPerfect.

Tell Me More

WordPerfect provides hundreds of printer definitions from which to choose. Definitions for many older printers and less popular printers are not available on the WordPerfect shipping disks. If the name appears dimmed on the list of available printers, you must order the printer disk from WordPerfect. You can reach WordPerfect's Customer Order Department at (800) 321-4566.

It is possible that a definition for your printer is not listed and therefore is not supported by WordPerfect. If your printer is not listed, WordPerfect suggests the following emulations:

PRINTER TYPE	POSSIBLE EMULATIONS
Dot matrix	Standard printer, IBM ProPrinter, IBM PC Graphics printer, Epson FX
Daisywheel	Standard typewriter, Diablo 630
Laser printer	HP Laser Jet III
PostScript printer	Apple LaserWriter

When you are using printer emulations, you may not have access to all your printer's capabilities.

If you are having difficulties printing, one of the first things you should do is verify that you have selected the correct printer.

HOW DO I. . . Print a Document?

One of the most important tasks in WordPerfect is printing your documents. WordPerfect offers several options for printing documents. You can print the full document displayed on-screen, a page in the document, a document on disk, specific pages in a document, or selected text.

Steps

➨To print all pages of the document currently on your screen:

1. Choose File➢Print *or* press F5. The Print dialog box is displayed.
2. Choose Print. WordPerfect returns you to the document screen.

➨To print only the page on which your insertion point is located:

1. Choose File➢Print *or* press F5.
2. Select Current Page.
3. Choose Print. WordPerfect returns you to the document screen.

➨To print specific pages in a document:

1. Choose File➢Print *or* press F5. The Print dialog box is displayed.
2. Select Multiple Pages and choose Print. The Multiple Pages dialog box is displayed, as shown in Figure 7–3.
3. Enter the pages you want to print separated by a comma in the Pages(s) text box. For information about the Print Multiple Pages options, see the following "Tell Me More" section.
4. Choose Print.

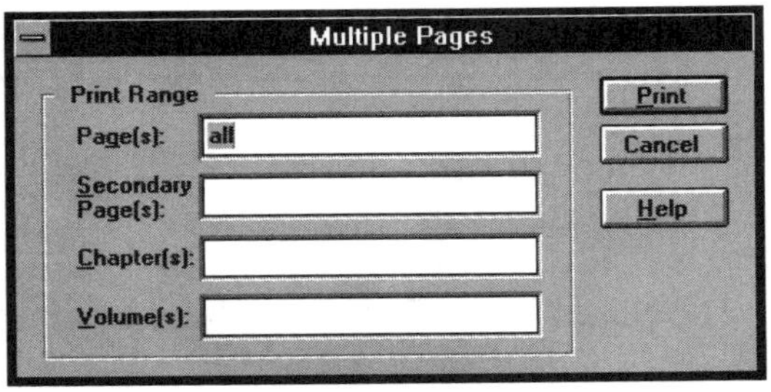

FIGURE 7–3
The Multiple Pages dialog box.

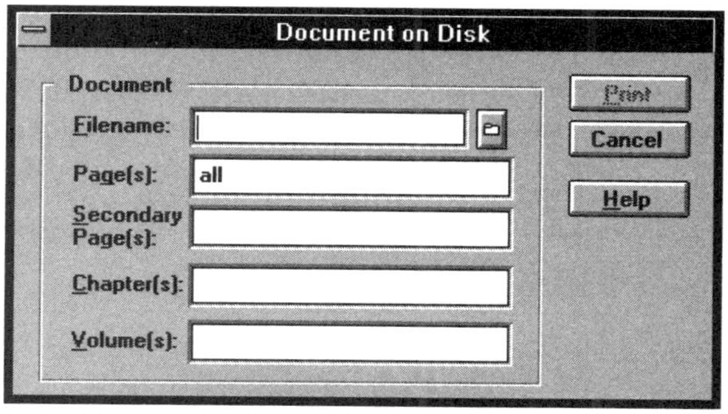

FIGURE 7–4
The Document on Disk dialog box.

➡ **To print selected text:**

1. Select the text you want to print.
2. Choose File ➢ Print *or* press F5. The Print dialog box is displayed.
3. Choose Print. WordPerfect returns you to the document screen.

➡ **To print a document saved on disk without retrieving it:**

1. Choose File ➢ Print *or* press F5.
2. Select Document on Disk and choose Print. The Document on Disk dialog box is displayed, as shown in Figure 7–4.
3. Enter the filename of the document, including the path (C:\DOCS\LETTER, for example).
4. To print all pages, choose Print. For information about the Print Multiple Pages options, see the following "Tell Me More" section.

You can also choose [icon] to open the Print dialog box.

Tell Me More

When you print the full document, WordPerfect prints the entire document that is on-screen from start to finish regardless of your insertion point location. When you print a page, WordPerfect prints only the page on which your insertion point is positioned.

The Document on Disk and Multiple Pages options give you precise control of which pages or section of a document you want to print. The following table describes each option on the Multiple Pages dialog box (refer to Figure 7–3):

OPTION	DESCRIPTION
Page(s)	Specifies the pages you want to print. To print a range of pages, enter the first page followed by a hyphen and then the last page, such as 4-8. To print from the beginning of the document to a specified page, enter a hyphen followed by the last page you want to print, such as -15. To print from a specified page to the end of the document, enter the first page you want to print followed by a hyphen, such as 5-. To print nonconsecutive pages, enter each page number followed by a comma, such as 1, 5, 8. Note: If you are specifying single pages, you must enter them in consecutive order; in the preceding example, you cannot enter 8, 5, 1, If you want to print several different ranges and pages, you can combine multiple techniques, such as 1, 4-6, 13.
Secondary Pages	If you have used the Page Numbering feature to create secondary pages, specifies the secondary pages to print.
Chapters	If you have used the Page Numbering feature to create chapters, specifies the chapters to print. WordPerfect prints only the pages in the specified chapters.
Volume	If you have used the Page Numbering feature to create volumes, specifies the volumes to print. WordPerfect prints only the pages in the specified volumes.

When you print selected text, WordPerfect prints the text at the exact location in which it appears on the page. If you select and print the last paragraph on a page, for example, the top portion of the printed page is blank and the text appears at the bottom of the page.

HINT

If you want selected text to print on the first line of a page, select the text, copy and paste it to another document window, and then print it.

HOW DO I. . . Preview a Document Before Printing?

The document window displays your text close to the way it will look when it is printed. By default, however, it does not display an entire page in the window so that you can see how the text will be positioned on the page. WordPerfect provides several Zoom options that enable you to display your document at different magnifications, such as Full Page, so that you can see the exact position of text and graphics in relation to the entire page. Other Zoom options enable you to magnify the entire page or sections of the page as well as select a specific section of your document and view it at a magnified level.

Steps

➡To view a document in Full Page mode:

1. With the document on-screen, choose View➢Zoom. The Zoom dialog box is displayed, as shown in Figure 7–5.
2. Select Full Page or any other Zoom option and choose OK.

POWER BAR

You can also choose the icon on the Power Bar to switch to a Full Page zoom. You can choose the 100% icon to display a pop-up list of Zoom options from which you can select. The percentage icon on the Power Bar displays your current Zoom percentage.

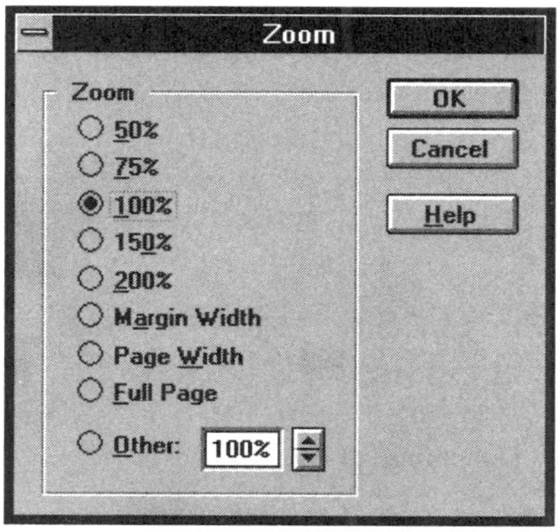

FIGURE 7–5
The Zoom dialog box.

Tell Me More

WordPerfect has several Zoom options that enable you to see different degrees of detail in your documents. The 100% Zoom option is the default display in the document window and is the actual size of the page. To give you an idea of the different magnifications, Figure 7–6 shows a document displayed with 50% zoom, and Figure 7–7 shows the same document displayed with 200% zoom.

If you want to see your document magnified at a level not listed in the Zoom dialog box, you can select the Other option and specify a percentage.

HOW DO I . . . Change the Print Quality?

WordPerfect gives you complete control over the quality of your printing. You can choose from high, medium, and draft qualities. Setting the Print Quality option to Draft may speed up the printing time for many dot-matrix printers.

Steps

➡ **To change the print quality:**

1. Choose File➢Print *or* press F5.
2. Select the quality you want from the Print Quality pop-up list.
3. Choose Print.

Tell Me More

Although you can change the print quality in WordPerfect, your printer must also have the capability to print in the selected quality. You should always set your printing quality in WordPerfect and not on your printer because WordPerfect uses the default settings on your printer and then sends the appropriate information to change the setting.

With most printers, when you change the quality of printing, you are changing the *resolution,* or the number of dots per inch on a page, of text and graphics. If you experience problems when you print on a laser printer a document that contains graphics, try changing the Print Quality setting. Sometimes a printer does not have enough memory to print the graphics in high quality; by selecting Medium or Draft, you may be able to print the document.

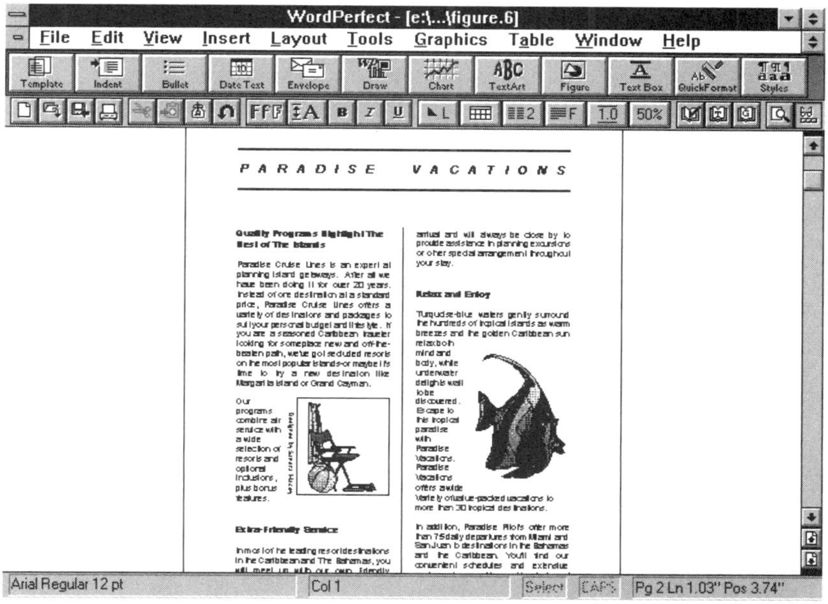

FIGURE 7–6
A document displayed using 50% zoom.

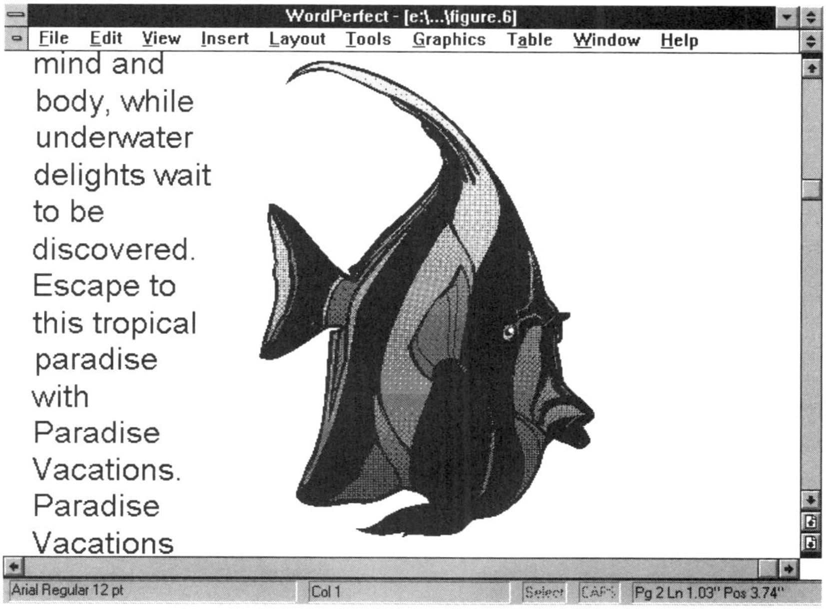

FIGURE 7–7
A document displayed using 200% zoom.

WordPerfect also offers the option of Do Not Print Graphics on the Print dialog box. This option lets you print just the text in a document. If you have a document that contains graphics, for example, and you want to edit just the text, printing just the text speeds up the printing of the document.

You can change the default settings for the Print Quality, Print Color, and Do Not Print Graphics options by choosing File➢Preferences, double-clicking the Print icon, and then specifying the default options you want WordPerfect to use for all documents you print.

HOW DO I... View the Status of Print Jobs?

The WP Print Job dialog box provides valuable information about the status of your print jobs. From the WordPerfect Print Job dialog box, you can see a great deal of useful information, such as which document is printing, which page is printing, and the percentage completed.

Steps

➨To view the status of print jobs:

1. After sending a document to the printer, choose File➢Print *or* press F5.
2. Choose Control.

Tell Me More

The WP Print dialog box does not display information after the print job has been passed to the Windows Print Manager; depending on the speed of your computer, therefore, you may not be able to open the WP Print dialog box before the job has been processed by WordPerfect. After the job is at the Print Manager, Windows displays any additional warning or error messages regarding the print job.

HOW DO I... Cancel a Print Job?

You can cancel print jobs from within WordPerfect's Print Job dialog box before it is sent to the Windows Print Manager. After the job is at the Print Manager, you can use the Print Manager to control the printing process.

Steps

➠To cancel a print job while you're in WordPerfect:

1. Choose File ➢ Print *or* press F5.
2. Choose Control Printer.
3. Choose Cancel Print Job.

Tell Me More

Sometimes it may not be possible to cancel a print job or you may be able to cancel only part of a job. If WordPerfect has already sent the information to the Print Manager, you cannot cancel it from within WordPerfect. If you want to cancel a job that is at the Print Manager, see your Windows manual for instructions. You know that the print job has been sent if it is not listed in the WordPerfect Print Job dialog box. The speed at which information is sent to the Print Manager and the amount of information sent depends on the speed of your computer and the memory of your printer.

HOW DO I... Print Multiple Copies?

You can print multiple copies of a document from WordPerfect. With the Number of Copies option, you can tell WordPerfect how many copies you want to print and whether you want WordPerfect, your printer, or the network to generate the copies.

Steps

➠To print multiple copies:

1. Choose File ➢ Print *or* press F5.
2. Specify the Number of Copies by entering a number or pressing the increment buttons to change the number of copies of each page you want.
3. If you want your printer rather than WordPerfect to generate the copies, select Printer from the Generated By pop-up list.

Tell Me More

If your printer (most laser printers) has the capability to control the number of copies, it is a good idea to change the Generated By option to

Printer. It is usually faster to have the printer generate the copies. When WordPerfect generates the copies, it sends the job for each copy generated, which takes more time. When WordPerfect prints multiple copies, it prints the document once and then prints it again so that your document is collated for you. If your printer generates the copies, it prints each page the specified number of times so that your document does not print collated.

HINT

If you want to print your document in reverse order, with the last page coming out of the printer first, you can choose File➢Print➢Options and then select Print in Reverse Order.

You can change the default settings for the Number of Copies and Generated By options by choosing File➢Preferences and then double-clicking the Print icon and specifying the default options you want WordPerfect to use for all documents you print.

HOW DO I... Edit Printer Setup Information?

If you want to change any of the options for your printer, you can edit the printer setup. Printer setup information includes the description of the printer, port and sheet-feeder information, and font information. You have to edit the printer setup whenever you are using a sheet feeder or purchase cartridges or printer fonts to use with your printer.

NOTE

You can edit WordPerfect and Windows print drivers. The information in this section is specific to editing WordPerfect drivers. For information about editing Windows print drivers, see your Windows manual.

Steps

➨To edit the printer setup:

1. Choose File➢Select Printer.
2. Highlight the printer you want to edit and choose Setup. The Printer Setup dialog box is displayed, as shown in Figure 7–8.
3. Choose the option you want and enter the necessary information.
4. Choose OK and Close until you return to the document window.

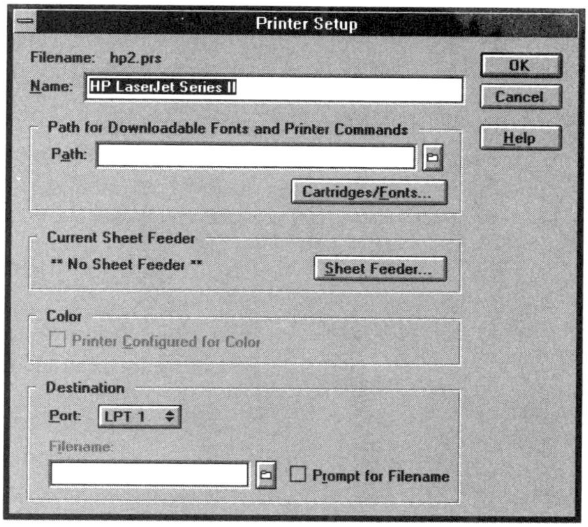

FIGURE 7–8
The Printer Setup dialog box.

Tell Me More

The Printer Setup dialog box lists the name of the PRS File and the Printer Name so that you know exactly which printer you are editing. The PRS (Printer Resource) file contains the specific codes your printer needs for printing. The following table lists the options in the Printer Setup dialog box and gives a description of each option:

OPTION	DESCRIPTION
Name	Lists the name WordPerfect uses to identify your printer. This name is displayed in the Current Printer field on the Print dialog as well as in many other places. You can change this name to help you more easily identify printers if you are using several printers. If you are on a network and can print to multiple laser printers, for example, you can change the description to Third Floor Laser Printer or Julie's Printer.

(continues)

Option	Description
Path for Downloadable Fonts and Printer Commands	Lists the directory in which soft font files and printer commands are stored. Soft fonts are software files that add additional fonts for your printer. This option is applicable and necessary only if you have purchased third-party soft fonts for your printer.
Current Sheet Feeder	Lists the currently selected sheet feeder. If your printer has a sheet feeder, you have to select it by using this option. After choosing this option, the Select Sheet Feeder dialog box is displayed and lists the available sheet feeders. Highlight your sheet feeder and choose OK. Note: Most laser printers with single-bin sheet feeders do not need a sheet-feeder definition.
Color	Specifies whether the printer can print in color.
Destination	Lists the current port, which is the device through which the computer sends information to the printer. The only time you have to change ports is if you change your computer configuration to print to a different port. You can also use this option if you want to print directly to a file. If you do not have a printer attached to your computer, you can print to a file. When you print to a file, WordPerfect inserts all the necessary formatting codes so that you can print the file from DOS, by using the DOS print command. After specifying the Port as a file, enter a filename in the Filename text box. The next time you print, WordPerfect prints all the text and formatting codes to this file. You can also select Prompt for Filename if you want WordPerfect to prompt you to enter a filename every time you print.

HOW DO I. . . Print in Color?

If you are using a color printer, WordPerfect has many options for inserting color in your document. If you do not have a color printer but you have a color monitor, you can still use color in your document to display color in the document window.

Steps

➠To change the color of text in a document:

1. Position the insertion point where you want to change the color.
2. Choose Font *or* press F9.
3. Click on the Color box and then select the color you want to use from the Color Palette.
4. Choose OK.

Tell Me More

If you are printing a draft of a color document or you decide that you do not want the document printed in color:

1. Choose File➢Print *or* press F5.
2. Select Black from the Print Color pop-up box. This option is dimmed if you don't have a color printer.

HOW DO I... Print on Both Sides of a Page?

If your printer supports duplex printing, you can have WordPerfect print on both sides of the paper. Duplex printing saves paper and gives you flexibility in the types of documents you can print. When you print on both sides of the paper, you can also specify a Binding Width so that you bind the document and have the text properly positioned.

Steps

➠To print on both sides of a page:

1. Move the insertion point to the page where you want duplexing to begin.
2. Choose Layout➢Page➢Binding-Duplex.
3. If you are going to be binding the document and want additional space for the binding width, select the appropriate Binding Width and then specify the Amount you need for binding.
4. From the Duplexing pop-up list, choose Long Edge if you are binding the document on the long edge of the page, or choose

Short Edge if you are binding the document on the short edge of the page.

5. Choose OK and then finish creating the document.
6. When you are ready to print the document, choose File➢Print *or* press [F5] and choose Print. The document automatically is printed on both sides of the paper.

Tell Me More

When you use the Binding Width, the amount you specify is added to the margin settings. It is important to use the Binding Width option rather than margin settings with duplex printing so that the adjustment is made correctly for both sides of a page.

NOTE

If you are binding a document that is not printed on both sides of the page, you should use the margin settings to move the text.

If your printer does not support duplex printing, you can reinsert the page back into the printer and print it on the other side. You can print on both sides of a page by using the Print Odd/Even Pages option.

➡To duplex-print by using a printer that does not support duplexing:

1. With the document in the document window, choose File➢Print *or* press [F5].
2. Choose Options.
3. Choose Odd from the Print Odd/Even Pages pop-up list and choose OK.
4. Choose Print.
5. Reinsert the pages properly in your printer.
6. With the document still in the document window, choose File➢Print➢Options.
7. Choose Even from the Print Odd/Even Pages pop-up list and choose OK.
8. Choose Print.

NOTE

Use caution when you reinsert paper in your printer. Some printers are sensitive to "used" paper, and reinserting the paper may cause paper jams.

HOW DO I. . . Select a Font Cartridge?

Depending on the type of printer you are using, you may be able to purchase font cartridges to enhance and expand the number and type of fonts you can use with your printer. Font cartridges are physical "cassettes" you insert in a slot in your printer. Font cartridges are sold by printer manufacturers and other companies; they do not come with WordPerfect.

Steps

➠To select a font cartridge:

1. Choose File➢Select Printer.
2. Highlight your printer and choose Setup.
3. Choose Cartridges/Fonts. The Select Fonts dialog box is displayed, as shown in Figure 7–9.
4. From the Font Source drop-down list, choose Cartridges.
5. Highlight the cartridge (or cartridges) you are using and select Cartridge Installed at the bottom of the dialog box *or* mark it with an asterisk (Shift+*).
6. If necessary, choose Total and enter the number of cartridge slots on your printer.

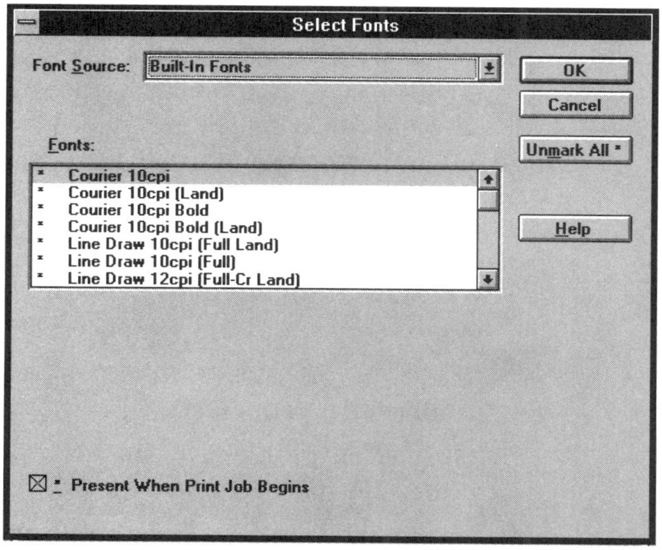

FIGURE 7–9
The Select Fonts dialog box.

7. Choose OK. During this time, a Please Wait dialog box is displayed while WordPerfect updates your printer drive and adds the new fonts.
8. Choose OK and Close until you return to the document window. The fonts on the cartridge are now available on the Font dialog box.

Tell Me More

When you insert a cartridge in your printer, make sure that it is inserted all the way. If the cartridge is not inserted securely, the fonts on the cartridge do not print properly. On most printers, you hear a click when the cartridge is correctly in place.

HOW DO I. . . Install Additional Fonts?

In addition to font cartridges, you can install graphics fonts and printer soft fonts. Graphics fonts work with any printer that has the capability to print graphics. Graphics fonts are *scalable,* which means that they can print in any size. WordPerfect ships Bitstream TrueType fonts, which are graphical fonts, with the program. When you're using a dot-matrix printer, graphics fonts may take much longer to print than do internal printer fonts. Graphics fonts, such as the TrueType fonts, can be used with any printer definition. To use the fonts, you simply install them by using the font manufacturer's instructions or the Windows Font Installation utility. These fonts are then automatically displayed on the Font dialog box.

Printer soft fonts, which print the text in a text mode, are specific font files you load in your printer's memory. Printer soft fonts must be installed on your computer and added to your printer definition in WordPerfect. Additional graphics fonts and printer soft fonts must be purchased separately from WordPerfect from a third-party vendor.

NOTE

Any fonts you have installed with Windows are available in WordPerfect.

Steps

➡**To install printer soft fonts:**

1. Install fonts for your computer by following the instructions from the font manufacturer or by using the Windows Font Installation utility.

2. Choose File➢Select Printer.
3. Highlight your printer and choose Setup.
4. Choose Cartridges➢Fonts. The Select Fonts dialog box is displayed.
5. From the Font Source drop-down list, choose Soft Fonts.
6. From the Font Groups, select the group that represents the font software you have purchased and installed. The Fonts group box displays the fonts in that font group.
7. From the Fonts list, highlight the name of each soft font file you have copied to your hard disk, and check the box for Present When Printer Initialized or Can Be Swapped out when Printing.
8. If necessary, choose Total and enter the correct amount of printer memory, listed in kilobytes. Enter 700, for example, if your printer has 700K of free memory. Check your printer manual for information about the memory in your printer.
9. Choose OK to return to the Printer Setup dialog box. During this time, a Please Wait dialog box is displayed while WordPerfect updates your printer drive and adds the new fonts.
10. Specify the Path for Downloadable Fonts and Printer Commands and choose OK. This is not a WordPerfect directory—it is where the font software installed the files.
11. Choose OK.
12. Choose Close until you return to the document window. The fonts on the cartridge are now available in the Font dialog box.

Tell Me More

This section gives you additional information about using graphics fonts and printer soft fonts.

Using Graphics Fonts

When you installed WordPerfect, you had the option of installing the Bitstream TrueType fonts. If you installed the fonts or have any other graphics fonts, they are displayed automatically when you choose Insert➢Font *or* F9.

HINT

If your printer has fonts similar to these, you may want to consider using the printer fonts rather than the graphics fonts to save printing time.

Using Printer Soft Fonts

After printer soft font files have been installed on your computer, they must be downloaded to your printer. Every time the printer is turned on, you must download the soft fonts. You should do this whenever your printer is turned off. If you turn your printer off at night, you should initialize the printer every morning.

To download the soft fonts:

1. Choose File➢Print *or* press F5.
2. Choose Initialize.

It may take several minutes to download the fonts, depending on the number of fonts and the size of the font files.

Soft font files can be permanently or temporarily downloaded to the printer. When you permanently download the fonts, they take up printer memory, but they are always ready for immediate use. When you temporarily download soft fonts, WordPerfect loads the font only when it is needed and then unloads it. Temporarily loading soft fonts takes printer memory only when the font is loaded, but it takes much longer to print documents.

WordPerfect distinguishes between permanent and temporary soft fonts by the way you mark them in the Select Font dialog box. An asterisk (*) indicates that the font is present when the job begins, and a plus sign (+) indicates that it must be loaded. If you have plenty of printer memory, mark your fonts with an *. If you have limited memory, mark those you use most with an * and those used less frequently with a +. You can also mark them with both an * and a +. Marking them with both allows WordPerfect to download as many fonts as possible and then unloads those not being used when it needs to download an additional font.

HOW DO I... Troubleshoot Printer Problems?

One of the most frustrating experiences in working with any software is the inability to print a document. Sometimes you may not be able to print at all, and at other times the printed page does not print correctly. The following sections list common printing problems and troubleshooting techniques you can use to solve the problem.

Printer Not Printing

If you cannot get your printer to respond after sending a job from WordPerfect, the first thing you should do is check the Control Printer screen. Follow any advice given in the Action field.

If you are still experiencing problems, follow these steps:

1. Verify that the printer is turned on and on-line.
2. Make sure that cable is inserted completely and correctly at both ends.
3. Print from a blank page. If the blank page prints, try saving your document and exit from WordPerfect. Reenter WordPerfect, retrieve your document, and try printing again.
4. Verify that the correct port is selected on the Printer Setup screen.
5. Try printing from another application. If you cannot print from another application, you may be experiencing hardware problems.
6. Try printing from DOS. At a DOS prompt, type **copy con lpt*n*** or **copy con com*n***, where *n* is the port number (which is usually 1). Then type **This is a test** and press Ctrl+Z followed by Enter. The Ctrl+Z keystroke appears as **^Z** on the command line and indicates the end of the text you want to send to the printer. If you have a laser printer connected to your computer, press Ctrl+L before pressing Ctrl+Z and then press Enter.

If the text does not print, you have a problem with your printer equipment; your printer may be connected to the wrong computer port, you may have incorrect equipment settings, or your computer or printer may have to be serviced. If the printer test does print from DOS but not from within WordPerfect, you probably have to change one or more printer setup options.

Printing Garbage

Sometimes your printed text may appear totally "garbaged." The characters are printed on top of each other or the wrong characters print. Several different software-configuration and hardware problems can cause printed text to be garbaged.

If your printer is printing garbage:

1. Verify that the correct printer is selected in WordPerfect. If you are using a sheet feeder, make sure that the correct definition is selected.
2. Turn the printer off for 30 seconds and try printing again.
3. If you are using a cartridge, make sure that it is inserted securely.
4. Type a single line of text on a blank document screen and try printing.
5. Verify that the printer dip switches are set to the factory default settings. *Dip switches* are settings on the printer that affect its configuration. You can find these settings in your printer manual.
6. Try printing with a different printer cable.

If the text does not print, you have a problem with your printer equipment; your printer may be connected to the wrong computer port, you may have incorrect equipment settings, or your computer or printer may have to be serviced.

Incorrect Margins

If your documents always print with an incorrect margin, usually top or left regardless of the margin settings in the document, your printer is adjusting the text. WordPerfect can compensate for these adjustments with the Text Adjustment feature. To set the Text Adjustment feature, you have to edit each Paper Size definition you use.

To edit a definition:

1. Choose Layout➢Page.
2. Choose Paper Size.
3. Highlight the Paper Definition you want to edit and choose Edit.
4. Specify the appropriate Text Adjustments by entering the measurement WordPerfect needs in order to adjust the text to have a correct top and left margin.
5. Choose OK and Close to return to the document screen.

"Out of Memory" Error Messages

"Out of memory" error messages appear if you attempt to print documents when you don't have enough computer memory or disk space available. When WordPerfect prints a document, it must perform several actions that require memory.

When an "Out of memory" message appears, you can try the following steps to free up memory in WordPerfect:

1. Try switching to Draft mode.
2. Close unused document windows.
3. Turn off the display of the Button Bar, Power Bar, Ruler, and Reveal Codes.

"Disk Full" Error Messages

When you print a document, WordPerfect uses disk space to prepare the document for printing. If not enough space is available, a "disk full" error message appears when your hard disk does not have enough available space for the printing operation.

To solve this problem of not having enough disk space:

1. Verify that WordPerfect is using your hard drive, choose File➢Open *or* press Ctrl+O and make sure that the highlighted directory is located on your hard drive. If the directory is not on the hard drive, enter your WordPerfect default directory and choose OK to return to the document screen and try printing again.
2. If the error is correct, try freeing up space on your hard drive. Use the Open File dialog box to delete or move files to floppy disks.

Text Is Printing in the Wrong Font

If text is printing in the wrong font when you change attributes or size or insert special characters, it means that the automatic font change WordPerfect is selecting has to be changed. When you print with certain fonts, WordPerfect may not be able to use certain attributes or print certain characters by using the selected font. When this occurs, WordPerfect makes an Automatic Font Change (AFC). WordPerfect tries to select the best font for the situation.

If you do not like the font WordPerfect selects, you can edit the automatic font changes:

1. Choose Layout➢Font *or* press F9.
2. Choose Font Map.

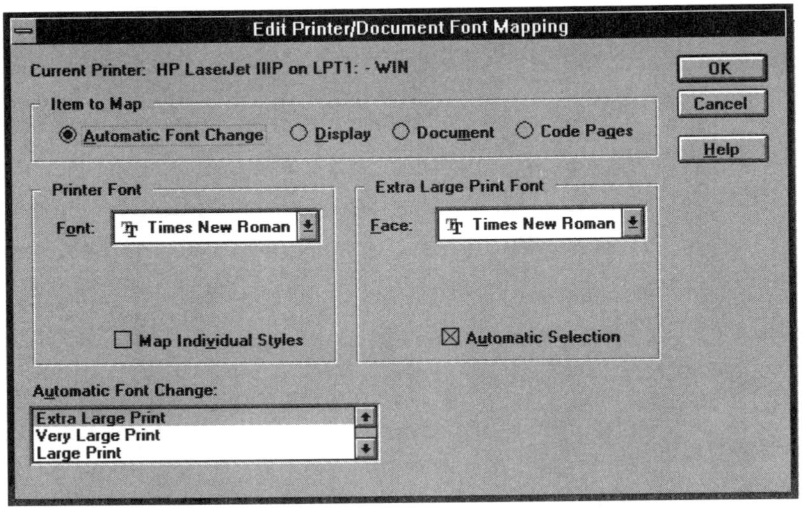

FIGURE 7–10 *The Edit Printer/Document Font Mapping dialog box.*

3. Select Automatic Font Change. The Edit Printer/Document Font Mapping dialog box changes, as displayed in Figure 7–10.
4. Choose the Font you want to change in the Printer Font group box. For example, if you want to change the Automatic Font Changes for Times Roman, select that font here.
5. Select the attribute, character set, or orientation that does not change to the right attributes when you change the text style in your document from the Automatic Font Change list.
6. Select the font you want to use as the new Automatic Font Change from the Face drop-down list.
7. Repeat steps 4–6 until you have changed all the desired automatic font changes.
8. Choose OK until you return to the document window.
9. Choose File➢Select Printer.
10. Choose Update. This adds the changes to the printer's .PRS file.

Chapter 8

Creating Tables, Formulas, and Charts

A powerful WordPerfect feature is its capability to create and manipulate tables within a document. A table is an effective and flexible tool for organizing and displaying any type of information. In this chapter, you learn how to create and edit the table and the information it contains. You learn how to change the structure of a table and how to format the information within a table.

This chapter covers the following table features:

- Creating a table
- Joining and splitting table cells
- Splitting a table
- Changing column width
- Inserting and deleting rows or columns
- Formatting cells, columns, rows, and tables
- Changing lines, borders, and fill patterns

- Formatting numbers in a table
- Moving and copying parts of a table
- Naming tables
- Creating formulas and using spreadsheet functions
- Linking spreadsheet files
- Creating a floating cell
- Creating charts

All the features used to create the table in Figure 8–1 are described in this chapter.

HOW DO I... Create a Table?

A table enables you to easily display and manipulate text, numbers, or formulas in a series of columns and rows. You can create a table anywhere in your document: within a column, on a separate page, or even within a graphics box. When you create a table, you specify how many rows and columns you want to begin with, but you can always insert (add) or delete additional rows or columns.

FIGURE 8–1
A sample formatted table.

expand our package service to several new destinations. Beginning April 1 we will be chartering flights to Cancun, Mexico. We plan to include special package rates for travel in the off- season. Also, We have lowered our original rate for the Las Vegas package to $743.00. The following table summarizes our current package offerings:

Travel Packages from San Francisco

Destination	*Flight*	*Hotel (6 nights)*	*Rental Car (per week)*	*Total*
Orlando	$299.00	$724.00	$145.00	$1,168.00
Cancun*	$579.00	$861.00	N/A	$1,440.00
	$449.00	$574.00		$1,023.00
Las Vegas	$213.00	$360.00	$170.00	$743.00
Seattle	$385.00	$839.00	$165.00	$1,389.00

*Less expensive package is for off-peak travel

New VACATION CONSULTING Service

It has always been our goal to offer the highest degree of service and convenience for vacationers. In addition to our new travel packages we will be offering a new vacation

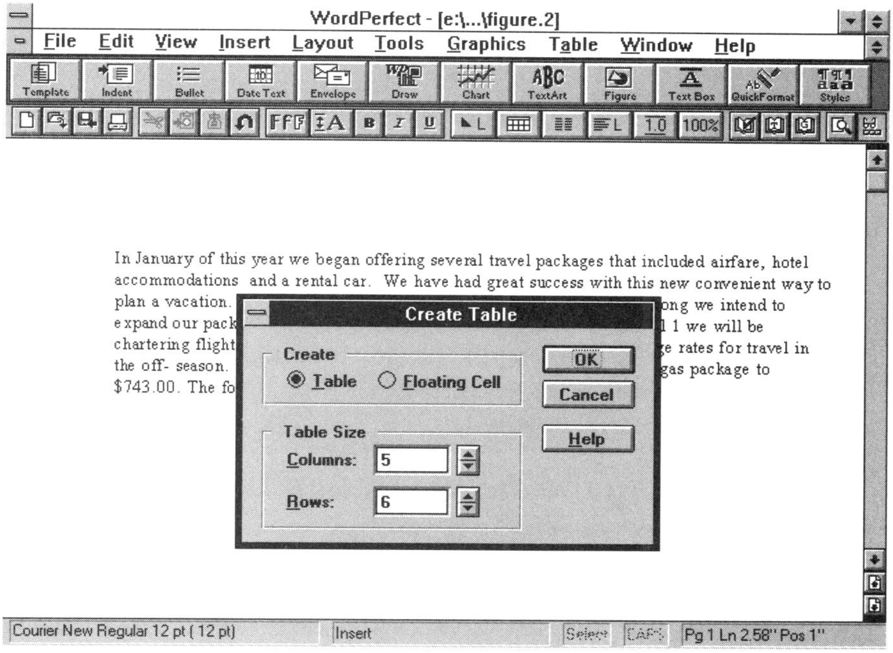

FIGURE 8–2
The Create Table dialog box.

Steps

➨To create a table:

1. Choose Table➢Create *or* press F12. The Create Table dialog box is displayed, as shown in Figure 8–2.
2. Select Table.
3. Enter the number of columns in the Columns entry box.
4. Enter the number of rows in the Rows entry box.
5. Choose OK.

You can also choose the icon from the Power Bar to create a table. Click the left mouse button and drag the mouse over the grid until you have selected the appropriate number of columns and rows and then release the mouse button.

Tell Me More

Figure 8–3 displays a basic table structure. A *table* is a structure composed of columns and rows. A *column* is a series of vertical boxes, and a *row* is a series of horizontal boxes. Columns are identified by letters beginning with *A* (column letters go from *A* through *Z* and then begin with *AA*, *AB*, and so on). You can have as many as 32 columns in a table. Rows are identified by a number beginning with 1; you can have as many as 32,767 rows in a table.

The intersection of a column and a row forms a *cell;* this relationship is shown in Figure 8–3.

Cells are identified by the letter of the column and the number of the row that intersect. This combination of column letter and row number is known as the *cell address.* WordPerfect always lets you know the insertion point position in a table by displaying the cell address in the status bar (notice the cell address of A1 in the status bar in Figure 8–3).

Using the Tables Button Bar

WordPerfect has a special Button Bar to allow you to access a number of Tables features quickly and easily. You should display the Tables Button Bar if you plan to work frequently with tables in your document. To

FIGURE 8–3
Empty table structure.

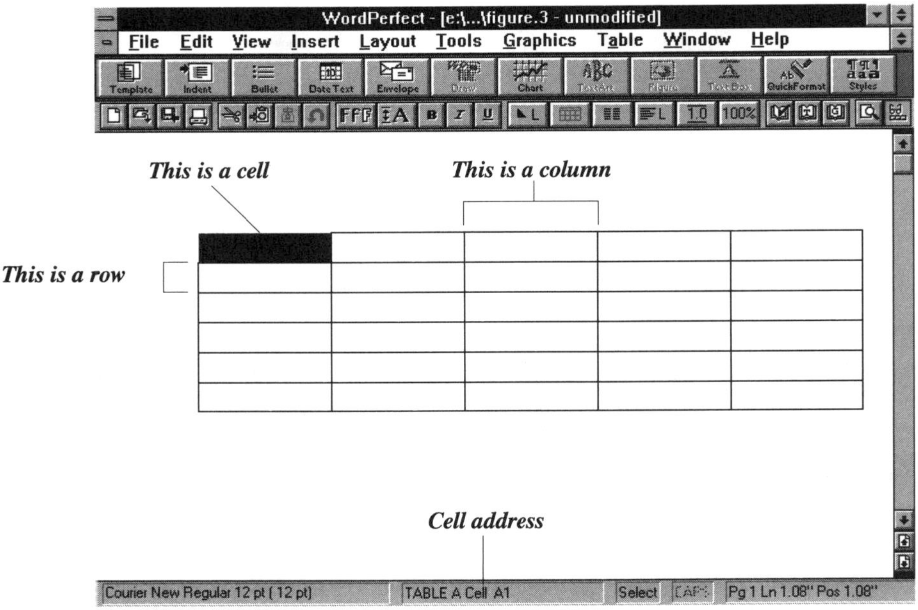

FIGURE 8–4
The Tables Button Bar.

display the Tables Button Bar, shown in Figure 8–4, simply position the insertion point anywhere on the current Button Bar, click the right mouse button, and then select Tables. Each of these buttons is described throughout this chapter.

HOW DO I. . . Enter Text in a Table?

After you have created a table in your document, you can type text or numbers within each cell of a table by using many of the same features described in Chapter 3. You can insert hard returns, for example, or have WordPerfect automatically wrap the text for you. You can also delete, select, copy, or move text. Figure 8–5 shows the basic table structure with some text and numbers typed in various cells.

Moving the Insertion Point in a Table

There are three basic methods to move the insertion point within a table: the mouse, the Tab and Shift+Tab keys, and the Alt+arrow-key combinations. A few shortcut keys also allow you to quickly move to certain parts of a table.

To use the mouse to move the insertion point, simply position the mouse pointer in any cell and click the left mouse button.

FIGURE 8–5
Text and numbers entered in a table.

Destination	Flight	Hotel (6 nights)	Rental Car (per week)	Total
Orlando	299	724	145	
Cancun				
Las Vegas				
Seattle				

The following table lists keystroke combinations you can use to move within a table:

KEYSTROKE	ACTION
Tab	Moves right one cell
Shift+Tab	Moves left one cell
Alt+↑	Moves up one cell
Alt+↓	Moves down one cell
Home, Home	Moves to first cell in row
End, End	Moves to last cell in row
Alt+Home	Moves to top line of text in a multi-line cell
Alt+End	Moves to bottom line of text in a multi-line cell

NOTE **Because pressing the Tab key moves the insertion point from cell to cell in a table, to use a regular tab within a table, you must insert a hard tab by pressing Ctrl+Tab.**

Using the Go To Feature in a Table

You can also use the Go To feature to move the insertion point to a specific location in a table or to move to another table in your document. To use this feature, choose Edit➢Go To *or* press Ctrl+G. You can select the following options:

OPTION	DESCRIPTION
Table	Moves the insertion point to the top of another table you select from the drop-down list
Cell/Range	Moves the insertion point to the specified cell or range of cells in the selected table

HOW DO I... Join Cells in a Table?

The Join feature lets you combine several cells within a table into a single cell. You can join cells from a row or column or both.

Steps

➡ **To join cells:**

1. Select the cells you want to join.
2. Click the right mouse button and Choose Join Cells from the QuickMenu.

Tell Me More

After you join a group of cells into a single cell, you can type text and numbers as you would in any other cell. This feature is helpful if you want to create, for example, a header for the information displayed in a table. Figure 8–6 shows a table with the cells in the first row being joined to form a single cell called cell A1. This cell is used as a table header row. For more information about creating a header row, see the section "HOW DO I... Format a Row?" later in this chapter.

Selecting in Tables

To use many of the features in this chapter, including the Join feature, you have to select parts of a table—a cell, a group of cells, several rows or columns, or even an entire table. To select several cells, rows, or

FIGURE 8–6
Text entered in a joined cell.

The cells in row 1 have been joined in a single cell

Travel Packages from San Francisco				
Destination	Flight	Hotel (6 nights)	Rental Car (per week)	Total
Orlando	299	724	145	
Cancun				
Las Vegas				
Seattle				

columns, you can move the mouse pointer close to any table line and display the selection arrow shown here:

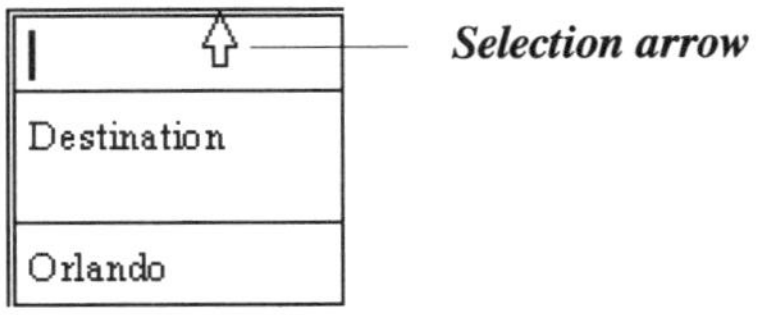

After the selection arrow is displayed, just click and drag until the areas you want are selected.

You can also use the following shortcuts with the selection arrow:

WHEN SELECTION ARROW IS	ACTION	WHAT IS SELECTED
↑ or ←	Single-click	Cell
↑	Double-click	Entire column
←	Double-click	Entire row
↑ or ←	Triple-click	Entire table

HOW DO I... Split a Cell into Columns or Rows?

The Split Cell feature lets you separate a cell into any number of rows or columns. You can also use Split as an "undo" feature for cells you joined inadvertently and want to return to their original structure.

Steps

➡To split a cell:

1. Position the insertion point in the cell to be split.
2. Click the right mouse button and choose Split Cell from the QuickMenu.

FIGURE 8–7
A table with split cells.

Travel Packages from San Francisco				
Destination	Flight	Hotel (6 nights)	Rental Car (per week)	Total
Orlando	299	724	145	
Cancun	579	861	N/A	
Las Vegas	213	360	170	
Seattle	385	839	165	

These cells have been split

3. Select either Columns or Rows and specify the number of columns or rows into which you want the cell to be split.
4. Choose OK.

Tell Me More

You can split several cells simultaneously into any number of columns or rows. To do this, you must first select all the cells you want to split and choose Table➢Split➢Cell. Each selected cell is split into the specified number of rows or columns. Figure 8–7 shows a table with three cells split into cells that each contain two rows.

HOW DO I... Join or Split Tables?

WordPerfect lets you join two separate tables to form a single table. Each table must have the same number of columns. You can also split a table into two separate tables.

Steps

➨To join two tables:

1. Position the insertion point anywhere in the first table.
2. Choose Table➢Join➢Table.

➨To split a table into two tables:

1. Position your insertion point in the row in which you want the table to split.
2. Choose Table➢Split➢Table.

Tell Me More

When you join two tables, the new table takes on the formatting options of the first table. The two tables you want to join must immediately follow each other in your document; there cannot be any text between the two tables. You also must make sure that no codes exist between the [Tbl Off] code in the first table and the [Tbl Def] code in the second table in Reveal Codes.

When you split a table, the row in which your insertion point is positioned becomes the first row of the new table. To separate the two tables, turn on Reveal Codes and insert a few hard returns between the [Tbl Off] code in the first table and the [Tbl Def] code in the new table.

HOW DO I... Change the Width of a Table Column?

You can change the width of a column in two ways. You can quickly change the width of a column by using the Ruler Bar or be more precise and specify an exact width measurement by using the Column or Table Format features.

Steps

➡To quickly change the column width by using the Ruler Bar:

1. Position the insertion point anywhere inside the table.
2. Choose View and select Ruler Bar *or* press Alt+Shift+F3. The Ruler Bar is displayed below the Power Bar, as shown in Figure 8–8.
3. Click and drag the column width marker (the arrow pointing down in the Ruler Bar, as indicated in Figure 8–8) to increase or decrease the width of a column.

HINT **You can also quickly change column width by using the table-sizing arrow. Position the mouse pointer over any column line until the mouse pointer is displayed as a double arrow pointing both left and right. Click and drag the arrow to change column width.**

➡To change a column width to an exact measurement:

1. Position the insertion point in the column you want to change.

FIGURE 8–8
The Ruler Bar displayed.

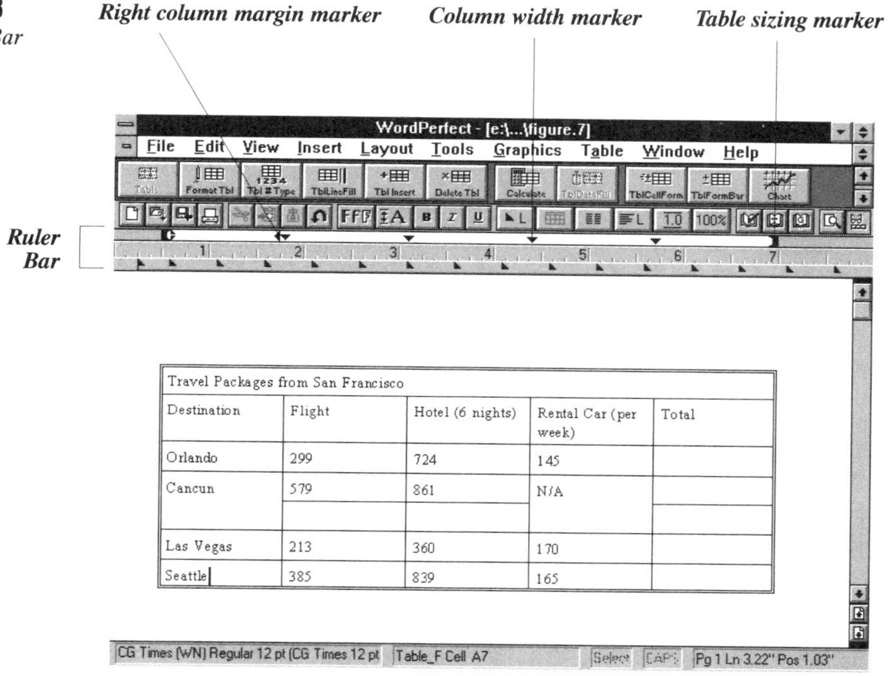

2. Click the right mouse button and choose Format from the QuickMenu. The Format dialog box is displayed, as shown in Figure 8–9.
3. Select Column.
4. Enter a measurement in the Width text box.
5. Choose OK.

Tell Me More

With the Ruler Bar displayed, you can also change the margins in a column or change the size of a table. To change column margins with the Ruler Bar, you click on either the left or right margin marker, as indicated in Figure 8–8, and drag the marker to the right or left to increase or decrease the margin. Margin markers are displayed for only the column in which the insertion point is located. You can also change the width of the entire table by clicking and dragging on one of the table sizing markers.

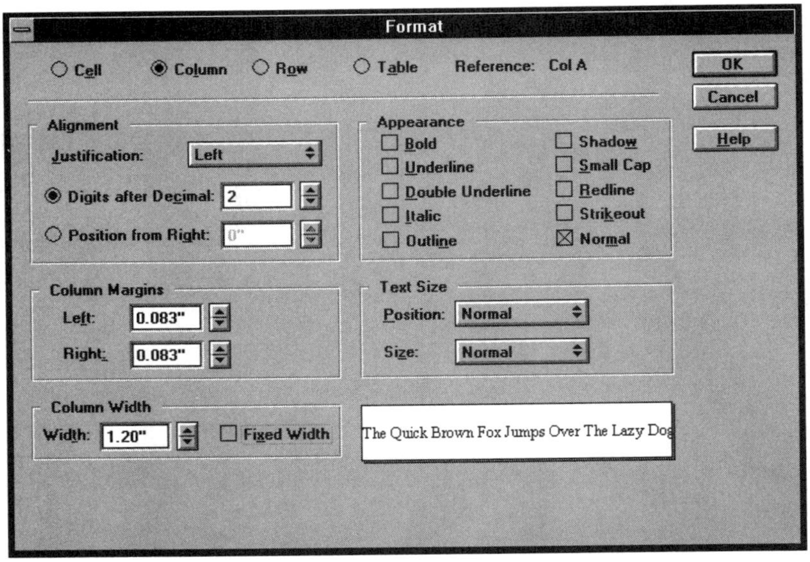

FIGURE 8–9
The Format dialog box with Column selected.

WordPerfect also lets you change the width of several columns simultaneously. To change the width of more than one column, you must use the steps for changing column width to an exact measurement. First select at least one cell in each column and then follow the preceding steps for changing the column width to an exact measurement.

HOW DO I... Insert and Delete Rows or Columns in a Table?

WordPerfect lets you insert or delete one or more rows or columns after you have created a table. You can insert or delete rows or columns before or after the insertion point position in your table.

Steps

➠To insert columns or rows:

1. Position the insertion point inside the table.
2. Click the right mouse button and choose Insert from the QuickMenu. The Insert Columns/Rows dialog box is displayed, as shown in Figure 8–10.

3. Select Columns or Rows and specify the number of columns or rows you want to add to your table.
4. Select Before (to insert a column to the left or a row above the insertion point position) or After (to insert a column to the right or a row above the insertion point position).
5. Choose OK.

BUTTON BAR

You can also choose the 

icon from the Tables Button Bar to display the Insert Columns/Rows dialog box.

HINT

A quick way to insert a single row at the bottom of a table is to position the insertion point in the far right cell of the last row and press Tab.

➡**To delete columns or rows:**

1. Position the insertion point in the column or row you want to delete.
2. Click the right mouse button and choose Delete from the QuickMenu.
3. Select Columns or Rows and specify the number of columns or rows you want to delete from the table.
4. Choose OK.

FIGURE 8–10
The Insert Columns/Rows dialog box.

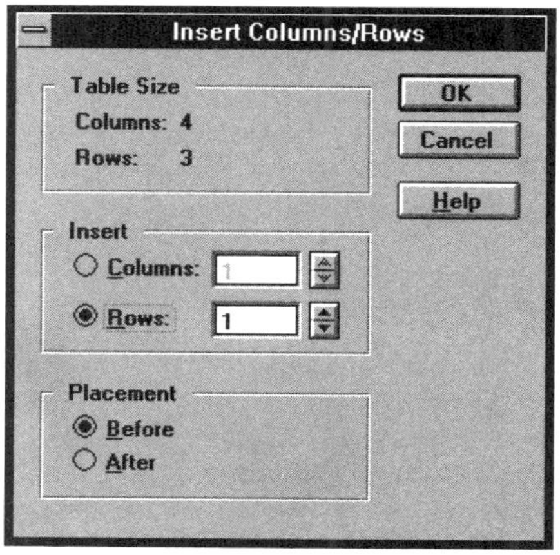

BUTTON BAR

You can also choose the  icon from the Tables Button Bar to display the Delete dialog box.

Tell Me More

When you specify more than one column to be deleted, the additional columns that are deleted are the ones to the right of your insertion point. If your insertion point is in column B and you specify to delete two columns, for example, columns B and C are deleted. Likewise, when you specify that you want to delete more than one row, you delete rows after the row in which your insertion point is positioned. You can also select any number of columns or rows to be deleted rather than specify how many.

To delete an entire table, you can select the entire table (triple-click the table-selection arrow in any location in the table) and choose Delete Tbl from the Tables Button Bar. You can select from the options displayed in Figure 8–11. You can also select the table and press the Delete key.

WordPerfect also lets you delete text or formulas in a table without deleting a row or column.

To delete only the contents of a cell or cells:

1. Position your insertion point in the cell or select cells from which you want to delete the contents.
2. Click the right mouse button and select Delete from the QuickMenu.
3. Select Cell Contents.
4. Choose OK.

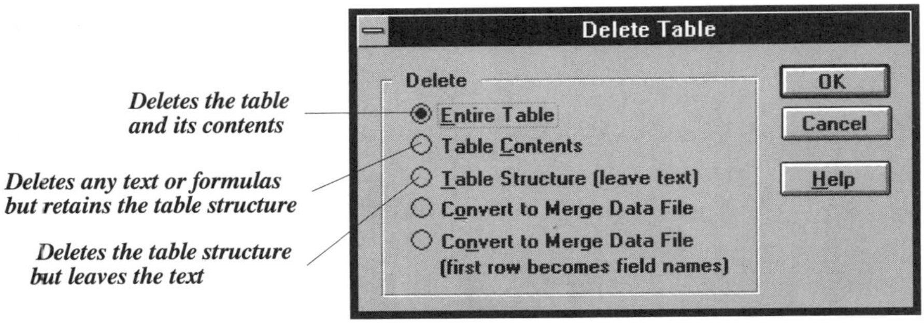

FIGURE 8–11
The Delete Table dialog box.

HOW DO I. . . Format a Row?

You can select specific options to customize the way text and formulas are formatted within a row. You can adjust the top and bottom margins, specify the height of a row, and specify the number of lines of text that can be entered in a row. With the row-formatting options, you can also create a header for your table.

Steps

➨To format a row:

1. Position the insertion point in the row you want to format or select at least one cell in each row if you want to format more than one.
2. Click the right mouse button and select Format from the QuickMenu.
3. Select Row and the Format dialog box displays the options shown in Figure 8–12.
4. Select the Row Format options you want to use and specify any necessary measurements for Fixed Row Height and Row Margins.
5. Choose OK.

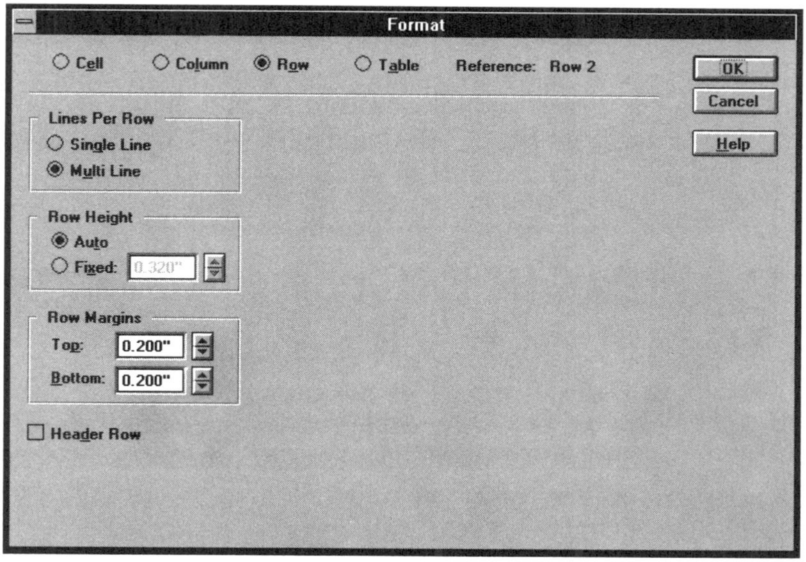

FIGURE 8–12
The Format dialog box with Row selected.

BUTTON BAR

**You can also choose the 

icon from the Tables Button Bar to display the Format dialog box.**

Tell Me More

The following table describes the Row Format options:

OPTION	DESCRIPTION
Lines Per Row	Specifies whether a single line of text or multiple lines of text can be typed in a row.
Row Height	Establishes a fixed height for the current row or lets the text height automatically determine the row height.
Row Margins	Defines the top and bottom margins within a row.
Header Row	Designates the current row as a Header Row for the table. If this option is activated, the header repeats every time the table flows to the next page. You can also designate several rows as header rows by selecting them before displaying the Format dialog box.

When you select a Row Format option, it affects all the cells in the current row or selected rows. Figure 8–13 shows a table with the top and bottom margins in row 2 set to .20 inch and multiple lines of text allowed.

HOW DO I... Format a Cell, a Column, or an Entire Table?

You can select specific options to customize the format of text within individual cells, columns, or an entire table. For example, Format options let you bold an entire column of information, center text in a header row, change the text size in a group of cells, establish column margins, and center a table on a page.

FIGURE 8–13
A table with row format changes.

Multiple lines per row

Row margins have been changed

Travel Packages from San Francisco				
Destination	Flight	Hotel (6 nights)	Rental Car (per week)	Total
Orlando	299	724	145	
Cancun*	579	861	N/A	
	449	574		
Las Vegas	213	360	170	
Seattle	385	839	165	

* Less expensive package is for off-peak travel

Steps

➨**To format a cell, column, or table:**

1. Position the insertion point in the cell or column you want to format or select a group of cells (the insertion point can be anywhere in the table if you are going to use table-formatting options).
2. Click the right mouse button and choose Format from the QuickMenu.
3. Select Cell, Column, or Table in the Format dialog box. Figure 8–14 shows the Table format options in the Format Dialog Box.
4. Select the formatting options you want to use and specify any necessary measurements.
5. Choose OK.

BUTTON BAR

You can also choose the Format Tbl icon from the Tables Button Bar to display the Format dialog box.

Tell Me More

Several formatting options can be used in a cell, a column, or an entire table. Other formatting options can be used in only a column or table. Finally, some formatting options are unique to cells or tables. The

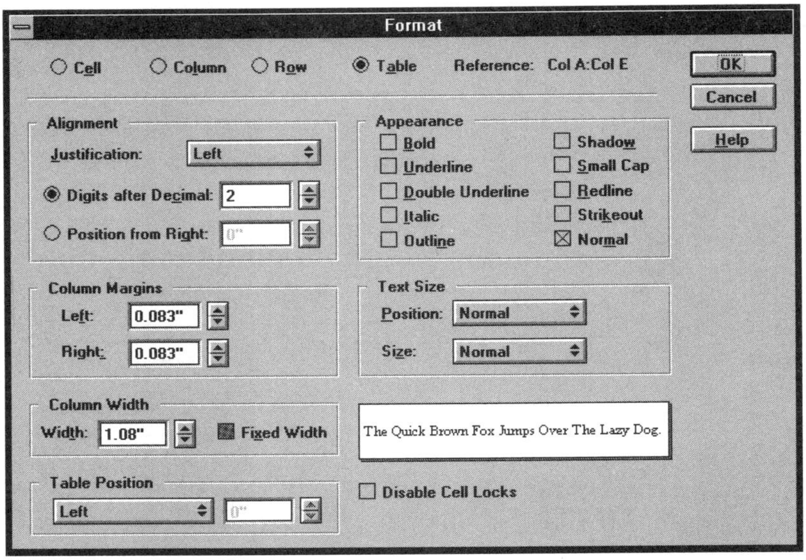

FIGURE 8–14
The Format dialog box with Table selected.

relationship among the Cell, Column, and Table Format options, as well as a description of each option, is shown in the following table:

OPTION	DESCRIPTION	APPLIES TO:		
		CELL	COLUMN	TABLE
Justification	Aligns the text horizontally	*	*	*
Appearance	Changes the appearance of text	*	*	*
Text Position	Allows text to appear as Subscript or Superscript	*	*	*
Text Size	Changes the size of text	*	*	*
Digits after Decimal	Limits the number of digits after a decimal		*	*
Position from Right	Sets the position of a decimal from the right side of the cell		*	*

(continues)

Option	Description	Applies to:		
		Cell	Column	Table
Column Margins	Defines exact measurements for left and right margins in a column	*	*	
Column Width	Defines an exact measurement for column width		*	*
Fixed Width	Maintains the specified column width regardless of width changes made to other column	*	*	
Vertical Alignment	Aligns text vertically at the top, center or bottom of a cell	*		
Use Column Justification/ Use Column Appearance and Text Size	Cancels current cell options and uses those defined for the column	*		
Cell Lock	Prevents information in a cell from being changed	*		
Ignore Cell When Calculating	Ignores cell contents when calculating formulas	*		
Table Position	Aligns the table horizontally on the page			*
Disable Cell Locks	Temporarily unlocks all locked cells for editing			*

The relationship between the formatting options common to cells, columns, or tables is simple: Cell format options selected for a particular cell (or group of cells) override any conflicting column or table format options; and column format options selected for a particular column override any conflicting table format options. If you have selected bold for the appearance of text in Table Format, for example, you can select

FIGURE 8–15
A table with Cell, Column, and Table format changes.

Appearance—bold

Vertical alignment—center

Travel Packages from San Francisco				
Destination	*Flight*	*Hotel (6 nights)*	*Rental Car (per week)*	*Total*
Orlando	299	724	145	
Cancun*	579	861	N/A	
	449	574		
Las Vegas	213	360	170	
Seattle	385	839	165	

* Less expensive package is for off-peak travel

Justification—center

Cell Format and change a particular cell to underline or italics. The rest of the table remains in bold except for the cell you have changed. Figure 8–15 shows examples of several cell, column, and table format options.

WordPerfect lets you lock a cell so that the text or formula it contains cannot be edited. When the Cell Lock option is selected, you cannot move the insertion point into that cell. It is important to understand, however, that locking a cell is not necessarily a security feature: Anyone who knows how to use tables can simply go in and unlock it.

HOW DO I. . . Change the Lines and Border in a Table?

The ability to change the lines and border of a table gives you tremendous flexibility in designing the appearance of your table. Each cell is surrounded by a line on the top, bottom, left, and right. You can change each of these lines individually for a single cell or group of cells, or you can change all the lines in the table simultaneously. You can also change the style of the border that appears around the outside of the table.

Steps

➡ **To change table lines:**

1. Position the insertion point in the cell you want to change or select a group of cells.

FIGURE 8–16
The Table Lines/Fill dialog box.

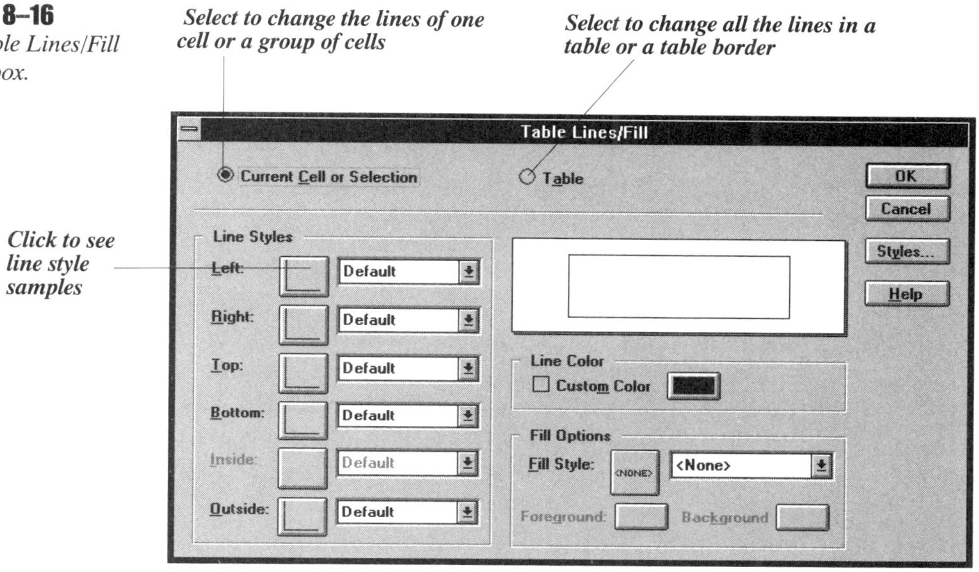

2. Click the right mouse button and choose Lines➢Fill from the QuickMenu. The Table Lines/Fill dialog box is displayed, as shown in Figure 8–16.
3. Select Current Cell or Selection to change the lines in a cell or group of cells, or select Table to change all the lines in the table.
4. Choose a line style by selecting from the Line Style palette *or* from the drop-down list for the lines you want to change.
5. Choose OK.

HINT

You can turn off table lines by selecting <None> as the line style for the current cell or an entire table.

➡To select a table border:

1. Position the insertion point anywhere in the table.
2. Click the right mouse button and choose Lines➢Fill from the QuickMenu.
3. Select Table.

4. Select a border from the Border palette *or* from the drop-down list.
5. Choose OK.

You can also choose the 

icon from the Tables Button Bar to display the Tables Line/Fill dialog box.

Tell Me More

The table lines and the table border are two separate lines. The border conceals the outside table lines from view, but they still exist underneath the border. If you have a border selected, the border is printed but not the outside table lines. If you do not select a border, the outside lines are visible and are printed with the table rather than a border, as shown here:

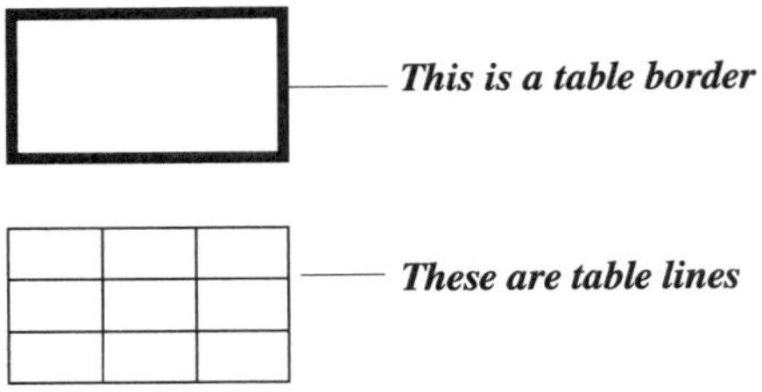

Each cell has its own top, bottom, left, and right lines. The bottom line of a cell, for example, is not the same line as the top line of the cell below it. It is important to remember this when you are changing the lines within the table. The following table illustrates this concept:

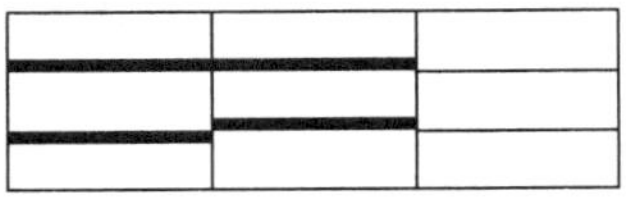

This table has four cells with line styles that have been changed to "thick." The bottom lines of both cells A1 and B1 were changed and line up well. The top line of cell A3 and the bottom line of cell B2 were

FIGURE 8–17
A table with Line Style and Border changes.

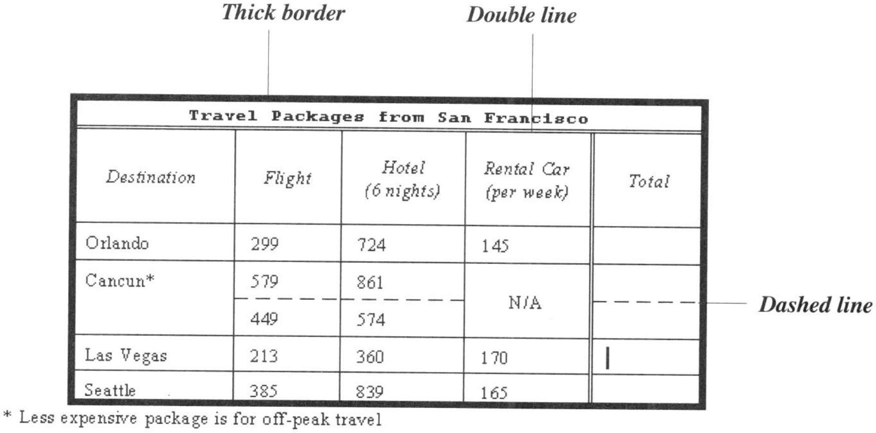

Travel Packages from San Francisco				
Destination	*Flight*	*Hotel (6 nights)*	*Rental Car (per week)*	*Total*
Orlando	299	724	145	
Cancun*	579	861	N/A	
	449	574		
Las Vegas	213	360	170	
Seattle	385	839	165	

* Less expensive package is for off-peak travel

changed, however, and you can clearly see that these are not the same lines and therefore do not align with each other.

Another feature that makes changing line styles simple and effective is the use of inside and outside lines. This feature is used when you select a group of cells to be changed and select either Inside or Outside from the Table Lines/Fill dialog box. The table below shows both inside and outside lines that have been changed in a group of cells.

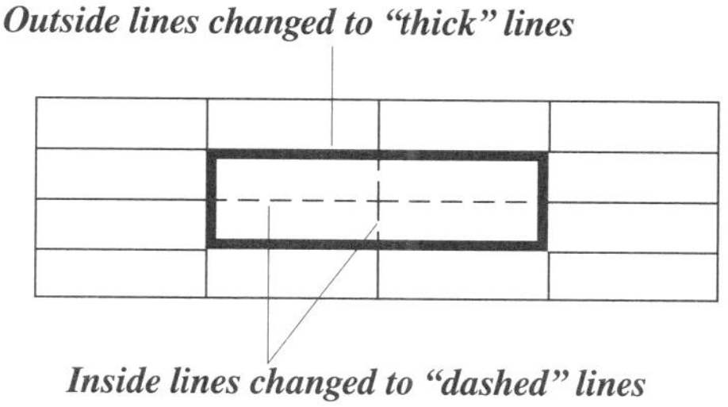

Figure 8–17 shows Line Style and Border Style changes that have been made to a table.

HOW DO I... Shade Parts of a Table?

WordPerfect lets you shade (or *fill*) areas to give you more control over the appearance of information within a table. By using a fill, for example, you can "highlight" and bring attention to critical information within a table. You can fill a single cell, a group of cells, or an entire table by using the Fill feature.

Steps

➡ **To fill a single cell, group of cells, or an entire table:**

1. Position the insertion point in the cell you want to fill or select a group of cells.
2. Click the right mouse button and choose Lines/Fill from the QuickMenu.
3. Select Current Cell to fill a single cell, select Selection to fill a group of cells, or select Table to fill all the cells in the table at a time.
4. Select a fill style from the Fill Style palette or the drop-down list.
5. Choose OK.

BUTTON BAR

You can also choose the  **icon from the Tables Button Bar to display the Tables Line/Fill dialog box.**

Tell Me More

You can edit the existing fill styles or create your own custom fill styles by choosing the Styles option from the Table Lines/Fill dialog box. Figure 8–18 shows a table with the header row filled with a 20% shaded fill.

HOW DO I... Format Numbers?

By using the Numbers Type options, you can change the way numbers are calculated and displayed within a table. With the integration of spreadsheet capabilities into tables, Number Type options provide for powerful flexibility. You can format numbers you enter as text in a cell or numbers that have been generated by a formula. Numbers can be formatted in a cell, a group of cells, columns, or an entire table. You can select from several standard number formats, such as currency, percent, or date format. After you have selected a standard number format, you can select options to customize the way the

FIGURE 8–18
A shaded header row.

20% shaded fill

Travel Packages from San Francisco				
Destination	*Flight*	*Hotel (6 nights)*	*Rental Car (per week)*	*Total*
Orlando	299	724	145	
Cancun*	579	861	N/A	
	449	574		
Las Vegas	213	360	170	
Seattle	385	839	165	

* Less expensive package is for off-season travel

number is displayed, such as parentheses for negative numbers, a specific date format for dates, or an international currency symbol for currency.

Steps

➡To format numbers:

1. Position the insertion point in a cell, column, or table or select a group of cells.
2. Click the right mouse button and choose Number Type from the QuickMenu. The Number Type dialog box is displayed, as shown in Figure 8–19.
3. Select Cell for a single cell or group of selected cells, Column or Table.
4. Select the number type from Available Types.
5. If necessary, choose Customize and select from the Customize Number Type options available for the number type you selected in step 4.
6. Choose OK twice.

BUTTON BAR

You can also choose the  **icon from the Tables Button Bar to display the Number Type dialog box.**

FIGURE 8–19
The Number Type dialog box.

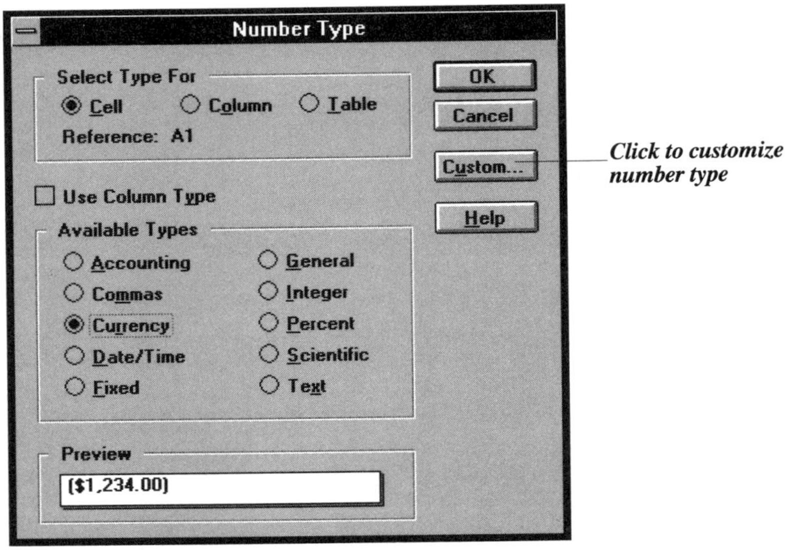

Tell Me More

The following sections describe the different number types, the Customize Number Type options, and custom date-and-time formats available for tables.

Number Types

The following table describes each number type and illustrates how the number 7820.2 would be displayed:

NUMBER FORMAT	DISPLAY	DESCRIPTION
Accounting	$7,820.20	Currency symbol used; as many as 15 decimal places; decimals aligned; currency symbol aligned to edge of column

(continues)

NUMBER FORMAT	DISPLAY	DESCRIPTION
Commas	7,820.20	Commas for thousands separators; as many as 15 decimal places; negative numbers in parentheses
Currency	$7,820.20	Currency symbol used; as many as 15 decimal places; decimals aligned
Date/Time	May 30, 1921	Converts numbers to date and time format
Fixed	7820.20	No thousands separator; as many as 15 decimal places; empty decimal places are filled with zeroes
General	7820.2	No thousands separator; no zeroes that fill empty decimal places
Integer	7820	Rounded to eliminate decimals
Percent	782020.00%	Value multiplied by 100; % sign used; as many as 15 decimal places
Scientific	7.82e+03	Uses exponential notation
Text	7820.2	Text is not recognized or calculated in formulas

Number Format Options

After you have selected the Number Type you want to use, you can choose from several options to customize the way the number is displayed. The following table describes these options:

OPTION	DESCRIPTION
Negative Numbers	Provides three options for formatting negative numbers (parentheses, a negative sign (–), or DR/CR symbols)
Currency Symbol	Turns on and customizes currency symbols

(continues)

OPTION	**DESCRIPTION**
Digits after Decimal	Changes the number of digits allowed after the decimal
Round to Number of Digits after Decimal	Rounds numbers to an integer rather than use the exact number entered
Use Commas	Enables you to use commas when you type a number in a cell

Date Format

If you select Date/Time as the Number Type you want to use, WordPerfect lets you select from several predefined date-and-time formats. After selecting the Date/Time number type, choose Customize and you can select from several formats from the Custom Date Types dialog box.

Figure 8–20 shows a table with several Number Type options selected.

FIGURE 8–20
A table with Number Type options.

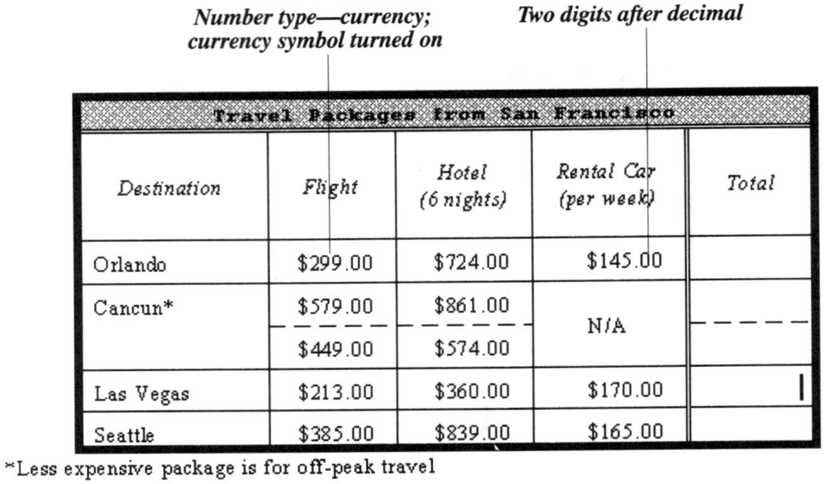

Travel Packages from San Francisco				
Destination	*Flight*	*Hotel (6 nights)*	*Rental Car (per week)*	*Total*
Orlando	$299.00	$724.00	$145.00	
Cancun*	$579.00	$861.00	N/A	
	$449.00	$574.00		
Las Vegas	$213.00	$360.00	$170.00	
Seattle	$385.00	$839.00	$165.00	

*Less expensive package is for off-peak travel

HOW DO I. . . Move or Copy a Cell, Column, or Row?

A feature that adds flexibility in creating and editing a table is the ability to move or copy the contents and structure of a cell, groups of cells, columns, or rows from one location to another within a table or between two tables.

Steps

➡ **To move or copy information in a table:**

1. Select the cells, columns, or rows you want to move or copy.
2. Click the right mouse button and choose either Cut (to move) or Copy from the QuickMenu. The Table Cut/Copy dialog box is displayed.
3. Select Selection to cut or copy the contents and structure of the cells you have selected *or* select Row or Column to cut or copy the contents and structure of a row or column *or* Select Cell to copy only one cell (then select To Cell to copy to another cell or specify how many cells down and to the right you want to copy the cell).
4. Choose OK.
5. Position the insertion point where you want to paste or move the cells, columns, or rows you selected in step 1.
6. Click the right mouse button and choose Paste from the QuickMenu.

POWER BAR

You can use the Cut, Copy, and Paste buttons from the Power Bar to move and copy text in tables.

Tell Me More

It is important to remember that when you move or copy a cell, column, or row, all the formatting is moved or copied to the new location. The formatting includes any line style changes, shading, formulas, number formats, or reference names.

HOW DO I. . . Create and Use Reference Names for Parts of a Table?

WordPerfect lets you name parts of a table so that they can be easily referenced. You can name a cell, block of cells, row, column, or an entire table. Names can add great convenience when you work with formulas or floating cells in a table (this subject is discussed later in this chapter). Table names also enable you to quickly reference a particular table in a document that contains multiple tables.

Steps

➠**To name a table:**

1. Position the insertion point anywhere in the table.
2. Choose Table➢Names. The Table Names in Current Document dialog box is displayed, as shown in Figure 8–21.
3. Select the default table name for the table you want to name (the current table is automatically selected) and choose Edit.
4. Enter the name you want for the current table.
5. Choose OK and Close.

➠**To name a cell, group of cells, row, or column:**

1. Select a group of cells or position the insertion point in a cell, row, or column.

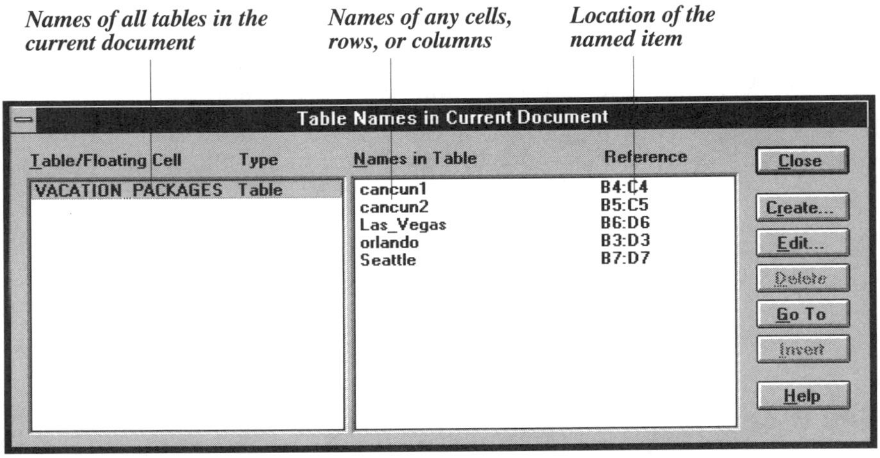

FIGURE 8–21
The Table Names in Current Document dialog box.

2. Choose Table➢Names.
3. Choose Create.
4. Select Cell➢Range, Row, or Column.
5. Enter the name in the Enter Name Manually text box.

Tell Me More

Figure 8–21 shows that several blocks of cells in the table VACATION_PACKAGES have been named: "orlando," "cancun1," and "Seattle," for example. These names reference the cells that contain prices for various aspects of travel packages to specific locations. These names can be used to create formulas in other cells in the table or in a floating cell. Notice that the names in a table are case-sensitive and must be referred to exactly as they were created when they are used in a formula or floating cell.

HOW DO I. . . Create a Formula?

One of the most powerful and flexible WordPerfect features is its capability to create and use formulas in a table. You can use nearly 100 predefined spreadsheet functions. You can also create your own formulas that are as simple as 1 + 1 or as complex as determining the net present value from a series of future cash flows. You do not have to be familiar with spreadsheets to take advantage of the efficiencies provided through the use of formulas. You can easily add a long column or row of numbers, for example, with a simple formula. If you are familiar with spreadsheets, however, you can use many formulas and functions in much the same way as you do with other spreadsheet programs.

Steps

➡To create a formula:

1. Position the insertion point in the cell in which you want to create a formula.
2. Click the right mouse button and choose Formula Bar from the QuickMenu. The Table Formula Feature Bar is displayed, as shown in Figure 8–22.
3. Click the mouse pointer once in the Formula Edit text box, which is located in the middle of the first line in the Feature Bar.

FIGURE 8–22
The Table Formula Feature Bar.

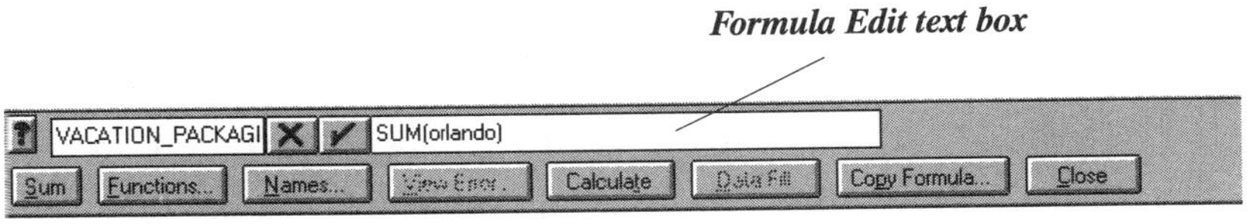

4. Enter a formula by using WordPerfect Spreadsheet Functions, table names, cell addresses, operators, and values. These options are discussed in the following "Tell Me More" section.
5. Click ✓ to insert the formula in your table, or click ✗ to cancel changes you have made to the formula.

BUTTON BAR

You can also choose the TblFormBar icon from the Tables Button Bar to display the Table Formula Feature Bar.

Tell Me More

This section is not intended to describe the specific use of all the spreadsheet functions included with WordPerfect. If you understand cash flow, however, there are functions for cash-flow calculations; if you understand addition and subtraction, you can use functions for addition and subtraction; if you understand logarithms, you can use functions to calculate logarithms; and so on.

To utilize the power of the spreadsheet functions in tables, it is helpful to understand some of the basic concepts of using and creating formulas and using spreadsheet functions. A formula is distinct from a function: A *formula* is a general term for an entry in a cell that performs a calculation or series of calculations based on commands you use to construct the formula; a *function,* on the other hand, performs a specific predefined calculation and can be inserted in a formula or used as a formula by itself. SUM(A1:A3) is a predefined function, for example, that provides the sum of the numbers in cells A1, A2, and A3 (in this example, the colon tells you that the function will include the values in all the cells from A1 to A3). This function can be inserted in a formula, such as 100 + SUM(A1:A3), which first adds the numbers in cells A1, A2, and A3 and then adds that result to the number 100.

When you create a formula, you can include numbers, specific cell references, names you have created in the current table or other tables, or predefined spreadsheet functions. The following table describes examples of basic formulas:

FORMULA	DESCRIPTION
1+3	3 is added to 1.
2*(1-4)	4 is subtracted from 1 and the difference is multiplied by 2.
A1+B3	The number in cell A1 is added to the number in cell B3.
E4*SUM(orlando)	The block of cells named "orlando" is added together (a predefined function), and the sum is multiplied by the number in E4.
SQRT(A5)/6	The square root of the number in cell A5 (a predefined function) is divided by 6.
MAX(cancun1)*10	The largest number in the block of cells named "cancun1" (a predefined function) is multiplied by 10.

Using Names in a Formula

You can insert names of cells, columns, rows, and so on into formulas. If you name a long column of numbers "cashflow," for example, you can refer to "cashflow" in a formula and not have to reference each cell (that is, the formula "SUM(cashflow)" gives you the sum of all the cells in the "cashflow" column).

To use a name in a formula, you can choose Names from the Table Formula Feature Bar and select any name from the list in the Table Names in Current Document dialog box.

Using Spreadsheet Functions in a Formula

Using spreadsheet functions in a formula is similar to inserting a name. Choose Functions from the Table Formula Feature Bar to list more than 100 spreadsheet functions predefined in WordPerfect. The Table Functions dialog box is displayed, as shown in Figure 8–23. Simply highlight the function you want to use in a formula and choose Insert. The Table

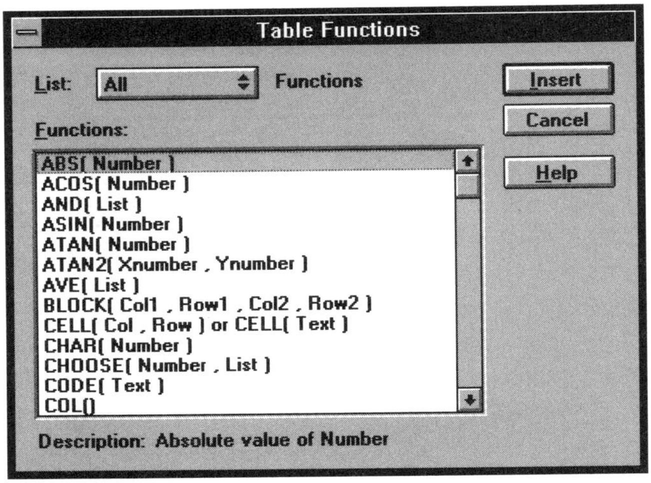

FIGURE 8–23
The Table Functions dialog box.

Functions dialog box provides a brief description of the calculation performed by the function.

Using the Data Fill Option

You can use Data Fill to continue a pattern of incrementing values in a table. If you have entered the numbers 2 and 4 in the first two cells of a row, for example, you can have WordPerfect automatically fill additional cells with 6, 8, and 10 by selecting the first two cells in addition to the cells in which you want the pattern to continue and choosing Data Fill from the Table Formula Feature Bar. You can do this with almost any incrementing values. Another example is days of the week: Fill the first two cells in a column with Mon and Tue, and Data Fill continues the rest of the column with Wed, Thu, Fri, Sat, and Sun.

Copying Formulas

After you have inserted a formula in a cell, you can copy the formula to other cells.

To copy a formula:

1. Position the insertion point in the cell of the formula you want to copy.
2. Select Table➢Copy Formula. The Copy formula dialog box is displayed.

3. Select To Cell to copy the formula to a specific cell or select Down or Right to copy the formula down a column or across a row.
4. Choose OK.

Calculating Formulas

Spreadsheets return the results of a formula by using an *order of precedence.* When WordPerfect performs calculations in a formula, it also follows an order of precedence. This term simply means that, within a formula, certain arithmetic operations are carried out before others. The order of precedence for basic arithmetic operations (add, subtract, multiply, and divide) is as follows: Multiplication and division operations are performed first; second, addition and subtraction operations are performed.

To break the order of precedence in a formula, you must insert parentheses () around an operation. Any calculations in parentheses always are performed first in a formula. To better understand this concept, consider the difference in the following formulas and their respective order of calculation:

FORMULA	ORDER OF CALCULATION
1+A2-B3*10/3	1. The value in cell B3 is multiplied by 10. 2. The product is divided by 3. 3. The quotient is subtracted from the value in cell A2. 4. The difference is added to 1.
1+(A2-B3)*10/3	1. The value in cell B3 is subtracted from the value in cell A2. 2. The difference is multiplied by 10. 3. The product is divided by 3. 4. The quotient is added to 1.

When you change the contents of any cells that are used in formulas, you can automatically update the formulas by using the Calculate function. This feature is accessed by choosing Calculate from the Table Formula Feature Bar or the Table menu.

Entering Formulas Directly into a Cell

The Cell Formula Entry feature allows you to enter a formula directly into a cell. Using this option eliminates the need to use the Table Formula Feature Bar if you just want to enter a simple formula in a single cell without using any Names or Functions. To activate this option, choose Table➢Cell Formula Entry. With the option activated, you simply enter a formula in a cell and then move the insertion point out of the cell.

Creating a Formula Example

Figure 8–24 shows a table with a series of basic formulas used to calculate column E, or "Total." The insertion point is in cell E3; the formula contained in this cell is SUM(orlando). This predefined function was used with the name "orlando" created earlier for the block of cells B3, C3, and D3. Each one of the other cells in column E has similar formulas, such as SUM(cancun1), SUM(Seattle), and so on.

FIGURE 8–24
Sample formulas.

This cell is calculated by using the formula SUM(orlando)

Travel Packages from San Francisco				
Destination	*Flight*	*Hotel (6 nights)*	*Rental Car (per week)*	*Total*
Orlando	$299.00	$724.00	$145.00	$1,168.00
Cancun*	$579.00	$861.00	N/A	$1,440.00
	$449.00	$574.00		$1,023.00
Las Vegas	$213.00	$360.00	$170.00	$743.00
Seattle	$385.00	$839.00	$165.00	$1,389.00

*Less expensive package is for off-peak travel

HOW DO I. . . Import a Spreadsheet into WordPerfect?

WordPerfect lets you import information from a spreadsheet file directly into a document. You can import a spreadsheet into a document one time or create a link between the document and spreadsheet that can be updated as you make changes in the spreadsheet. You can import spreadsheet information into your document as a table or as text. If you import a spreadsheet as a table, you do not have to create a table—WordPerfect automatically creates a table for you.

Steps

➡To import information from a spreadsheet:

1. Position the insertion point in your document where you want to import spreadsheet information.
2. Choose Insert➢Spreadsheet/Database.
3. Choose Import to copy the information from the spreadsheet into your document once or choose Create Link to be able to update your document as information in the spreadsheet changes.
4. Select Table, Text, or Merge Data File from the Import As or Link As pop-up list.
5. Type the name of the spreadsheet file to be linked or imported in the Filename text box or click the file button and choose from the Select File dialog box.
6. Enter any specific ranges from the spreadsheet.
7. Choose OK.

Tell Me More

When you import a spreadsheet, you cannot automatically update changes you make to the information in the spreadsheet. WordPerfect allows you to create a link, however, that will update your document as spreadsheet information changes.

If a spreadsheet is linked to your document, you have two options for updating any changes you make in the spreadsheet. First, you can activate the Update on Retrieve option by choosing Insert➢Spreadsheet/Database and then choosing Options. If you select Update on Retrieve, the information from the linked spreadsheet is updated every time you open the WordPerfect document. You can also manually update spreadsheet information by choosing Spreadsheet/Database from the Insert menu and then choosing Update.

WordPerfect-Supported Spreadsheet Formats

WordPerfect supports the linking or importing of spreadsheets from these programs:

- PlanPerfect versions 3.0 through 5.1
- Quattro Pro versions 3.0 and 4.0
- Quattro Pro for Windows version 1.0
- Lotus 1-2-3 versions 2.01, 2.3, 2.4, 3.0, and 3.1
- Excel versions 2.1, 3.0, and 4.0

HOW DO I... Use Floating Cells?

The Floating Cell feature allows you to reference information from a table, column, row, or range of cells in the text of a document.

Steps

➡To create a floating cell:

1. Place the insertion point in a document where you want to create a floating cell.
2. Choose Table➢Create.
3. Select Floating Cell.
4. Choose OK.

Tell Me More

A floating cell is not like a table cell; rather, it is a pair of codes ([Flt Cell] and [Flt Cell]) inserted into your document wherever the insertion point is positioned when you create the floating cell. You can display Reveal Codes to see the [Flt Cell] codes inserted. A floating cell can be used to reference table cells, columns, or rows outside a table within the body of a document.

Similar to a table, the number type used in a floating cell can be edited. Simply choose Number Type from the Table menu and select a number type and any options you want, as explained earlier in this chapter.

HOW DO I. . . Create a Chart?

A great new WordPerfect feature is its capability to create charts in your document. You can create a chart by using data from a table or a spreadsheet file or by entering new data in a worksheet when the chart is created. Charts are created by using the Chart Editor in WordPerfect Draw. This feature allows you to use predefined templates for simple charts or to select from a number of options to customize almost any aspect of a chart.

Steps

➠**To create a chart and insert it in your document:**

1. Position the insertion point where you want a chart located in your document.
2. Choose Graphics➢Chart. The Chart Editor opens, as shown in Figure 8–25, with default sample data and a sample chart.
3. Enter or import data in the worksheet of the Chart Editor; these options are described in more detail in the following "Tell Me More" section.
4. Customize the chart by selecting a chart type, adding a title or a legend, choosing layout options, and so on; these options are described in more detail in the following "Tell Me More" section.
5. Choose File➢Close and Return and then choose Yes, or choose Return at the bottom of the window and then choose Yes, to insert the chart into your document.

BUTTON BAR

You can also choose the 

icon from the Tables Button Bar to enter the Chart Editor from your document.

Tell Me More

The following sections describe the basics of entering data in a worksheet and selecting basic options to customize a chart.

FIGURE 8–25
The Chart Editor in WordPerfect Draw.

Worksheet with sample data

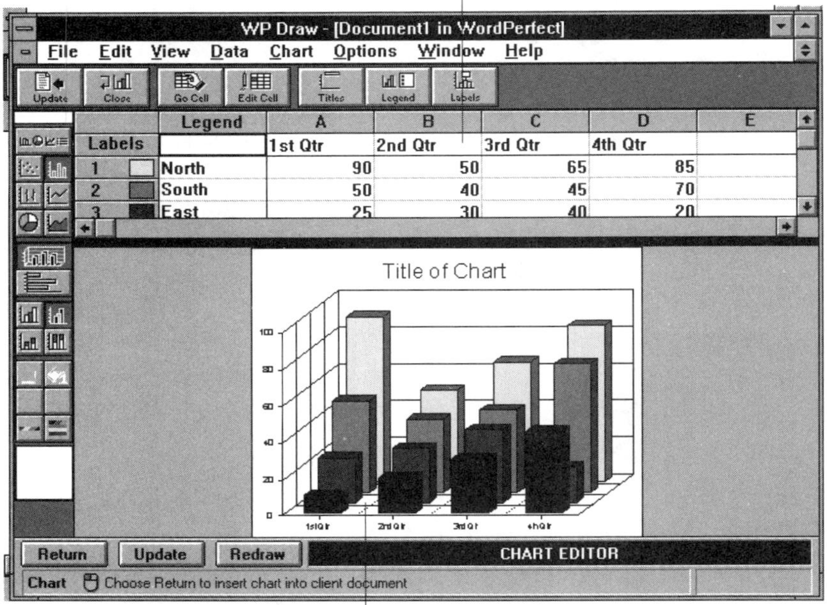

Sample chart derived from worksheet data

Entering or Importing Data into the Worksheet

You have three basic options for entering data in the Chart Editor: Use data from a WordPerfect table in your document, enter new data in the worksheet, or import data from a spreadsheet.

Using data from a WordPerfect table in your document is easy and effective. All you do is select the table data and then enter the Chart Editor by following the preceding steps. The data is automatically inserted into the worksheet in the Chart Editor. You can even select table column and row headings to be used as a chart legend or as chart labels.

To enter new data, you must first clear the sample data in the worksheet.

To clear existing data:

1. From the Chart Editor, choose Edit➢Select All.
2. Press the Delete key to display the Clear dialog box.
3. Select Data and choose OK.

You may have to click the Redraw button at the bottom of the window to update the chart. After the existing data is cleared, you can click in any worksheet cell and enter data. Figure 8–26 shows some of the data from the table that was used earlier in the chapter.

You can also import data into the Chart Editor worksheet from an existing spreadsheet file.

To import data from a spreadsheet:

1. Click in the cell in the worksheet where you want to import the data.
2. Choose File➢Import. The Import Chart Data dialog box is displayed.
3. Enter the name of the spreadsheet file in the Filename text box and choose Import. The Import Spreadsheet dialog box is displayed, as shown in Figure 8–27.
4. Enter the cell coordinates you want to import in the Range text box or select a predefined Range Name. Cell range coordinates must be entered similarly to coordinates in a formula (A1:C10, for example).
5. Select Clear Current Data if you want the existing data in the worksheet to be cleared and replaced with the spreadsheet data.
6. Choose OK.

FIGURE 8–26
A chart with data from a WordPerfect table.

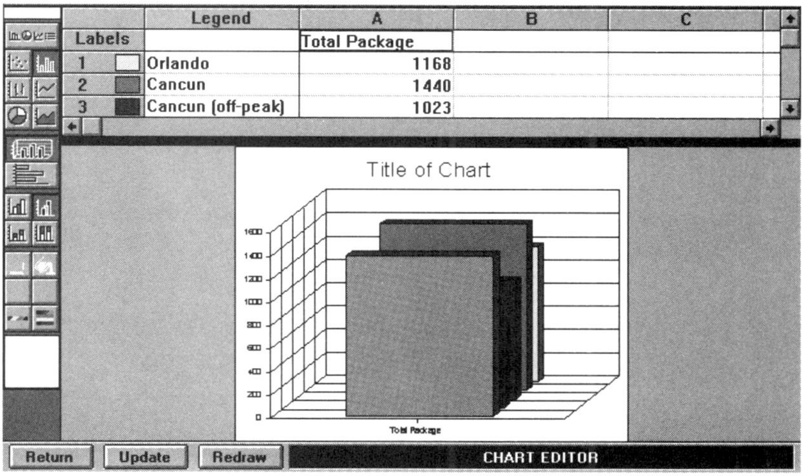

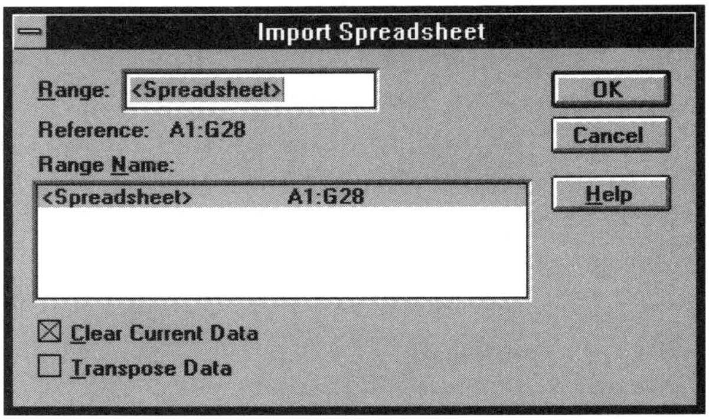

FIGURE 8–27
The Import Spreadsheet dialog box.

WordPerfect allows you to import data into the Worksheet from the following popular spreadsheet programs:

- PlanPerfect versions 3.0 through 5.1
- Quattro Pro versions 2.0 through 4.0
- Quattro Pro for Windows version 1.0
- Lotus 1-2-3 versions 2.01 through 3.1
- Lotus for Windows
- Microsoft Excel versions 2.1 through 4.0

NOTE

The program versions supported for importing into the worksheet in the Chart Editor are slightly different from those supported for importing and linking to a WordPerfect table.

Inserting and Deleting Rows and Columns in the Worksheet

As you enter data in a worksheet, you can insert or delete entire columns or rows of cells.

To delete a column or row:

1. Select the entire column or row by clicking on the column letter or row number in the worksheet.
2. Choose Edit➢Delete.
3. Choose OK.

You can also select several columns or rows to be deleted simultaneously.

To insert a column or row:

1. Select the entire column to the right of where you want the column inserted, or select the entire row below where you want the row inserted.
2. Choose Edit➢Insert.

You can also insert several columns or rows simultaneously by selecting several columns to the right of where you want the columns inserted or by selecting several rows below where you want the new row inserted. If you select 2 rows and choose Edit➢Insert, for example, two new rows are inserted above the selected rows.

Basic Customization Options

The options available for customizing a chart are extensive. To get an idea of the flexibility provided in the Chart Editor, you should spend some time going through the menus. The following sections describe a few basic options that allow you to effectively create great-looking charts.

Selecting a Chart Type

You can select a chart type before or after you have entered data in the worksheet. It is easier to choose a chart type for your particular data, however, if you have entered data in the worksheet first. You can select from the following chart types:

- Area
- Bar
- Hi-lo
- Line
- Pie
- Scatter

If you know which type of chart you want, you can select it by choosing Chart and selecting from the chart type options that are displayed. You can also select a chart type by choosing one of the following buttons from the chart palette:

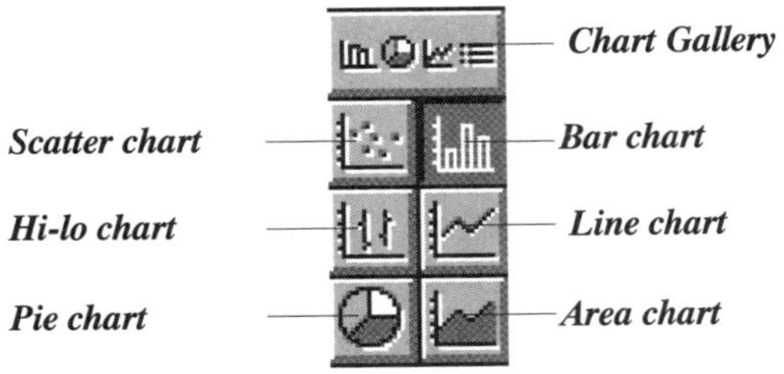

If you are uncertain which type of chart you want, you can view samples of all the chart types by using the Chart Gallery, shown in Figure 8–28.

To display all chart types in the Chart Gallery:

1. Choose Chart➢Gallery *or* click the Chart Gallery button. The Chart Gallery dialog box is displayed with several different chart styles for one particular chart type.
2. Choose Chart Types to display a sample chart for all six different chart types, as shown in Figure 8–28.

To select a chart type from the Chart Gallery:

1. Select the chart type you want by clicking on the sample chart.
2. Choose Retrieve.

FIGURE 8–28
The Chart Gallery dialog box.

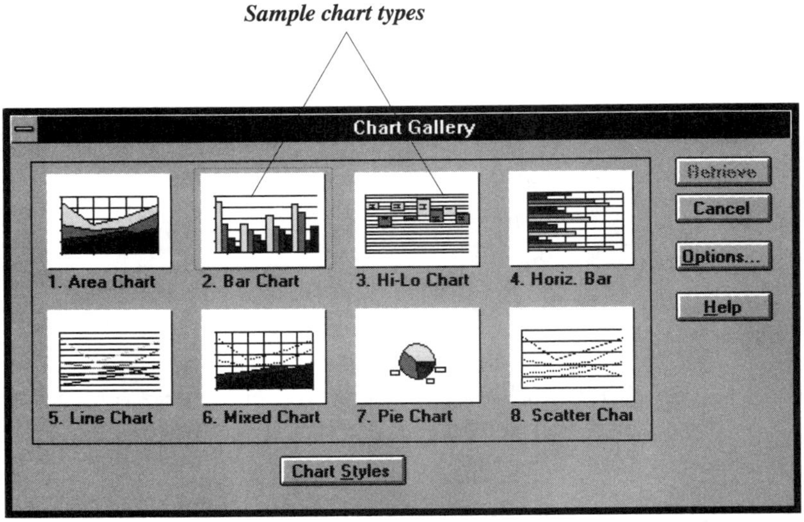

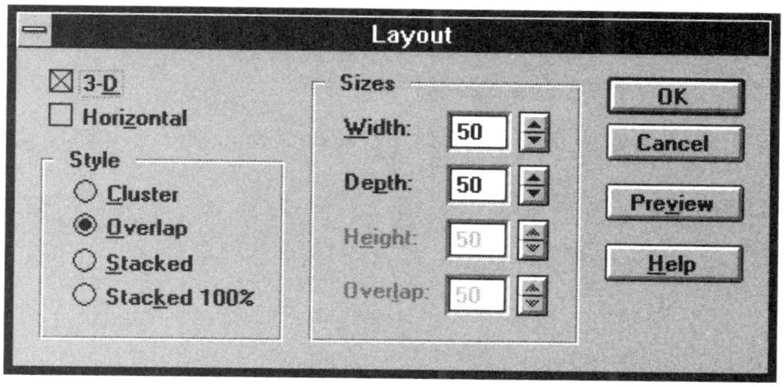

FIGURE 8–29
The Layout dialog box.

Changing the Chart Layout

Depending on which chart type you select, different layout options are available. If you have selected a bar chart type, for example, the following layout options are available:

- Three-dimensional bars
- Horizontal bar orientation
- Bar style
- Bar size

To change the layout options:

1. Choose Options➢Layout. The Layout dialog box is displayed, as shown in Figure 8–29.
2. Select the options you want to use.
3. Choose OK.

To change layout options, you can also choose any of the following buttons:

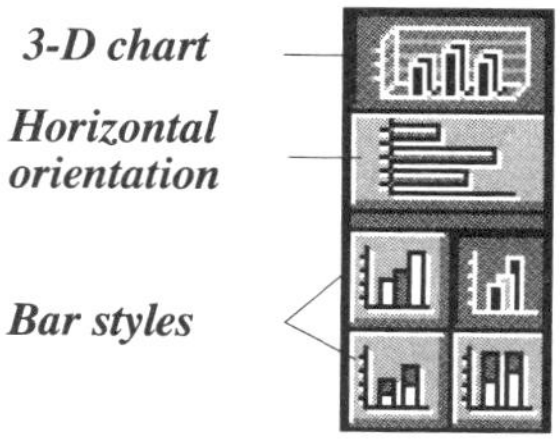

These buttons change depending on the chart type that is selected. The bar chart in Figure 8–30 illustrates several layout changes.

FIGURE 8–30
A chart with layout changes.

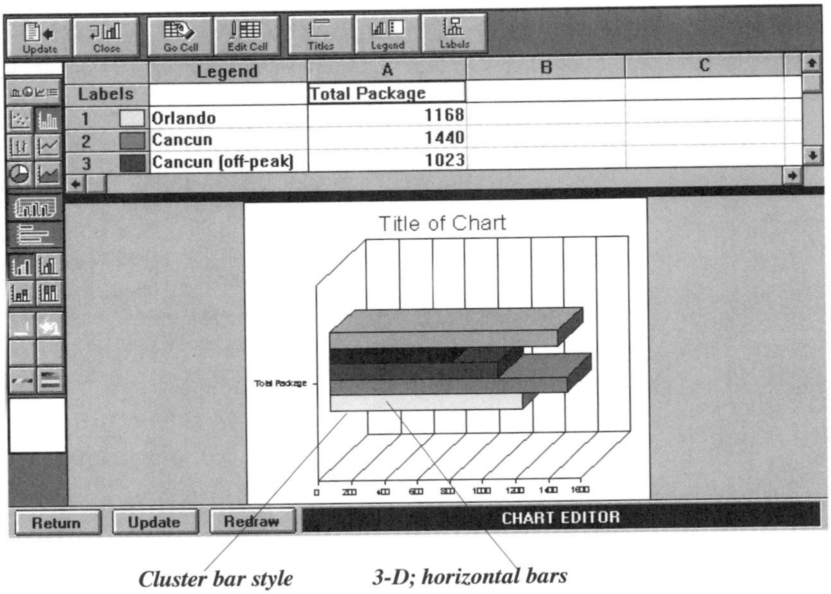

Adding Chart Titles and Legend

To add a chart title:

1. Choose Options➢Titles. The Titles dialog box is displayed, as shown in Figure 8–31.
2. Enter any titles you want to use.
3. Choose OK.

FIGURE 8–31
The Titles dialog box.

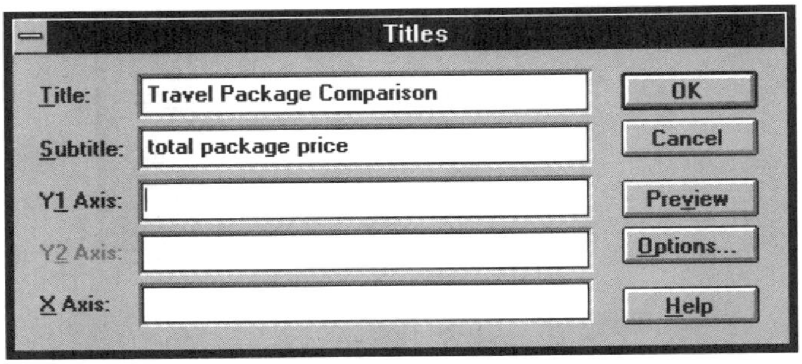

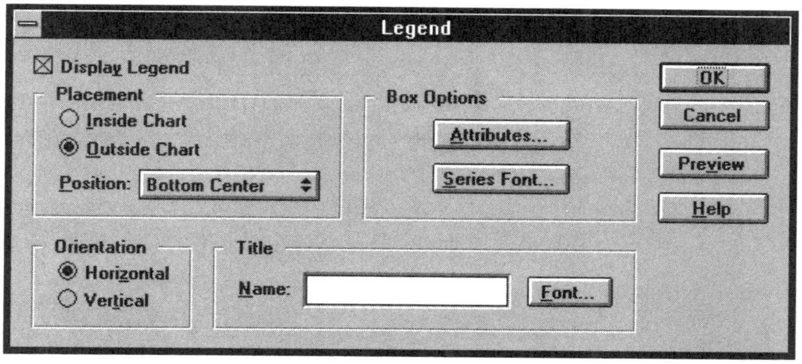

FIGURE 8–32
The Legend dialog box.

BUTTON BAR

You can also choose the  **icon from the Chart Editor button bar to display the Titles dialog box.**

From the Titles dialog box, you can enter a Title and a Subtitle in addition to titles for both the X axis and Y axis of your chart.

A legend can be used with a chart to identify each row of data. To use a legend with your chart, you must add legend titles in the worksheet as well as select the legend display options you want to use. Legend titles are added directly into a worksheet in the Legend column (Notice in Figure 8–26 that the legend titles correspond with the vacation packages "Orlando," "Cancun," "Las Vegas," and "Seattle.")

To display the legend with the chart and select display options:

1. Choose Options➢Legend. The Legend dialog box is displayed, as shown in Figure 8–32.
2. Select Display Legend.
3. Select any options you want to use.
4. Choose OK.

Editing a Chart in a Document

When you return the chart to your document, you have saved the chart as a part of your WordPerfect document. When the chart is returned to your document, some text may be automatically wrapped around the chart, as shown in Figure 8–33. With the chart returned to your document you can click and drag the chart to position it anywhere you want

FIGURE 8–33
A chart inserted in a document.

Cancun*	$579.00	$861.00	N/A	$1,440.00
	$449.00	$574.00		$1,023.00
Las Vegas	$213.00	$360.00	$170.00	$743.00
Seattle	$385.00	$839.00	$165.00	$1,389.00

*Less expensive package is for off-peak travel

New VACATION CONSULTING Service

It has always been our goal to offer the highest degree of service and convenience for vacationers. In addition to our new travel packages we will be offering a new vacation consulting service. This service will include an analysis of your interests, hobbies, athletic interests, family status and several other factors. Our vacation consultants will provide you with vacation alternatives based on this analysis.

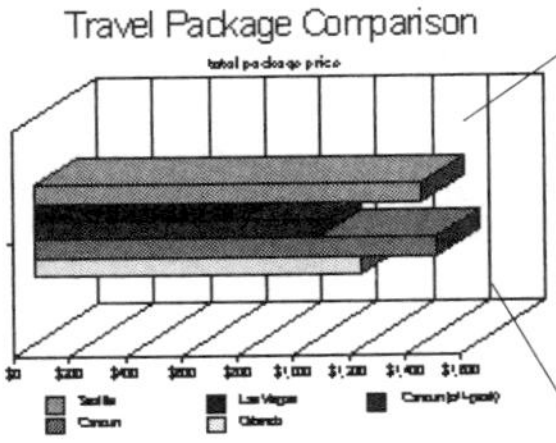

in the document. You can also return to the Chart Editor and edit the chart by double-clicking anywhere on the chart.

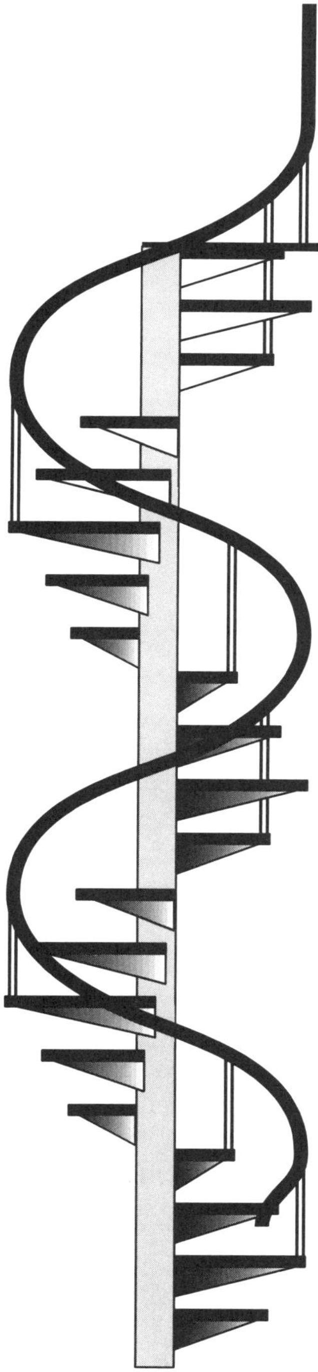

Chapter 9

Enhancing Documents with Graphics

WordPerfect offers many ways to enhance your documents with graphics features. You can use graphics images, graphics lines, TextArt, borders, watermarks, and equations. You can use graphics to create illustrations for term papers or scientific papers. Or you can add graphics just to give readers a little enjoyment. Graphics can be used in any document in which you want to add variety and enhance the quality and appeal of your documents.

WordPerfect ships several graphics images with WordPerfect 6; by default, they are copied in your C:\WPWIN60\GRAPHICS directory when you install WordPerfect. To help you become familiar with the graphics images shipped with WordPerfect, all figures and illustrations in this chapter use the graphics files shipped with WordPerfect 6. In addition to these graphics files, you can use many other graphics files, such as bit-mapped graphics (BMP), encapsulated PostScript (EPS), PC

Paintbrush graphics (PCX), tagged-image file format (TIFF), and several others.

This chapters answers questions about the following graphics features:

- Adding a graphics image
- Creating a text box
- Creating a graphics box
- Editing a graphics box
- Creating a caption
- Positioning a graphics box
- Changing the size of a graphics box
- Changing the border and fill of a graphics box
- Changing the position of text around a graphics box
- Editing a graphics image
- Using TextArt
- Using WP Draw
- Creating graphics lines
- Creating borders
- Creating an equation
- Creating watermarks
- Enhancing the display of graphics

HOW DO I... Add a Graphics Image to a Document?

The simplest and quickest way to add a figure to your document is with the Graphics Figure option. This option automatically inserts the graphics image in a figure box and adds it to your document. When you use the Graphics Figure option, you just specify the name of the graphics image and WordPerfect does the rest.

Steps

➡ **To retrieve a graphics image directly into your document and have it inserted in a figure box:**

1. Choose Graphics➢Figure. The Insert Image dialog box is displayed.
2. Enter the filename of the graphics image and choose OK *or* click on a directory that contains graphic images and then double-click on the filename.

BUTTON BAR

You can also click the  **icon to open the Insert Image dialog box.**

Tell Me More

When you insert a graphics image directly in your document, WordPerfect uses the default settings for a figure graphics box. The figure box containing the graphics image is positioned to the right of the current paragraph (if one exists) and is surrounded by a single line border on all sides, as shown in Figure 9–1. The text in the paragraph wraps on the left side of the figure for most figures.

The figure box is selected when it is inserted into your document. With the figure box selected, you can edit the settings of the figure

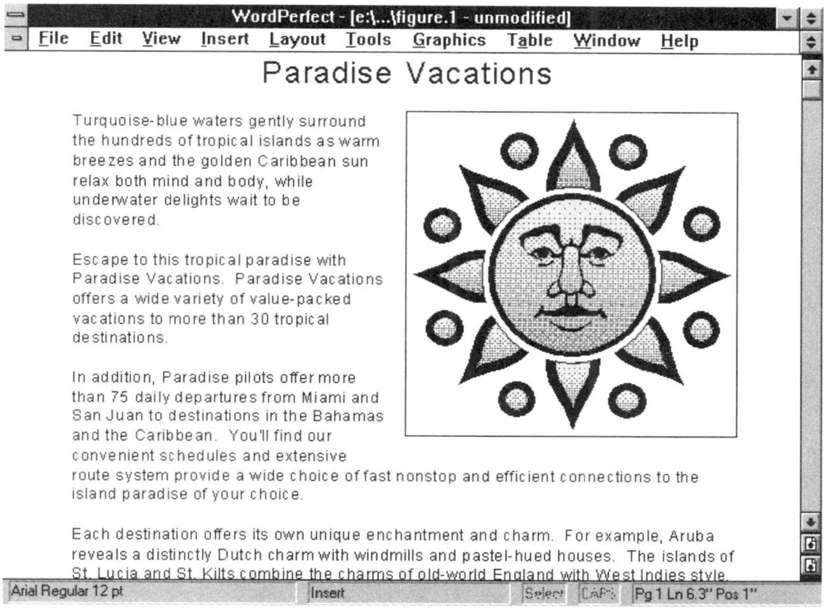

FIGURE 9–1
An image inserted in a figure box.

graphics box by choosing any of the options on the Graphics Feature Bar. For information about editing a graphics box, see the section "HOW DO I... Edit a Graphics Box?" later in this chapter.

NOTE

To deselect the graphics box and close the Graphics Feature Bar, choose Close from the Feature Bar.

HOW DO I... Create a Graphics Box That Contains Text?

You can place text, columns, and tables in graphics boxes. Inserting text in a graphics box offsets it from the rest of the document to add special emphasis. In addition, placing text in a graphics box lets you easily move and position the text in your document. You can type the text directly into a graphics box or retrieve a file you have already created.

NOTE

If you want to use special text effects, such as changing the shape of the text, see the section "HOW DO I...Create Fancy Text?" later in this chapter.

Steps

➨To create a graphics box that contains text:

1. Choose Graphics ➢ Text Box.
2. Enter the text you want to include in the box. The text box is displayed, as shown in Figure 9–2.
3. Make any changes to the text box by using the Feature Bar options.
4. Click outside the box to deselect it *or* choose Close from the Feature Bar.

BUTTON BAR

You can also choose the Text Box icon to quickly create a text box.

Tell Me More

When you enter text in a text box, you can make any necessary formatting changes. If you want to center the text, for example, you can do

FIGURE 9–2
A text box inserted in a document.

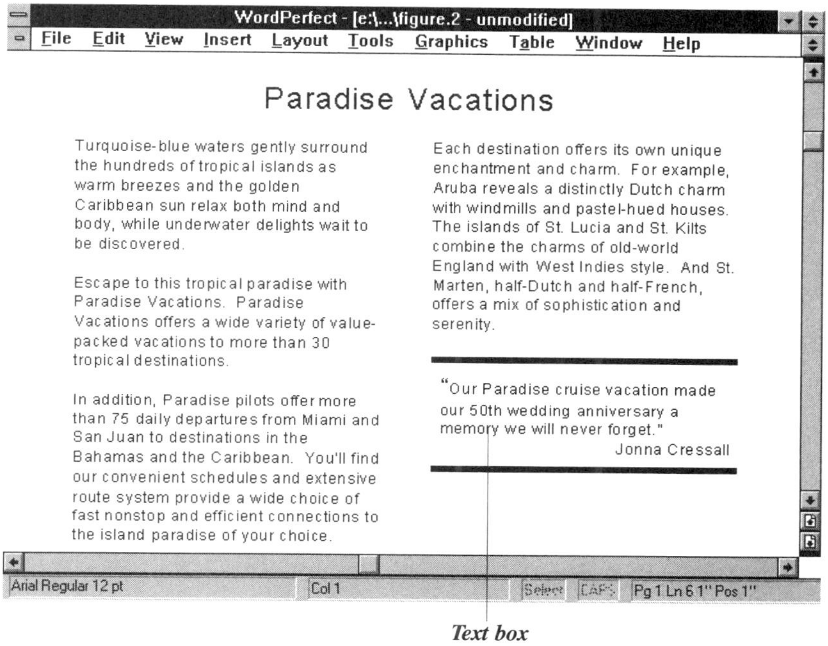

so as you would do in a regular document. Options that are not available are dimmed on the pull-down menus.

If you want to insert the contents of a file in the text box:

1. After creating the text box, choose Content from the Feature Bar.
2. Enter the name of the file in the Filename Text Box and choose OK until you return to the document window.

Using the Filename option gives you the flexibility to create the text first and then insert it in a graphics box.

Inserting columns and tables into a text box (or any kind of graphics box) can be extremely beneficial because you can easily move the information anywhere within the document. You can create the graphics box without any borders or fill so that the text appears as though it is normal text and not inserted in a graphics box.

Figure 9–3 shows a table in a graphics box without any borders or fill. For information about modifying the Borders/Fill options, see the section "HOW DO I... Change the Border and Fill of the Graphics Box?" later in this chapter.

FIGURE 9–3
A table inserted in a graphics box with no borders.

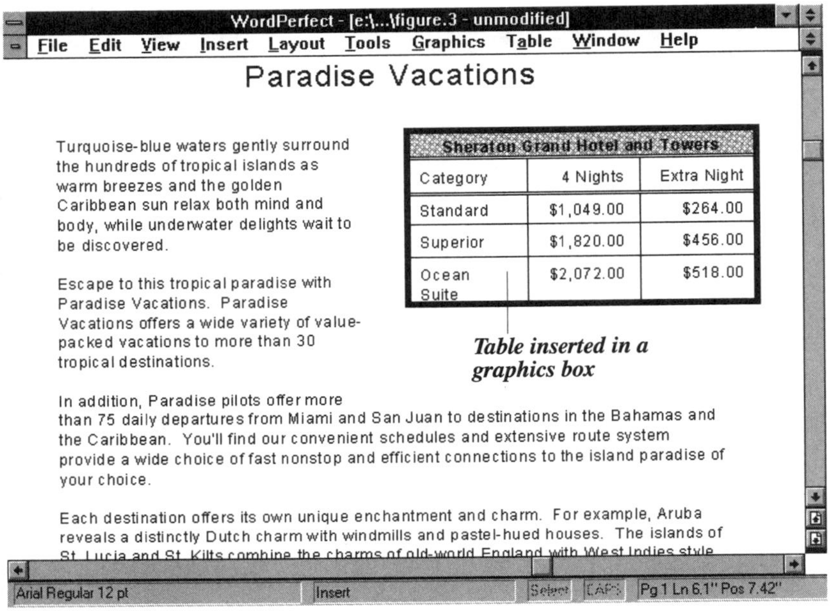

Another powerful feature of a text box is the capability to rotate text. You can create personal or business stationery, for example, that displays your name down the left edge of the page, as shown in Figure 9–4.

➡To create a text box similar to the one that was shown in Figure 9–4:

1. Choose Graphics ➢ Text Box *or* click the Text Box Button Bar icon.
2. Select the font type and size you want and set Justification to All.
3. Type your name in the box.
4. Choose Content from the Feature Bar. The Box Content dialog box is displayed, as shown in Figure 9–5.
5. Select 90 Degrees for the rotation and choose OK.
6. Choose Border/Fill from the Feature Bar, change the Border Style to No Border, and choose OK.
7. Choose OK. You can then size the box or move it to a new location.

FIGURE 9–4
Rotated text in a text box.

Julie Marsh

Dear Friends and Family:

We are happy to inform you that we are now in our new house. We love the neighborhood and are enjoying the extra space and our lovely back yard.

FIGURE 9–5
The Box Content dialog box.

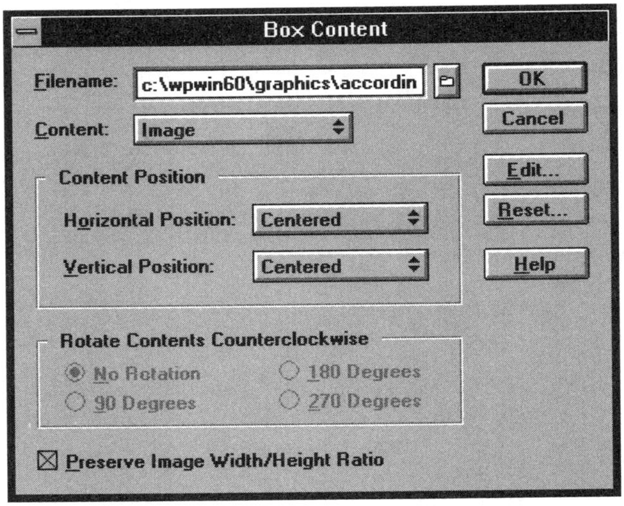

HOW DO I... Create a Graphics Box?

WordPerfect has several types of graphics boxes:

- Figure box
- Text box
- Equation box
- Table box
- User box
- Button box
- Watermark image box
- Inline equation box
- OLE box

All these boxes are graphics boxes; the only difference is that they all use different graphics box options. A figure box has a single border around the box, for example, and a text box has a thick border on the top and bottom. You can insert graphics or text into any box; just because it is a figure box does not mean that you have to insert a figure in it. In addition, you can change any of the options associated with a box.

FIGURE 9–6
The Custom Box dialog box.

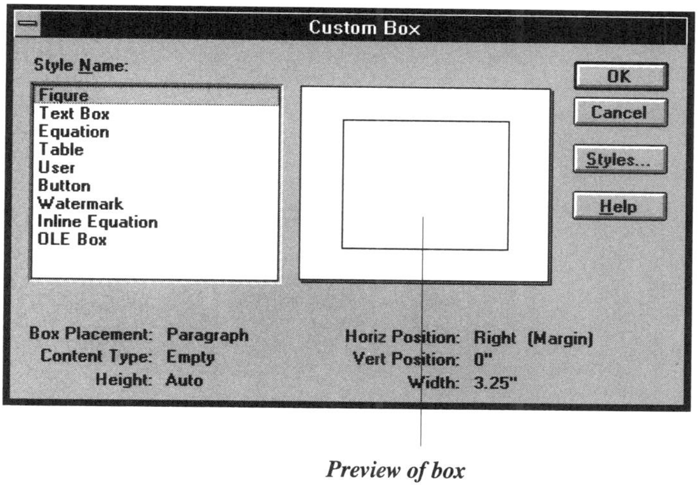

Steps

➡To insert a graphics box:

1. Choose Graphics and then select the graphics box type from the pull-down menu. If the box type you want to use is not listed, choose Custom Box; the dialog box shown in Figure 9–6 is displayed. Highlight the box you want to use and choose OK.
2. Use the Feature Bar to make any changes to the graphics box.
3. When you are finished editing the box, choose Close to remove the Feature Bar.

Tell Me More

The following sections explain how to use the Graphics Feature Bar and QuickMenu, how to specify the contents of a graphics box, and how to add graphics box types to the graphics pull-down menu.

Using the Graphics Feature Bar and QuickMenu

The Graphics Feature Bar (displayed in Figure 9–7) and the Graphics QuickMenu (displayed in Figure 9–8) provide you with all the options you need to customize and edit your graphics box.

FIGURE 9–7
The Graphics Feature Bar.

Graphics Feature Bar

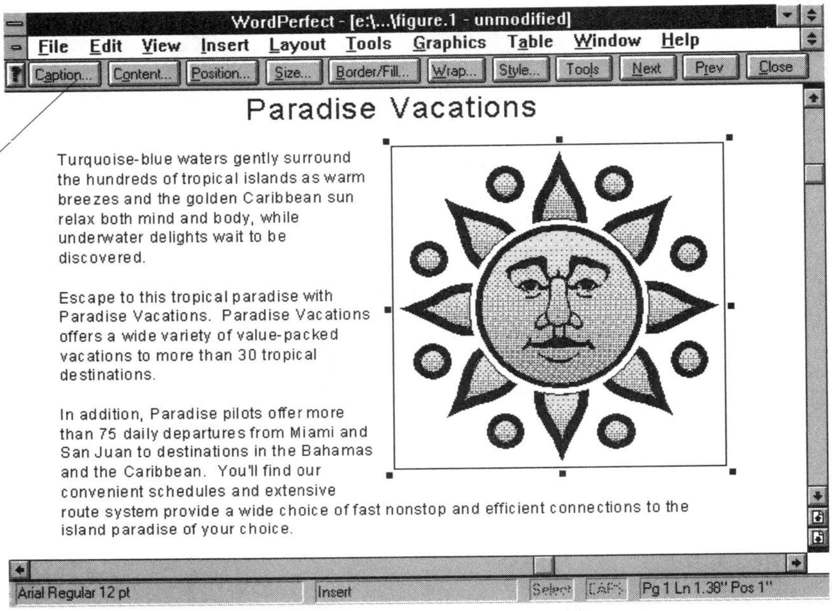

FIGURE 9–8
The Graphics QuickMenu.

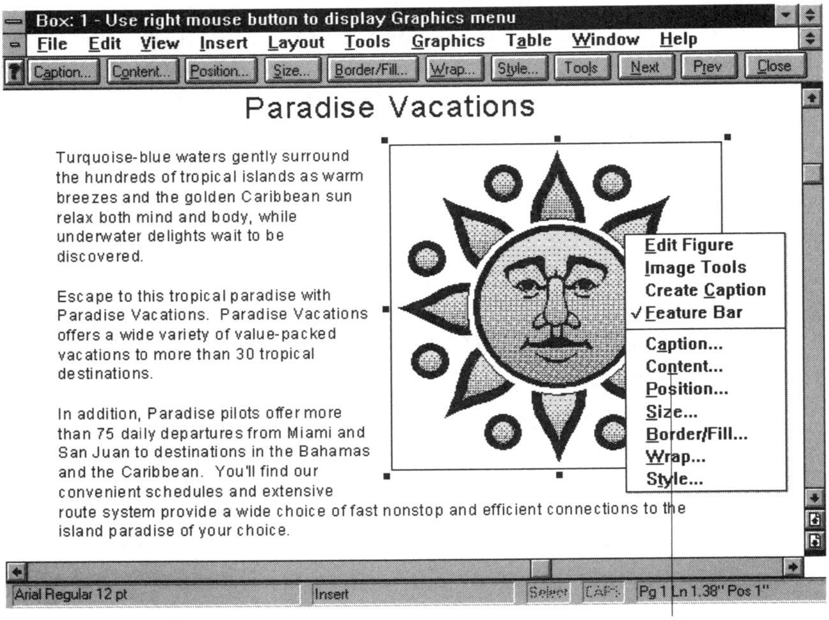

Graphics QuickMenu

The Graphics Feature Bar is displayed when you are creating a new graphics box. You can also display the Feature Bar by selecting Feature Bar from the Graphics QuickMenu. If you will do extensive editing on a graphics box, you may want to display the Feature Bar for quick and easy access to the features.

The following table gives a brief description of the options available on the Graphics Feature Bar and the Graphics QuickMenu (more detailed information about these options is found throughout this chapter):

OPTION	DESCRIPTION
Caption	Allows you to create a caption and change the position, format, and style for the caption.
Content	Specifies the contents of the graphics box. You can select from Empty, Image, Text, Equation, and Image on Disk. You can also specify the position of the box contents.
Position	Specifies the placement and position of the box. With the position options, you specify the exact horizontal and vertical position of the graphics box. You can also use the mouse to position a graphics box.
Size	Specifies the width and height of the graphics box. You can set a specific size or you can have WordPerfect automatically determine an appropriate width and height based on the contents of the box. You can also use the mouse to size a graphics box.
Border/Fill	Specifies the style of the lines surrounding the graphics box and the color and pattern of the fill, or shading, within the box.
Wrap	Specifies how text wraps around a graphics box. You can specify how you want the text to flow around the box and where you want the text positioned in relation to the graphics box.
Style	Allows you to select a different box style, such as Figure, Text, or User, for the current graphics box.
Tools	If your graphics box contains a graphics image, the Tools option lets you edit the graphics image.

(continues)

OPTION	DESCRIPTION
Next	Moves to the next graphics box in the document.
Prev	Moves to the previous graphics box in the document.
Close	Closes the Graphics Feature Bar.

Specifying the Contents of a Graphics Box

Most of the graphics boxes have a default content specified. The content for a text box, for example, is text. There may be times, however, when a box does not have a content specified or you want to change the content.

The following table describes the different types of Contents you can select:

OPTION	DESCRIPTION
Empty	Use this option if you do not want to include anything in the graphics box. You can use the Empty option if you want to create a graphics box that contains a special seal or sticker that must be physically attached to the page after printing the document. You may also create an empty box to create an actual page layout for a newsletter. You can then insert a photo or other hard copy of art in the box.
Image	Specifies a graphics file as the contents.
Image on Disk	Specifies a graphics file on disk as the Contents. When you select Image on Disk, WordPerfect references the graphics you specify in the Filename entry field in the document but stores the actual file on disk. This option is useful if you want to reduce the size of documents that contain large graphics files or if you plan to edit the graphics file and you want the image in the document to automatically include the changes.
Text	Specifies text as the contents. You can enter the text in the text box or retrieve a file that contains text.
Equation	Specifies equation as the contents.

FIGURE 9–9
Additional graphics box types added to the Graphics pull-down menu.

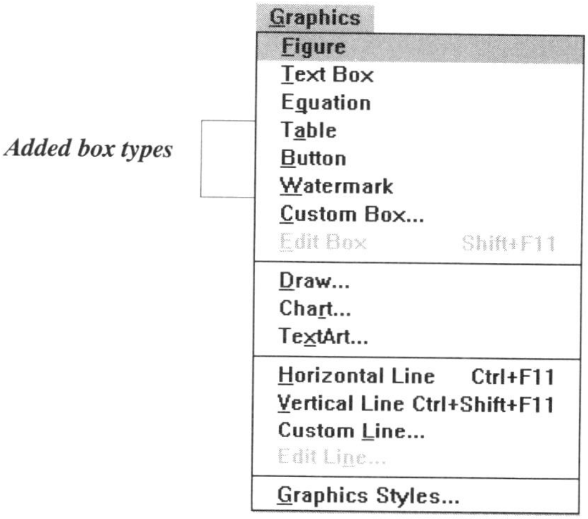

Adding Additional Graphics Box Types to the Graphics Menu

By default, when you open the Graphics pull-down menu, the only graphics boxes listed are Figure, Text, and Equation. To access the other types, you choose Custom Box and then select the box type.

If you want to add another graphics box type to the Graphics pull-down menu, as shown in Figure 9–9, you can do so with the following steps:

1. Choose Graphics ➢ Custom Box ➢ Styles.
2. Choose Menu.
3. Select the graphics box types you want to include and choose OK.
4. Choose Close and OK to return to the document window.

HOW DO I. . . Edit a Graphics Box?

After you create a graphics box, you can easily change any of the options associated with the box. If you create a figure box, for example, and you want to change the way the text wraps around the box, you can easily edit the figure box and change the Wrap Text options.

Steps

➡To edit a graphics box:

1. Right-click anywhere on the graphics box you want to edit to select it and display the QuickMenu. A selected graphics box displays "markers" on each side of the box.
2. Choose an option from the QuickMenu and make the necessary changes.

Tell Me More

If you are going to edit several features of the graphics box, you may want to display the Graphics Feature Bar by selecting it from the QuickMenu and then choosing the options from the Feature Bar.

If you have several graphic boxes in your document, you can quickly move to the next or previous graphics box by choosing the Next and Prev buttons on the Feature Bar.

NOTE **If you have several graphics boxes in a document, you can choose Graphics ➢ Edit Box *or* press Shift + F11 to display a dialog box from which you can choose the box you want to edit.**

HOW DO I... Create a Caption?

Captions enable you to label a graphics box for easy reference in your documents. If you create a graphics box with a chart that displays average seasonal temperatures in Bermuda, for example, you can create a caption that reads "Average Temperatures in Bermuda." You can specify the position and format of a caption by using Caption options.

Steps

➡To create a caption:

1. Right-click anywhere on the graphics box you want to edit and choose Create Caption. The appropriate default caption appears for the box style you are using in the Caption Editor, such as **Figure 1**, **Table 1**, **1**, **(1)**, and so on. Enter the text you want in the caption.
2. Choose Close. The caption appears directly below the graphics box, as shown in Figure 9–10.

FIGURE 9–10
A graphics box with caption.

Take a break--skydive in the Cayman Islands

Tell Me More

WordPerfect does not automatically insert captions for you; you must create a caption when you are creating or editing the graphics box. WordPerfect inserts a default caption in the caption-editing window. If you enter the caption-editing window and do not want to use the default caption, you must delete it. Although WordPerfect displays a default caption, it uses it only if you enter the caption-editing window and accept the default.

The caption-editing window is just like a document window. When you enter your caption, you can make any necessary formatting changes. If you want your caption in a smaller font, for example, you can change the font in the caption-editing window. By default, WordPerfect uses your document's initial font. Options that are not available when you are editing a caption are dimmed on the pull-down menus.

WordPerfect provides several options to customize the position, width, and styles of captions.

➨To make changes to the Caption options:

1. Right-click on the graphics box and choose Caption. The Box Caption dialog box is displayed, as shown in Figure 9–11.

The following sections describe the caption options.

HINT **If you want to change the Captions back to their original settings, you can choose Reset from the Box Caption dialog box.**

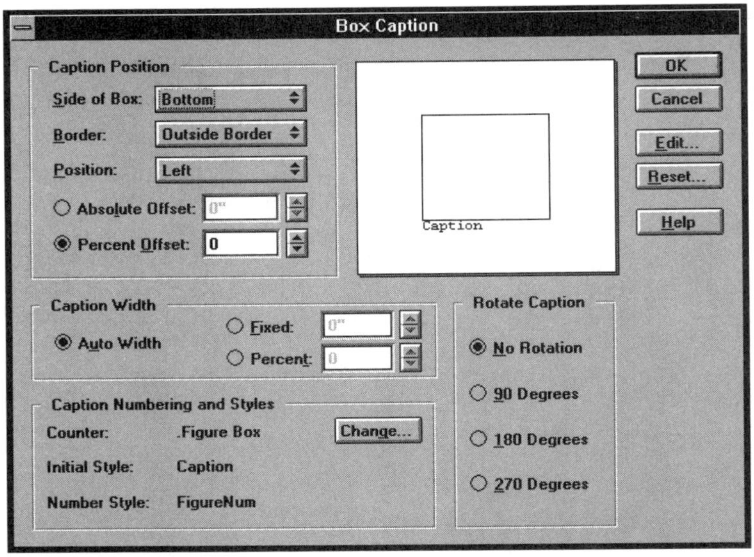

FIGURE 9–11
The Box Caption dialog box.

Changing the Caption Position

You can specify the exact location in which you want to position a caption. By default, WordPerfect inserts the caption in the top left or bottom left of the box, depending on the type of graphics box you are using. The following table describes the options you can use to change the position of a caption:

OPTION	DESCRIPTION
Side of Box	Specifies where to insert the caption in relation to the graphics box. You can choose Bottom, Top, Left, or Right. If you want the caption to be placed directly above the graphics box, for example, choose Top.
Border	Specifies where to insert the caption in relation to the border of the graphics box. You can choose Outside, Inside, or On. If you want to place the caption inside the graphics box border, for example, choose Inside. When a caption is outside the graphics box, it is still considered part of the box.

(continues)

OPTION	DESCRIPTION
Position	Specifies the alignment of the caption. You can choose Center, Left, or Right. The Position setting is in relation to the Side of Box setting. If you choose Top for the Side of Box and Center for the Position, for example, the caption looks like this: Figure 1: Hummingbird 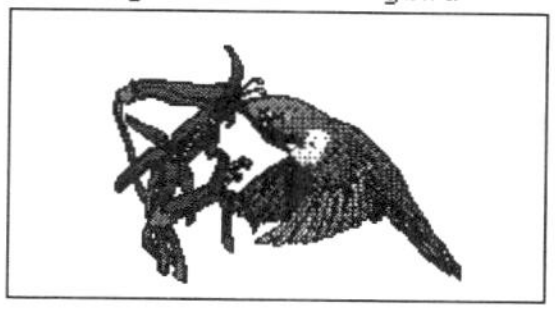
Absolute or Percent Offset	Specifies the distance from the Position option. By default, the offset is 0, which means that the caption aligns exactly center, left, or right. You can select Set or Percent. If you choose Set, you must enter the distance you want to shift the caption text from the position. If you choose Percent, type the percentage (from –100 to 100) that you want to shift the caption text.

Changing the Caption Width

You can change the width of the caption to eliminate unnecessary white space when the caption is lengthy and is positioned on the left or right side of the graphics box.

To change the caption width from the Box Caption dialog box:

1. Select Auto Width (Based on Caption), Fixed, or Percent. If you choose Auto Width, the width of the caption is adjusted automatically.

If you choose Set, type a measurement. You are limited to the width or height of the box. If you choose Percent, type a percentage of the box width you want the caption to occupy (from 1 through 100).

Rotating the Caption

Rotating the caption enables you to change the orientation of the text so that it takes up less room on the page or makes it easier to read, depending on the location of your graphics box in the document.

To rotate a caption:

FIGURE 9–12
A caption rotated 90 degrees.

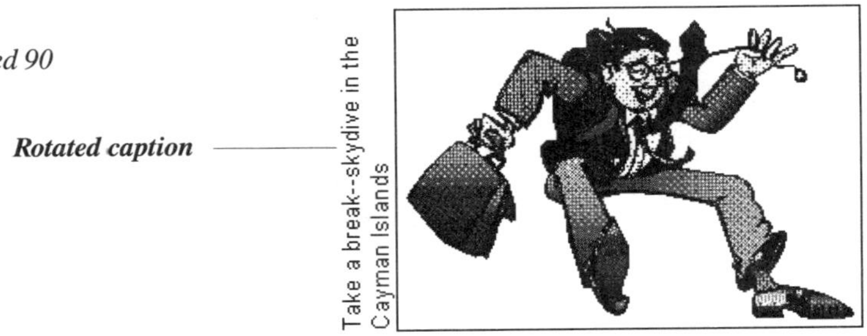

1. Select one of the following options from the Rotate Caption group box: No Rotation, 90°, 180°, or 270°. The caption rotates counterclockwise.

Figure 9–12 shows an example of a caption that has been rotated 90 degrees so that the text flows along the left border. In this example, the caption has been positioned on the Left side of the box, and Bottom has been selected for Position.

HOW DO I... Position a Graphics Box?

WordPerfect gives you complete control over where you want to position a graphics box. You can use the mouse to drag an existing graphics box to a new location. You can also position a graphics box by using the Box Position dialog box and entering the exact placement and measurements. Using the mouse to position a graphics box is quick and easy. Using the Box Position dialog box allows you to specify exact measurements for the location.

Steps

➡To position an existing graphics box by using the mouse:

1. Point to the graphics box and hold down the left mouse button—the mouse pointer will look like this:

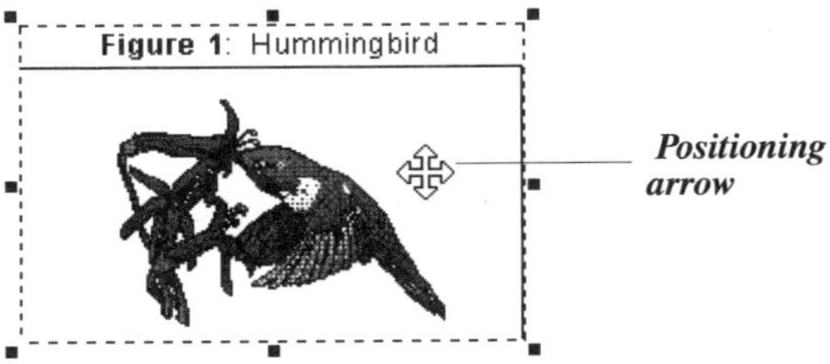

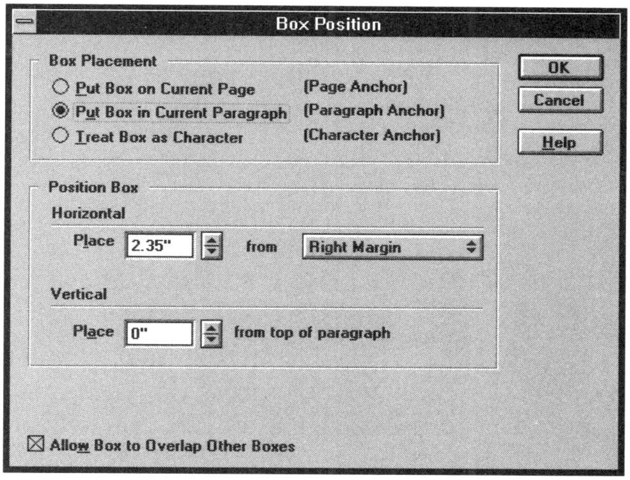

FIGURE 9–13
The Box Position dialog box.

2. Drag the box to the new position and release the mouse button. As you drag the box, the box is surrounded by dashed lines to aid you in positioning the box.

NOTE

If you need to deselect a graphics box, click anywhere outside the box.

➨**To position a graphics box by using the Box Position dialog box:**

1. Right-click on the graphics box and choose Position. The Box Position dialog box is displayed, as shown in Figure 9–13.
2. Select a box-placement option. This item specifies what you want to serve as the "anchor" for your graphics box.
3. Specify a Horizontal Place and from which location the placement occurs.
4. Specify a Vertical Place measurement.
5. Choose OK to return to the document window.

Tell Me More

Using the mouse to drag-and-drop to position your graphics is easy and quick. After you move a graphics box with the mouse, the box remains in a fixed position on the page unless you move it again with the mouse. Any text you enter above or below the graphics box does not affect its position.

When you change the position of a graphics box by using the Box Position dialog box, you must specify to which element you want to attach, or *anchor*, the graphics box. You can attach a graphics box to a page, paragraph, or character. When you attach a graphics box, the option you choose determines in part where the box is positioned and how the box moves when text is inserted in the document. The following sections explain each attachment option.

Attaching and Positioning a Graphics Box to the Current Paragraph

Attaching a graphics box to a paragraph causes the graphics box to remain with a paragraph or, if no text is in the paragraph, allows the box to move as though it is a paragraph (when you press Enter, for example, the box moves down one line). You should attach a graphics box to a paragraph with text when the information contained in the graphics box has to accompany the information in the paragraph. If the graphics box contains a table that is explained in the text of the paragraph, for example, you attach the graphics box to the paragraph. The code for the graphics box is placed at the beginning of the paragraph. If you add text to the document before the paragraph that causes the paragraph to move to a new page, the graphics box also moves to a new page.

By default, the graphics box aligns with the top of the current paragraph, as shown in Figure 9–14. You can change the position of the graphics box by using the Box Position options.

The following table describes the Box Position options that are available when you attach a graphics box to a paragraph:

Option	**Description**
Horizontal	Specifies the way the graphics box is positioned: Left Edge of Page, Left Margin, Right Margin, or Center of Paragraph. The Left and Right Margin options align the graphics box with the appropriate margin. The Left Edge of Page option positions the graphics on the edge of the page without regard to the left margin. The Center of Paragraph option centers the graphics box between the margins; however, the text flows according to the Wrap Text option. You can also specify a measurement in the Place field to indicate an offset from the Horizontal Position.

(continues)

FIGURE 9–14
A graphics box aligned with the top of a paragraph.

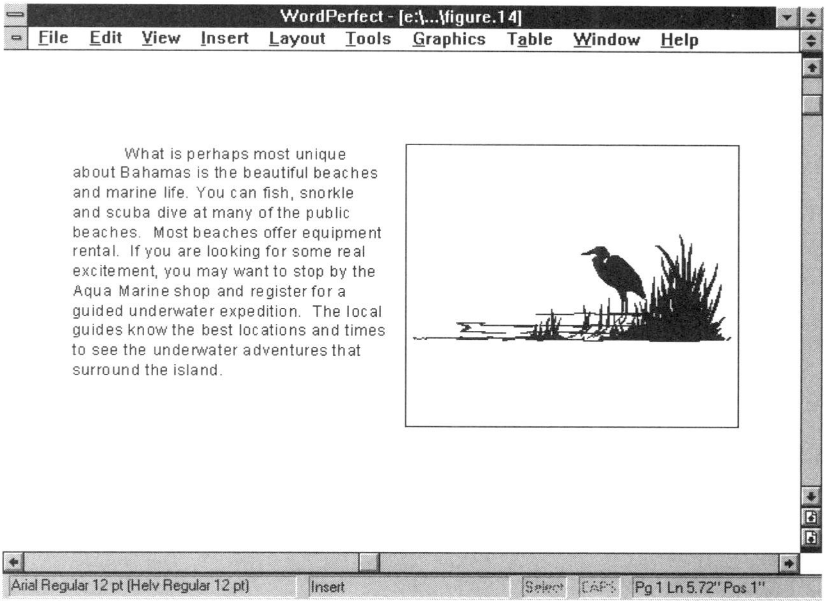

OPTION	DESCRIPTION
Vertical	Specifies the distance the graphics box is located from the top of the paragraph.
Allow Box to Overlap Other Boxes	Allows graphics box to overlap other boxes.

Attaching and Positioning a Graphics Box to the Current Page

Attaching a graphics box to a page causes the graphics box to remain with the text on the page or, if there is no text on the page, allows the box to span an entire page. You should attach a graphics box to a page when the information contained in the graphics box has to accompany the information on the page. The code for the graphics box is placed at the beginning of the page. By default, the graphics box is aligned with the top right margin of the page. You can change the position of the graphics box by using the Box Position options.

The following table describes the Box Position options that are available:

OPTION	DESCRIPTION
Horizontal	Specifies whether the graphics box is positioned at the Left Edge of Page, Left Margin, Right Margin, or Center of Paragraph. The Left and Right Margin options align the graphics box with the appropriate margin. The Left Edge of Page option positions the graphics from the edge of the page without regard to the left margin. The Center of Paragraph option centers the graphics box between the margins; however, the text flows according to the Wrap Text option. You can also specify a measurement in the Place field to indicate an offset from the Horizontal Position. You can select Across Columns if you want the horizontal position relative to the Columns. If you choose Across Columns, type the column numbers you want the box positioned between.
Vertical	Specifies the vertical position of the graphics box. You can choose Top of Page, Top Margin, Bottom Margin, or Center of Margins. You can also specify an offset from the Vertical Position option by entering a measurement in the Place field.
Allow Box to Overlap Other Boxes	Allows the graphics box to overlap other paragraph boxes.

Attaching and Positioning a Graphics Box to a Character

Attaching a graphics box to a character position enables you to keep the box with a specific line of text. The graphics box is treated as a single character regardless of the size of the graphics box. Every time the word *frog* is used in a story you are writing, for example, you can insert a graphics image of a frog, as shown here:

I am not a  I am a prince!!

By default, a graphics box attached to a character aligns with the top of the current text line, and the size of the graphics box changes the line height of the entire line. You can change the position of the graphics box by using the Box Position options. The following table describes the Box Position options that are available when you attach to a character:

OPTION	DESCRIPTION
Position Box	Specifies where the box aligns on the line of text. You can choose Top, Centered, Bottom, or Content Baseline. If you choose Top or Center, the top or center of the graphics box is aligned with the baseline of the document text. If you choose Content Baseline, the bottom of the contents of the graphics box is aligned with the baseline of the document text.
Box Changes Text Line Height	Prevents other lines of text from being inserted around the graphics box if it is larger than the text line height.

HOW DO I... Change the Size of a Graphics Box?

WordPerfect automatically calculates the width and height of a graphics box by taking several factors into account, such as the box style, the contents of the box, and what the box is attached to. You can easily change the size of a graphics box to meet the specifications of your document by using the mouse or the Box Size dialog box. Using the mouse to size is quick and easy. Using the Box Size dialog box allows you to enter exact measurements.

Steps

➡ **To size a graphics box by using the mouse:**

1. Click anywhere on the graphics box to select it.
2. Move the pointer over one of the markers so that it is displayed as a sizing handle, as shown here:

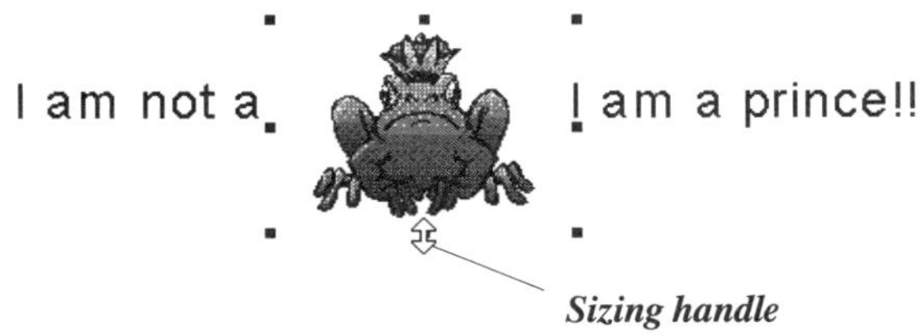

3. Drag the handle until the box is the size you want.

HINT

You can change the horizontal and vertical size of the box simultaneously by dragging a corner of the box.

➨To size a graphics box by using Box Size dialog box:

1. Right-click the graphics box and choose Size. The Box Size dialog box is displayed, as shown in Figure 9–15.
2. Select a Width option. If you select Set, specify a measurement.
3. Select a Height option. If you select Set, then specify a measurement.
4. Choose OK.

FIGURE 9–15
The Box Size dialog box.

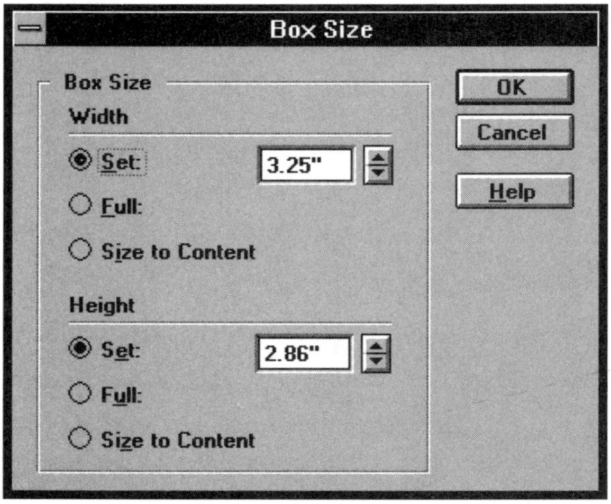

Tell Me More

When WordPerfect sets the size for graphics boxes containing images, it automatically preserves the original shape of the image. If you change the Set Width or Set Height options, the possibility exists that the graphic may be displayed and printed out of proportion. If you choose to set the width of the graphics box but leave the height automatically selected, or if you choose to set the height of the graphics box but leave the width automatically selected, WordPerfect calculates the height or width of the box automatically to keep the figure from distorting.

If you are sizing with the mouse and want to maintain the proportion of the image, you should size the image by dragging only the corner handles. When you drag the corner handles, you size both the width and the height simultaneously.

HOW DO I. . . Change the Border and Fill of the Graphics Box?

Each graphics box style has a predefined border and fill. A *border* consists of the lines that surround the box; the color and pattern within the box comprise the *fill,* or shading. A figure box, for example, has a single line border and no fill. A text box has a thick top and bottom border and no fill. Figure 9–16 shows the default borders and fill of a figure box and a text box. If the predefined borders and fill styles do not meet the needs of your document, you can edit the Box Border/Fill Styles to change the style and thickness of the lines surrounding the graphics box in addition to the style of the fill.

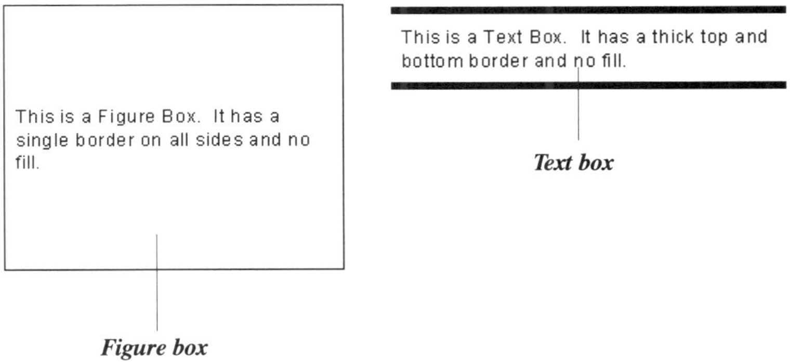

FIGURE 9–16
Default borders and fill of a figure box and a text box.

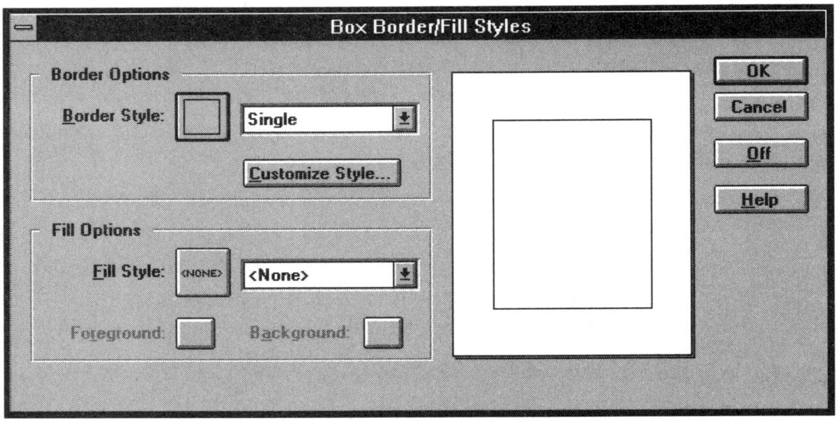

FIGURE 9–17
The Box Border/Fill Styles dialog box.

Steps

➨To change the Box Border/Fill Style:

1. Right-click on the graphics box and choose Border/Fill. The Box Border/Fill Styles dialog box is displayed, as shown in Figure 9–17.
2. Click the Border palette button and select a new Border Style *or* select an option from the drop-down list.
3. Click the Fill palette button and select a new Fill Style *or* select an option from the drop-down list.
4. If necessary, change the Foreground and Background options. The preview box displays a sample of your selections.
5. Choose OK to return to the document window.

HINT

If you do not want the graphics box to contain a border or fill style, choose Off.

Tell Me More

If the styles available for the Border option do not contain the selections you are looking for, you can choose the Customize Style option to display additional options for customizing the Border style.

Figure 9–18 shows a graphics box with a 10 percent fill style and a drop shadow (which is in the Customize Border dialog box).

FIGURE 9–18
A graphics box with a 10 percent fill style and a drop shadow.

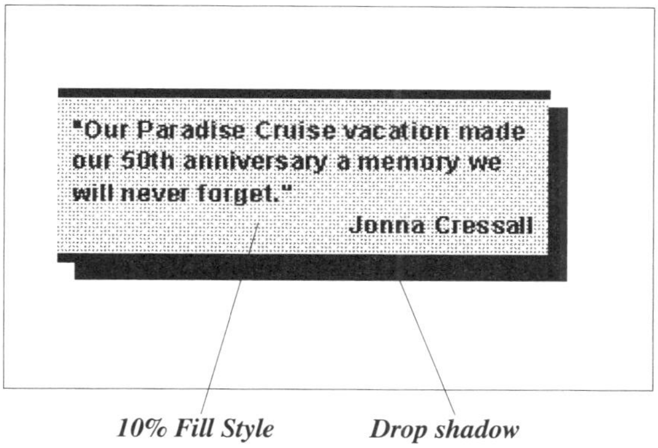

HOW DO I. . . Change the Positioning of Text Around a Graphics Box?

When you insert a graphics box in a document that also contains text, you can choose how you want the text to flow around the box. You can also specify whether you want the text to follow the contour of the box. Using the Wrap options lets you offset a graphics box from the text or make a graphics box blend in with the text.

Steps

➠To specify how the text wraps around a graphics box:

1. Right-click on the graphics box and choose Wrap. The Wrap Text dialog box is displayed, as shown in Figure 9–19.
2. Select a Wrapping Type option: Square, Contour, Neither Side, or No Wrap.

FIGURE 9–19
The Wrap Text dialog box.

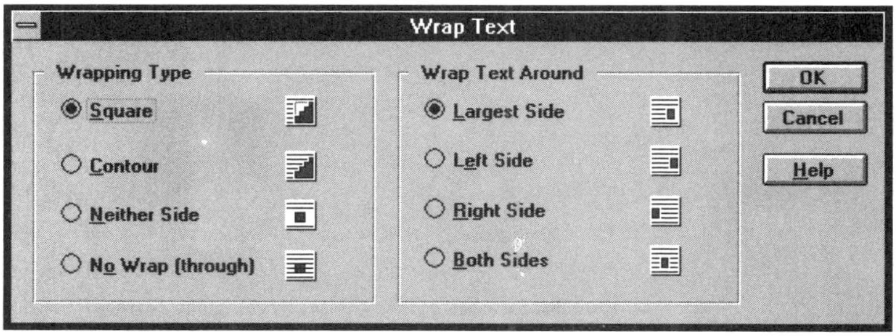

3. If you selected Square or Contour for the Wrapping Type, select a Wrap Text Around option: Largest Side, Left Side, Right Side, or Both Sides.
4. Choose OK.

Tell Me More

The Wrapping Type options specify how the text will wrap around the graphics box. The Square option simply wraps the text around the border of the graphics box.

The Contour option is useful if you want the graphics to blend in and have a more subtle appeal in the document and eliminate excessive white space around a graphics box. If you choose the Contour option, WordPerfect removes the left, right, top, and bottom lines and any fill styles from the graphics box. The text then follows the contour of the image within the graphics box, as shown in Figure 9–20.

NOTE

If a graphics box has rounded corners, this option contours the text to the borders of the graphics box. If the graphics box has only top and bottom lines, this option contours the text to only the left and right sides of the image within the graphics box.

FIGURE 9–20
Wrapping Type set to Contour.

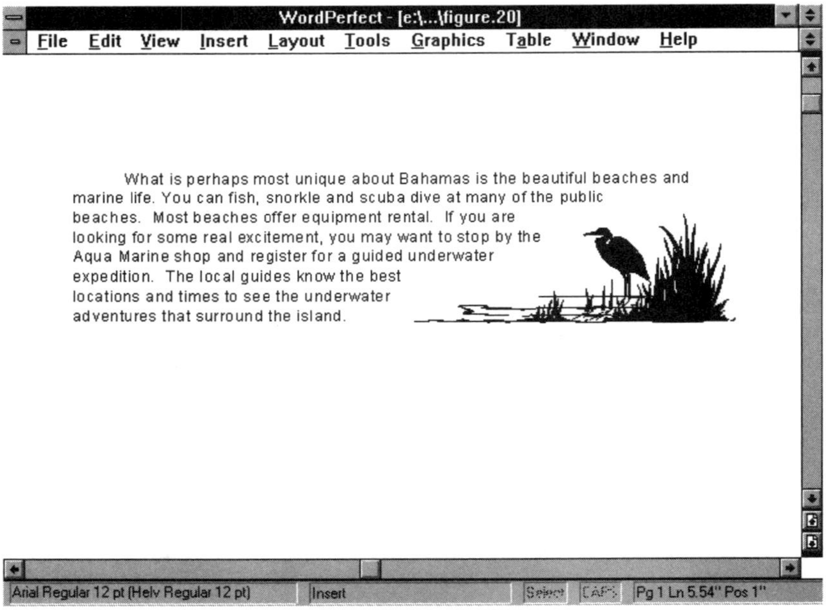

If you choose Neither Side, the text skips the graphics box and continues below the box. This option enables you to set off the graphics box from the rest of the text.

The No Wrap option allows text to be placed directly on top of the graphics box. If you have modified the image to have a light fill pattern, you can insert the text on top of the image and still be able to read the text.

The Wrap Text Around options let you determine around which sides of the graphics box you want to wrap the text. If you choose Largest Side, the text flows on the side of the graphics box that has the most white space unless the box is centered between the left and right margins on the page. In that case, the text flows on the left side.

HOW DO I... Edit a Graphics Image?

WordPerfect lets you edit graphics images you have retrieved into a graphics box by using special Image Tools. You can use the Image Tools to edit bit-mapped and vector-type graphic images. You can change appearance attributes, color brightness and contrast, the position of the image within the graphics box, the fill, and the print parameters. In addition, you can also use WP Draw to edit the image. For more information about WP Draw, see the section "HOW DO I... Use WP Draw?" later in this chapter.

Steps

➨ **To edit a graphics image:**

1. Right-click on the graphics box and choose Image Tools. The Tools palette is displayed next to the graphics box, as shown in Figure 9–21.
2. Choose the editing item from the Tools palette and make the changes you want.
3. Click outside the graphics box to deselect the box and remove the Tools palette.

Tell Me More

When you edit an image, you are editing only the image inside the graphics box—you are not editing the file that contains the original image. The following table describes all the options available when you edit a graphics image:

OPTION	DESCRIPTION
Rotate Image	Specifies the degrees the image is rotated.
Move Image	Moves the image inside the graphics box.
Select	Re-enables mouse pointer.
Zoom	Scales image.
Invert Color	Converts colors to their complementary colors. You can use this option if you have a dark image and you want to lighten its appearance.
Black and White	Displays the image in black and white rather than in color.
Contrast	Specifies the contrast of an image.
Brightness	Specifies the brightness of an image.
Reset	Resets all image attributes.

(continues)

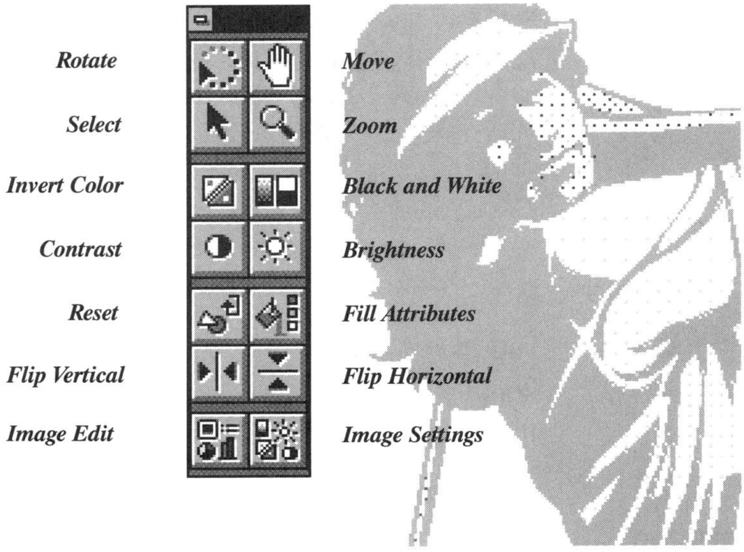

FIGURE 9–21
The Tools palette.

OPTION	DESCRIPTION
Fill Attributes	Specifies the appearance of the fill of the image. You can choose Normal, Transparent, or White. If you choose Transparent, the fill is removed from the image and leaves only the lines. If the figure is heavily shaded, choosing Transparent can considerably speed up the printing of the image. The background of the image shows through the image. If you choose White, the fill color changes to white and leaves only black lines.
Flip Horizontal	Displays a "mirror" image of the original image.
Flip Vertical	Displays the reverse side of the image; in some cases, it simply turns the image upside down.
Image Edit	Opens the WP Draw program for additional editing.
Image Settings	Displays a dialog box for editing all attributes of an image.

The Image Tools options may seem overwhelming when you view them as a whole, but using even one or two of the options gives you great versatility in using graphics images. Figure 9–22 shows the same graphics image that was used in Figure 9–21, but the image has been edited using the Image Tools. The image has been flipped vertically so that it is facing the opposite direction, and the Fill Attributes option has been changed to Transparent so that only the outline of the figure appears.

HOW DO I... Create Fancy Text?

The TextArt feature lets you create fancy text you can use for titles or headings. Figure 9–23 shows some examples of what TextArt can do.

Steps

➠To create TextArt:

1. Choose Graphics ➢ TextArt. The TextArt dialog box is displayed, as shown in Figure 9–24.
2. Choose the Font and Style you want to use for the text.
3. Select All Capitals if you want the text to be in all caps.

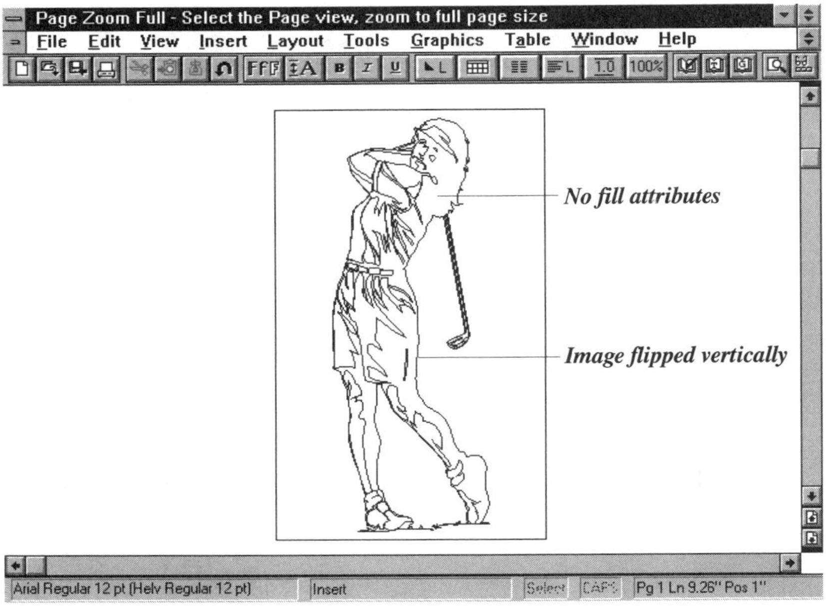

FIGURE 9–22
A graphics image edited with Image Tools.

FIGURE 9–23
Samples of TextArt.

4. Type the text in the Enter Text field. You can include as many as 58 characters and have as many as three lines.
5. Change the shape of the TextArt image by clicking on a shape in the dialog box. The text follows the pattern of the selected shape.
6. Choose File ➢ Exit & Return to WordPerfect, and choose Yes to exit and insert the TextArt image in WordPerfect.

You can also click the  **icon to display the TextArt dialog box.**

Tell Me More

The TextArt image is inserted into a graphics box, so after you return to WordPerfect, you can select the box and make any modifications to the size, position, or any other graphics box setting.

If you want to edit the content of the TextArt, you can double-click on the TextArt to display the TextArt dialog box.

FIGURE 9–24
The TextArt dialog box.

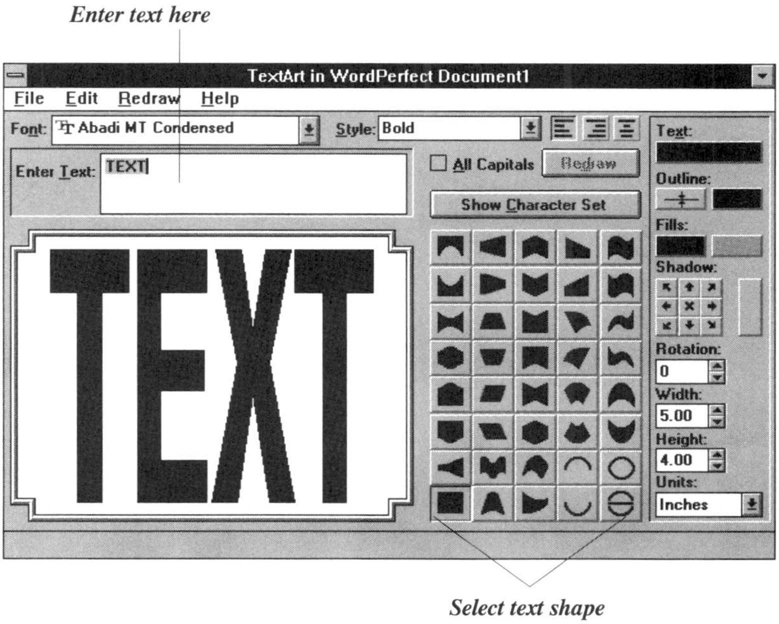

The following table lists several additional Text Art options you can use to jazz up your text:

OPTION	DESCRIPTION
Text	Specifies the color of the text
Outline	Specifies the thickness of the outline of the text and the color of the outline
Fill	Specifies the fill pattern and color for the text
Shadow	Specifies the location and color of a shadow on the TextArt
Rotation	Specifies the number of degrees to rotate the text; this option is useful if you want a line of text to be printed down the side of the page, for example, and all other text across the page
Width	Specifies the width of the TextArt
Height	Specifies the height of the TextArt
Units	Specifies the type of measurement you want to use to specify the width and height

HOW DO I... Use WP Draw?

WP Draw is WordPerfect's built-in graphics programs. By using WP Draw, you can create text, draw objects, and create charts. For information about creating charts, see Chapter 8, "Creating Tables, Formulas, and Charts." You can also use WP Draw to edit or add to existing graphic images. Figure 9–25 shows a graphics image shipped with WordPerfect that has been modified using WP Draw.

Steps

➡**To create a new drawing or text with WP Draw:**

1. Choose Graphics ➢ WP Draw. If you want to edit an existing image, double-click the graphics box.
2. Create the drawing or text *or* modify the existing image by using the palette tools shown here:

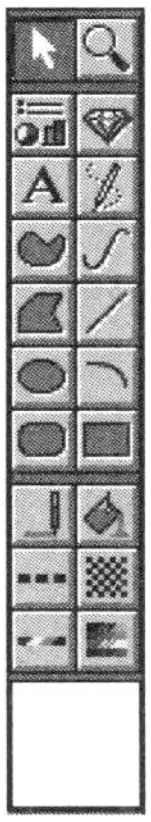

3. Choose File ➢ Exit and Return to Document to update the image in WordPerfect.

BUTTON BAR

You can choose the  icon to open the WP Draw program.

Tell Me More

WP Draw is a powerful program. The following list shows a few of the capabilities WP Draw offers you:

- Combine existing graphics images
- Edit individual segments of graphic images

FIGURE 9–25
A graphics image modified using WP Draw.

- Change the color and outline of objects
- Combine images and text
- Draw shapes and lines
- Draw freehand (excellent for creating maps)
- Create charts (see Chapter 8 for more information)

Using the palette makes performing these tasks relatively simple. This section by no means covers all the capabilities of WP Draw, but now that you know how to access it and what it can do for you, you are ready to do some exploring.

HOW DO I... Create Graphics Lines?

Graphics lines enable you to offset information and draw attention to specific text in a document. You can create both horizontal and vertical graphics lines anywhere in a document. You can customize the thickness, size, style, color, and spacing for each line. Graphics lines are simple to create and can add that little extra touch that makes your documents more appealing.

Steps

➡To insert a graphics line:

1. Move the insertion point to the position where you want to insert the line.
2. Choose Graphics ➢ Horizontal Line or Vertical Line *or* press Ctrl+F11 for a Horizontal Line *or* Ctrl+Shift+F11 for a Vertical Line. WordPerfect inserts the graphics line into the document.

Tell Me More

By default, a graphics line is inserted at the location of the insertion point and spans the length of your margins (a horizontal line spanning the left and right margins and a vertical line spanning the top and bottom margins).

The following sections explain the numerous options you can use to position, size, and change the style of graphics lines. Figure 9–26 shows a basic document that uses graphics lines to enhance its appearance.

FIGURE 9–26
A document with graphics lines.

Horizontal line

EMILY JACOBS

OBJECTIVE To obtain gainful employment in the teaching profession.

EDUCATION Stanford University, Palo Alto, California. B.A. in Elementary Education. 3.2 GPA on a 4.0 scale. Graduation April 1990.

Roswell High School, Roswell, Georgia. President of Girls' Chorus

EXPERIENCE February 1989 to April 1989

● **Student Teacher**, Sunset View Elementary, Provo, Utah.
● Responsible for educational instruction of forty-five fourth grade students as well as keeping a record of each student's progress.

Vertical line

September 1986 to April 1989
● **Bindery and Press worker** for Print Services.
● General bindery and press work as well as some data entry.

September 1980 to 1984, and Summers of 1985 and 1986

● **Administrative Secretary**, Rio Georgia, Marietta, GA.
● Responsible for office supervision as well as secretarial, clerical, and bookkeeping for real estate-mortgage company.

August 1972 to September 1980
● **Sales Representative,** Iron Pony Sales, Woodstock, GA.
● Responsible for sales and merchandise displays in various parts of the country at sporting goods events and trade shows. Accountable for daily cash register balance.

BACKGROUND Basic knowledge of WordPerfect products. Extremely confident in sales and phone conversations. Personal characteristics include hardworking, responsible, honest, self motivated.

REFERENCES Available upon request.

Positioning and Sizing a Graphics Line

You can easily position a graphics line by using the mouse. To use the mouse to position the line, simply click the mouse pointer directly on the line and then drag the line to a new location. When you click on the line, you see the sizing markers; as you drag the line, you see the line's outline.

To size the line with the mouse, click the mouse directly on the line and then drag one of the sizing handles shown here:

You can size both the width and the length of a line depending on the marker over which you position the mouse.

You can also use the Edit Graphics Line dialog box, displayed in Figure 9–27, to specify the exact measurements for the position and size of a line.

To open the Edit Graphics Line dialog box:

1. Select the line and click the right mouse button to open the QuickMenu.

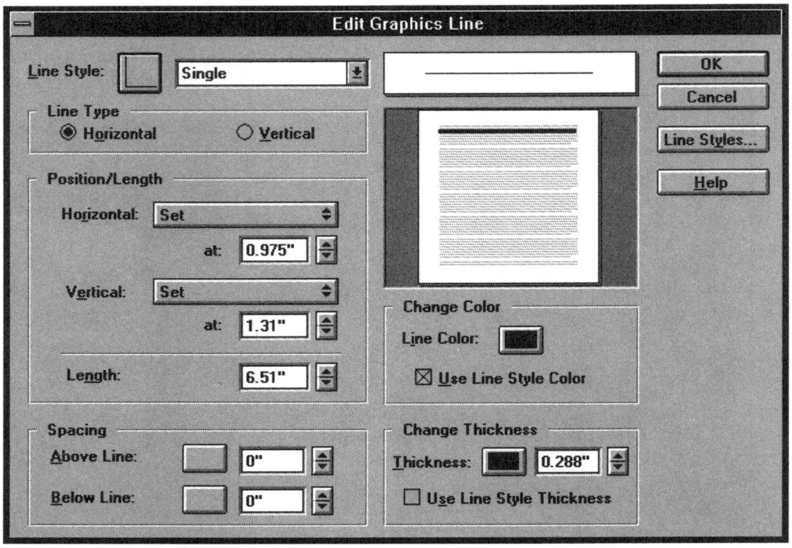

FIGURE 9–27
The Edit Graphics Line dialog box.

2. Choose Edit Line and make the necessary changes to the Position and Length options. The preview box in the top right corner of the dialog box displays a sample of the line you are editing so that you can easily see your changes.
3. Choose OK.

When you create a horizontal line, you can set a Horizontal position at Full, align it with the left or right margin, center it between the margins, or set a specific position. If you specify a horizontal position of Full, WordPerfect automatically creates the graphics line equal to the margin width of the page.

If the horizontal position is anything other than full, you can specify a length for the line. By default, a horizontal line aligns vertically with the baseline of the current insertion-point position. You can adjust the vertical position, for example, if you want the line slightly lower.

When you create a vertical graphics line, you can vertically position the line down the full page, align it with the top or bottom margin, center it between the margin, or set a specific position. If you specify a vertical position of Full, WordPerfect automatically creates the graphics line equal to the space between the top and bottom margins.

If the vertical position is anything other than full, you can enter an exact length for the line. By default, a vertical line aligns horizontally at the position of the insertion point. You can change the horizontal position to the right margin or centered between the margins or between columns, or you can set a specific horizontal position.

Changing the Line Style, Thickness, and Color

The default line style for graphics line is a single line. WordPerfect offers several different line styles, however, from which you can choose. A few of the styles include a single line, thick line, dashed line, and double line. You can simply change the thickness of a line by sizing the line or you can use the Edit Graphics Line dialog box to specify an exact width for the line. You can also change the color of a line to add emphasis in the Edit Graphics Line dialog box.

To change the line style, thickness, or color:

1. Right-click on the line and choose Edit Line from the QuickMenu.
2. Select a Line Style from the Style palette or drop-down list.
3. Select a Thickness from the Thickness palette *or* specify a measurement in the Thickness text box.

4. Select a Color from the Color palette.
5. Choose OK to return to the document window.

Changing the Line Spacing

By default, a horizontal line does not have any space above or below it, which means that the text is close to the line. If you want to add space around the line, you can specify the amount of space you want above and below the line in the Edit Graphics Line dialog box.

HINT **You can click the buttons next to the Above and Below line options to view and select examples of different spacing options. When you select an option, WordPerfect inserts the correct spacing.**

When a vertical line is positioned on the left or right margin, you can enter the amount of space you want to offset the line from the margin. If you want the line to be directly on the margin, enter 0.

HOW DO I... Create Borders?

Borders consist of graphics lines used to offset and emphasize information. You can place a border around a paragraph or page or between columns. You can insert a border around existing text or create the border and then enter the text. Figure 9–28 shows a document that uses several borders.

Steps

➡ To create a border around existing text:

1. Move the insertion point to the paragraph, page, or column where you want to insert the border.
2. Choose Layout ➢ Paragraph or Page or Columns ➢ Border/Fill. The appropriate Border dialog box is displayed, as shown in Figure 9–29.
3. Select a Border Style from the palette or drop-down list.
4. Select a Fill Style from the palette or drop-down list. The preview box shows a sample of the border.

FIGURE 9–28
A document with graphics borders.

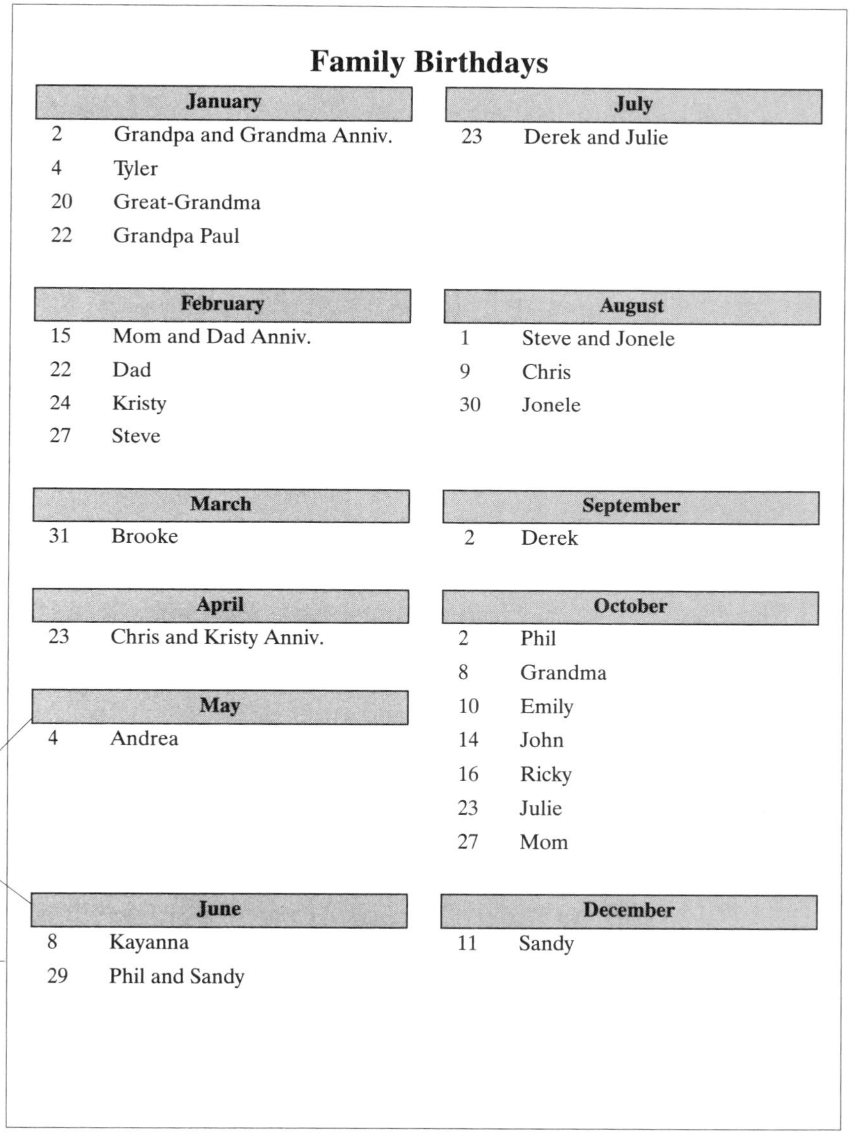

Family Birthdays

	January
2	Grandpa and Grandma Anniv.
4	Tyler
20	Great-Grandma
22	Grandpa Paul

	February
15	Mom and Dad Anniv.
22	Dad
24	Kristy
27	Steve

	March
31	Brooke

	April
23	Chris and Kristy Anniv.

	May
4	Andrea

	June
8	Kayanna
29	Phil and Sandy

	July
23	Derek and Julie

	August
1	Steve and Jonele
9	Chris
30	Jonele

	September
2	Derek

	October
2	Phil
8	Grandma
10	Emily
14	John
16	Ricky
23	Julie
27	Mom

	December
11	Sandy

5. Deselect Apply border to current paragraph (or page) only, if you want all subsequent paragraphs or pages to have a border.
6. Choose OK.

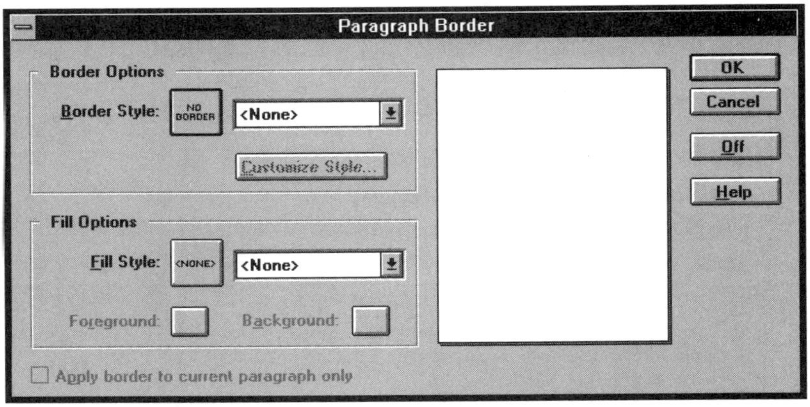

FIGURE 9–29
The Paragraph Border dialog box.

NOTE

You can create a paragraph border first and then enter the text. If you create the border before entering the text or if you insert a border around existing text without selecting it, you must turn off the border when you want it to end. Before turning off the border, press Enter to create a blank line. The extra line is removed after you turn off the border. To turn off the border, follow step 2 and then choose Off.

HINT

If you want to have multiple paragraphs surrounded by one border, you can select the paragraphs first and then follow the preceding steps.

Tell Me More

Editing text within a border is just like editing text in a document. To delete a border, you can highlight the code in Reveal Codes and then delete it or, with your insertion point inside the text surrounded by a border, choose Off from the Border dialog box. A paragraph border code looks like this: [Para Border]. WordPerfect deletes only the border—not the text—which is an advantage of using a border rather than a graphics box.

You can customize the border style and the fill style used in the border.

➠To customize the appearance of a border while creating the border:

1. Choose Layout ➢ Paragraph or Page or Columns ➢ Border/Fill.

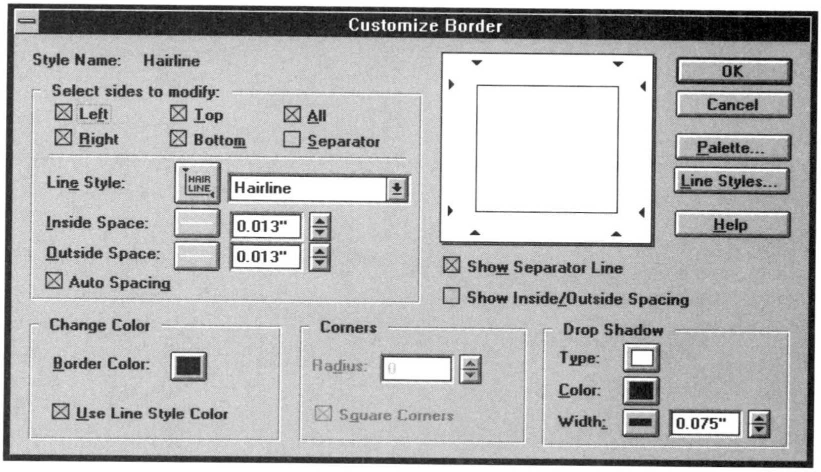

FIGURE 9–30
The Customize Border dialog box.

2. Choose Customize Style and make any changes you want to options in the Customize Border dialog box, displayed in Figure 9–30.
3. Choose OK twice to create the border with the new settings.

HOW DO I. . . Create an Equation?

WordPerfect's Equations feature helps you easily create mathematical and scientific equations. Equations are inserted in graphics boxes. You can change the style of the graphics box, however, or use the Inline Equation Box that does not include a border around the box. The Equation Editor helps you easily enter and format the equation correctly. Equations use graphical fonts to display and print scientific and mathematical symbols. Figure 9–31 shows a few examples of equations created in WordPerfect.

Steps

➨ **To create an equation:**

1. Choose Graphics ➢ Equation. The Equation Editor is displayed, as shown in Figure 9–32.
2. From the pop-up list to the left of the window, select the set of equation symbols and keywords you want to use, such as

FIGURE 9–31
Sample equations.

$$\frac{5}{7} \qquad 5\cos\sqrt{27} \qquad \left(\sqrt{\frac{ax+b}{2}}\right)^{10}$$

Greek or Symbols. Figure 9–33 shows some of the commands in the available equation sets.

3. Double-click on the items you want to insert in the equation. Or for some items, you can insert the keyword rather than the symbol by clicking once on the item and choosing Keyword.

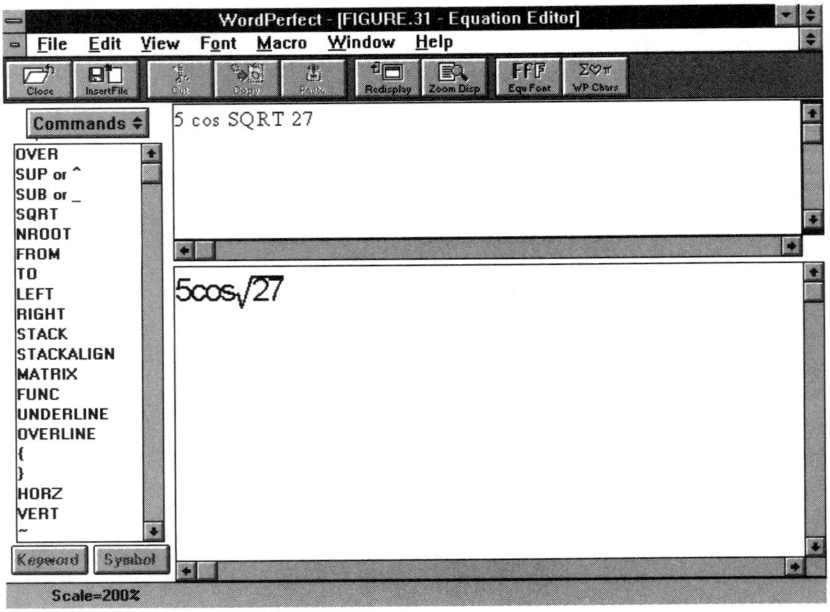

FIGURE 9–32
The Equation Editor.

FIGURE 9–33
Equation sets.

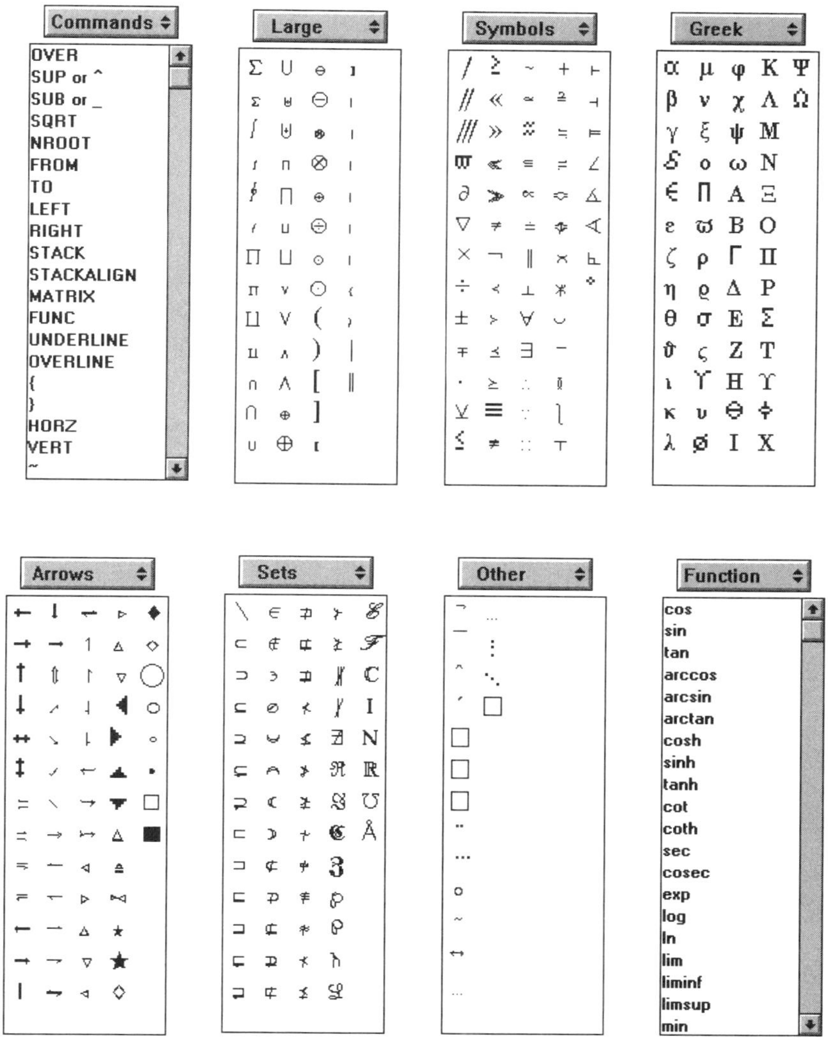

The items are inserted into the upper window of the Equation Editor.

4. To view the equation, choose Redisplay from the Button Bar.
5. After entering the equation, choose Close from the Button Bar to exit from the Equation Editor.

HINT

If you cannot get an equation to display in the lower window, check the validity and syntax of the equation. You can check the status bar for an error message describing the problem in the equation. WordPerfect verifies the syntax of all equations.

Tell Me More

The Equation Editor provides pull-down menus and a Button Bar to help you quickly access the options. The top window in the Equation Editor is where you enter the contents of the equation and it displays the equation in a text format. The bottom window displays the equation as it will look in the document.

When you click on a command in the Equation Editor, you can view a description of the command in the lower left corner of the window. This description helps you determine the function of the command if you are not familiar with the symbol. You can insert commands as symbols or as keywords. After highlighting the command you want, choose Keyword or Symbol. You can choose, for example, to display the Greek alpha character as a symbol or as a keyword, as shown here:

Equations always appear as symbols regardless of the way you enter them in the Equation Editor.

When you first enter the Equation Editor, WordPerfect displays the equation at 200 percent magnification. If you want to see how the equation will look in the document, choose the Zoom Disp icon on the Button Bar and select 100%. You can display the equation at many different magnifications within the Equation Editor.

You can move, size, position, and edit the graphics box containing the equation just as you do with any other graphics box.

FIGURE 9–34
A sample watermark

HOW DO I. . . Create Watermarks?

WordPerfect can print a graphics image behind the text in a document by using the Watermark feature. You can use watermarks to include a company logo on letters, for example. Figure 9–34 shows one of the pre-defined graphics images shipped with WordPerfect that can be used as a watermark. You can use any graphics image as a watermark; WordPerfect automatically adjusts the shading. You can also use text as a watermark.

Steps

➠**To insert a watermark:**

1. Choose Layout ➢ Watermark.
2. Select Watermark A or Watermark B.
3. Choose Create. The Watermark Feature Bar is displayed, as shown here:

4. To insert a graphics figure, choose Figure, specify the name of the graphics file you want to use as the watermark image, choose OK, and then choose Close. *Or* choose File and specify the name of a text file you want to use as the watermark.
5. Choose Placement and select Odd Pages, Even Pages, or Every Page.
6. Choose Close to remove the Feature Bar.

NOTE **Watermarks do not display in Draft mode.**

Tell Me More

Watermarks are displayed on all specified pages until you turn off the watermark. You can turn off a watermark on any page.

➡To turn off a watermark:

1. Position the insertion point on the page where you want to turn off the watermark.
2. Choose Layout ➢ Watermark and select the watermark you want to turn off.
3. Choose Discontinue. The watermark is turned off from that page to the end of the document.

HINT **You can also use the Suppress option to turn the watermark off for a single page.**

HOW DO I... Enhance the Display of Graphics?

When you start WordPerfect, the text in your document is displayed at about 100 percent magnification. It may be difficult to see some graphics attributes at this magnification. The details of graphics lines and some detailed graphics images, for example, may be easier to see at 200 percent magnification. Changing the Zoom settings enables you to see the document at a different magnification. Zoom settings affect only the display of text; they do not affect your printed document.

Although you can view graphics on-screen, every time the screen rewrites, the graphics are rewritten also, which decreases the speed at which you can move through your document. To increase the speed when you're working with documents containing graphics, WordPerfect lets you turn off the display of graphics while you are editing text.

Steps

➡To reduce or enlarge the size of the document screen:

1. Choose View ➢ Zoom and then select one of the percentages or choose Margin Width to see a complete view of the current page from left margin to right; *or* choose Page Width to see a complete horizontal view of the entire page from one edge to the other; *or* choose Full Page to see the entire page.
2. Choose OK.

POWER BAR

You can also choose the [icon] to zoom to full-page size or choose [100%] to select a Zoom option.

➡To disable the display of graphics:

1. Choose View ➢ Graphics.

NOTE

This is a toggle. Choose View ➢ Graphics to redisplay graphics.

Tell Me More

Many of the WordPerfect graphics features enable you to change the color of different elements of a graphics element. If you are using a color monitor, this capability greatly enhances the display. The different features print in color, however, only if you have a color printer.

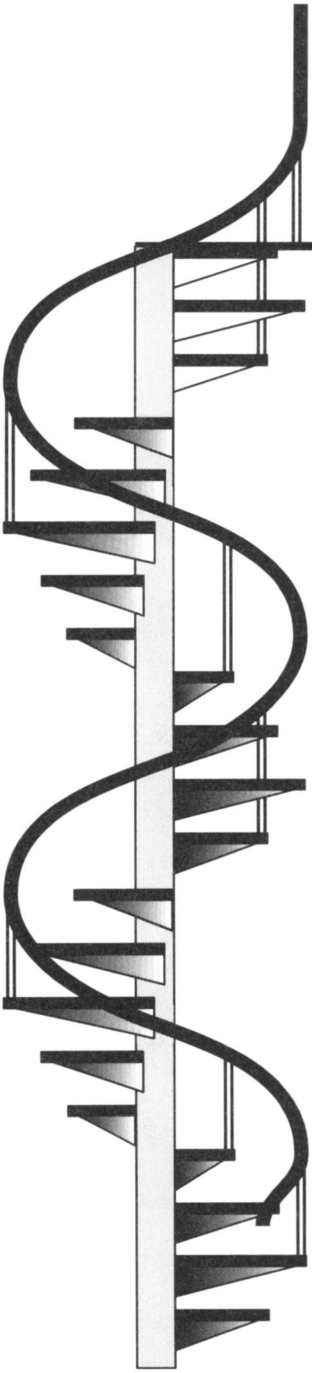

Chapter 10

Managing Files and Documents

WordPerfect has several file-management and document-management tools to help you organize and use your files and documents more efficiently. This chapter answers questions about the following file- and document-management features:

- Displaying directory and file lists
- Creating a QuickList
- Viewing a file
- Selecting files
- Copying files
- Moving and renaming files
- Deleting files and directories
- Printing file and directory lists
- Changing the attributes of files
- Assigning a password to a document

- Customizing the file list display
- Creating a directory
- Finding files
- Creating a QuickFinder index
- Entering QuickFinder search information
- Converting documents
- Creating a summary of a document
- Comparing two documents
- Linking documents

NOTE

WordPerfect has several file-management dialog boxes, such as the Open File dialog box, Save As dialog box, and Insert Image dialog box. Many of the features described in this chapter can be performed from any of these dialog boxes. To make the steps easy to follow, the Open File dialog box is used as the example.

HOW DO I... Display a List of Directories and Files?

By using the file-management dialog boxes in WordPerfect, you can display a list of directories, all the files in a directory, your QuickList, and a drive list. The Open File dialog box displayed in Figure 10–1 and the Save As dialog box displayed in Figure 10–2 are examples of a file-management dialog boxes. From the various file-management dialog boxes, you can perform many functions, such as deleting and copying files.

The main elements of a file-management dialog box are the directory list, file list, QuickList, and drive list. The *directory list* displays a list of directories and subdirectories. The *file list* displays the files that are in a selected directory. The *QuickList* is a customized listing of files and directories you use most often. The Drives drop-down list displays all available drives.

Steps

➡To display a list of files and directories:

1. Choose File➢Open *or* press Ctrl+O.

FIGURE 10–1
The Open File dialog box.

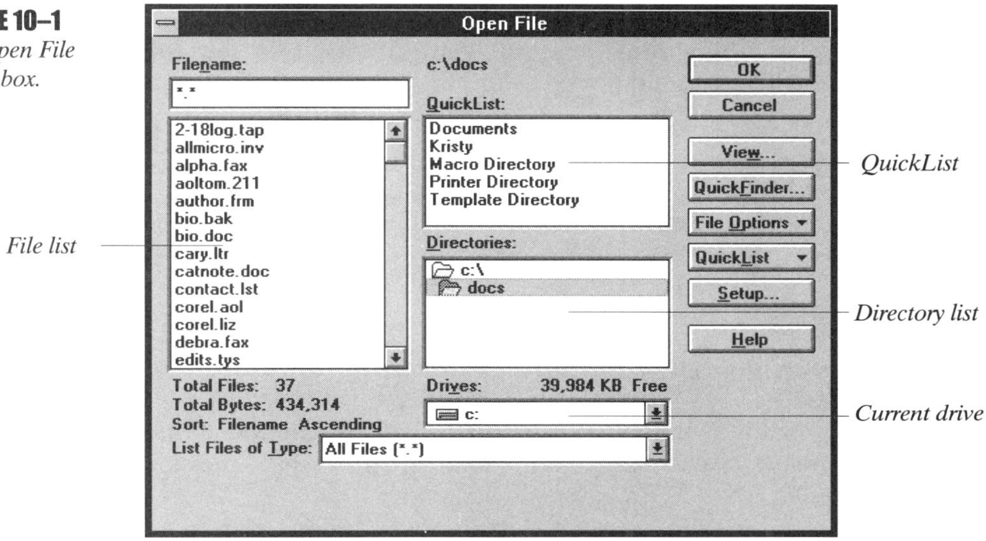

FIGURE 10–2
The Save As dialog box.

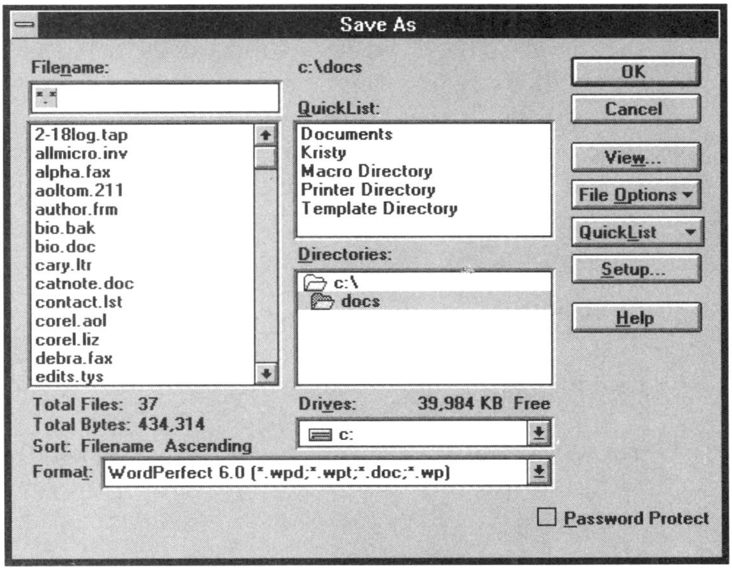

2. From the Directories list or the QuickList list, double-click on the directory you want to display. The filenames in the selected directory are displayed in the file list.
3. To return to the document window without performing any other actions, choose Cancel.

POWER BAR

You can also click on the to display the Open File dialog box.

Tell Me More

The following sections give detailed information about the different elements displayed in the file-management dialog boxes.

NOTE

In addition to displaying useful information, the file-management dialog boxes give you many powerful options to manipulate and organize your files. These options are listed when you choose File Options and are discussed individually in subsequent sections of this chapter.

Using the File List

At the top middle of the file-management dialog box, WordPerfect displays the directory being listed in the file list. The file list displays the name of all files in the directory. Below the file list is the total number of files in the directory, the number of bytes being used by the files in the directory, the method used for sorting the files, and the type of files being displayed. You can change which types of files are displayed in the file list by selecting an option from the List Files of Type drop-down list. To select a file in the file list, simply click on the file.

HINT

If you want to see additional information about a file, such as when the file was last modified, select the file. In the lower left corner of the dialog box, WordPerfect displays the date and time the file was last modified and the size of the file.

If you want to quickly move to a file, you can use the Name Search feature in the file list. After clicking anywhere in the file list, simply begin typing the first few characters of the filename. The letters are displayed below the file list, and the first file that matches the letters you typed is highlighted.

You can use *wildcard characters* to limit which files are displayed in the file list. WordPerfect uses two wildcard characters: the question mark (?) and the asterisk (*). The ? represents only one character, and the * represents zero or more characters. A *zero character* simply means that there is no character. If you name all your letter files with a .LET extension, for example, you can enter **C:\DOCUMENTS*.LET** in the Filename text box to have WordPerfect display only those files with a .LET extension.

Using the Directory List

By default, the Directories list box displays your WordPerfect default document directory and subdirectories along with the directory one level above your document directory. If you have not specified a document directory, the default directory is your WordPerfect directory.

Directories and subdirectories help you better organize your files. They are often compared to a filing cabinet, in which the entire cabinet is the *root directory* (C:\, for example) and the individual drawers of the filing cabinet are the *subdirectories* (C:\WPWIN60, for example). The main dividers within the drawers are also subdirectories (for example, C:\WPWIN60\GRAPHICS), and the items in the folders are the files. Just as you would never throw all your information into one big drawer, you do not want to put all your computer files in one directory.

If you want to view the files and subdirectories contained within a directory, simply double-click on the directory name. The file list to the left of the dialog box displays the names of the files stored in the selected directory. If you want to see all the directories on your C:\ drive, for example, simply double-click on that entry. When you select a directory, the directory list also updates and displays the selected directory, the parent directory (which is the directory one level above), and any subdirectories contained in the directory.

If you display a directory from a file-management dialog box and then choose OK or close the dialog box by using the control menu, the directory you were displaying becomes your default directory; any files you save without specifying a full path are therefore saved to the new default directory (unless you've specified WordPerfect not to change the default directory).

In addition, when you open files, WordPerfect tries to retrieve the files from the new default directory unless you specify a full path.

If you do not want WordPerfect to automatically change your default directory:

1. Choose Setup from a file-management dialog box.
2. Deselect Change Default Directory to turn off the option.

Using the QuickList

The QuickList is also displayed in the file-management dialog boxes. Your QuickList is a customized listing of files and directories you use most often. When you first start WordPerfect, the information for the QuickList is taken from the information specified for File Preferences. To display information in the file list for a QuickList item, double-click on the item. The QuickList makes it easy to display file lists without scanning through the entire directory list. For information about adding and deleting an entry on the QuickList, see the section "HOW DO I... Create a QuickList Entry?" later in this chapter.

Using the Drives List

The Drives list allows you to display the contents of another drive in the file list and directory list. Choose the Drives option and select the drive you want to display. WordPerfect lists all available drives, including disk drives, RAM drives, and network drives. The total number of available bytes on the selected drive is listed.

HINT

Knowing the amount of free disk space is especially useful when you want to copy files to a floppy disk. You can list the files on the disk in the floppy drive and compare the amount of free space to the size of the files you want to copy. By checking this information, you don't get the frustrating "Disk Full" error message that is displayed when there is not enough room to copy files.

Customizing the Display

WordPerfect allows you to customize several elements of the file-management dialog boxes. You can choose whether you want to display both the QuickList and the directory list or one or the other.

To change which lists are displayed in the file-management dialog boxes:

1. Choose File➢Open *or* press Ctrl+O.

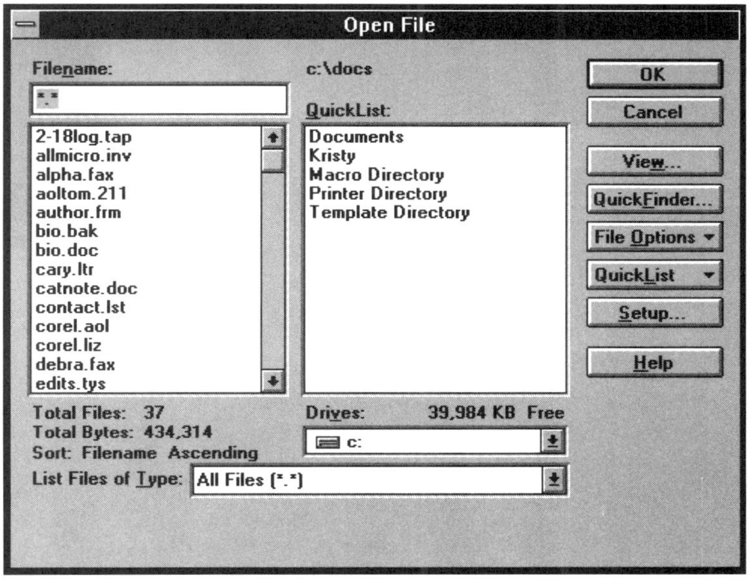

FIGURE 10–3
The Open File dialog box with only the QuickList and file list.

2. Choose QuickList.
3. Select Show QuickList to display only the QuickList and file list, select Show Directories to display only the directory list and file list, or select Show Both to display all three lists. Figure 10–3 shows the Open File dialog box with only the QuickList and file list.
4. Choose OK.

Any changes you make to the setup of a file-management dialog box takes effect for all file-management dialog boxes. If you change the setup to display the QuickList from the Open dialog box, for example, the QuickList is also displayed in the Save As dialog box.

HOW DO I... Create a QuickList Entry?

A QuickList is a customized, descriptive list of directories and files. The QuickList is displayed in all file-management dialog boxes and enables you to display in one list the directories and files you use most often. With the QuickList, you can use descriptive names for files and directories and therefore eliminate the need to remember exact directory names and filenames. From the QuickList, you can display a directory listing, certain files in a directory, or a single file in a directory.

Steps

➠**To create a QuickList entry:**

1. Choose File➢Open *or* press Ctrl+O.
2. With your mouse pointer in the QuickList, press the right mouse button *or* choose the QuickList button.
3. Choose Add Item.
4. Specify the path to the directory or files in the Directory/Filename text box, such as **C:\LETTERS** *or* use the Browse button and select a directory from the Select Directory dialog box and choose OK.
5. Specify a description for the directory or files in the Description text box, such as **Personal Letters**.
6. Choose OK to return to the QuickList. The new entry is inserted in the QuickList.

Tell Me More

The QuickList displays an alphabetical listing of the descriptive names you have given to a directory or file. When you click on a QuickList entry, WordPerfect displays the full directory path for the highlighted item in the Filename text box. When you double-click on an item from the QuickList, WordPerfect displays the information for the QuickList in the file list.

Creating QuickList Entries

When you create a QuickList entry, your description can contain as many as 39 characters, which is much more than the number of characters allowed for a directory name. For example, you could create an entry called Brooke's Expense Reports. With this description, you do not have to remember in which directory the reports are located—you simply use the QuickList.

You have many options for entering information in the Filename/Directory entry box. If you use a large number of files from a particular directory, you can enter a directory path, such as **C:\DOCUMENTS**. When you select this entry from the QuickList, WordPerfect displays all the files in this directory. If you frequently use a single file, you can enter a directory path and filename, such as **C:\DOCUMENTS\MEMO**. When you select this entry from the QuickList, WordPerfect displays only this file. From here, you can quickly open the file by double-clicking on the file in the file list.

Using the Default QuickList and Deleting QuickList Items

WordPerfect creates a default QuickList for you during the installation process. The QuickList contains the options and directories from your File Preferences. If you have not specified a directory for an option in the File Preferences dialog box, it is not included in the QuickList. If you do not want one or more of these entries displayed on your QuickList, you can delete them.

To delete an entry from the QuickList:

1. Choose File➢Open *or* press Ctrl+O.
2. Select the entry in the QuickList and press the right mouse button to display the QuickMenu.
3. Choose Delete Item.
4. Choose Yes to delete the item from the QuickList.

Using Wildcard Characters in a QuickList Entry

You can use *wildcard characters* to limit which files are displayed in a selected directory. WordPerfect uses two wildcard characters: the question mark (?) and the asterisk (*). The ? represents only one character, and the * represents zero or more characters. A *zero character* simply means that there is no character. If you name all your letter files with a .LET extension, for example, you can enter C:\DOCUMENTS*.LET in the Filename/Directory text box to have WordPerfect display only those files with a .LET extension.

Using a QuickList Entry as a Pattern

You can also use entries in the QuickList as a pattern for displaying directories. If you have a QuickList entry called Clients for your C:\CLIENTS directory, for example, but you want to display files for only a specific client you have named with a .CRE extension, you can use your Clients QuickList entry as a pattern.

To use a QuickList entry as a pattern by using the preceding example:

1. Choose File➢Open *or* Ctrl+O.

2. Click on the QuickList item you want to use as a pattern.
3. Add to or change the information in the Filename text box. In the example, you add ***.CRE** to the end of the line, as shown here, and press Enter:

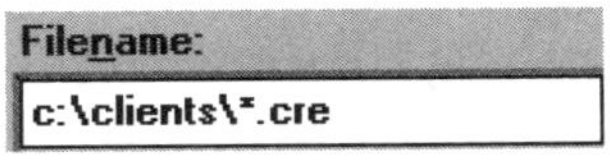

The selected directory and files are displayed in the file list.

Using an existing entry as a pattern can save you a great deal of time, especially if you are working with long directory paths.

HOW DO I... View a File Without Opening It?

You can use the Viewer to look at the contents of a file without opening the file. This feature is helpful if you are not sure whether the file you are highlighting is the file you want to open. You can look at the file to verify the contents. You can also copy and print information for a file displayed in the Viewer. You can view the contents of many type of files, including spreadsheet files, graphics files, and all WordPerfect document files. The Viewer does not display all formatting, but it does give you a good idea of the contents of the file.

Steps

➡To view the contents of a file without opening the file:

1. Choose File➢Open *or* press Ctrl+O.
2. Select the file from the file list you want to see and choose View. The Viewer window is displayed, as shown in Figure 10–4.
3. To close the Viewer window, double-click on the control menu.

Tell Me More

When you display the contents of a file, the Viewer window displays the filename on the title bar and the file type (if it is known) in the lower left corner. If the file contains text, the Viewer displays the text in addition to many of the codes (bold, underline, indent, and tab) from the

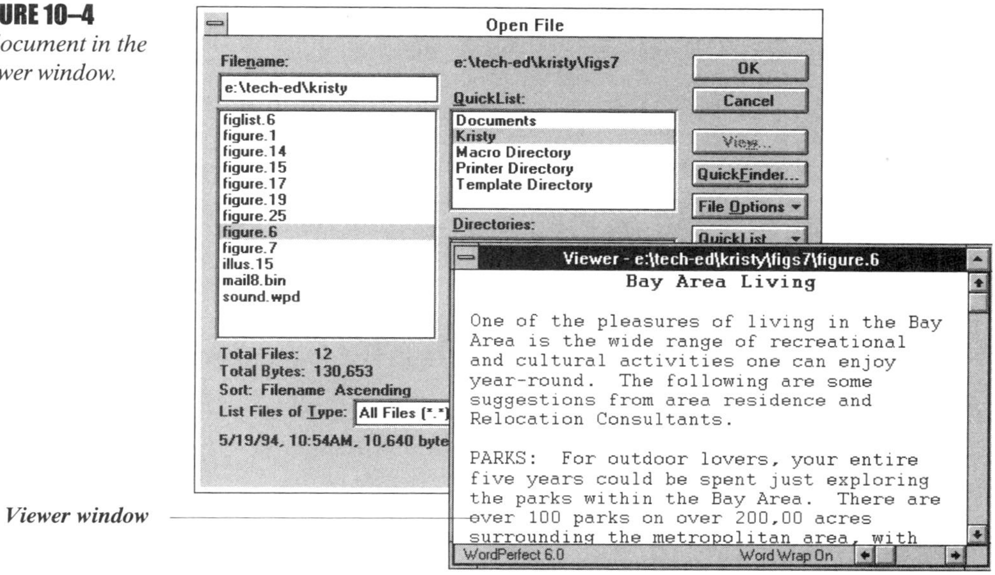

FIGURE 10–4
A document in the Viewer window.

document. If the file is a graphics image, the Viewer displays the image. The ability to view the contents of a graphics file without retrieving the file saves time and helps you to identify files quickly.

The QuickMenu for the Viewer window, displayed in Figure 10–5, allows you to perform several actions while viewing a file. You can find a

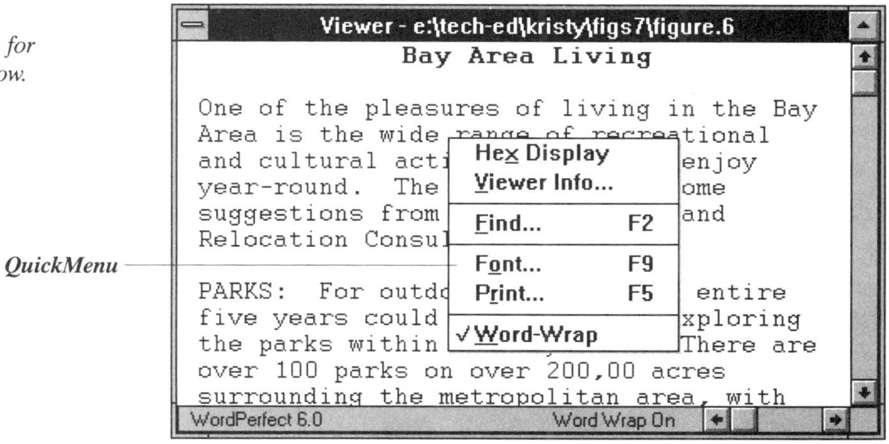

FIGURE 10–5
The QuickMenu for the Viewer window.

specific word or phrase, change the font, print the file, copy selected text to the Clipboard, and display the Document Summary if you have created one for the current document. You can also turn off Word Wrap if you want the text to scroll beyond the Viewer window.

HINT **Finding text is especially useful because it enables you to quickly look for and read information in a file without retrieving it. It also helps you to verify that the file is the one you want to retrieve.**

HOW DO I... Select Multiple Files?

Selecting files lets you perform a function on more than one file at a time. You can copy, move, delete, print, and change attributes for selected files. Selecting files avoids having to repeat functions over and over again.

Steps

➡ **To select a file:**

1. Choose File➢Open *or* press Ctrl+O.
2. Press the left mouse button and drag the pointer across all the files you want to select, as shown in Figure 10–6, *or* if you want to select a noncontinuous range of files, press the Ctrl key while clicking on the files. You can also select a file and then point to a file and press Shift+click, and all the files between the selected file and the mouse pointer are selected. This capability is useful for selecting a continuous range of files.
3. Choose the function you want to perform on the selected files.

HINT **To deselect all files, click on any file in the list. To deselect a single file, press the Ctrl key and click on the file.**

Tell Me More

The file-management box displays the total number of selected files directly under the file list along with the number of bytes in the selected files.

FIGURE 10–6
Selected files in the file list.

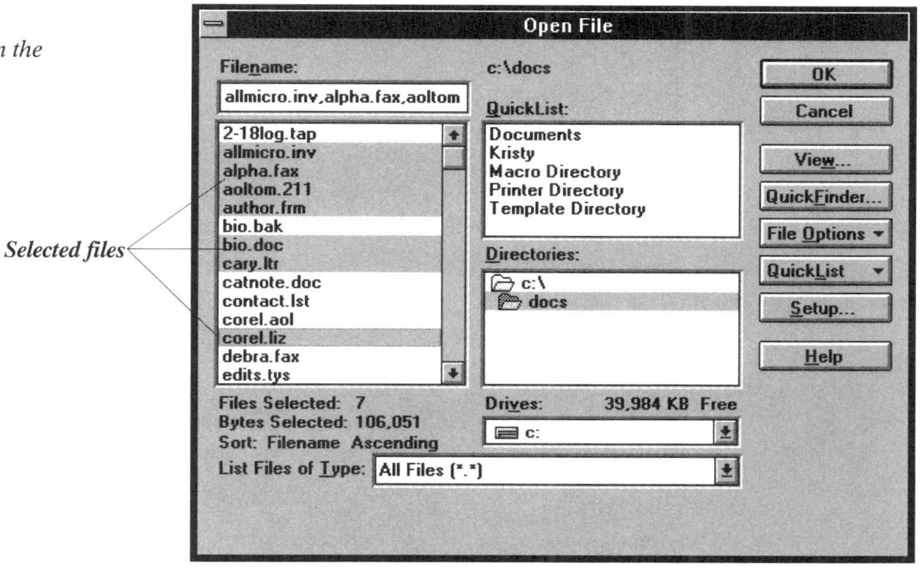

HOW DO I. . . Copy Files?

With the file-management dialog boxes, you can copy a single file or all selected files to a specified drive or directory. When you copy a file, a duplicate file is created in the specified drive or directory. The Copy feature is useful for copying files to a floppy disk.

Steps

➨**To copy a file:**

1. Choose File➢Open *or* press Ctrl+O.
2. Select the file (or files) from the file list you want to copy.
3. With the mouse pointer in the file list, press the right mouse button and choose Copy *or* choose Copy from File Options.
4. In the To text box, type the drive or directory in which you want the file (or files) copied. To copy the file to a floppy disk in drive A, for example, type **a:**.
5. Choose Copy. The file (or files) is copied to the destination directory.

Tell Me More

If a file with the same name exists in the destination drive or directory, WordPerfect displays the Confirm File Replace dialog box. Choose Yes to All to replace all duplicate files or choose Yes to replace only the file listed in the dialog box.

HINT **If you know that the exact files exist in the destination directory, you can select the "Don't replace files with the same size, date, and time" option so that WordPerfect does not replace the files and does not prompt you if these conditions are met.**

HOW DO I... Move and Rename Files?

The Move and Rename features help you rearrange files and directories. With the Move and Rename features, you can change the name of a file or directory, move a file or selected files to a different directory, and simultaneously move a file to a different directory and change the name of the file.

Steps

➡To rename a file:

1. Choose File➢Open *or* press Ctrl+O.
2. Select the file from the file list you want to rename.
3. With the mouse pointer in the file list, press the right mouse button and choose Rename *or* choose Rename from File Options. The Rename dialog box is displayed, as shown in Figure 10–7.
4. Specify a new filename in the To text box.
5. Choose Rename.

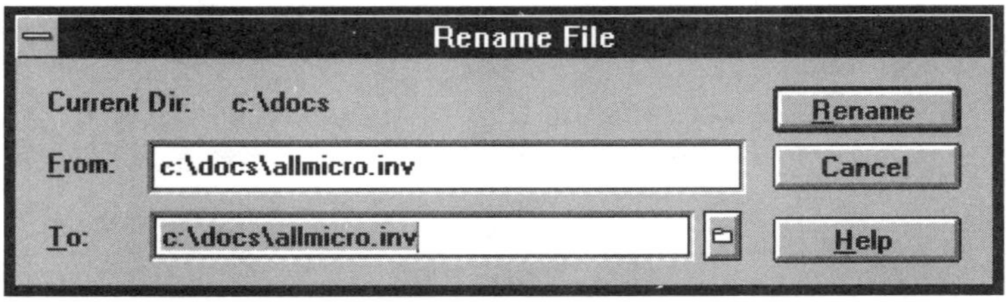

FIGURE 10–7
The Rename dialog box.

➠**To move a file or selected files:**

1. Choose File➢Open *or* press Ctrl+O.
2. Select the file (or files) from the file list you want to move.
3. With the mouse pointer in the file list, press the right mouse button and choose Move *or* choose Move from File Options. The Move File dialog box is displayed.
4. Specify the directory to which you want to move the file (or files).
5. Choose Move.

HINT **When you rename a file, you can also move it to a new directory by specifying a different directory in addition to a new filename.**

Tell Me More

Renaming a file is useful if you want to give more descriptive names to certain files. If you name all your reports REPORT.1, REPORT.2, REPORT.3, and so on, for example, after a few days you may forget what is contained in each report. You can use the Rename feature to change the names to COST.RPT, SALES.RPT, and PROFIT.RPT. All this can be done within WordPerfect with a few easy steps.

Moving files is useful if you want to move files to make room on your hard drive but still want a copy of the files. WordPerfect copies the files to the new directory, such as a floppy disk, and then deletes them from the original directory.

HINT **WordPerfect creates a new directory for you if you attempt to move files to a directory that does not exist.**

HOW DO I... Delete Files and Directories?

You can use the Delete feature in the file-management dialog boxes to delete unwanted files and directories. Deleting files and directories helps you keep your drives and directories from becoming cluttered with unneeded and unwanted files. If you regularly delete unnecessary files, you can avoid taking up valuable space on your hard drive.

CAUTION

If you delete a file, you cannot undelete it by using WordPerfect. You can use DOS or other third-party utility programs to undelete files.

Steps

➡To delete files:

1. Choose File➢Open *or* press Ctrl+O.
2. Select the file (or files) from the file list.
3. With the mouse pointer in the file list, press the right mouse button and choose Delete *or* choose Delete from File Options.
4. WordPerfect displays a dialog box to confirm the deletion. Choose Delete.

Tell Me More

Along with deleting files, you can delete directories. When you delete a directory, any subdirectories and files in the directory are also deleted.

➡To delete a directory:

1. Select the directory from the Directories list.
2. Press the right mouse button and choose Remove Directory. The following dialog box is displayed:

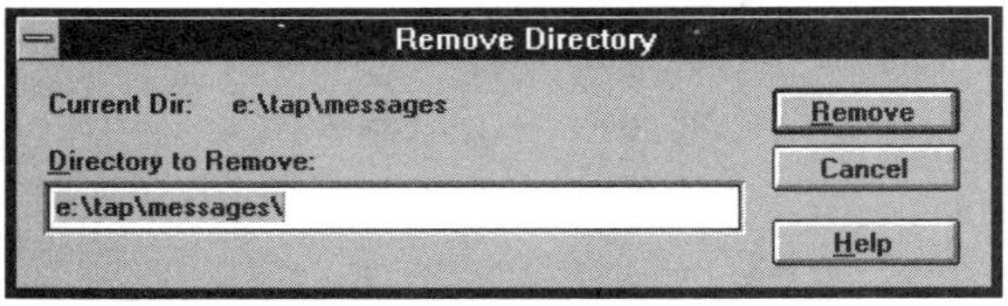

3. The directory you selected is displayed in the dialog box. Choose Remove. If the directory contains files or subdirectories, WordPerfect displays a warning. Choose Yes to confirm that you want to delete all files and subdirectories in the directory.

HOW DO I... Print a File List, QuickList, or Directory List?

From within a file-management dialog box, you can print a copy of a file list, QuickList, or directory list. This feature is useful if you are working on a network, for example, and you want all the users to know the structure of the network drives and where directories and files are located.

Steps

➡ To print a file list, QuickList, or directory list:

1. Choose File ➢ Open *or* press Ctrl + O.
2. With the mouse pointer in the list box you want to print, press the right mouse button.
3. Choose the appropriate Print List option.
4. Choose Print.

NOTE **If you have selected items, you can choose whether you want to print only the selected items or the entire list.**

Tell Me More

When you print a file list, WordPerfect prints the current date and time, the name of the directory, the total number of files, the amount of free disk space, and a list of all the files. When you print a directory list, WordPerfect prints a list of all the files in the selected directory. (Figure 10–8 shows an example of a printed file list.) If you have more files or directories than will fit on one page, the printout may span several pages; WordPerfect inserts a page number in the upper left corner.

HINT **You can also print the contents of a file from a file-management dialog box. Simply select the file and choose Print either from the QuickMenu *or* from File Options and choose Print again. WordPerfect prints the document just as though you used the Print dialog box. If you want to print multiple files, you can use a file-management dialog box to quickly select the files and then print them.**

FIGURE 10–8
A printed file list.

```
 1                          Print File List
                          5/21/94   7:33AM
                        C:\WPWIN60\GRAPHICS

Total Files:  134
Total Bytes:  1,487,883

accordin.wpg
approved.wpg
asap.wpg
bord01l.wpg
bord01p.wpg
bord02l.wpg
bord02p.wpg
bord03l.wpg
bord03p.wpg
bord04l.wpg
bord04p.wpg
bord05l.wpg
bord05p.wpg
bord06l.wpg
bord06p.wpg
bord07l.wpg
bord07p.wpg
bord08l.wpg
bord08p.wpg
bord09l.wpg
bord09p.wpg
bord10l.wpg
bord10p.wpg
bord11l.wpg
bord11p.wpg
bord12l.wpg
bord12p.wpg
bord13l.wpg
bord13p.wpg
bord14.wpg
bord15.wpg
bord16.wpg
bord17.wpg
bubbles.wpg
buck.wpg
buterfly.wpg
centerpc.wpg
certify.wpg
chanukah.wpg
cheetah.wpg
classifi.wpg
conductr.wpg
confiden.wpg
confirm.wpg
copyrite.wpg
cowboy.wpg
coyote.wpg
crane_j.wpg
crest.wpg
dontcopy.wpg
draft.wpg
```

HOW DO I. . . Change the Attributes of a File?

There are several DOS file attributes you can assign to a file from a file-management dialog box: Read-Only (r), Hidden (h), Archive (a), and System (s).

Steps

➡ **To change the attribute of a file:**

1. Choose File➢Open *or* press Ctrl+O.
2. Select the file from the File List.
3. With the mouse pointer in the file list, press the right mouse and choose Change Attributes *or* choose Change Attributes from File Options. The Change File Attributes dialog box is displayed, as shown here:

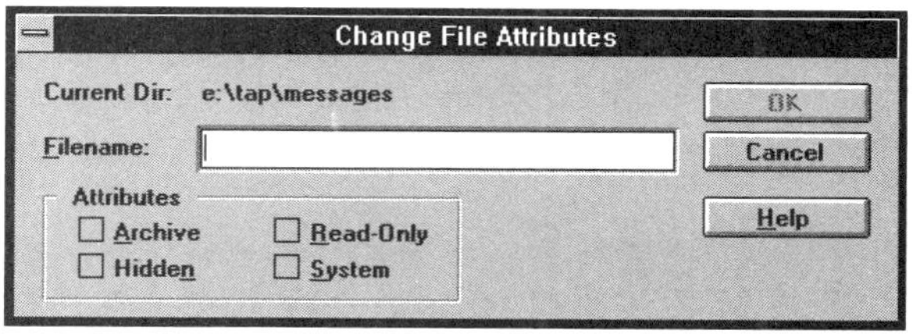

4. Select the attribute or attributes you want and then choose OK.

NOTE

If you do not select a file before opening the Change File Attributes dialog box, you can specify a file in the Filename text box.

Tell Me More

When a file is marked Read-Only (r), it cannot be deleted or modified, but it can be copied, moved, and renamed. If you are on a network and save files to a directory to which many users have rights, it may be a good idea to change to Read-Only the attribute of files you do not want modified. You have to be sure that you remove the Read-Only attribute before you try to modify the file (or files).

When a file is marked Hidden (h), it is not displayed when you use the DIR command from DOS to display a directory list or in the file list in WordPerfect. You can still perform all file operations, such as move, copy, delete, and so on, on a hidden file if you know the filename, but a hidden file is not easily accessible to those who do not know the filename. Marking a file as Hidden is a good way to prevent novice users from tampering with it.

Each time you create or modify a file, it is marked with the Archive (a) attribute. This attribute informs backup programs which files have been modified since the last backup. The backup may be performed with the DOS BACKUP command or with a backup utility program. After a backup copy or archive of the file is created, the Archive attribute is removed. This removal helps you quickly identify which files have changed since your last backup, therefore alleviating the need to back up all files every time you perform a backup.

A file marked as System (s) signifies that the file is necessary in order to run your computer. System files are not displayed when you use the DIR command from DOS to display a directory list. By default, system files are not displayed in WordPerfect. You should not modify or delete system files.

HOW DO I... Assign a Password to a Document?

Assigning a password to a document locks the document so that only those who know the password can retrieve, view, print, copy, move, or rename the file while using WordPerfect. You can delete a file that is password-protected, however, without knowing the password. Assigning a password to a file adds security to confidential files. If you are using a network and you save files in a shared directory or share a computer, assigning a password ensures that other users cannot retrieve and modify your document unless they know the password.

Steps

➠To assign a password:

1. With the file in the document window, choose File➢Save As *or* press F3.
2. If the document has not been saved, specify a filename.

FIGURE 10–9
The Password Protection dialog box.

3. Select Password Protect and choose OK. The Password Protection dialog box is displayed, as shown in Figure 10–9.
4. Specify a password.
5. Select a Protection Option if necessary.
6. Choose OK.
7. Reenter the password. WordPerfect asks you to reenter the password to ensure that you entered it correctly the first time.
8. Choose OK.

➡**To remove a password:**

1. With the file in the document window, choose File➢Save As *or* press F3.
2. Deselect Password Protect and choose OK.
3. Choose Yes when you are prompted to replace the file.

Tell Me More

Every time you try to retrieve, print, copy, or view a file with a password, you are prompted to enter the password. The password applies only when you save the document in WordPerfect 6 and 5.*x* versions.

HOW DO I. . . Customize the File List Display?

When you display a file-management dialog box, only the filename is displayed in the file list; the date and time the file was last modified and the size of the file are displayed in the lower left corner of the dialog box. If you want to see more information for each file in the file list, you can customize the display. For example, you can display the filename, size, date, and time in the file list. You can also change the way files are sorted in the file list.

Steps

➡**To change the file list display:**

1. Choose File➢Open *or* press Ctrl+O.
2. Choose Setup. The Open/Save As Setup dialog box is displayed, as shown in Figure 10–10.
3. Select a display option from the Show pop-up list. Choose Filename to display only the filename (the default setting).
   - Or choose Filename, Size, Date, or Time to display more information in the file list.
   - Or choose Descriptive Name, Filename to display and sort the file list by using the Document Summary Descriptive Name followed by the actual filename.
   - Or choose Custom Columns if you want complete control over what information is displayed in the file list and how it is displayed.
4. Choose OK.

NOTE

If you choose the Descriptive Name, Filename option or Custom Columns, an additional option is displayed in the dialog box. With the Create Speedup Files option selected, WordPerfect creates speedup files in the specified directory containing the Descriptive Name from the Document Summary. This option greatly decreases the amount of time

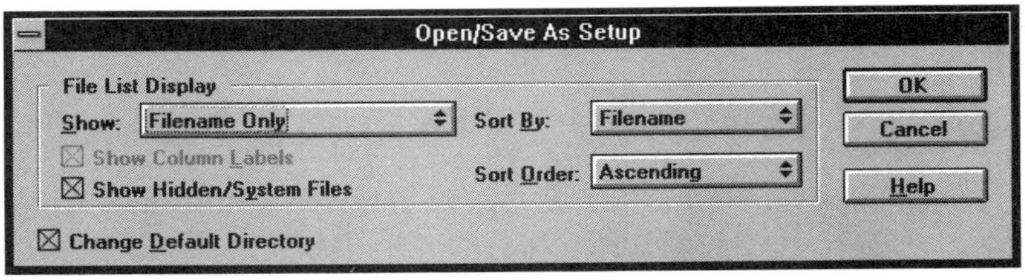

FIGURE 10–10
The Open/Save As Setup dialog box.

it takes to display a file-management dialog box that uses Descriptive Names because it does not have to scan each Document Summary.

Tell Me More

The following sections explain how to use custom columns in the file list and how to change the order in which files are sorted in the file list.

Using Custom Columns

When you're using the Custom Columns option, the file list may look something like the screen shown in Figure 10–11.

You can change the order, size, and type of information displayed in the file list. To move a column of information to a different location in the file list, point to the column heading with the mouse pointer, hold down the mouse button, and drag the column heading to a new location at the top of the list. To change the size of a column, move the mouse pointer to the edge of the column heading you want to size. When the mouse pointer changes to a double arrow, drag the box to the size you want.

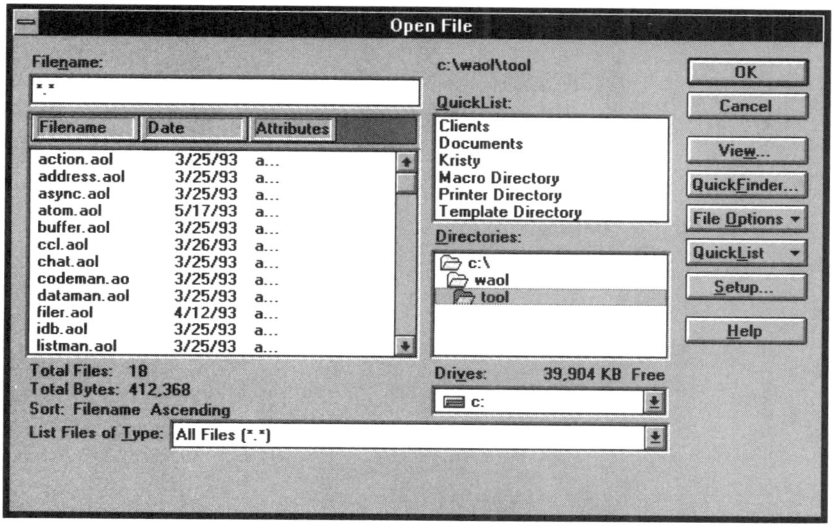

FIGURE 10–11
The Open File dialog box with Custom Columns.

If you want to remove a column from the file list, simply use the mouse pointer to drag the column heading off the heading bar. To add information to the file list, point to a blank space on the heading bar and hold down the right mouse button. If a blank space is not visible, use the scroll arrow to scroll to a blank area. The following pop-up list displays the available column headings:

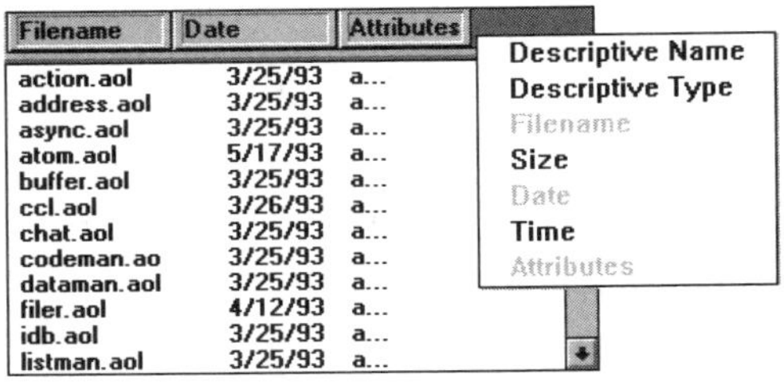

Choose an item from the pop-up list to add a column of information to the file list window. If a column heading is already used in the current file list window, the corresponding item appears gray in the pop-up list and cannot be selected. After you choose an item from the pop-up list, a column for that information is added to the file list.

If you display more file information than can be viewed in the file list box, the direction buttons (< and >), at the left edge of the column headings window, allow you to scroll horizontally through the information. You cannot change the size of the file list box.

HINT

If you do not want to display the title of each column, such as Filename, Size, etc., deselect the Show Column Labels option in the Open/Save As Setup dialog box.

Changing the Sort Order

From the Open/Save As dialog box, you can change the sort order of the files displayed in a file list.

To change the sort order:

1. Choose Setup from a file-management dialog box.
2. Select from the Sort By pop-up list the item by which you want the list sorted.

3. Select from the Sort Order pop-up list (Ascending or Descending) the order by which you want the file list sorted. Change this option to Descending, for example, if you want to display filenames that begin with the letter *Z* before filenames that begin with the letter *A*. This option is most useful when you are sorting filenames by date and time. When this option is selected, the most recently created files are displayed before the older files.
4. Choose OK. The file list is automatically updated to reflect the changes you made.

By default, the file list is sorted by Filename. You can also sort according to the date and time files were last modified. If you want to see all files that were modified within the past two weeks, for example, you can display these files chronologically on the list. When you're using the Sort option, you can specify only one field as the key for sorting.

HOW DO I. . . Create a Directory?

WordPerfect gives you the ability to create a new directory from within WordPerfect. Whenever you copy or move files, you can specify a directory that does not exist and WordPerfect creates it. You can also create a directory without performing any other actions by using the Create Directory option. This option is useful if you want to save a file to a directory that doesn't exist, for example. You can use the Save As dialog box to create the directory and then save the file within WordPerfect.

Steps

➨**To create a directory from the Open File dialog box:**

1. Choose File➢Open *or* press Ctrl+O.
2. Choose File Options.
3. Choose Create Directory and specify the full path and name of the directory you want to create, such as **C:\REPORTS\SALES**.
4. Choose Create.

NOTE **You can also create a directory from the Save As dialog box.**

Tell Me More

You cannot save a file to a directory that does not exist. After a directory is created, you can save files to it.

HOW DO I... Find Files?

The QuickFinder is a powerful tool that helps you find files that match certain search criteria. Using the QuickFinder can be as simple as finding a file in a directory containing the name Brooke Taylor or as complicated as searching selected directories and finding all the files that contain the word *Florida* but not the word *California* that were created between 9/1/95 and 10/1/95. With the QuickFinder, you can search specific directories, drives, and even customized indexes you create. After you narrow down where you are going to search, you specify what you are going to search for.

Steps

➨**To use the QuickFinder:**

1. Choose File➢QuickFinder. The QuickFinder dialog box is displayed, as shown in Figure 10–12. You can also choose QuickFinder from a file-management dialog box.
2. If necessary, specify in the File Pattern text box a directory and file pattern for which you want to search. For example, C:\LETTERS*.LET would search only the files in the LETTERS directory that ended with a .LET extension. You can

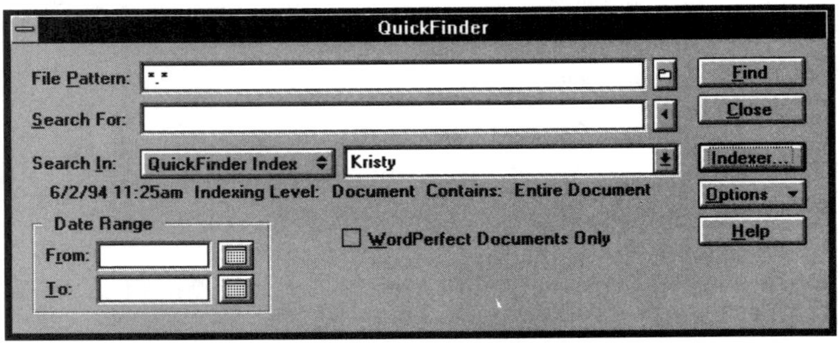

FIGURE 10–12
The QuickFinder dialog box.

combine multiple filename patterns by separating them with a comma. If you do not enter anything in the File Pattern text box, all files are searched.

3. If you want to find files with specific text, enter the text in the Search For text box. For more information on what you can enter in the Search for text box, see the section "HOW DO I... Enter QuickFinder Search Information" later in this chapter.
4. From the Search In pop-up list, select Directory, Disk, Subtree, or QuickFinder Index to specify where you want to search. The Subtree option searches all subdirectories below a specified directory. For more information about QuickFinder indexes, see the section "HOW DO I... Create a QuickFinder Index?" later in this chapter.
5. If necessary, enter a Date Range in the From and To text boxes. You can click the calendar icon to display the current month's calendar and select a date from it. You can use the arrows on the calendar to move to different months and years. Entering a Date Range can speed up a search because WordPerfect has to search only the files last modified during a certain period of time.
6. Select WordPerfect Document Only if you want to search only documents created in WordPerfect.
7. Choose Find to begin the search. After completing the search, WordPerfect displays the Search Results List, which contains a list of all files that met the criteria specified.

Tell Me More

The Search Results dialog box, displayed in Figure 10–13, is similar to the other file-management dialog boxes in WordPerfect and contains many of the same options.

The file list displays the names of all files that meet the specified search criteria along with the Full Path of the file and several other columns of file information. You can open a file or view its contents. Viewing the file can help you further determine whether the file is the one for which you are looking. You can also choose File Options and perform several other actions on a file, such as copying, deleting, and even printing the file.

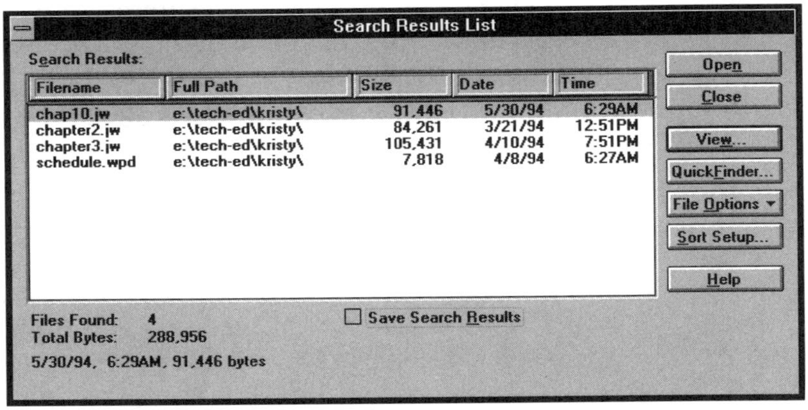

FIGURE 10–13
The Search Results List dialog box.

HOW DO I. . . Create a QuickFinder Index?

In addition to searching specific files and directories, you can also create your own indexes to search. Creating a QuickFinder index greatly increases the searching speed of the QuickFinder. In addition, creating your own indexes allows you to include only those files and directories you need in a search. After the index is created, you can use the QuickFinder to quickly search the information contained in the index for specific files and text. Using the QuickFinder allows you to expand your search to include multiple directories. It also allows you to limit your search to only specific files from specific directories.

Steps

➡To create a QuickFinder index definition:

1. Choose File➢QuickFinder.
2. Choose Indexer. The QuickFinder File Indexer dialog box is displayed.
3. Choose Create. The Create Index Name dialog box is displayed.
4. Enter a name for the Index, such as **Employee Expense Reports**, and choose OK. The Create Index dialog box is displayed, as shown in Figure 10–14.

5. Specify in the Add Directory or File text box a directory or filename you want to include in the index and then choose Add. You can use the Browse option to list files and directories from which you want to choose. You can also select the Include Subdirectories option to automatically include all subdirectories under the specified directory.
6. Repeat step 5 until you have added all directories and files you want to include in the index.
7. Choose Generate to create the index file. WordPerfect displays the Generating Index dialog box followed by the Index Completed dialog box.
8. Choose OK and then choose Close.

➡**To use a QuickFinder Index in a search:**

1. From the QuickFinder dialog box, select QuickFinder Index from the Search In pop-up list.
2. Select the Index you want from the Search In drop-down list.
3. Enter any additional information in the QuickFinder dialog box and then choose Find.

Tell Me More

Whenever you make changes to the files or directories in an Index, you have to update the index to reflect the changes. When you update the index, WordPerfect reads the files and directories and updates the index file.

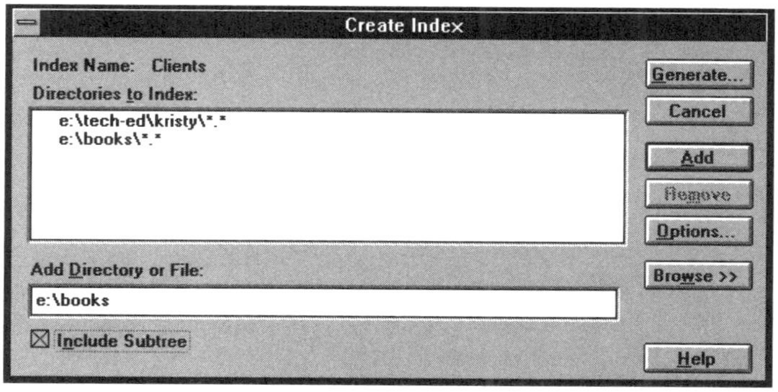

FIGURE 10–14
The Create Index dialog box.

➡To manually update your indexes:

1. Choose File➢QuickFinder.
2. Choose Indexer➢Generate. The Index Method dialog box is displayed, as shown here:

3. Select Update Indexes With New or Modified Files or Index All Files to completely rebuild the index.
4. Choose OK and Close to return to the document window.

NOTE

You can also use the KickOff utility in the WordPerfect program group to automatically update your indexes. Consult the on-line help for specific information about KickOff.

HOW DO I... Enter QuickFinder Search Information?

WordPerfect gives you numerous options for defining the search criteria when you're using the QuickFinder. You can specify logical operators, which components of the document you want to search, case sensitivity, and how thorough you want the search to be.

Steps

➡To use the QuickFinder:

1. Choose File➢QuickFinder.
2. If necessary, specify in the File Pattern text box a directory and file pattern for which you want to search.
3. Enter the necessary information in the Search For text box.
4. From the Search In pop-up list, select Directory, Disk, Subtree, or QuickFinder Index to specify where you want to search.
5. Choose Find to begin the search.

Tell Me More

The following sections describe the different options available for specifying search criteria.

Using Logical Operators

In addition to entering words and phrases in the Search For text box, you can also use the Operators option to limit your search even more. Sometimes the word or word pattern you are looking for is not clear-cut. For example, you may want to find files with two words that are not always displayed together, or you may want to find files that do not contain a certain word. These and other situations are handled by logical operators. *Logical operators* are text strings which tell WordPerfect that certain conditions exist. To access the operators, choose Operators from the Search For drop-down list.

The following table lists the operators available, the corresponding text string that is inserted, and a description and example of how each operator functions.

OPERATOR	TEXT STRING	FUNCTION
AND	&	Finds files which contain the word pattern that is on each side of the **&**. For example, enter **Defendant & Charles Morgan** to find all files with both **defendant** and **Charles Morgan**.
OR	|	Finds files that contain the word pattern on each side of the **|** or files that contain either word pattern. For example, enter **Profits | Deficits** to find files with both profits and deficits or files with either word.
NOT	!	Finds files that do not contain the word following the **!**. For example, enter **! April** to find all files that do not contain the word April.
Followed By	..	Finds files that have the first word preceding the second word somewhere in the document. For example, enter **rain..February** to find all files that contain the word rain somewhere in the document before the word February.

(continues)

OPERATOR	TEXT STRING	FUNCTION
Group	()	Finds files that contain specific words or phrases in various groupings.
Match Single Character	?	Finds words containing a single wildcard character. For example, enter **report?** to find report1, report2, report3, etc.
Match Multiple Characters	*	Finds words containing multiple wildcard characters. For example, enter **sail*** to find sail, sailor, sailboat, sails, etc.

Several logical operators can be combined to limit the search even more.

Specifying the Parts of a Document to Search

You can specify exactly which parts of the document you want searched when you're using the QuickFinder. Choose Document Components from the Search For drop-down list.

The following table describes the available options:

DOCUMENT COMPONENT	DESCRIPTION
Entire	Searches the entire document, including headers, footers, footnotes, and the Document Summary
Text Only	Searches the text body of the document but does not search headers, footers, and Document Summaries
First Page	Searches the first page of the document and the Document Summary
Summary Only	Searches only Document Summary fields
Summary Fields	Searches selected Document Summary fields

Specifying Case Sensitivity

When you enter text in the Search For text box, WordPerfect ignores all case sensitivity. If you want the search to be case-sensitive, choose Case Sensitivity from the Search For drop-down list and then choose Case Sensitive.

Specifying the Search Level

If you are searching for word patterns, you may want to change the level at which WordPerfect finds your search criteria. From the Search For drop-down list, choose Closeness of Words and then choose the level you want WordPerfect to search for word patterns. Document is the most global option. The more specific the level of searching, the longer the search will take. In the table example that used *defendant* and *Charles Morgan,* if you choose Page, both words would have to be found on the same page.

HOW DO I. . . Convert Documents to and from Other Formats?

WordPerfect has a powerful conversion feature that enables you to open documents created in other applications, such as Microsoft Word and Ami Pro. You can also save documents in a format other than WordPerfect 6.

Steps

➨**To open a non-WordPerfect file:**

1. Choose File➢Open *or* press Ctrl + O.
2. Type the filename.
3. Choose OK. The Convert File Format dialog box is displayed, as shown in Figure 10–15.

FIGURE 10–15
The Convert File Format dialog box.

4. Choose OK. If the correct file format is not displayed in the Convert File Format From text box, select the correct format. The document is converted and opened in a new document window.

HINT

If you want to preserve the original format of the file, make sure that you save the converted file with a different filename. If you save it with the same filename, it overwrites the existing file and the file will be in WordPerfect format.

➡To convert a WordPerfect 6 file to another format:

1. Choose File➢Save As *or* press F3.
2. Type the filename.
3. Select the format you want from the Format drop-down list.
4. Choose OK.

Tell Me More

When you open or retrieve the file, WordPerfect automatically converts files created in WordPerfect 5.0 and 5.1 for DOS and WordPerfect 5.1 and 5.2 for Windows. All codes are preserved in the conversion.

WordPerfect converts several other file formats. When you convert a file created in a non-WordPerfect application, you may lose some formatting codes not supported by WordPerfect 6. Although your document may not be formatted exactly the way it was, you do not lose text in the conversion process. If you are creating documents in non-WordPerfect applications and you know that you will retrieve the document into WordPerfect 6, it is helpful to keep the formatting of the document as simple as possible or use features that you know WordPerfect 6 supports. By doing so, your document does not change drastically in the conversion process.

You can also convert WordPerfect 6 files to other file formats, such as WordPerfect 5.1 and Microsoft Word 5.5, by selecting the format in the Save As dialog box. Features specific to WordPerfect 6, however, are not preserved in the conversion.

HOW DO I… Create a Summary of a Document?

A document summary gives you a quick overview of a document without reading or even opening the document; it also displays information usually not found in the text of the document. A document summary can contain helpful information, including when it was created, when it was last edited, the author, the typist, the subject, and a descriptive name.

After creating a document summary, you can view the contents while looking at a document in the Viewer or when the document is on-screen.

Steps

➠To create a document summary:

1. Choose File➢Document Summary. The Document Summary dialog box is displayed, as shown in Figure 10–16.
2. Specify the information you want included in the Document Summary fields *or* choose Options and select Extract Information From Document.
3. Choose OK to return to the document window.

➠To view a document summary:

1. Choose File➢Open *or* press Ctrl+O.
2. Select the file and choose View.
3. Position the mouse pointer in the View window, press the right mouse button, and select Document Summary. The Document Summary is displayed in the Viewer window. The Document Summary option is available only if you are displaying a WordPerfect document.

FIGURE 10–16
The Document Summary dialog box.

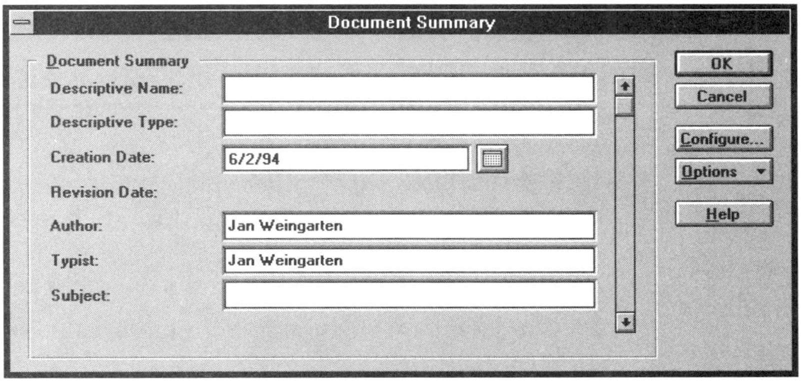

Tell Me More

Document summaries are especially useful when you are saving files on a network on which many people have access to the files. If users want to open a file saved on a network drive, they can look at the document summary and make sure that they have the correct file. You can print a document summary, save it to its own file, and delete it from the Document Summary dialog box. The following sections provide detailed information about the Document Summary fields and setup options.

Document Summary Fields

WordPerfect has several default fields for a document summary. The following table briefly describes the default fields and the type of information that generally is entered.

Document Summary Field	Description
Descriptive Name	A descriptive name of the document; you can display files by their Descriptive Name within file-management dialog boxes
Description Type	A description of the type of document, such as letter, memo, brief, or proposal
Creation Date	Date originally created
Revision Date	Date of last edit
Author	Name of author
Typist	Name of typist
Subject	The subject matter contained in the file

WordPerfect has several other fields you can include in a document summary to help you customize the document summary for your own needs.

To add, move, or remove fields in the document summary:

1. Choose File➢Document Summary.

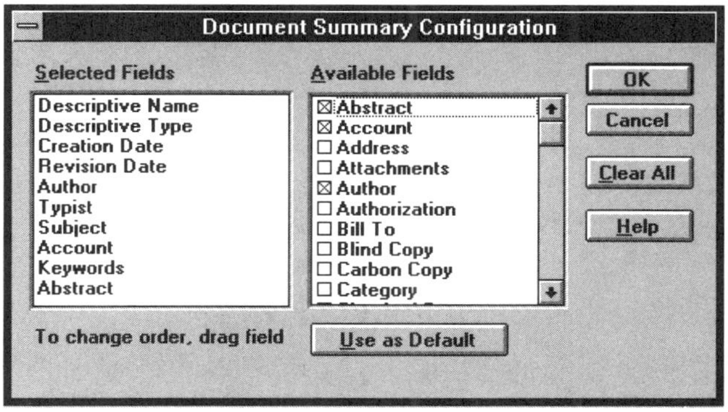

FIGURE 10–17
The Document Summary Configuration Fields dialog box.

2. Choose Configure. The Document Summary Configuration dialog box is displayed, as shown in Figure 10–17.
3. To include a field in the summary, select the field from the Available Fields list.
4. To move a field, drag the field name to the desired location in the Selected Fields list.
5. To use the new fields as the Default Summary Fields for all new documents, choose Use as Default and choose Yes.
6. Choose OK to return to the Document Summary dialog box.

Document Summary Preferences

WordPerfect offers several useful preference options for Document Summary. When you change the Document Summary preferences, the new options become the defaults for all future document summaries.

To change the Document Summary preferences:

1. Choose File➢Preferences.
2. Double-click the Summary icon. The Document Summary Preferences dialog box is displayed, as shown in Figure 10–18.
3. In the Default Subject Text text box, enter text that will precede the subject in your document. Because the default is RE, for example, when WordPerfect finds RE in your document, it inserts the text following RE in the Subject field.
4. In the Default Descriptive Type field, specify a default value, such as Letter.

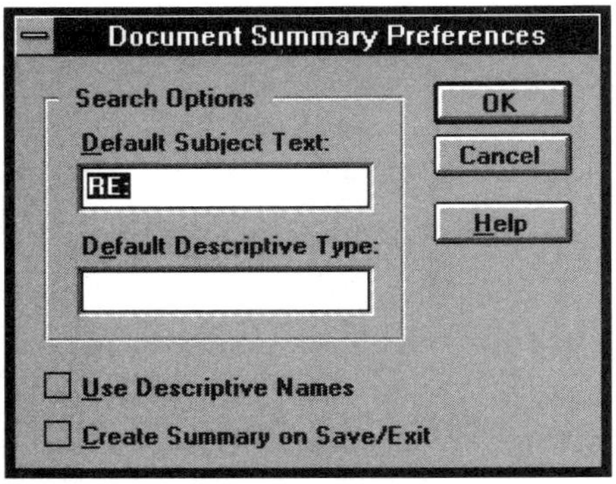

FIGURE 10–18
The Document Summary Preferences dialog box.

5. Select Use Descriptive Names if you want to enter descriptive names that are longer than the filenames.
6. Select Create Summary on Exit/Save to have WordPerfect display the Document Summary dialog box every time you exit from or save a document. After you have created a summary, the dialog box is not displayed.

HINT

You can also specify default values for the Author and Typist fields by choosing File➢Preferences➢Environment and specifying your name in the Name text box.

HOW DO I... Compare Two Documents?

WordPerfect has the capability to compare two documents and display text that has been added and text that has been deleted. The Document Compare feature is useful when you edit a document and you want to see what you have changed since you last saved the document.

Steps

➨To compare two documents:

1. With the newest version of the document you want to compare on-screen, choose File➢Compare Document.
2. Choose Add Markings.

FIGURE 10–19
An example of a compared document.

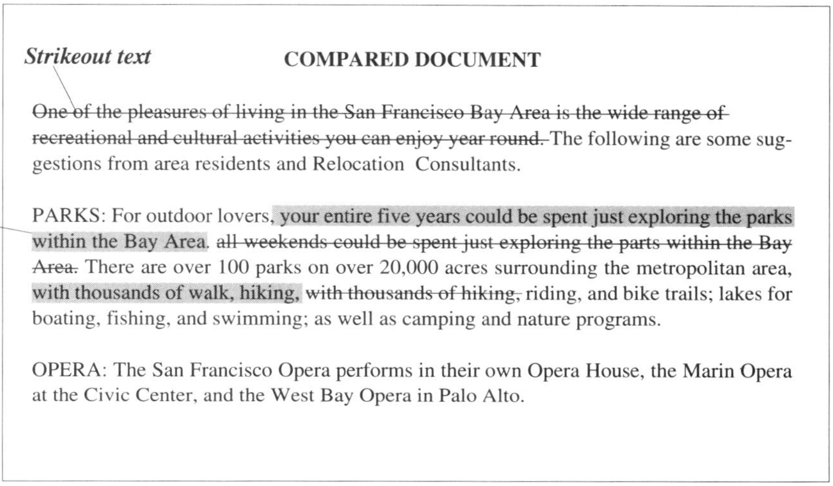

COMPARED DOCUMENT

~~One of the pleasures of living in the San Francisco Bay Area is the wide range of recreational and cultural activities you can enjoy year round.~~ The following are some suggestions from area residents and Relocation Consultants.

PARKS: For outdoor lovers, your entire five years could be spent just exploring the parks within the Bay Area. ~~all weekends could be spent just exploring the parts within the Bay Area.~~ There are over 100 parks on over 20,000 acres surrounding the metropolitan area, with thousands of walk, hiking, ~~with thousands of hiking,~~ riding, and bike trails; lakes for boating, fishing, and swimming; as well as camping and nature programs.

OPERA: The San Francisco Opera performs in their own Opera House, the Marin Opera at the Civic Center, and the West Bay Opera in Palo Alto.

3. Specify the name of the document you want to compare. By default, WP uses the most recently saved version of the current document.
4. Select the method of comparison: Word, Phrase, Sentence, or Paragraph.
5. Choose OK. The Document Compare Status dialog box is displayed while the documents are being compared.

➡ **To remove the markings after comparing documents:**

1. Choose File ➢ Compare Document.
2. Choose Remove Markings.
3. Select Remove Redline Markings and Strikeout Text or Remove Strikeout Text Only.
4. Choose OK.

Tell Me More

Figure 10–19 shows an example of a document after being compared with an earlier version. If you see redline (shaded) text, it indicates that the text has been added to the document. If you see strikeout text, it indicates that the text has been deleted from the document.

The following table explains the differences between the methods of comparison:

METHOD	DESCRIPTION
Word	Compares text that ends with a space, comma, colon, semicolon, period, question mark, exclamation point, hard return, hard page break, and footnote or endnote number
Phrase	Compares text that ends with a comma, colon, semicolon, period, question mark, exclamation point, hard return, or hard page break
Sentence	Compares text that ends with a period, question mark, exclamation point, hard return, or hard page break
Paragraph	Compares text that ends with a hard return or hard page break

Changing the Redline Method and Character

You can change the way redline text is marked by using Redline Method and Redline Character.

The default Redline Method is Printer Dependent. When you redline your text, it is printed according to your printer's specification. Most printers print redline by either shading the text or, if you have a color printer, printing red text.

To specify the redline method and change the redline character:

1. Choose Layout➢Document➢Redline Method.
2. Select Printer Dependent, Mark Left Margin, Mark Alternating Margins, or Mark Right Margin.
3. If you select any option other than Printer Dependent, you can type a new character in the Redline Character text box. The default redline character is a vertical bar (|).
4. Choose OK.

If you specify Left as the redline method, the redline character is inserted in the left margin. On the other hand, if you specify Right, the redline character is inserted in the right margin. The Alternating option inserts the redline character in the left margin for even-numbered pages and in the right margin for odd-numbered pages.

HOW DO I... Link Documents?

When you are working on a lengthy document, it is sometimes easier and more efficient to divide the document into several smaller documents. Using several documents decreases the size of the document, which in turn speeds up many of WordPerfect's formatting features. After dividing a document into smaller documents, you can link them together to form one master document. You can create a master document by creating several documents initially or by dividing an existing document into several files. A master document can be condensed so that it lists just the names of the other files it contains or it can be expanded to include the text from all files.

Steps

➠**To divide a large document into smaller documents:**

1. Select the section of the document you want to save as a smaller file.
2. Choose File➢Save As *or* press F3 and enter a name for the file.
3. Press Delete to delete the selected text from the original document.
4. Repeat steps 1 through 3 until you have created all your subdocuments.

➠**To create a master document:**

1. If necessary, divide the document into smaller documents by following the preceding steps.
2. Move the insertion point to the location in the master document where you want to insert the smaller document.
3. Choose File➢Master Document➢Subdocument.
4. Specify the name of the document and choose Include. WordPerfect inserts an icon into the master document, as shown here:

Subdocument icon

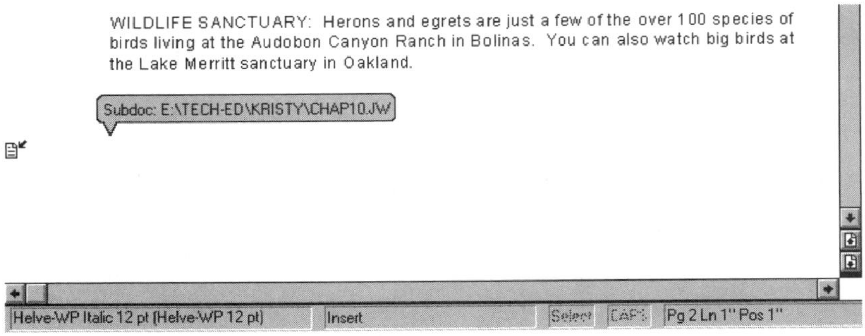

If you click on the icon, the name of the subdocument is displayed.

5. Repeat steps 1 through 4 for each subdocument.

➠**To expand or condense a master document:**

1. Retrieve the master document.
2. Choose File➢Master Document➢Expand Master or Condense Master.

HINT **You can also double-click the subdocument icon to expand or condense a subdocument.**

Tell Me More

A master document can include text in addition to subdocuments. You can have one subdocument or multiple subdocuments in a master document—it all depends on your needs.

Suppose that you have created a document which contains information about all the U.S. Virgin Islands. Each island is discussed in a section of more than 30 pages. You can create a master document that contains subdocuments for each island. Then when you want to edit information about one island, you have to retrieve only the document for that island.

You can also create a master document with only one subdocument. You create a master document with only one subdocument if you have a document with a lengthy section. For example, a document you have created that contains information about the Bahamas has several sections, but the tourism section is 70 pages long. By using the Master Document feature, you can create a subdocument for just the tourism section. Your master document includes all the other text in the document in addition to the tourism subdocument.

You must expand the master document before you can print all the information in all the subdocuments. You can retrieve individual subdocuments and edit them, however, without doing anything to the master document. The changes you make to the subdocuments are reflected in the master document the next time you expand it.

When you print a master document, it prints just as though it were one long document. For example, page numbering and footnote numbering is continuous. If you edit a subdocument when a master document is expanded, you have to make sure that you save the subdocument when you condense the master document.

➡To save changes you make to an expanded subdocument:

1. Double-click the subdocument icon you want to save.
2. From the dialog box, select the document (or documents) you want to save and condense and choose OK. Depending on what you choose, WordPerfect condenses the subdocuments and saves the changes.

Chapter 11

Automating Tasks and Optimizing WordPerfect

WordPerfect provides numerous way to optimize and automate many of the tasks you perform with WordPerfect. Several tools make creating documents easier and faster. This chapter answers questions about the following features:

- Using QuickFormat
- Using abbreviations
- Repeating keystrokes, commands, and macros
- Creating Button Bars
- Remapping the keyboard
- Using predefined macros
- Using and creating macros
- Merging documents
- Sorting text
- Creating templates

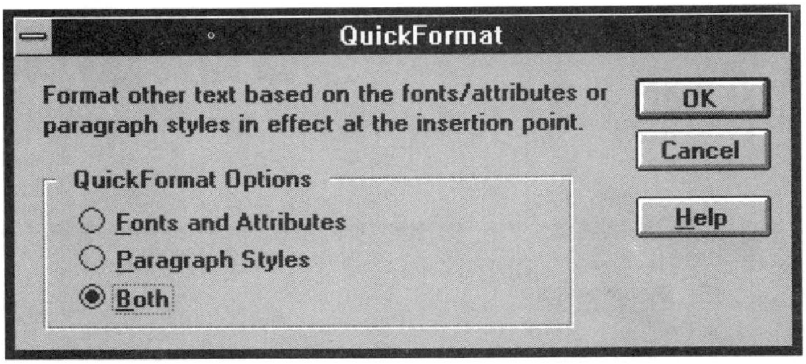

FIGURE 11–1 *The QuickFormat dialog box.*

- Creating styles
- Faxing documents

HOW DO I. . . Apply Existing Formatting to Other Text?

The QuickFormat feature lets you take the fonts, attributes, and paragraph styles for existing text and apply them to text in another part of the document. If you have inserted a quote in your document, for example, and have changed the font and inserted a paragraph style, you can use QuickFormat to apply the formatting codes to another quote you use in the document. QuickFormat is a great way to eliminate repeating the same steps over again.

Steps

➡To copy existing fonts, attributes, or paragraph styles to other text:

1. Position the insertion point on the text containing the formatting you want to copy.
2. Press the right mouse button and choose QuickFormat. The QuickFormat dialog box is displayed, as shown in Figure 11–1.
3. Select the desired QuickFormat option and choose OK. The mouse pointer now is displayed like this:

4. Drag the icon over the text to which you want to copy the formatting codes.
5. Press the right mouse button and select QuickFormat to deactivate the feature.

BUTTON BAR

You can also click the QuickFormat button to open the QuickFormat dialog box.

Tell Me More

You can use QuickFormat to format multiple areas of text. You simply drag the icon over the different areas of text. This feature makes it easy to quickly format multiple parts of a document at one time.

HOW DO I. . . Use Abbreviations?

Abbreviations let you type a short abbreviation for information you frequently use in your documents. If you frequently type your name, address, and ZIP code, for example, you can create an abbreviation called Address. Then each time you want to insert your name, address, and ZIP code in a document, all you have to type is **Address**. After entering the abbreviation in the document, you have to expand it so that all the information is displayed.

NOTE

If you used macros in previous versions of WordPerfect to insert text, you may want to use abbreviations.

Steps

➡To create an abbreviation:

1. Select the text you want to include in the abbreviation.
2. Choose Insert➢Abbreviations.
3. Choose Create, type the name of the abbreviation, such as **Address**, and choose OK and then choose Close.

➡To expand an abbreviation:

1. Move the insertion point to the abbreviation and press Ctrl+A.

HINT

WordPerfect ships a predefined macro that automatically expands all abbreviations in a document. Using the macro is much faster than manually expanding an abbreviation. To use the macro to expand your abbreviations, choose Tools➢Macro➢Play *or* press Alt+F10, specify EXPNDALL for the Name, and choose Play.

Tell Me More

When you create an abbreviation, you should make it as concise as possible. Abbreviations are case-sensitive, so be sure to type them exactly as you have created them. Abbreviations are assigned to the current template you are using. If you want to use an abbreviation in a different template, you can copy the abbreviation.

HOW DO I... Automatically Repeat a Keystroke, Command, or Macro?

The Repeat feature lets you automatically repeat a keystroke, command, or macro. Using the Repeat feature can eliminate repetition in your work. If you want to use the dollar sign ($) to make a border at the top of your document, for example, you can use the Repeat feature to have it automatically insert a specified number of dollar signs to fill the entire line.

Steps

➡To repeat a keystroke, command, or macro:

1. Choose Edit➢Repeat.
2. Enter a new value in the Number of Times to Repeat Next Action text box, if you want. The default value is 8.
3. Choose OK.
4. Enter the keystroke, command, or macro you want to repeat.

➡To change the default repeat value:

1. Choose Edit➢Repeat.
2. Enter the new repeat value and choose Use as Default.

Tell Me More

The Repeat feature works with insertion-point movement, deletion commands, characters, and many other WordPerfect features. Some keystrokes that may be useful to use with Repeat are Delete, the arrow keys (←, →, ↑, ↓), and the Spacebar.

You can use Repeat with a macro to execute a macro a certain number of times. For example, you can create a macro that selects a line of text and then moves it to another document screen. If you want to move several lines of text, you can repeat the macro a specific number of times rather than play the macro for each line.

HOW DO I. . . Create a Button Bar?

In addition to the many predefined Button Bars described in Chapter 2, "Setting Up WordPerfect," you can create your own customized Button Bars. Creating your own Button Bar enables you to control exactly which menu items, features, and macros you include on a Button Bar. You can create a Button Bar for specific types of documents you create. If you write articles for a magazine or newsletter, for example, you can create a Button Bar that contains buttons for the menu items, features, and macros you use every time you create an article. You can also edit the predefined Button Bars. Creating and editing Button Bars makes your use of them flexible and personalized.

Steps

➨**To edit or create a Button Bar:**

1. Click the right mouse button while pointing to the Button Bar to display the Button Bar QuickMenu.
2. Choose Preferences or, if you want to edit the current Button Bar, choose Edit and skip to step 4.
3. Highlight the Button Bar you want to edit and choose Edit or choose Create and specify a name for the Button Bar and choose OK. The Button Bar Editor dialog box is displayed, as shown in Figure 11–2.
4. Select Activate a Feature to add a WordPerfect feature to the Button Bar. Choose the pull-down menu on which the feature is located and then select the feature from the Features list and choose Add Button from the Feature Categories drop-

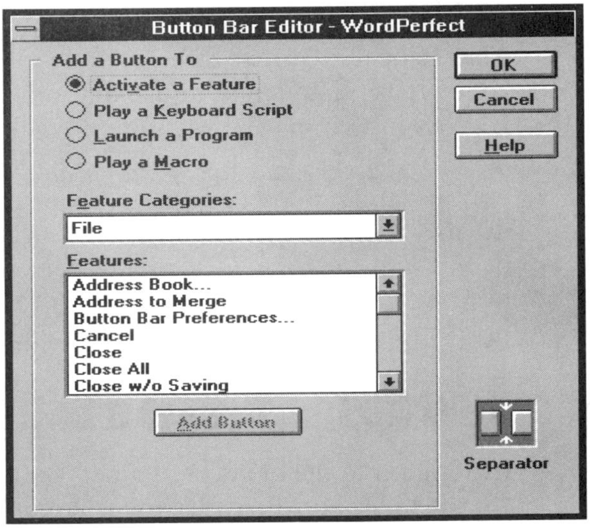

FIGURE 11–2
The Button Bar Editor dialog box.

down list. As you highlight the features, WordPerfect displays the icon that will be used and a brief description of the feature at the bottom of the dialog box.

- Or select Play a Keyboard Script and type the text you want WordPerfect to insert in the document window when you choose the button and choose Add Script. For example, you can type your name and title so that every time you want to insert it in a document, you simply click the appropriate Button Bar icon.
- Or select Launch a Program to start another program while you're in WordPerfect. Then choose Select File, specify the name of the executable file of the program, and choose OK. To start WordPerfect Office, for example, enter **OFWIN.EXE**.
- Or select Play Macro and choose Add Macro. Specify the name of the macro *or* choose the file icon, select the macro, and choose OK.

HINT

Adding a feature to a Button Bar is especially helpful if a feature you often use is located several levels deep on a menu.

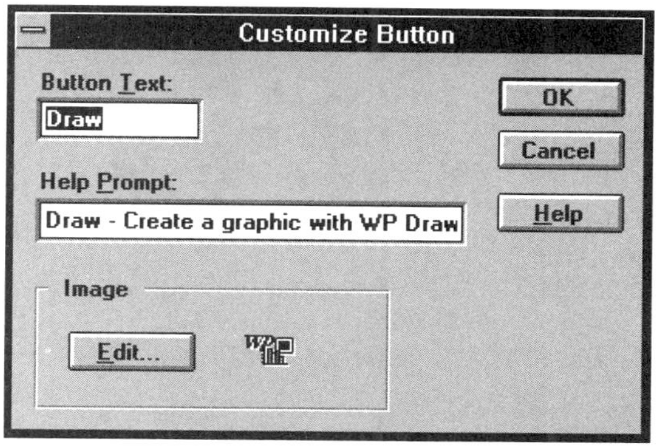

FIGURE 11–3
The Customize Button dialog box.

5. If necessary, drag the buttons to the desired location on the bar or drag a button off the bar to delete it. The newly created bar is displayed above the dialog box during the creating and editing process.

NOTE

If you want to separate buttons, you can drag the Separator to the desired location on the Button Bar.

6. After you have added and arranged all the items on your Button Bar, choose OK to return to the document window.

Tell Me More

When you edit and define a new Button Bar, you can edit the icon and text that represent the menu items, features, and macros on it.

➡To change the icon and text on a Button Bar item:

1. With the Button Bar Editor displayed, double-click the button you want to change. The Customize Button dialog box is displayed, as shown in Figure 11–3.
2. If you want to change the description on the button, enter the new text in the Button Text text box.
3. If you want to change the help prompt that is displayed when you point to the button with the mouse pointer, enter the information in the Help Prompt text box.
4. If you want to change the icon that is displayed, choose Edit to display the Button Bar Image Editor, as displayed in

FIGURE 11–4
The Button Bar Image Editor.

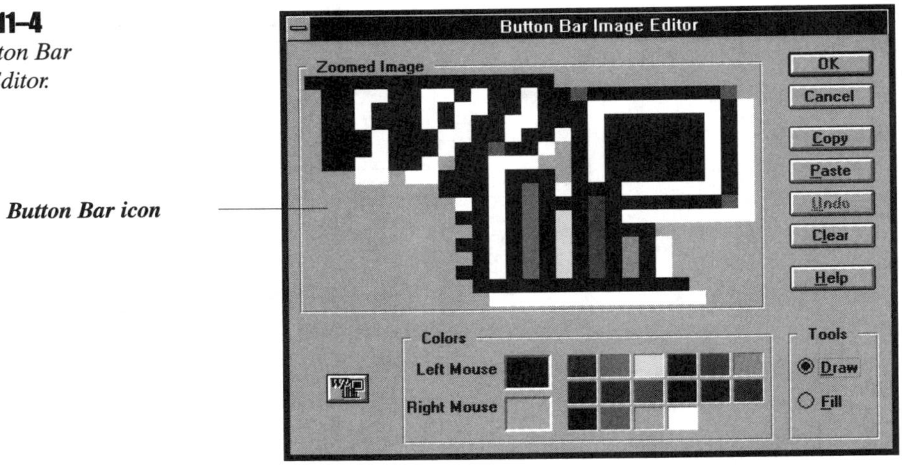

Figure 11–4. You can draw a new image, change colors, or paste information from the Clipboard.

5. Choose OK until you return to the document window.

NOTE

When you create a Button Bar, you create it for the current template you are using. If you want to use it in more than one template, you can copy it by using the Copy button in the Button Bar Preferences dialog box. If you are not sure which template you are using, the name of the template is displayed at the bottom of the Button Bar Preferences dialog box.

HOW DO I... Remap My Keyboard?

WordPerfect provides three predefined keyboards. You can use any one of the predefined layouts, create a new keyboard layout to remap your keyboard any way you want, and edit a keyboard you have created. You cannot edit the existing keyboards. Remapping your keyboard enables you to include specialized keyboard functions, such as inserting specific text with the touch of one or two keystrokes, performing a command with a keystroke that is more comfortable to you, launching a program, or playing a macro. Using keyboards can save you time and gives you complete control over the use of your keyboard.

Steps

➡To create or edit an existing keyboard definition:

1. Choose File➢Preferences and double-click the Keyboard icon. The Keyboard Preferences dialog box is displayed.
2. Highlight the keyboard you want to edit and choose Edit or choose Create and specify the name of the keyboard and choose OK. The Keyboard Editor is displayed, as shown in Figure 11–5.
3. Type any character or keystroke combination from the keyboard you want to change.

HINT **You can also click on the key combinations in the Choose a Key to Assign or Unassign list box or on the keyboard displayed at the bottom of the dialog box.**

FIGURE 11–5
The Keyboard Editor.

Name of current keyboard

Actions available to keystroke

Current keystroke assignment

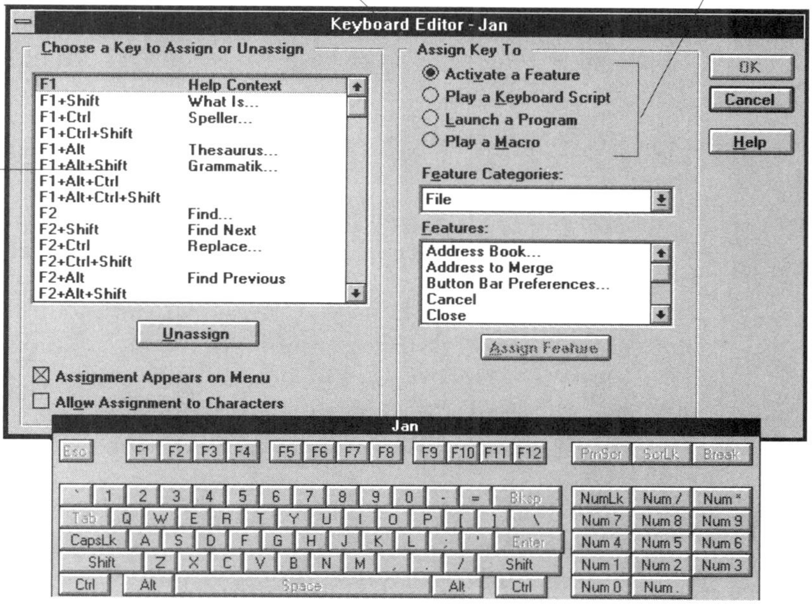

4. Select Activate a Feature to assign a WordPerfect feature to the keyboard. Choose the pull-down menu on which the feature is located from the Feature Categories drop-down list and then select the feature from the Features list and choose Assign Feature. As you highlight the features, WordPerfect displays a brief description of the feature at the bottom of the dialog box.
   - Or select Play a Keyboard Script and type the text you want WordPerfect to insert in the document window when you press the key assignment and choose Assign Script.
   - Or select Launch a Program to start another program while you're in WordPerfect. Then choose Select File, specify the name of the executable file of the program, and choose OK. Every time you press the assigned key combination, you launch the specified program.
   - Or select Play Macro and choose Assign Macro. Specify the name of the macro *or* choose the file icon, select the macro, and choose OK.
5. Repeat steps 4 and 5 until you have assigned the desired keys.
6. If you want to unassign a key combination, highlight the combination and choose Unassign. You do not have to unassign a key before assigning a new action.
7. Choose OK and then choose Select to activate the new keyboard.

Tell Me More

When you assign keys, you can specify a function key (F9 or F2, for example), a keystroke combination (Alt, Shift, or Ctrl plus another keyboard character or function key), or a keyboard character (*a, 1,* or +, for example). To assign a keyboard character, you must select Allow Assignment to Characters from the Keyboard Editor dialog box.

NOTE

If you assign an action to a character, the key no longer functions as the character—it performs the assigned action. If you assign the character a to type your address, for example, it no longer inserts the letter *a* in your document.

Activating a Feature

One of the many strengths of WordPerfect is its flexibility. The Keyboard Editor allows you to assign features to keys that are most efficient and familiar to you. If you want the Print feature to be assigned to Shift+F7, for example, you can do so. You can assign or change as many keys as necessary. If learning new keystrokes is slowing you down, simply create your own keyboard.

Playing a Keyboard Script

You can create a key to insert specific text in your document at the touch of a button. For example, you might regularly write scientific papers that include many medical terms (*staphylococcus aureas,* for example). Because scientific terms are often long and difficult to spell, you can create a key that enables you to type the term only one time and then recall it with a simple keystroke or keystroke combination.

You can then press they key anywhere in your document to insert the text. This is just one of the different types of text you can assign to a key. You can create as many text keys as there are keystroke combinations. However, you can assign only one action to a keystroke or keystroke combination for a specific keyboard layout.

Launching a Program

If you use many programs for performing your tasks throughout the day, you can launch those programs directly from WordPerfect by assigning them to a keyboard definition. If you use Lotus 1-2-3 to perform spreadsheet functions, for example, you can assign the keys Alt+L to launch Lotus 1-2-3. This keystroke is faster than returning to the Program Manager, and you can select a keystroke that is easy for you to remember.

Playing a Macro

You can play a macro at the touch of a button by defining a key or keystroke combination as a macro. Although you can play individual macros with simple keystroke combinations, there are advantages to assigning groups of macros to a specific keyboard layout. Suppose that you create memos and letters every day. You have automated the creation of these documents by using macros. You can create a keyboard layout that includes all the macros you use for creating memos and letters. With a specific keyboard defined, you can group the macros together and play each macro at the touch of a button.

HOW DO I... Use Predefined Macros?

WordPerfect ships several predefined macros to enhance and automate the performance of certain functions within the program. For example, there are macros for saving all open documents, converting endnotes to footnotes, inserting a page number in the "X of Y" format, and many others. In addition to automating various tasks, these macros serve as examples and templates for creating your own advanced macros.

Steps

➠**To play a predefined macro:**

1. Choose Tools➢Macro➢Play *or* press Alt+F10.
2. Enter the name of the predefined macro and choose Play.

NOTE **You can click the file icon *or* press F4 to display a list of all macros in the macro directory.**

Tell Me More

When you use the predefined macros, you simply play the macro and then follow the on-screen prompts. By default, these macros are stored in your C:\WPWIN60\MACROS directory. The following table describes several of the most useful predefined macros. Take some time to experiment with these macros—they provide quick access to some powerful features.

MACRO NAME	DESCRIPTION
ABBREV.WCM	Displays the Abbreviations dialog box so that you can insert multiple abbreviations without having to type them; you simply select them from a list.
ALLFONTS.WCM	Types the names of all fonts for the selected printer in their respective typefaces.
CAPITAL.WCM	Capitalizes the first letter of the current word.
CLIPBRD.WCM	Opens the Windows Clipboard Viewer so that you can quickly view or edit the contents.

(continues)

MACRO NAME	DESCRIPTION
CLOSEALL.WCM	Closes all opened document windows. The Close All Documents dialog box is displayed so that you can select which documents you want to save and specify a filename if necessary.
DROPCAP.WCM	Creates a large capital letter (or *drop cap*) for the first character of the current paragraph, as shown in Figure 11–6. The macro inserts a larger size of the character into a graphics box.
ENDFOOT.WCM	Converts existing endnotes to footnotes.
EXPNDALL.WCM	Expands all Abbreviations in the current document window.
FILESTMP.WCM	Creates a footer or header with the document name. When you play this macro, you can customize several options, as shown in the File Stamp Options dialog box, displayed in Figure 11–7. This is a quick and easy way to insert the document name on documents.
FONTDN.WCM	Decreases the current font by two points.
FONTUP.WCM	Increases the current font by two points.
FOOTEND.WCM	Converts existing footnotes to endnotes.
GOTODOS.WCM	Opens a DOS window. To return to WordPerfect, type **exit**.
PAGEXOFY.WCM	Inserts page numbering in a document in the format of Page 1 of 10, for example. You can select the exact format and position of the page numbering.
PARABRK.WCM	Inserts character or graphical markers at the end of the current paragraph. Figure 11–8 shows an example of the Floral paragraph break.
PGBORDER.WCM	Creates fancy page borders from graphics images. Figure 11–9 shows an example of the pencil page border.

(continues)

MACRO NAME	DESCRIPTION
PLEADING.WPM	Creates legal pleading paper. It creates and inserts a style in your document that includes the codes necessary to create the pleading paper. After playing this macro, you can easily enter your text to create your legal document.
SAVEALL.WCM	Saves all currently opened documents.
WATERMRK.WCM	Automates the process for inserting a graphics image into a watermark.

HOW DO I... Create Macros?

A *macro* is a file that contains functions which are automatically invoked when you play the macro. A macro can contain keystrokes, text, and macro commands. Macros enable you to combine multiple tasks in a single file to be used over and over again to help automate repetitive tasks. If you frequently change one of your Display Preferences, for example, you can record the information to make the changes in a macro

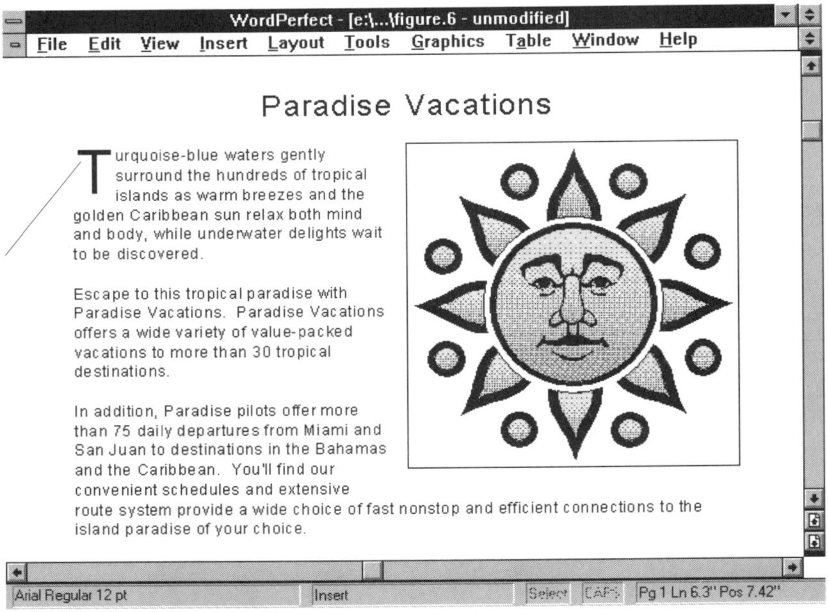

FIGURE 11–6 *A drop cap created with the DROPCAP.WCM predefined macro.*

Drop cap

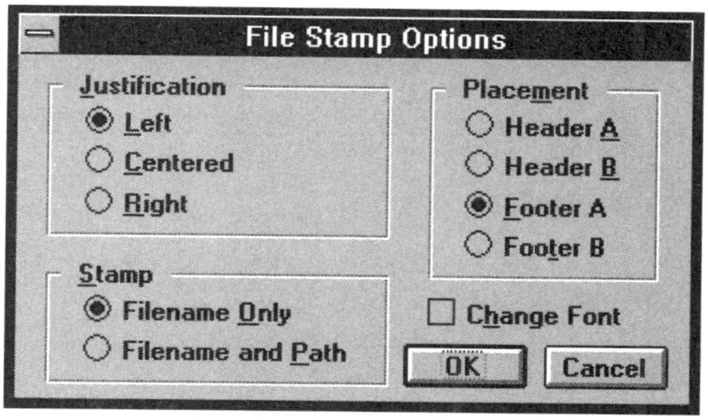

FIGURE 11–7
The File Stamp Options dialog box.

rather than perform several steps every time you want to change the option.

When you want to create a macro, you *record* the information in the macro. When you want to use a macro, you *play* the macro. Playing a macro simply means that the selected macro performs the tasks for which it was defined. Macros save time and can greatly increase the efficiency with which you perform repetitive tasks.

Steps

➠To record a macro:

1. Choose Tools➢Macro➢Record *or* press Ctrl+F10.
2. Enter a name for the macro and choose Record. See the section "Naming Macros" later in this chapter for more information.

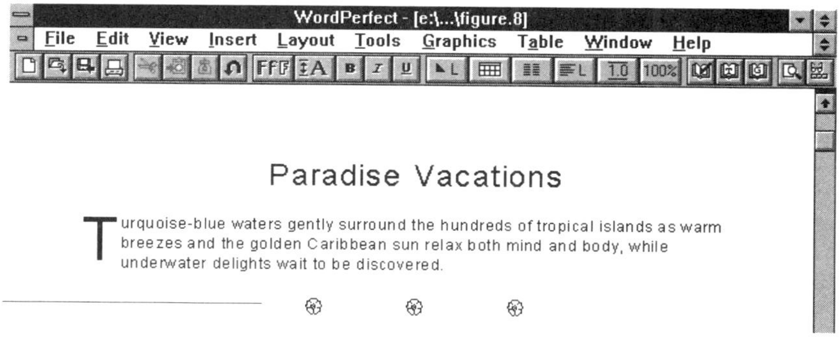

FIGURE 11–8
A Floral paragraph break inserted by using the PARABRK.WCM predefined macro.

Floral paragraph break

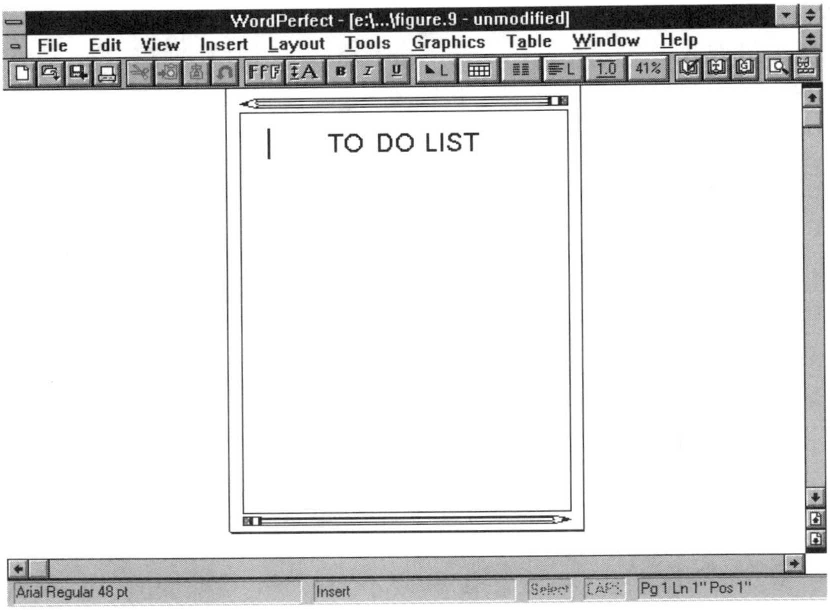

FIGURE 11–9
A pencil page border inserted by using the PGBORDER.WCM predefined macro.

3. You are returned to the document window, where you can enter the text and perform the functions you want to include in the macro. While you are recording a macro, the words "Macro Record" are displayed in the middle of the status line. Any and all actions you perform are recorded in the macro.
4. Choose Tools➢Macro➢Record *or* press Ctrl+F10 to end the recording.

➠To play a macro:

1. Choose Tools➢Macro➢Play *or* press Alt+F10.
2. Specify the name of the macro. WordPerfect plays the macro. You can also click on the file icon *or* press the ↓ key to display the macros in your default macro directory (C:\WPWIN60\MACROS).
3. Choose Play.

HINT

You can choose Tools➢Macro and select the last macro you played from the menu.

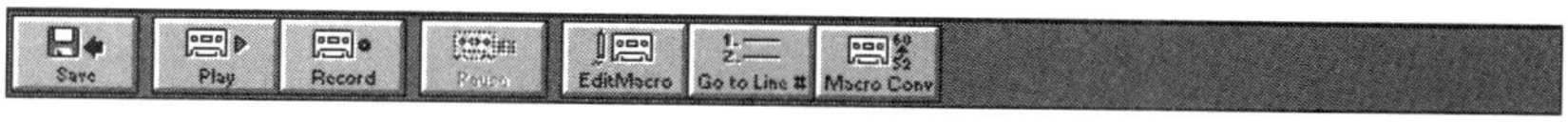

FIGURE 11–10
The Macro Button Bar.

Tell Me More

The Macro Button Bar displayed in Figure 11–10 is useful if you will be creating and editing many macros. To display the Macro Button Bar, point to the Button Bar, click the right mouse button, and then select Macro Tools.

The following sections explain how to name, record, and edit a macro. In addition, instructions for creating and using a temporary macro are included.

Naming a Macro

When you name a macro, it must meet the DOS filenaming requirement of eight characters or fewer. You should use descriptive names for your macros so that they are easy to remember when you want to run them. WordPerfect automatically adds a .WCM extension to the macro. You do not have to enter the extension when you are recording or playing a macro; WordPerfect automatically inserts the extension. By default, WordPerfect saves your macros in the C:\WPWIN60\MACROS directory. You can use the Location of Files option to designate a different directory. Also, if you have saved a macro in a different directory, you must specify the entire path to the macro file in the Play Macro dialog box.

Recording a Macro

Recording a macro is easy: You simply enter text or access features in the same way as you do when you create a document. WordPerfect records the tasks you perform in the macro. If you make a mistake, you can delete text and it is not recorded.

When you create a macro, try to perform the tasks in the most efficient way. If you want to bold the text, for example, turn bold on, enter the text, and then turn bold off rather than select and bold the text. The results of the actions you perform are recorded in the macro; the more efficient you are in creating your macros, the faster your macros play.

To pause temporarily while recording a macro so that you can perform another task on the current document window or another document window:

1. While recording a macro, choose Tools➢Macro➢Pause.

BUTTON BAR **You can also choose the Pause button from the Macros Button Bar.**

2. To continue recording, choose Tools➢Macro➢Pause. You can also choose Record from the Macros Button Bar.

Editing a Macro

You can easily edit macros you have created.

To edit a macro:

1. Choose Tools➢Macro➢Edit.
2. Type the name of the macro you want to edit and choose Edit. WordPerfect retrieves the contents of the macro file into a document window and displays the Macro Feature Bar, as shown in Figure 11–11.

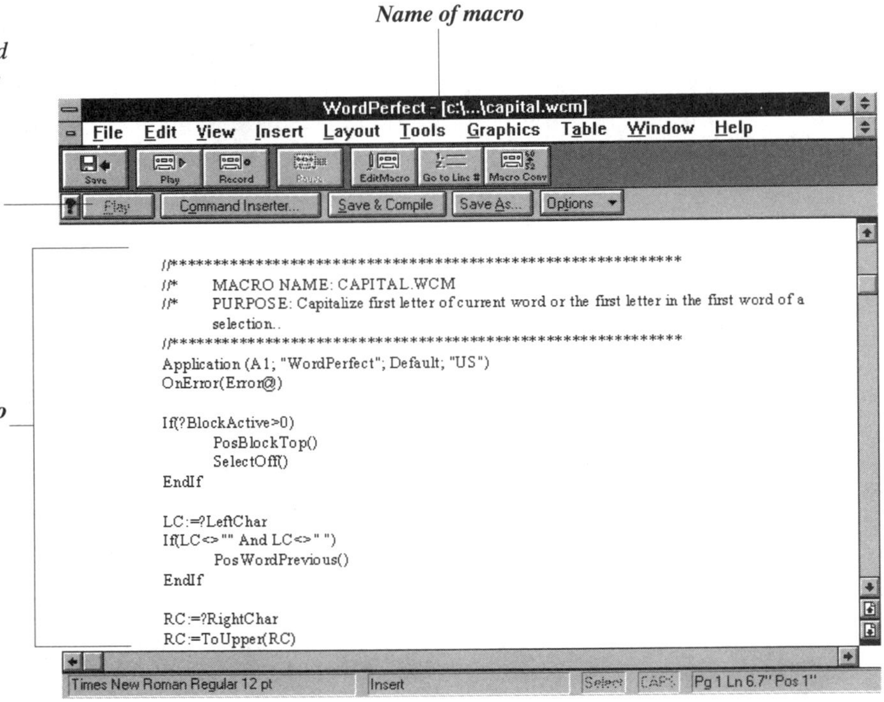

FIGURE 11–11
The macro file and the Macro Feature Bar.

3. Make the necessary changes directly in the document window.
4. Choose Options from the Macro Feature Bar and choose Close Macro. Choose Yes to save the macro file and return to the preceding document screen.

When you edit a macro, you can type additional text after the **Type("")** command. Insert the text inside the quotation marks, as shown here:

Insert text here

```
HardReturn()
Font(FontInfo[Count])
Type("aAbBcCdDeEfFgGhHiIjJkKlLmMnNoOpPqQrRsStTuUvVwWxXyYzZ12345678
90`'""~!@#$%^&*()_+-=:;,.?/\|<>[]{}")
BlockProtect(Off!)
HardReturn()
```

You can also access additional advanced macro codes while you're recording or editing macros. These powerful commands allow you to perform complicated and powerful tasks. For example, with the macro commands, you can pause a macro, display a question, and then perform additional functions according to the response to the questions. Detailed information about the macro-programming commands are included in the WordPerfect on-line help.

To insert macro commands, you use the WordPerfect Macro Command Inserter. You can display it by choosing Command Inserter from the Macro Feature Bar when you're editing a macro. As you highlight a macro command, a brief description of the command is displayed at the bottom of the dialog box. Highlight the macro command you want to use and then choose Insert. If the macro code requires additional parameters, the Parameters text box lists them. Type the additional information in the Command Edit text box and then choose Insert. The macro code is inserted at the insertion-point position in the document window.

Creating a Temporary Macro

You can create a temporary macro by choosing Record rather than enter a name for the macro. You might want to perform a certain task within a document a multiple number of times, for example, such as bold the word *Cruise* wherever it appears in the document but only for the current document. You can create a regular macro and then delete the macro when it is no longer needed. Or you can record this information in a temporary macro.

The temporary macro is stored in the macro directory with all other macros; WordPerfect names this macro WP{WPC}.WCM. Whenever you do not enter a name for the macro when you are recording a macro, the information in the temporary macro is replaced with the new information.

To play a temporary macro, choose Tools➢Macro➢Play and then choose Play without entering a name.

HOW DO I... Use Merge?

The Merge feature enables you to merge two files to combine the information in both files. You can use Merge to automate the process of creating envelopes, labels, form letters, and many other types of documents. To create and send a letter to 100 people, for example, you can create a file that contains the names and addresses of those to whom you want to send the letter. You can then create one letter and merge the two files to automatically create a letter for each of the 100 people. This section is designed to help you understand the concepts and terminology associated with the use of Merge.

Understanding Merge Terminology

To fully understand how the Merge feature works, it is important to know some of the terminology that relates to Merge features. The following table describes all the terms you need to know to use the Merge feature.

MERGE TERM	DESCRIPTION
Data file	In previous versions of WordPerfect, this file was referred to as the secondary file. It contains the information you want to merge with another document. There are two types of data files: data text files and data table files. You can use either type of file when you create a data file. In the preceding example, the data file is the document that contains the names and addresses of those who receive the letter.

(continues)

MERGE TERM	DESCRIPTION
Data text file	Includes fields and records and displays the text followed by merge codes. Use a data text file when you want to see all the merge codes on-screen.
Data table file	Includes fields and records. This type of file is displayed in table format and does not display the merge codes. You use a data table file when you do not want to worry about entering merge codes manually; this type of file is especially useful if a multiple number of people will enter the information in the file.
Form file	In previous versions of WordPerfect, this file was referred to as the *primary file.* Contains all the formatting codes and information with which you want to merge your data. If you are merging a letter, the file that contains the text and formatting codes for the letter is the form file. A form file includes fields to match the fields in the data file.
Fields	Contains the specific information within a record—if you are creating a data file that consists of the name, address, city, state, and ZIP code, each of these items can be an individual field.
Record	A series of repeating common fields. In the preceding example, each person is considered a record. If you enter information for 100 people, you have 100 records.

Steps

➠To perform a merge, you follow three primary steps:

1. Create a data file (using a data text file or a table text file).
2. Create a form file.
3. Merge the two files.

The next three heading questions outline the specific steps for performing each of these steps.

HOW DO I... Create a Data File?

A data file includes the information that will be merged into a form file. For example, a data file might contain all the names and addresses of those people to whom you want to send a letter. The data file can be in a text format or entered in a table format. The data file contains fields and records. Each record in the data file must contain the same number of fields.

Steps

➡**To create a data file:**

1. From an empty document window, choose Tools➢Merge. The Merge dialog box is displayed, as shown in Figure 11–12.
2. Choose Data. If you want the data file in a table format, select Place Records in A Table. The Create Data File dialog box is displayed, as shown here:

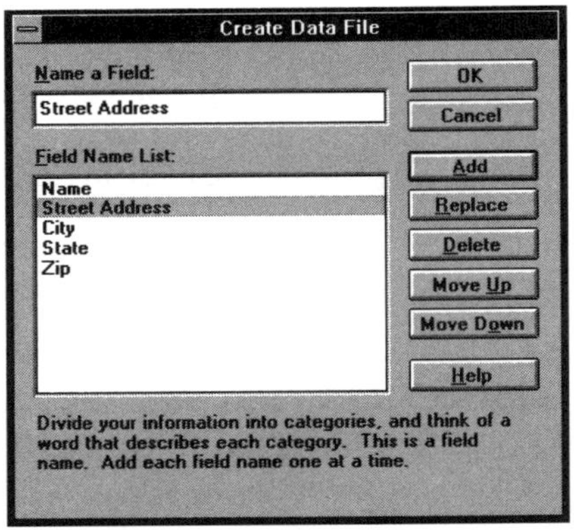

3. Enter the name of a field and choose Add. The Field Name is a word that describes the type of information you will enter, such as name, street, and city.
4. Repeat step 3 for each field you want to include in the data file.

HINT

The order in which you enter the names is how they appear in the data file. You can use the Move Up and Move Down

FIGURE 11–12
The Merge dialog box.

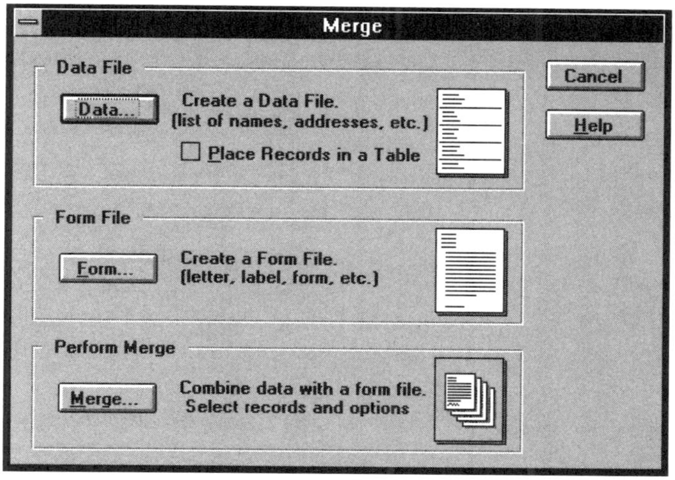

options to change the order. You can also Delete and Replace field names.

5. Choose OK to display the Quick Data Entry dialog box, displayed in Figure 11–13.
6. Enter the information for the first record. To move to the next field in the record, you can press Enter *or* you can click the mouse button in the desired field *or* choose Next Field.
7. When you have finished entering all the information, press Enter *or* choose Next Record and enter the information for the second record. Repeat this step until you have added all the information to your data file.

NOTE

If you want to insert a new line in a field, press Ctrl + Enter. If you are entering the street, city, and state all in one field, for example, you press Ctrl + Enter after entering the street information.

8. When you have added all the records to the data file, choose Close and choose Yes to save the changes. Specify a filename for the data file and choose OK. It is a good idea to save data files with a specific extension, such as .DAT, so that you can easily identify them. Your data file is displayed in the docu-

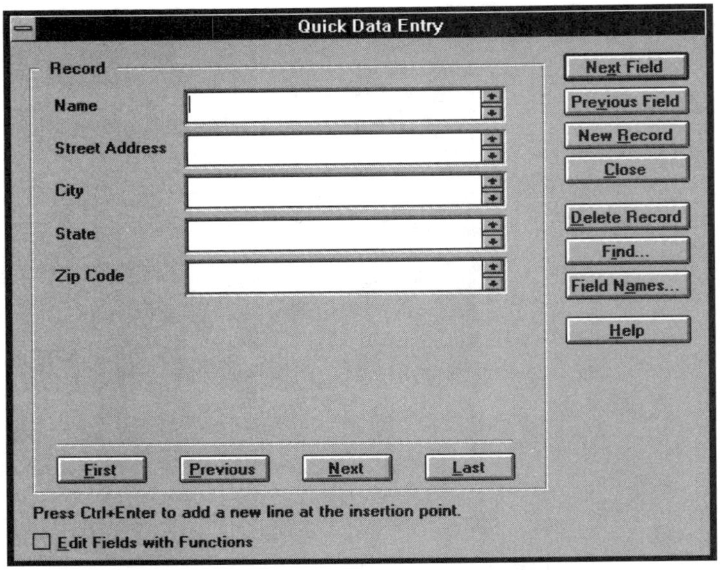

FIGURE 11–13
The Quick Data Entry dialog box.

ment window. Figure 11–14 shows a text data file, and Figure 11–15 shows a table data file.

9. Choose File➢Close or choose an option from the Merge Feature Bar.

Tell Me More

After you have created a data file, you can use the file with many different form files. This capability is especially useful if you include the same information for many documents—for example, if you use the Merge feature to send several different letters to the same group of people. You have to create the data file only one time and then create a series of form files (the letters) with which to merge the data file. A data file can contain a maximum of 65,535 records or as many as disk space allows.

Editing Data Files

After initially creating the data file, you may periodically have to edit the information. For example, an address may change or you may want to add some more records to the file.

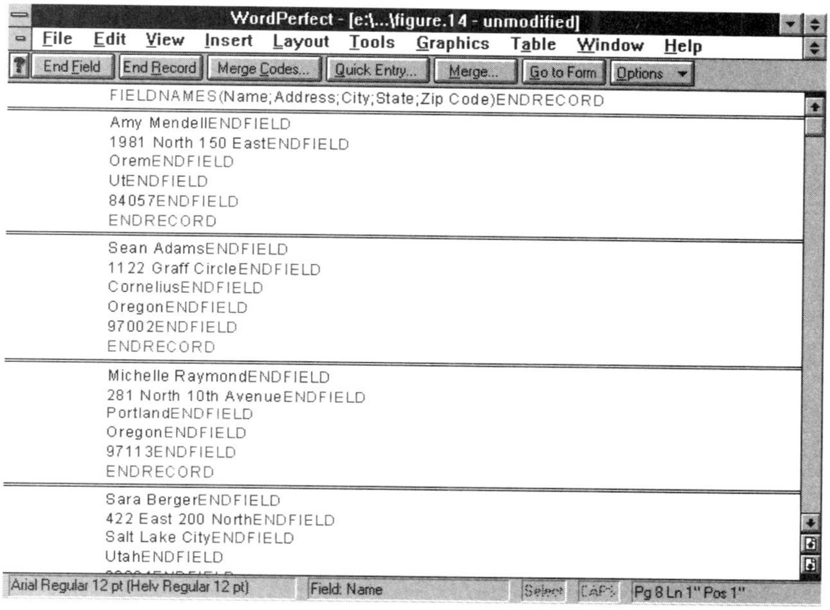

FIGURE 11–14
A text data file.

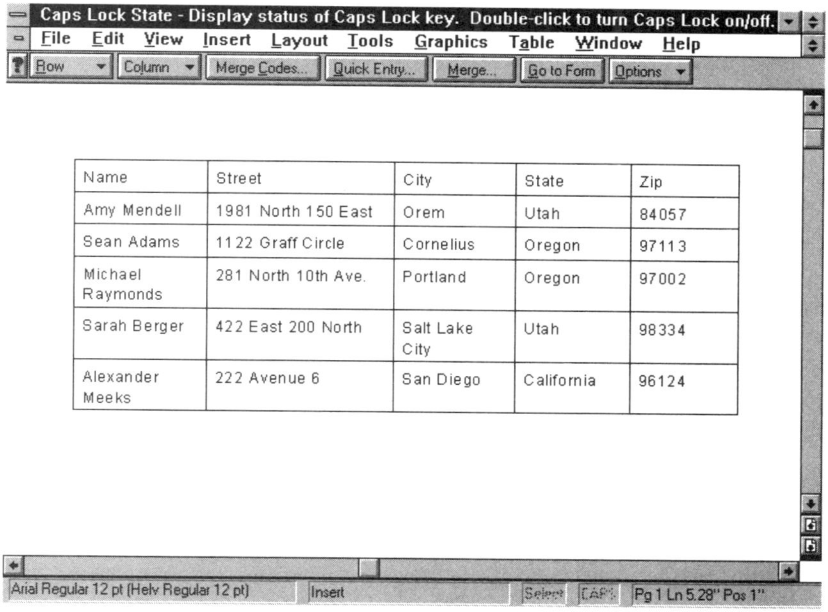

FIGURE 11–15
A table data file.

To add or delete new records to a data file:

1. Open the data file.
2. Choose Quick Entry from the Merge Feature Bar, shown here:

3. Enter the new information by using the Quick Data Entry dialog box *or* use Find to find the record you want to delete or edit and choose Delete Record *or* make the necessary changes to the record.
4. After making the necessary changes, choose Close. After choosing Yes, the data file is updated.

If you want to edit existing information, you can make the changes directly from the document window. If you are not using a data table file, be careful not to delete the merge codes that display as **ENDFIELD** and **ENDRECORD**.

HINT **If you want to hide the merge codes or display them as symbols, choose Options from the Merge Feature Bar and select Display as Markers or Hide Codes.**

HINT **If you have a large data file and want to edit specific records, you can use the Find feature to quickly locate a key word in the record you want to edit.**

If your data file is in a table format, you can quickly add or delete a single record.

To add a record:

1. Choose Row from the Merge Feature Bar.
2. Choose Insert.
3. Select where you want to insert the row.
4. Enter the information for each field. Each field is a column. To move to the next field, press Tab.
5. Save the file.

To delete a record from a table data file:

1. Position the insertion point in the row you want to delete.
2. Choose Row from the Feature Bar.
3. Choose Delete and choose Yes.

NOTE **You can use also use the Column option to add a field to the data file or to delete a field from it.**

Using Field Numbers and Names

When you create a data file, you are prompted to create field names. You can however, choose OK when the Create Data File dialog box is displayed and enter the number of fields you want in the data file. The advantage of using field names is that when the data file is displayed in the document window and you move to a field, the status line displays the name of the field. If you are using a data table file, the column headings display the name of the field. This capability is helpful if you need to quickly edit information in the data file and are not sure which information is supposed to be contained in the field.

Whether you use field names or numbers, you must include the same number of fields in every record in order for the data file to merge correctly.

HOW DO I... Create a Form File?

The form file contains all the formatting codes, such as margins, fonts, and paper size, and information with which you want to merge your data. If you are merging a letter, the file containing the text and formatting codes for the letter is the form file. A form file includes fields to match the fields in the data file. The form file consists of formatting codes and merge codes.

Steps

➡ **To create a form file:**

1. Insert all necessary formatting codes for the document just as though you were creating a regular document.
2. Place the insertion point where you want the first field to appear.
3. Choose Tools➢Merge.

4. Choose Form. If necessary, select New Document Window.
5. If you want to link a specific data file with this form file, specify the name in the Associate a Data File text box or select None and then choose OK. When you associate a data file and form file, it simplifies many of the steps for creating a form file.
6. Choose Insert Field from the Merge Feature Bar. The Insert Field Name or Number dialog box is displayed, as shown in Figure 11–16.
7. Select the field you want to insert into the form file and choose Insert. The **FIELD**(*field name or number*) code is displayed, as shown here:

```
July 28, 1995

FIELD(Name)
FIELD(Street)
FIELD(City)FIELD(State)FIELD(Zip)

DearFIELD(Name):
```

NOTE

If you did not associate a data file with the form file, you have to enter a field name or number and then choose Insert.

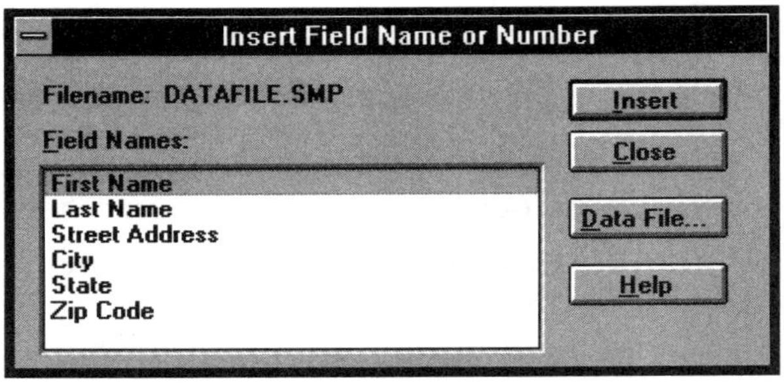

FIGURE 11–16
The Insert Field Name dialog box.

8. Move the insertion point to the location where you want to insert the next field and follow step 7. Repeat steps 7 and 8 until you have inserted all the fields you need in the form file. You do not have to use all the fields in the form file; use only the field you need.
9. Enter any additional information you want in the document, such as the text of a letter, and save the document as normal. It is a good idea to save a form file with a specific extension, such as .FOR, so that you can easily identify the file.

Tell Me More

When you create a form file, you have to lay out the information exactly the way you want the document to look when you merge it. If you are creating a letter, for example, you have to type it exactly the way you would type a letter you were mailing to one individual, with one exception: Rather than type a name, address, city, state, ZIP code, and salutation, you include merge codes. Figure 11–17 displays a letter that has been created as a form file.

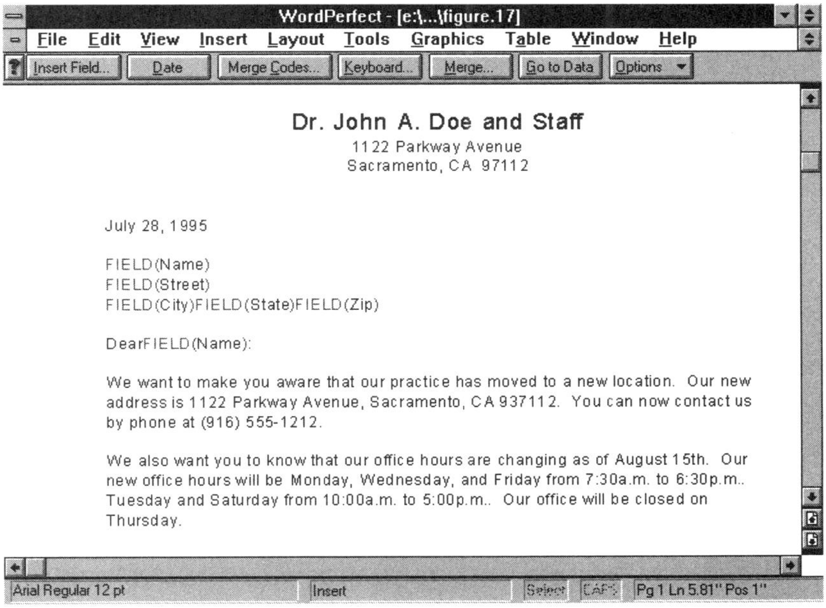

FIGURE 11–17
A form file.

Using the Merge Feature Bar

When you create a form file, the Merge Feature Bar, shown here, is displayed:

The following table describes the options on the Feature Bar:

OPTION	DESCRIPTION
Insert Field	Inserts a field at the location of the cursor. If you have associated a data file, you can choose from the fields in the data file.
Date	Inserts a date code that is updated to reflect the current date every time you merge the document.
Merge Codes	Displays a list of advanced merge codes you can insert to add power and flexibility to the merge. See the section "Using Merge Codes and Performing a Keyboard Merge" later in this chapter.
Keyboard	Inserts a command that prompts the user for text during a merge. See the section "Using Merge Codes and Performing a Keyboard Merge" later in this chapter.
Merge	Displays the Merge dialog box, from which you can merge the form file and data file.
Go to Data	If you have associated a data file with the form file, displays the contents of the data file. You can then choose Go to Form to display the form file again.
Options	Allows you to remove or change the merge codes to icons. With a form file, it is easier to display the codes in full form so that you know exactly which information is in the form file. You can also remove the Feature Bar.

Using Merge Codes and Performing a Keyboard Merge

In addition to inserting the field codes in your form file, you can insert other merge codes to further customize your merge.

To insert other merge codes:

1. Choose Merge Codes from the Merge Feature Bar.
2. Select the option you want.

There are several advanced merge codes you can use in a form file. These advanced merge codes give you great power and flexibility when you are merging. As you highlight each merge code in the Insert Merge Codes dialog box, a brief description of the code is displayed below the list box. To insert a code, highlight the merge code you want and then choose Insert. If the merge code requires additional information, type the information in the entry field that is displayed and then choose OK. The merge code is inserted at the insertion-point position in the document window. The following sections explain a few of the common merge codes.

You can allow user input when you are merging two documents by using the Keyboard merge code. Suppose that you have a form letter for scheduling interviews, but you want to enter a different interview time for each recipient. Move to the location in the letter where you want to insert the time. Choose Keyboard from the Merge Feature Bar, type **Enter the interview time** in the Enter Prompt text field, and choose OK. When you merge this form file with your data file, WordPerfect displays a dialog box at the bottom of the document window. Type the time of the interview and then choose Continue from the Merge Feature Bar. You are prompted for the time for each record.

You can insert comments in your data and form files to explain the codes in the file. Suppose that you have created a complex form file for your company and you plan to take an extended vacation. The person covering for you is unfamiliar with merges. You can include comments throughout the form file to help the new person understand each code. Simply choose Merge Codes and then select Comment and choose Insert. Type the comment and then choose OK. When you merge the form file, the comment is not displayed in the merged file.

HOW DO I... Merge a Form File and a Data File?

After creating a data file and a form file, the final step of a merge is to physically merge the two files. Before you merge the documents, you have to be sure that one file is in data format and the other is in form format. Merging documents creates a third file.

Steps

➠To merge two documents:

1. From either the data file or the form file, choose Merge from the Feature Bar and then choose Merge again *or* choose Tools➢Merge➢Merge. The Perform Merge dialog box is displayed, as shown in Figure 11–18.
2. If necessary, enter the name of the form file and the data file.
3. Choose OK. The two documents are merged to create a new document.

HINT

To cancel a merge, you can press Esc or Ctrl+Break at any time while the documents are merging.

Tell Me More

Performing a merge creates a new document that contains information from both the data file and the form file. Suppose that you merge a data file which consists of 100 addresses with a letter form file. After completing the merge, you end up with a new file containing 100 copies of the letter that includes a different address for each record. A hard page break is inserted between each copy of the letter in the new document.

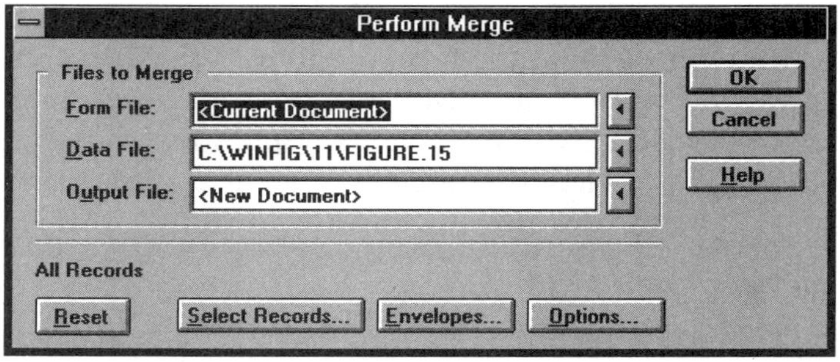

FIGURE 11–18
The Perform Merge dialog box.

FIGURE 11–19
The Perform Merge Options dialog box.

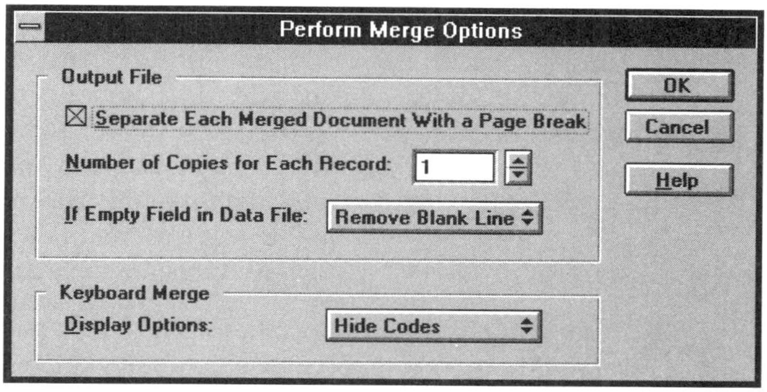

By default, when you merge a document, the document is written to a new document window. You can specify where the merged file ends up by selecting a different option from the Output File pop-up list in the Perform Merge dialog box (refer to Figure 11–18). If you choose Current Document, the file is displayed in the document window you are in after executing the merge. If you choose Printer, the file automatically prints without being written to the document window. If you choose Select File, the Select Output File dialog box is displayed and lets you specify a filename.

Using Merge Options

From the Perform Merge dialog box, you can choose Options to set specific options for the merge. If you make changes to these options, you can change all options back to their original settings by choosing Reset from the Perform Merge dialog box. The following table describes the options on the Perform Merge Options dialog box, displayed in Figure 11–19:

Option	Description
Separate Each Merged Document with a Page Break	By default, WordPerfect automatically inserts a hard page break between records after completing a merge. You can eliminate the hard page breaks by deselecting this option. This option is useful, for example, if you want to create a list that contains names and addresses from a data file and you don't want each name and address on a separate page.

(continues)

Option	Description
Number of Copies for Each Record	Specifies the number of copies you want of each record in the data file. Suppose that you are merging mailing labels and know that you will mail information to the same people at least four times in the next two weeks. You can type **4** in the entry field to duplicate the address four times.
If Empty Field in Data File	Specifies what to do with blank fields. When you create a data file, there are instances in which each record may not have to have all fields you have specified. In that case, you must still enter an END-FIELD code in the data text files, even if there is no text for that field. When you perform a merge, you can choose the way the merge handles blank fields. If you do not want the blank field to be displayed, choose Remove Blank Line. If you want the blank field to display as a blank line in the merged document, choose Leave Blank Line.
Display Options	When you perform a Keyboard Merge, specifies how to display merge codes. You can Hide Codes, Show Codes, or Show Codes as Markers.

Merging Envelopes

If you want to create envelopes for each record in the Merge, you can choose Envelopes from the Perform Merge dialog box. This option is especially useful if you are merging a letter with an address list. A letter is not only created for each address but also an envelope so that you don't have to merge the data file a second time with an envelope form file.

To generate an envelope for each record:

1. Choose Envelopes from the Perform Merge dialog box.
2. Fill in the necessary information in the Envelope dialog box that is displayed.
3. For Mailing Address, choose Field and insert the fields in the correct location.
4. Choose OK twice to begin the merge. When you merge the document, the envelopes are displayed after all the letters.

Selecting Records to Merge

Sometimes you may not want to merge all the records in a data file, for example, if you have a large mailing list and you only want to send flyers to people with a certain ZIP code. You can use the Select Records feature to specify the conditions and merge only those records that meet the conditions.

To select records that meet a certain condition:

1. Choose Select Records from the Perform Merge dialog box. The Select Records dialog box is displayed, as shown in Figure 11–20.
2. Select Specify Conditions.
3. If you want to limit which records you are specifying conditions for, select Record Number Range and enter a value in the From and To text box.
4. Select the field for which you want to specify a value. If you want to select records according to ZIP code, for example, select ZIP code for the Field in the first column. You can specify several fields if necessary.

FIGURE 11–20
The Select Records dialog box.

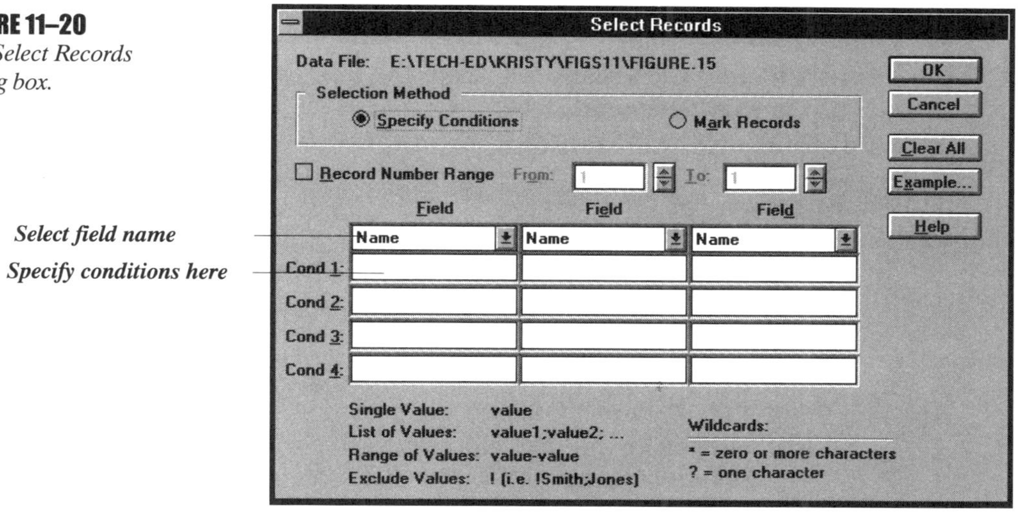

5. Enter a condition for the field. For example, enter the ZIP code here. You can enter as many as four conditions for each field.
6. Choose OK twice to perform the merge.

HINT

If you do not have exact conditions for selecting records but you want to merge only a few of the records, you can select Mark Records. When you select Mark Records, a list of all the records in the data file is displayed and you can mark the ones you want to use in the merge. This is a fast and easy way to select a few records from a long list.

The Select Records feature is powerful. WordPerfect has provided several examples of the type of information you can enter and how the selection is performed. You can see these examples by choosing Example from the Select Records dialog box.

HOW DO I... Sort Text?

The Sort feature can perform basic functions in addition to complicated and sophisticated functions, depending on your needs. For example, the Sort feature enables you to do simple tasks, such as alphabetizing a list of names, and complicated tasks, such as sorting a data file for all ZIP codes greater than a certain number. No matter what your needs are, the Sort feature can greatly automate the task of organizing and arranging text in your documents.

Steps

➡To sort a document:

1. With the document in the document window, choose Tools➢Sort *or* press Alt+F9. The Sort dialog box is displayed, as shown in Figure 11–21.
2. If necessary, specify a name for the Input File and Output File. If you want to sort the document displayed in the current document window and have the results displayed in the current document window, leave the options as is.
3. Select a Sort By option. You can select from Line, Paragraph, Merge Record, Table Row, or Column. Table Row and Col-

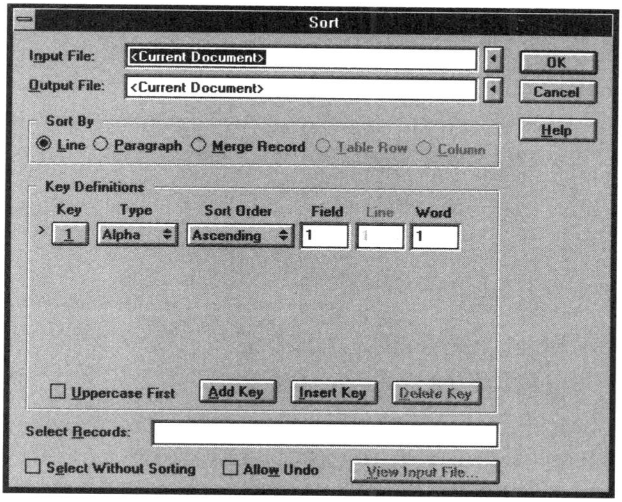

FIGURE 11–21
The Sort dialog box.

umn are available only if the document is a table or in columns.

4. If necessary, add or edit the Key Definitions. For more information about adding and editing key definitions, see the section "Using Key Definitions" later in this chapter.
5. If you want to be able to "undo" the sort, select Allow Undo.
6. Choose OK to sort the file. You can also choose View Input File if you want to see the results of the Sort before sorting the document.

Tell Me More

When you are sorting a document, you have to select the type of sort you want to perform, such as line or paragraph, and define the parameters for the sort. WordPerfect generally defaults to the correct sort type based on the format of the text you are sorting. After these elements are selected, several options help you customize and optimize the sorting of your documents.

Selecting a Sort Type

When you perform a sort, the first selection you must choose is the type of records you are sorting. A *record* is the text group that is sorted. You can sort by Line, Paragraph, Merge Data Files, Table Rows, or Columns. The following table defines each of these record types:

RECORD TYPE	DEFINITION
Line	Each line that ends with a hard return is viewed as an individual record
Paragraph	Each paragraph followed by two or more hard returns is viewed as an individual record
Merge Record	Each record in a merge file ending with an ENDRECORD code is viewed as an individual record
Table Row	Each row of cells is viewed as an individual record
Column	Each column is viewed as an individual record

Using Key Definitions

After you define the type of records you are sorting, you must define the way you want the records sorted. The Key Definitions enable you to specify the options used for the sort. Depending on the record type you select, you may see only some of the sort keys.

The following table describes the available sort keys:

SORT KEY	DESCRIPTION
Key	Specifies the order in which the sort conditions are used for each record. You can have as many as nine sort keys; 1 is given first priority.
Type	Specifies whether the search is alphabetic or numeric.
Ord	Specifies whether the search is in ascending or descending order.
Line	Indicates which line to sort; a line ends with a hard return or a soft return if you are sorting a paragraph.

(continues)

SORT KEY	DESCRIPTION
Field	Specifies which field to sort; a field ends with an END-FIELD code in a Merge Data File (if you are sorting a data file and you want to sort by ZIP code, for example, you specify the field in which the ZIP code is listed). In a non-merge file, each line is a field. Tabs and indents divide a line into multiple fields.
Word	Specifies which word to sort by

When you first enter the Sort dialog box, only one sort key is defined. You can add another sort key, insert a sort key, edit the existing sort key, or delete a sort key. Adding a sort key adds it to the end of any previously defined sort keys so that it takes a lower priority. Inserting a sort key inserts the key with an arrow to the far left, which gives it a higher priority.

When you select the Uppercase First option, WordPerfect sorts identical words with uppercase letters before words with lowercase letters.

Selecting Records

After you have selected a record type and defined the sort keys, you can further customize your sort with the Select Records option. The Select Records option lets you select records that meet certain criteria you define—for example, if you have a mailing list that contains all the companies with which you do business. Using this mailing list, you want to send fliers to only the companies in Florida. You can use Select Records to sort through a mailing list and find only those located in Florida. Figure 11–22 shows the defined sort key and the selection statement you would use for the preceding example.

The following table describes the operators you can use in your selection statement when you use the Select Records option:

OPERATOR	DESCRIPTION
=	Selects records that have the same information for the specified key
< >	Selects records that do not have the same information for the specified key

(continues)

OPERATOR	DESCRIPTION
>	Selects records that are greater than the information for the specified key
<	Selects records that are less than the information for the specified key
>=	Selects records that are greater than or equal to the information for the specified key
<=	Selects records that are less than or equal to the information for the specified key
| or OR	Selects records that meet either statement listed
& or AND	Selects records that meet both statements listed

When you are using Select Records, you can also choose the Select Without Sorting option to have the records that meet the criteria selected but remain unsorted. The selected records are displayed in the current document window or in the output file depending on the Output File option. This procedure saves time if you want to find only certain

Selection statement

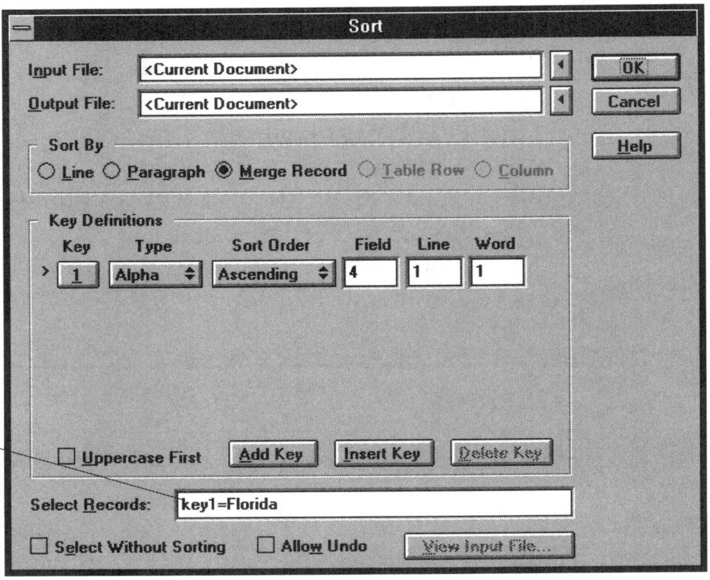

FIGURE 11–22
A sort example.

records but don't want them sorted. You must always have sort keys defined, however, in order to use the Select Records feature.

HINT

If you want to select records based on a word that is displayed anywhere in the record, not just in a specific line, field, or word, you can use the global key in the Select Records text box. The global key is defined as *key g.* Enter key g=*text* in the Select Records text box and all records containing the specified text are selected.

HOW DO I... Create a Template?

All documents in WordPerfect use templates. A template can include formatting codes and text. You can also associate specific styles, macros, abbreviations, Button Bars, keyboards, and menu bars with templates. WordPerfect has several predefined templates, but you can also create your own templates for specific types of documents you frequently create. If you have a particular layout for a newsletter you create, for example, you can create a customized template for the newsletter that includes all the features and tools needed to create the newsletter. Using templates helps ensure consistency between similar documents.

Steps

➨To create a template:

1. Choose File➢Template *or* press Ctrl+T.
2. Choose Options➢Create Template. The Create Document Template dialog box is displayed, as shown in Figure 11–23.

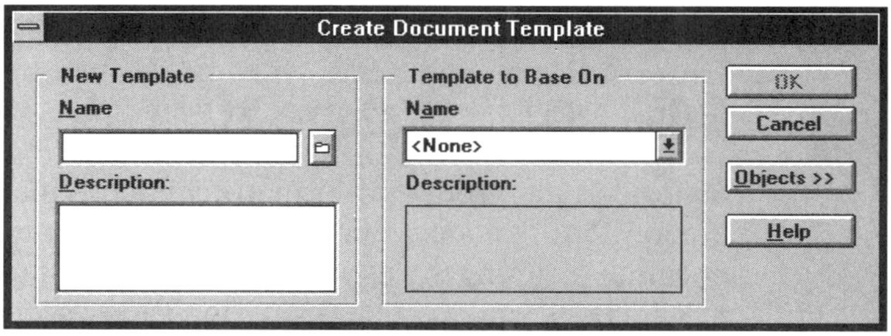

FIGURE 11–23
The Create Document Template dialog box.

3. Specify a name and description for the template. All templates have a .WPT extension. You do not have to add the extension.
4. If you want to use another template as a pattern, select a template from the Template to Base On drop-down list and choose OK.
5. From the document window, enter the formatting codes and text you want to include in the template, just as you would with a regular WordPerfect document.
6. You can also choose items from the Template Feature Bar. You can choose Create Object, for example, and create styles, macros, abbreviations, Button Bars, keyboards, and menu bars to associate with the template.
7. When you have finished creating the template, choose Exit Template from the Feature Bar.

Tell Me More

You can create a template from an existing document. To do so, simply add a .WPT extension to the filename and move the document to your template directory. You can also edit existing templates that are shipped with WordPerfect so that they better fit your needs.

➡**To edit an existing template:**

1. Choose File➢Template *or* press Ctrl+T
2. Highlight the template you want to edit.
3. Choose Options➢Edit Template.

NOTE **If you want to delete a template, you can choose Delete Template at this point.**

4. Make the necessary changes to the template and choose Exit Template from the Feature Bar.

HOW DO I... Create Styles?

Styles contain groups of formatting codes you use frequently in a document. You create your own styles and then insert them in your documents. Using Styles saves time because you don't have to remember which codes you used, and you don't have to insert all the codes every time you want to use them; you simply select the style. For example, you can create a style that contains all the formatting codes for a brochure. The style can contain the font type and size, margin settings, line spacing, page numbering, and so on. Every time you create a brochure, you select the brochure style and begin entering your text and therefore eliminate the need to remember and enter all the formatting codes. WordPerfect automatically updates all the styles in your document whenever you edit the style.

In addition to user-created document styles, WordPerfect has styles for many features, including graphics box styles, graphics line styles, fill styles, outline styles, and table of contents styles (there are styles everywhere!). The abundance of "feature" styles may seem overwhelming, but the power and versatility it adds to WordPerfect is immense.

You can use QuickCreate to create a style from formatting codes you have already entered in a document. You can also create a style in the Styles Editor.

Steps

➡**To create a style based on formatting codes in the current document:**

1. Position the insertion point on the formatted text.
2. Choose Layout➢Styles *or* press Alt+F8. The Style List dialog box is displayed, as shown in Figure 11–24.
3. Choose QuickCreate.
4. Specify a Name for the style name. This name is used as the filename for the style.
5. Specify a Description that will help you identify what the style is used for, such as Brochure Formatting.
6. Select a Style Type. You can select Paragraph or Character.

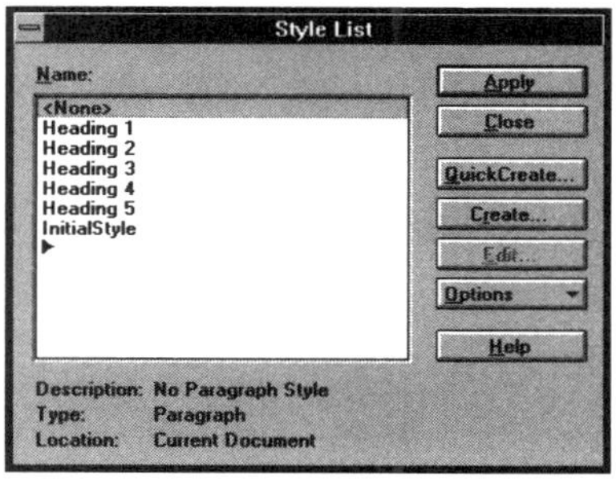

FIGURE 11–24
The Style List dialog box.

7. Choose OK. The style is added to the Style List.
8. Choose Close to return to the document window.

➠To create a style in the style editor:

1. Choose Layout➢Styles *or* press Alt+F8.
2. Choose Create. The Styles Editor dialog box is displayed, as shown in Figure 11–25.
3. Specify a Name for the style name.
4. Specify a Description that will help you identify what the style is used for, such as Brochure Formatting.
5. Select a Style Type. You can select Paragraph, Character, or Document.
6. In the Contents text box, enter the information you want to include in the style. You can use the pull-down menus and function keys to access features and functions you want to include in the style. If the menu item is not available, it appears dimmed.
7. Choose OK to return to the Style List dialog box, where the new style is listed.

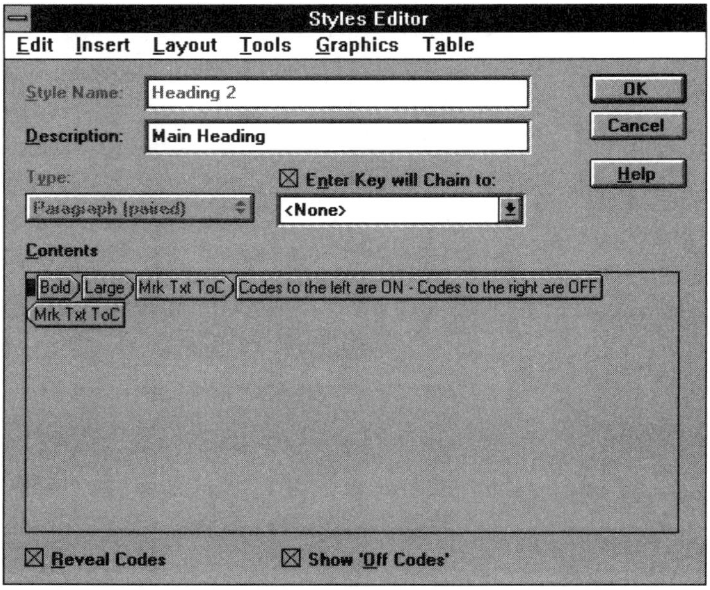

FIGURE 11–25
The Styles Editor dialog box.

8. Choose Apply to insert the style in your document or choose Close to return to the document window.

➠**To insert a style in your document:**

1. Position the insertion point where you want to insert the style; if it is a paragraph style, position the insertion point anywhere in the paragraph; if it is a character style, select the text you want to be affected by the style; and if it is a document style, position the insertion point where you want the style to take effect.
2. Choose Layout➢Styles *or* press Alt+F8.
3. Highlight the style you want to use.
4. Choose Apply.

BUTTON BAR

You can also choose the Style button from the Button Bar to open the Style List dialog box.

Tell Me More

After you create a style and then save the document, WordPerfect saves the style with your document. You can also create styles for templates. Every time you retrieve the document or template, the styles created for the document or template are displayed in the Style List, which is displayed by choosing Layout➢Styles *or* pressing Alt+F8.

In addition to the styles you create, WordPerfect lists several default styles on the Style List. You cannot delete these default styles, but you can edit them.

NOTE

You can reset the default styles to their original content by choosing Options➢Reset and choosing Yes.

When you create a style, you must choose the type of style you want to create. The following sections describe each style type and give examples of when you use the specific style type.

Using a Paragraph Style

A *paragraph style* affects all text from the last hard return code ([HRt]) or hard page code ([HPg]) until the style is turned off. If you apply a paragraph style to existing text, it affects only the current paragraph or

FIGURE 11–26
A paragraph style inserted in a document.

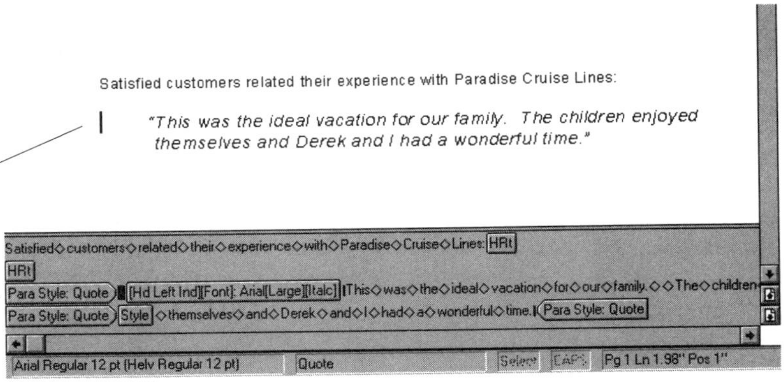

Formatted by using a paragraph style

Style in Reveal Codes

selected text. Paragraph styles are useful for formatting codes that you want to affect only specific sections of a document. For example, you can create a paragraph style for inserting long quotations. The style can select a smaller font and double-indent the text. After typing the quote, you press the Enter key to turn off the style. Figure 11–26 shows an example of a paragraph style inserted in a document.

To turn off a Paragraph style that is not automatically turned off by pressing the Enter key:

1. Choose Layout➢Style *or* press Alt+F8.
2. Highlight **<None>** in the Style List and choose Apply.

The None style ends the current paragraph style. You should press Enter before selecting the None style; otherwise, the style ends after the last hard return or hard page code. When you turn off the style in WordPerfect, the appropriate off codes are inserted automatically. In the preceding example, WordPerfect inserts the appropriate codes to return to the normal font in the ending [Para Style] code, after you select the None style, as shown here:

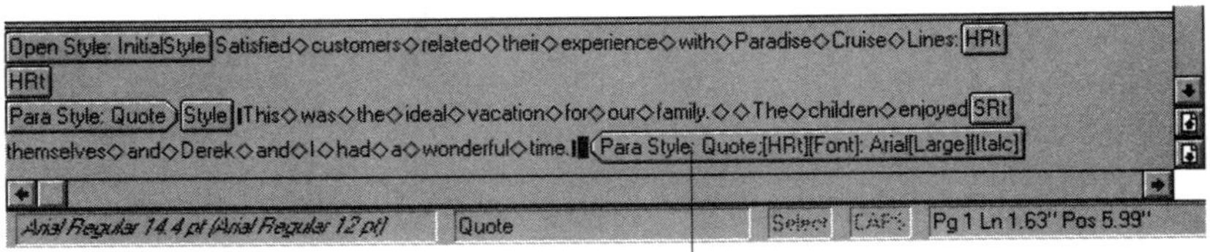

<None> style used to turn off paragraph style

By default, WordPerfect turns the paragraph style off and then back on when you press Enter. This feature is for use primarily with styles that insert outline numbers and when you want to use the style continually to update the outline number. WordPerfect provides several options for turning off a paragraph style when you use the Enter key.

To choose the action of the Enter key with a paragraph style or character style:

1. Choose Layout➢Styles *or* press Alt+F8.
2. Highlight the paragraph style you want to edit.
3. Choose Edit.
4. To have the Enter key simply insert hard returns and not affect the style, deselect the Enter Key will Chain to option.
   - Or to have the Enter key turn off the style, select <None> from the drop-down list below the Enter Key option.
   - Or to have the Enter key turn the style off and back on again, select <Same Style> from the drop-down list.
   - Or to have the Enter key turn the style off and turn on another style, select the style name from the drop-down list.
5. Choose OK and Close to return to the document window.

In the preceding example of the quote style, the Enter key will chain to <None>, so as soon as you finish entering the quote, you can press Enter and resume creating your document.

Using a Character Style

A character style affects all selected text or all text you type until you turn off the style. Character styles are useful for changing the appearance of text. For example, you can create a character style that italicizes and superscripts the text.

Like paragraph styles, character styles also have on and off codes. Unlike the paragraph style, however, the character style inserts both the on and off codes in the document when you select the style. You can then easily turn off the style by displaying Reveal Codes and moving your insertion point past the Style Off code. The following illustration shows the Character Style On and Character Style Off codes in a document:

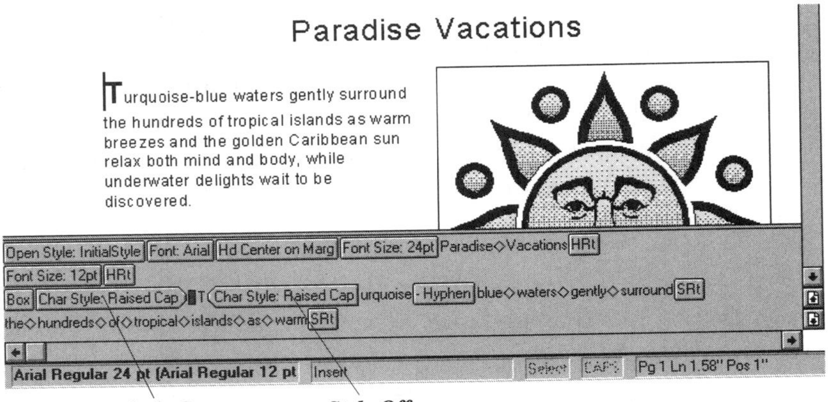

If you do not want to move manually past the Style Off code in Reveal Codes, you can press the Enter key to turn off character styles. See the section "Using a Paragraph Style" earlier in this chapter for information about using the Enter key to turn off a character style.

Using a Document Style

A *document style* affects all text from the insertion point on. Open styles are useful for initial formatting codes that you want to affect the entire document. If you have certain formatting codes you use for creating interoffice memos, for example, such as a specific typeface, margin settings, justification, and hyphenation, you can put all that information in an open style.

All the formatting codes in an open style remain in effect until you insert another formatting code that replaces it. For example, if you set the left margin to .5 inch and then want to set it to 1 inch for a specific section of the document, you can simply change the margin setting in your document. The new margin setting remains in effect until you change it again.

Retrieving and Saving Styles

When you create a style, it is saved with the current document or the document template you are creating or editing. If you want to use a style you created in another document, you can simply retrieve the style with the following steps:

1. Choose Layout➢Styles *or* press Alt+F8.

2. Choose Options➢Retrieve.
3. Enter the name of the document or template that contains the styles you want to use.
4. Select User Styles if you want to see only the styles you created.
5. Choose OK.
6. Choose Yes to overwrite the current styles in the Style List or No to display both sets of styles.
7. Highlight the style and choose Apply.

If you will be using styles with multiple documents and multiple templates, you can save the styles to a style file. This way, the styles are not specific to a document or template and can be retrieved when needed.

To save a list of styles:

1. Create the styles by using the steps outlined earlier.
2. From the Style List, choose Options➢Save As.
3. Specify a name for the style list, such as **TECH.STY**. You should use the .STY extension so that you can easily identify your style files.
4. If you want to save only the styles you created, select User Styles. To save all styles in the list, select Both or select System Styles to save only the system files.
5. Choose OK.

Now whenever you want to use the style list, you simply follow the steps outlined previously for retrieving styles.

HOW DO I. . . Fax a Document from WordPerfect?

If you have a fax program and fax driver that work with Windows, you can fax documents directly from WordPerfect.

Steps

➡To fax a document from within WordPerfect:

1. Choose File➢Print *or* press F5.
2. Choose Select.

3. From the Printers list, highlight your fax driver and choose Setup. Enter the necessary setup information by using the information from your fax driver manual.
4. Choose OK and then choose Select to select the fax driver.
5. Choose Print and the document in the current document window will be printed.

NOTE

You have to perform steps 2–4 only if the fax driver is not your selected printer.

Tell Me More

When you fax a document, you can select any of the Print Selection options in the Print dialog box. For example, you can fax selected pages or a document on disk. You can use the WordPerfect Print Job dialog box to cancel a fax just as you would cancel a normal print job.

Index

A

B

C

E

F

G

H

M

N

O

Q

R

S

T

Z